An Introduction to the

Canadian Labour Market

FOURTH EDITION

An Introduction to the

Canadian Labour Market

FOURTH EDITION

Helmar Drost
YORK UNIVERSITY

H. Richard Hird
DURHAM COLLEGE

Updated by Eric Moon
UNIVERSITY OF TORONTO

NELSON

NELSON

An Introduction to the Canadian Labour Market, Fourth Edition
by Helmar Drost and
H. Richard Hird
Updated by Eric Moon

COPYRIGHT © 2014, 2013 by Nelson Education Ltd.

Printed and bound in Canada
3 4 5 6   22 21 20 19

For more information contact Nelson Education Ltd., 1120 Birchmount Road, Toronto, Ontario, M1K 5G4. Or you can visit our Internet site at nelson.com

Statistics Canada information is used with the permission of Statistics Canada. Users are forbidden to copy this material and/or redisseminate the data, in an original or modified form, for commercial purposes, without the expressed permissions of Statistics Canada. Information on the availability of the wide range of data from Statistics Canada can be obtained from Statistics Canada's Regional Offices, its World Wide Web site at <http://www.statcan.gc.ca>, and its toll-free access number 1-800-263-1136.

ISBN-13: 978-0-17-667002-3
ISBN-10: 0-17-667002-5

Cover Design:
EDHAR/Shutterstock

To Maria

H.D.

To my students

R.H.

Brief Contents

Preface xvi

Acknowledgments xix

About the Authors xx

PART I: INTRODUCTION AND OVERVIEW 1
Chapter 1: The Economist's Study of Labour 5

Chapter 2: Overview of the Labour Market 21

Chapter 3: Institutional Aspects of the Labour Market 47

PART II: TRENDS AND RECENT DEVELOPMENTS IN THE CANADIAN LABOUR MARKET 65
Chapter 4: Trends in the Canadian Labour Force 69

Chapter 5: Employment 105

Chapter 6: Unemployment 141

Chapter 7: Trends in Labour Compensation 181

PART III: MICROECONOMIC THEORY OF THE LABOUR MARKET 207
Chapter 8: Labour Market Decisions of Households 211

Appendix 8A: Indifference Curve Analysis of Labour Supply 234

Chapter 9: Labour Market Decisions of Firms 241

Chapter 10: Wage Rate and Employment Determination 267

Appendix 10A: Wage Rate Changes and Unemployment 293

Chapter 11: Wage Rate Differentials 295

Chapter 12: Education, Training, and Earnings Differentials 315

Appendix 345

Glossary 349

Index 355

Contents

Preface xvi

Acknowledgments xix

About the Authors xx

PART I: INTRODUCTION AND OVERVIEW 1

Chapter 1: The Economist's Study of Labour 5

Chapter Learning Objectives 5

Vignette: The Role of Government in a Market Economy 6

The Relevance of Labour Economics 7

Labour Markets and the Employment Relation 7

Some Basic Economic Concepts 8

    Scarcity and Opportunity Cost 9

    Optimal Decision Making 10

Labour Market Outcomes and Labour Market Process 11

    Market Forces 11

    Institutional Forces 12

    Sociological Forces 13

Economists as Policymakers 14

    Evaluating Positive and Normative Statements 14

    Links Between Positive and Normative Economics 15

Labour Market Issue 1.1: Efficiency Versus Distribution—A Matter of
    Value Judgment 15

Summary 16

Key Terms 17

Weblinks 17

Discussion Questions 17

Using the Internet 18

Exercises 18

References 19

Chapter 2: Overview of the Labour Market 21

Chapter Learning Objectives 21

Vignette: Globalization and Human Resources Management 22

The Market Mechanism (Or How the Market Works) 23

    The Demand Side 24

    The Supply Side 26

    Price Determination 28

    Price Elasticity 30

Special Features of the Labour Market 33

The Labour Market and the National Economy 37

The Flow Approach to the Labour Market 39

Labour Markets in a Global Economy 41

Labour Market Issue 2.1: A Canadian-Made Automobile? 42

Summary 43

Key Terms 44

Weblinks 45

Discussion Questions 45

Using the Internet 45

Exercises 46

Chapter 3: Institutional Aspects of the Labour Market 47

Chapter Learning Objectives 47

Vignette: Maternity and Parental Leave 48

Jurisdiction 49

Government Involvement in the Labour Market 50

    Employment Standards 50

Labour Market Issue 3.1: Enforcing Employment Standards on Home Workers 51

Labour Market Issue 3.2: The Rationale for Severance Pay 54

    Human Rights 56

    Health and Safety 57

    Workers' Compensation 57

    Employment Insurance 57

    Union–Management Relationships 58

Union Membership 59

Labour Market Issue 3.3: A Comment on Government Intervention in the Labour Market 59

Summary 61

Key Terms 62

Weblinks 62

Discussion Questions 63

Using the Internet 63

Exercises 63

PART II: TRENDS AND RECENT DEVELOPMENTS IN THE CANADIAN LABOUR MARKET 65

Chapter 4: Trends in the Canadian Labour Force 69

Chapter Learning Objectives 69

Vignette: Brain Gain or Brain Waste? 70

The Labour Force 71

The Population Base 75

    Growth of the Domestic Population 75

Labour Market Issue 4.1: The Fertility Gap Between Canada and the U.S. 76

    Changes in the Age Composition of the Labour Force 76

Labour Market Issue 4.2: Aging of the Labour Force and Absences from Work 80

    Immigration 81

Changes in Labour Force Participation 88

    Labour Force Activity of Men 90

    Female Participation Trends 90

    Changes in the Gender Composition of the Labour Force 95

    Labour Force Participation of Youth 97

    Provincial Labour Force Participation Rates 98

Summary 99

Key Terms 100

Weblinks 101

Discussion Questions 101

Using the Internet 101

Exercises 102

References 103

Chapter 5: Employment 105

Chapter Learning Objectives 105

Vignette: Outsourcing in the Computer Services Industry 106

Aggregate Labour Demand 107

Changes in Level of Employment 107

Shifts in the Composition of Employment 111

    The Shift to Service-Sector Employment 111

Labour Market Issue 5.1: Are All Industrial Nations Becoming Service Economies? 115

    Occupational Shifts 117

The Growth of Non-Standard Employment 120

    Part-Time Work 121

Labour Market Issue 5.2: Four Young People and Ten Jobs 124

    Multiple Jobholding 125

    Own-Account Self-Employment 126

    Temporary Work 127

    Why Has Non-Standard Employment Been on the Rise? 128

Hours of Work 132

What Caused the Changes in Standard Working Hours? 134

Changes in the Distribution of Standard Working Hours 135

Summary 136

Key Terms 136

Weblinks 137

Discussion Questions 137

Using the Internet 138

Exercises 138

References 139

Chapter 6: Unemployment 141

Chapter Learning Objectives 141

Vignette: Discouraged Workers in Newfoundland 142

How Is Unemployment Measured? 143

Do the Official Unemployment Figures Measure What They Ought To? 144

Inactive Job Seekers 144

Discouraged Workers 145

Underemployed Workers 146

Marginal Workers 146

The Unemployment Rate as a Measure of Economic Hardship 147

An Alternative Measure of the Utilization of Labour 149

Characteristics of Canadian Unemployment 150

The Incidence of Unemployment 151

The Duration of Unemployment 153

Demographic Differences in Unemployment 155

Youth Unemployment 155

Female Unemployment 157

Other Factors 157

Regional Differences in Unemployment 158

Unemployment in Canada and the United States Compared 160

Macroeconomic Performance 160

Employment Insurance 161

Differences in the Measurement of Unemployment 163

Types of Unemployment 164

Frictional Unemployment 164

Labour Market Issue 6.1: Commercial Employment Agencies 165

Seasonal Unemployment 166

Structural Unemployment 166

Cyclical Unemployment 168

Why Has the Natural Rate of Unemployment Shifted Upward? 169
    Demographic Shifts 169
    Employment Insurance 170
Labour Market Issue 6.2: Unemployment Hysteresis 172
    Industrial Restructuring 173
    Technological Change 173
Summary 174
Key Terms 175
Weblinks 176
Discussion Questions 176
Using the Internet 177
Exercises 177
References 179

Chapter 7: Trends in Labour Compensation 181
Chapter Learning Objectives 181
Vignette: Canada's Low Wage Earners 182
Introduction 182
Concepts and Measures 183
    Labour Income 184
    Nominal Wages Versus Real Wages 184
Changes in Total Labour Income and Labour's Share 188
Labour Market Issue 7.1: Labour's Share Rises in Recessions 191
Changes in Average Labour Income 191
Changes in Average Weekly Earnings and Hourly Wages 193
Changes in Nominal and Real Wage Rates 194
Earnings Gaps 197
    The Gender Gap 197
    The Age Gap 198
    Occupational Earnings Polarization 199
Labour Market Issue 7.2: Bargaining Structure and the Relative Wage
    Decline Among Unskilled Workers 201
Summary 202
Key Terms 203
Weblinks 203
Discussion Questions 203
Using the Internet 204
Exercises 204
References 205

PART III: MICROECONOMIC THEORY OF THE LABOUR MARKET 207

Chapter 8: Labour Market Decisions of Households 211

Chapter Learning Objectives 211

Vignette: Part-Time Work 212

Introduction 213

The Work/Leisure Tradeoff 213

    The Decision to Work 215

Labour Market Issue 8.1: Mandatory Retirement 217

Labour Market Issue 8.2: Employment Earnings and Welfare Benefits 221

The Individual Supply Curve 222

Labour Market Issue 8.3: Tax Laws and Childcare Decisions 223

    Wage Rate Elasticity of Labour Supply 225

Labour Market Issue 8.4: Marginal Tax Rates and the Decision to Work 226

Market Supply Curve for Labour 227

Labour Market Issue 8.5: The Brain Drain 229

    Economic Rent 230

Summary 231

Key Terms 232

Weblinks 232

Discussion Questions 232

Using the Internet 233

Exercises 233

Appendix 8A: Indifference Curve Analysis of Labour Supply 234

Chapter 9: Labour Market Decisions of Firms 241

Chapter Learning Objectives 241

Vignette: The Demand for Truck Drivers 242

Introduction 242

The Demand Curve for Labour 243

    The Short Run 243

    The Long Run 249

Wage Elasticity of Labour Demand 251

Labour Productivity 255

    The Structure of the Economy 258

    Economic Conditions 258

    Government Policies 259

Labour Market Issue 9.1: Literacy and Wages 259
   The Scale of Business Operations 260
Labour Market Issue 9.2: International Trade and the Labour
  Market 261
   Management Techniques 262
   Quality and Quantity of Capital 262
   The Labour Force 262
Quasi-Fixed Labour Costs and the Demand for Labour 263
Summary 264
Key Terms 265
Weblinks 265
Discussion Questions 265
Using the Internet 266
Exercises 266

Chapter 10: Wage Rate and Employment Determination 267
Chapter Learning Objectives 267
Vignette: Espanola: Paper, Logging, and Monopsony 268
Introduction 268
Wage Rate and Employment Determination in a Competitive Labour
  Market 269
Wage Rate and Employment Determination Under Conditions of
  Monopsony 271
The Impact of Government Policies on the Labour Market 274
   Minimum Wage Rate 274
Labour Market Issue 10.1: The Minimum Wage Rate and Poverty 276
   Payroll Taxes 277
   Wage Subsidy 281
The Impact of Unions on Wage Rates and Employment 282
   The Impact of Unions on the Demand for Labour 282
   The Impact of Unions on the Supply of Labour 283
   Empirical Evidence 285
Causes of Unemployment 286
   Job Search 286
   Wage Rate Rigidity 287
Summary 290
Key Terms 291
Weblinks 291
Discussion Questions 291
Using the Internet 291
Exercises 292

Appendix 10A: Wage Rate Changes and Unemployment 293

Chapter 11: Wage Rate Differentials 295
Chapter Learning Objectives 295
Vignette: Paralegals: A Case of Occupational Licensing 296
Introduction 297
Adjustment Lags 297
Labour Market Barriers 299
Compensating Wage Differentials 303
Labour Market Issue 11.1: Legislation Related to Risk in the
    Workplace 304
Personal Characteristics 305
Discrimination and Male–Female Wage Differentials 306
    Empirical Evidence on Male–Female Wage Differentials 306
    Theories of Discrimination 307
    Discrimination as a Result of Imperfect Information 308
    Policies to Combat Discrimination 309
Labour Market Issue 11.2: Bell Canada Settles Pay Equity
    Dispute 311
Summary 312
Key Terms 313
Weblinks 313
Discussion Questions 314
Using the Internet 314
Exercises 314

Chapter 12: Education, Training, and Earnings Differentials 315
Chapter Learning Objectives 315
Vignette: The Rise in Student Debt 316
Introduction 316
The Pattern of Education and Earnings 317
Investment in Education 317
    The Investment Decision 318
    Private and Social Rates of Return 324
Labour Market Issue 12.1: Who Should Pay for Higher
    Education? 325
Implications of Human Capital Theory 326
Changes in Private Returns Over Time 327
Education and the Distribution of Individual Earnings 329
The Link Between Education and Earnings 331
    Education as a Signal 331

The Job Competition Model 332

Empirical Evidence 333

On-the-Job Training 334

Labour Market Issue 12.2: A Training Tax to Solve the Free Rider
Problem 335

General and Specific Training 335

Benefits and Costs of On-the-Job Training 336

Implications of On-the-Job Training 338

Summary 339

Key Terms 340

Weblinks 340

Discussion Questions 341

Using the Internet 341

Exercises 342

References 343

Appendix 345

Glossary 349

Index 355

Preface

The tremendous growth in the field of human resources management has fuelled a growing interest in the Canadian labour market. Human resources (HR) professionals must have an understanding of the market conditions that influence the determination of earnings and the hiring and training of employees. The professional HR manager also needs to know how changes in government legislation are likely to affect the labour market. In the last 50 years, governments have been very active in implementing policies designed to regulate working conditions. Laws have been written concerning pay equity, severance pay, safety in the workplace, and so on.

The fourth edition of *An Introduction to the Canadian Labour Market* introduces students, especially those in the human resources field, to the economic issues affecting the market for workers. The book is also suitable as a reference for professionals who require an understanding of Canada's labour market.

This book has four goals. The first is to inform the reader about the major trends and developments in the Canadian labour market. The second is to provide some explanation for these real-world developments and labour market outcomes. For example, why are unemployment rates for youth higher than for adults? Why has there been an increase in employment in the service sector of our economy? What factors are responsible for the earnings gap between men and women? Since these questions often have more than one answer, the third goal is to show why economists sometimes disagree. Finally, the fourth goal is to teach the reader to apply labour market theory to analyses of current events and labour policy issues, and in so doing learn to assess the relevance of theory.

The text is divided into three parts.

- **Part I: Introduction and Overview (Chapters 1 to 3)**
  Many students taking a course in labour economics have no previous exposure to the discipline of economics. The introduction provides an overview of how economists approach real-world problems. The central concept of a market and the principles underlying demand and supply are explained. The unique features of the labour market are outlined and an explanation is given of how labour markets interact with other markets in the Canadian economy. International influences are also discussed. The third chapter presents the legislative and institutional framework of the labour market. It reviews the role of government in regulating the labour market, various labour legislation, and the extent of unionization of the Canadian labour force.

- **Part II: Trends and Recent Developments in the Canadian Labour Market (Chapters 4 to 7)**
  This part presents the major labour market trends and developments in Canada since World War II. The purpose is to establish those macroeconomic developments in the Canadian labour market

that will be explained in later chapters. The trends cover the changes in the Canadian labour force, employment, unemployment, and labour compensation.

- **Part III: Microeconomic Theory of the Labour Market (Chapters 8 to 12)**
  This part of the text explains the labour market behaviour of households and business firms. Households represent the supply side of the labour market and offer their services to employers. Business firms represent the demand side of the labour market. Business firms want the services of workers in order to provide goods and services to the marketplace. The interaction of the buyers and the sellers in the labour market determines the wage rate. Since workers and jobs are not the same, wages differ. The final chapters of the text shed some light on the reasons for these wage differentials. Special attention is paid to the impact of education, training, and discrimination on wage rate differentials.

Labour economics has become increasingly technical over the last two decades. It has also come to be distinguished by the use of highly sophisticated statistical techniques. Most textbooks on labour market economics are aimed at the student who has a solid background in economic principles. This text addresses the needs of those with no, or very little, previous economics training. The concepts and economic relationships are presented in non-technical language without relying on mathematical equations. The text does, however, use graphs and figures to illustrate economic trends and labour market principles. Although used sparingly, we believe that students should become accustomed to using graphs in their analysis of labour market issues. If you can trace one variable in a time series graph, and if you can identify positive and negative relationships on a graph, your knowledge of graphs is sufficient for this text.

This book will help the reader understand the aspects of the labour market that play a central role in the determination of employment and earnings in Canada. Toward that end, various learning tools, retained from the previous edition, appear throughout the book. These are:

- *Chapter Learning Objectives*: Every chapter begins with a list of learning goals. These objectives provide a good study guide and help students to focus on the key lessons presented in the chapter.
- *Key Terms*: When important concepts are introduced in the text, they are boldfaced. A list of key terms appears at the end of each chapter and a glossary defining each key term appears at the end of the text.
- *Labour Market Issue boxes*: Economic theory is useful and interesting only if it can be applied to understanding actual events and policies. The boxes throughout the book contain interesting issues and applications of the theory.
- *Summaries*: Each chapter ends with a brief summary that reminds students of the most important lessons that they have just learned. The chapter summaries provide a review for exams.

- *Exercises*: At the end of each chapter are questions for review and discussion as well as for learning. Students can apply their newly acquired knowledge to these exercises. They can also use the exercises for examination preparation.

In addition to the updating of data and incorporating some new material, several other features have been retained from the previous edition of the text. They are:

- *Opening vignettes*: Each chapter starts with a short discussion of a topic relevant to that chapter. Many vignettes cover current issues in the labour market.
- *Weblinks*: Internet references are provided for some of the topics discussed in the text.
- *Discussion Questions*: The questions at the end of the chapter have been divided into discussion questions and exercises.
- *Using the Internet exercises*: Each chapter contains at least one exercise using the Internet. These exercises should be particularly beneficial for those students taking a course using laptop computers.
- *Appendix on Indifference Curve Approach to Labour Supply*: For those who prefer the use of indifference curves to explain the labour supply curve, this material is included as an appendix to Chapter 8.

For instructors, this edition is accompanied by both an Instructor's Manual, with test questions, and PowerPoint™ slides, which can be downloaded directly from www.hrm.nelson.com.

We hope that students and instructors find these changes as exciting as we do and that they help to facilitate and maximize learning.

Acknowledgments

A textbook is rarely the product of the authors alone. Our book is no exception. In writing this text we have benefited greatly from the comments, suggestions, and support of a number of people. We and the publishers would like to thank the following people, who provided their valuable comments during the development of our book: Mary MacKinnon, McGill University; Stephen Havlovic, Simon Fraser University; Richard Delaney, Fanshawe College; Peter Fortura, Algonquin College; Ihor Sokolyk, Humber College; and Michael Walker, Georgian College. We would especially like to thank the following reviewers for their helpful suggestions: John Hayfron, Coquitlam College; Lori Prsa, Sheridan College; Robert Scharff, Kwantlen University College; Norm Smith, Georgian College; and Simon Woodcock, Simon Fraser University. Yang Lin provided valuable research assistance in updating the time series.

Finally, there are our families. Their patience and emotional support, which made everything go more smoothly, was greater than we had any right to expect.

About the Authors

Helmar Drost

Dr. Helmar Drost is Professor of Economics and Social and Political Thought at York University. He received a Master of Arts in economics from the University of Cologne in 1965 and a Ph.D. in economics from the University of Bochum in 1968. He joined the faculty at York University in 1969 after a year as postdoctoral fellow at the University of Toronto.

He has held appointments as Full Professor at the Technical University of Berlin, as Visiting Professor at the University of Toronto at Scarborough and the University of Konstanz, and as director of York's Graduate Program in Social and Political Thought. He has acted as consultant to the federal governments of Canada and Germany.

Dr. Drost has taught introductory and advanced courses in microeconomic and macroeconomic theory, labour economics, the economics of education, and business cycle and growth theory. His research has primarily been in the areas of labour economics and macroeconomics. His current research focuses on labour market outcomes in Canada, in particular unemployment and income of minority groups, and the links between the educational system and the labour market. He is the author of two books on social policy and growth theory as well as numerous articles in professional journals in Europe and North America.

H. Richard Hird

Mr. Hird is a Professor of Economics and Statistics in the Business School at Durham College in Oshawa, Ontario. He earned his Bachelor's and Master's degrees in economics at the University of Windsor, where he specialized in labour economics. Prior to joining Durham College in 1977, he was an economist with the Ontario Ministry of Labour, the Ontario Ministry of Community and Social Services, and the Canada Department of Manpower and Immigration. Mr. Hird has helped draft legislation in the area of employment standards, written research reports on the labour market, and evaluated government initiatives in the labour market.

Mr. Hird has taught at Atkinson College, York University and currently teaches part-time for Trent University. He is the author of an introductory economics text (*Working With Economics*, Seventh Edition) and the co-author of an introductory statistics text (*Understanding Business Statistics*). He is an examiner and course author for the Certified General Accountants Association of Canada and an examiner for the Human Resources Professional Association of Ontario.

Eric Moon

Mr. Moon is an international economic policy analyst who has managed research projects for governments around the world. He has lectured extensively at universities and colleges in Canada, the United States, and Korea, in the areas of economics, business statistics, and operations management. He is a member of both the Canadian and American Economic Associations.

Introduction and Overview

1. THE ECONOMIST'S STUDY OF LABOUR

2. OVERVIEW OF THE LABOUR MARKET

3. INSTITUTIONAL ASPECTS OF THE LABOUR MARKET

PART I

Introduction and Overview

Many people like to dip their toes into the swimming pool to test the water temperature; they do not want to jump in without information about the condition of the pool.

Your introduction to the Canadian labour market is analogous to dipping your toes in the water. The first three chapters establish a framework for analyzing the labour market. Chapter 1 explains the differences between human resources management, labour relations, and labour market analysis. It provides an overview of the economist's way of thinking and of the economic, institutional, and sociological forces that determine labour market outcomes.

The labour market is one of several markets in the economy. Before analyzing the labour market in detail, we must first understand how markets work in general. Chapter 2 introduces the concept of a market and the two major components of any market: demand and supply. The labour market has special features that distinguish it from other markets; Chapter 2 discusses these features and places the labour market into the context of the national and global economy.

Governments and unions play a major role in regulating the labour market. Chapter 3 outlines the legislative framework of the labour market. It refers to legislation concerning employment standards, human rights, health and safety, workers' compensation, and employment insurance. For approximately one-third of the Canadian labour force, wages and other conditions of employment are determined by collective bargaining. Changes in union membership are discussed in the concluding part of the chapter.

Chapter 1

The Economist's Study of Labour

Chapter Learning Objectives

After completing this chapter, you should be able to:

- identify the differences between human resources management, labour relations, and labour market analysis
- describe how society deals with the scarcity of resources
- explain the concept of opportunity cost and rational decision making
- describe the difference between command, free-market, and mixed economies
- explain the economist's view of optimal decision making
- discuss how market, institutional, and sociological forces determine labour market outcomes
- distinguish between positive and normative economics

THE ROLE OF GOVERNMENT IN A MARKET ECONOMY

Labour economists analyze how wages and employment are determined in the labour market through the exchange of labour services. The central decision makers in the exchange are households supplying labour services and firms demanding labour services. A third decision maker is the government. Governments at the federal and provincial levels enact legislation that regulates and thereby constrains the decision making of households and firms in the labour market.

One of the questions continually debated by economists is to what extent governments should interfere in the free operation of markets, be these labour markets, commodity and service markets, or financial markets.

Those who argue that government should interfere as little as possible in markets value individual freedom most. They further claim that markets left on their own provide the best solution to the problem of scarcity. Markets coordinate individual decisions through the price mechanism in a way that allocates scarce resources to their best possible use. A market economy is said to be efficient in that it produces things people want to buy at prices they are willing to pay. Government, by interfering with the price mechanism, would reduce efficiency.

Those who are in favour of more government presence point out that efficient exchanges in markets only occur under certain ideal conditions, which are rarely fulfilled in reality. Inefficiencies are likely to result whenever these conditions are not met. For example, involuntary unemployment constitutes a waste of human resources. It is the result of labour market failure. Government policies designed to reduce unemployment aim at improving labour market outcomes rather than reducing efficiency. Possible market failures and the resulting inefficiencies are not the only basis on which one might argue for government intervention. The operation of unfettered market forces often leads to large income inequalities, which violate the principle of equity and fairness and threaten the political and social stability of a society. Also, labour market outcomes may be efficient and yet may involve discrimination against certain workers on the basis of gender, race, or age. If one values equity more than efficiency, government policies might be justified to prevent discriminatory practices.

The position taken in the debate about the appropriate role of government in a market economy depends on the values held by individuals. People who value equity and fairness most tend to be in favour of more rather than less government intervention. People who value individual freedom and efficiency most tend to prefer as little government regulation as possible. Differences in value judgments ultimately cannot be resolved by scientific methods.

The Relevance of Labour Economics

"With Good Jobs Scarce, More Young People Stay in School," "Middle Income Families Losing Ground," "Hockey Star Signs Multimillion $ Contract," "Federal Government Tightens Eligibility for Employment Insurance Benefits," "Canadian Union of Public Employees Threatens Strike," "Car Plant Closing."

Barely a day goes by without a newspaper headline or radio or TV report addressing issues related to work. The world of work is the focus of labour economics—who is working, what types of jobs are available, and what determines the pay people receive. These issues are not just of academic interest: they are central to our daily lives. Most people spend large parts of their lives working. The lion's share of income received by households is derived from employment. Compensation of employees—that is, wages, salaries, and fringe benefits—accounts for about 70% of total national income generated each year in Canada. Not only is work central to one's ability to provide income, but it also plays an important part in shaping one's self-esteem and role in society.

The prominence of work and its financial remuneration is reflected in a multitude of public policy debates. Should the minimum wage be raised? Should mandatory retirement be abolished? Can the reduction of overtime through higher overtime premiums create new jobs? Are wage subsidies paid by the government to firms an appropriate tool to increase the employment of disadvantaged groups? Should legal restrictions on union formation be increased or reduced? Should employment insurance benefits be reduced for repeat users? Do increased employment standards reduce the competitiveness of Canadian firms? As we will see throughout this text, labour economics provides a very useful framework in which to analyze these questions.

Labour Markets and the Employment Relation

Economics is concerned with the determination of prices and levels of production in the economy. Labour economics deals with one particular aspect of this process: the determination of wages and employment in the labour market and the resulting distribution of labour income among individuals and households. In a market, buyers and sellers exchange a good or a service; the quantity of the good to be exchanged is determined and the price is set in the market. In the labour market, labour services are exchanged. The buyers are the employers and the sellers are those who are seeking employment. The price is the wage rate, or salary, that is agreed upon by both parties.

Labour economics is not the only discipline concerned with the interaction of employers and employees. Other fields that study the relationship between employers and employees are human resources management and labour relations.

Human resources management (HRM) deals with an organization's structure and processes aimed at attracting, motivating, and retaining employees of an organization. HRM views the relationship between an individual organization (the employer) and an individual employee from the perspective of the organization and aims at increasing the efficiency of its employees. HRM involves recruitment, performance assessment, compensation methods, training, job design, and health and safety.

Labour relations, or industrial relations, focuses on the interaction between an employer, or a group of employers, and the representatives of the employees (the union or professional association). Labour relations studies how employers and unions structure their relationship through the collective bargaining process. Topics covered include dispute resolution and the contents of collective agreements. While HRM focuses on improving the productivity of employees, labour relations tilts toward the equity aspect of the employment relationship.[1] Historically, the lack of balance between equity and efficiency in the workplace was a major factor in the rise of unions, whose goal has been to promote equitable, or fair, treatment of their members by employers.

Of the three fields dealing with the interaction between employers and employees, labour economics takes the broadest approach. HRM focuses on the employment relationship within an individual company, government agency, or not-for-profit organization. Labour relations focuses on a particular subset of employees, namely members of unions or professional organizations. It studies the interaction between unions and employers in the collective bargaining process. Labour economics deals with all workers, whether unionized or nonunionized. Its main emphasis is on the interaction between workers and employers in a market setting. The exchange of labour services is studied in occupational, industrial, or regional labour markets or the economy at large. Conditions in labour markets have a significant impact on HR policies and the collective bargaining process. A shortage of workers in a particular trade, for example, will affect the recruiting, training, and compensation decisions of companies in need of skilled tradespeople. It will also strengthen the bargaining position of trade unions representing workers in that particular trade.

Some Basic Economic Concepts

Labour market analysis constitutes the core of modern labour economics. Since the subject of this book is labour economics, we focus on the analysis of Canadian labour markets. Before plunging into the substance and details of labour economics, however, it is helpful to understand some basic economic concepts and the way economists reason.

Scarcity and Opportunity Cost

Almost everything in this world has a limit. There are only 24 hours in a day. There is only so much money in your pocket, or in your bank account. There are only so many doctors to provide medical services. Companies have only so much space within which to manufacture products. There is only so much land in Canada. Economists refer to the limitation of human and physical resources as **scarcity**.

As a result of scarcity, decisions must be made. You must decide how you will use the 24 hours in a day. You must decide what you will do with your money. Society has to decide how much to spend on the training of doctors. Companies must plan how to use the space available to them. Canadians must decide how to use the land that we have available. Economics is the study of how these decisions are made.

Just as scarcity implies the need for choice, so choice implies the existence of cost. A decision to have more of something implies having less of something else. Economists define **opportunity cost** as the value of the item that has to be given up when a decision is made. For example, if you decide to spend 12 hours in class per week then you give up the opportunity to spend these 12 hours working for pay. The pay you forgo is the opportunity cost of attending class. If you spend some money on lunch, you cannot spend the same money on another item. The value of the item you did not purchase represents the opportunity cost of buying lunch. If you spend money from your bank account, you lose the opportunity to earn interest on the money.

When you spend money on an item, you may argue that there are many other ways to dispose of your money. What is the opportunity cost when there are many alternatives? The opportunity cost represents the value of the best, or most valuable, forgone alternative. For example, the opportunity cost associated with spending money on an item is the amount of interest that could have been earned had that money been left in the bank.

Note that you cannot escape opportunity costs. Every time you make a decision to use your resources in a specific way, you sacrifice the alternatives. If you decide, for example, to pursue a career as a human resources professional, you will sacrifice the opportunity of a career in some other field. A knowledge of opportunity cost encourages you to consider all the alternatives.

Societies must contend with the scarcity of resources available to them. All societies face a limited amount of land, people, machinery, and equipment. If Canadians use land to build a college, for example, the land cannot be used for an apartment building at the same time. Choices have to be made, but who makes them?

In some economies, the decisions regarding the use and distribution of resources are largely made by the state. Decision making is highly centralized and often determined by long-term economic plans. These are **command economies** or centrally planned economies. In command economies, there is very little individual freedom and the society's resources are owned by the state. In other societies, decisions about resource use are largely made by individuals. Resources are privately owned and the decision-making process is

scarcity
limitation of a society's resources

opportunity cost
value of the best forgone alternative when a decision is made

command economy
an economy in which the decisions about resource allocation are made by the state

free-market economy

an economy in which the decisions about resource use are made by private households and firms

mixed economy

a combination of the command system and the free-market system

decentralized. Individual decisions are coordinated through the market. Such a system is known as a **free-market economy**, or a market economy. Free-market economies are characterized by a great deal of individual freedom.

No country offers an example of a pure command or market economy. In reality, economies combine elements of both systems. We call an economy in which some decisions are made by households and firms and some by the government a **mixed economy**: Canada has a mixed economy and this is evident in the labour market. For example, individuals are basically free to pursue careers of their choice. Governments in Canada have put restrictions on the numbers of people who can practise in certain occupations, however. For example, there are restrictions on the numbers of dentists, physicians, or veterinarians who can practise their profession, as there are restrictions on the numbers of taxicab operators and people who fish for lobster. Governments also impose restrictions on the employment arrangement. Laws have been enacted to set minimum wage rates, restrict hours of work, regulate safety conditions, and so on. Much of the discussion about labour markets in this text focuses on the impact of government regulation.

Optimal Decision Making

The basic decision makers in a market economy are households and firms. How do they make decisions? A central principle in economics is that households and firms optimize—they do the best they can for themselves given their objectives and the constraints they face. When households decide which items to purchase or how much to spend today and how much to save for the future, they make choices designed to maximize their well-being, or **utility**. When firms decide how many goods to produce or whether to build a new factory, they make choices designed to maximize the difference between revenues and cost, that is their **profit**. When exchanging labour services in the labour market, households choose to allocate their time between paid work and other activities in such a way as to maximize their level of satisfaction, and firms hire labour services to maximize profit.

A key point in making optimal decisions is that households and firms compare the cost and benefits of their decision *at the margin*. The relevant costs and benefits in economic decisions are the additional costs and additional benefits that result from a decision. Economists use the term *marginal* when referring to additional changes. **Marginal cost** is the additional cost over and above the costs already incurred. If a firm decides to produce one unit more of an item the marginal cost would be the addition to total cost resulting from the increased production. Likewise **marginal benefit** is the additional benefit over and above the benefits already achieved. The optimal decision rule in economics is:

utility

the satisfaction or well-being a household receives from consuming a good or service

profit

the difference between revenues and costs

marginal cost

the additional cost resulting from doing something

marginal benefit

the additional benefit

If the marginal benefit of doing something exceeds the marginal cost, go ahead and do it.
If the marginal cost exceeds the marginal benefit, don't do it.

We can apply the optimal decision rule, for example, to the hiring decision of a firm. A firm considering whether to hire an extra worker must evaluate the marginal cost of the worker (the extra wages and benefits that must be paid) and weigh it against the marginal benefit of the worker (the increase in revenue that will be generated by the extra worker). If the marginal benefit of hiring the additional worker exceeds the marginal cost, the firm should hire the worker.

Labour Market Outcomes and Labour Market Process

A useful distinction in studying labour economics is that between labour market outcomes and the labour market process.[2] The distinction underlies the structure of this book in Part II and Part III. In Part II we study labour market outcomes, and in Part III we study the labour market process. Labour market outcomes are the events and developments in the labour market that we are trying to understand and to explain. They are the results of the operation of the labour market.

There are a great number of labour market outcomes. In Part II of the book we focus in particular on four outcomes:

- the changing level and composition of labour supply
- the changing level and composition of labour demand
- the changing level and composition of unemployment
- the changing level and structure of earnings

In order to understand labour market outcomes, one has to understand the process that gives rise to them. In other words, one has to understand how the labour market works. The labour market process involves three broad forces that together determine the labour market outcomes: market forces, institutional forces, and sociological forces.

Market Forces

A key concept in economics is scarcity. Most things in life are available in only limited supply. Scarcity requires rationing; that is, a mechanism must be chosen to determine who gets what. In college and university courses with limited enrollments, the mechanism is a first-come, first-served rule. Once the course is filled, no further students are admitted. In market economies, the most widely used rationing mechanism is the price mechanism. When there is a shortage of gasoline, gasoline prices increase. When there is a shortage of electrical engineers, salaries of electrical engineers increase. When the demand for mortgages exceeds the supply of mortgage funds, mortgage rates increase. Prices move in the opposite direction when there is a surplus. When there is a glut in the housing market, housing prices decrease. When the supply of graduates from education programs exceeds the demand, starting salaries of teachers decline. Market forces ration the available supply by changing prices.

invisible hand

the price mechanism that coordinates individual actions in a market

internal labour market

personnel policy of firms by which job openings are filled from within the ranks of firms' own employees

A substantial part of this book is devoted to analyzing how the labour market coordinates the decisions of households and firms through changes in compensation. The wage mechanism is the price mechanism in labour markets. It guides like an **invisible hand** the decisions and actions of households and firms involved in the exchange of labour services.

Institutional Forces

Institutional forces reflect the influence of organizations such as unions, government agencies, and large corporations on the process of wage and employment determination. These institutions affect labour market outcomes in various ways. One way is through rules and regulations in the form of collective agreements, government legislation, or corporate policies. Corporations, for example, often follow a policy of filling job openings in preset promotion ladders from within the firm rather than hiring people from outside. Such a policy creates an **internal labour market** by limiting competition for jobs to individuals already employed in the firm.[3] As workers move up the job ladder, vacancies open at the bottom—"the port of entry." Through entry-level jobs, the internal labour market becomes connected to the external labour market. Individuals in the external market compete for the entry-level jobs. Once they have been hired by the company, they can move up on internal job ladders. Internal labour markets are characterized by long-term employment relationships in which seniority provides some degree of protection against layoffs.

Corporate personnel policies are not the only policies that create restrictions and barriers in labour markets. Seniority rules in union contracts contain provisions specifying which employees have first rights of refusal with respect to new job vacancies or which employees will be laid off first when companies experience lower sales. The operation of hiring halls in construction trades and longshoring restricts competition for newly opened jobs largely to union members. Similarly, government legislation in the form of protective labour laws prevents certain groups from entering particular jobs. By creating barriers to entry and segmenting the labour market, institutions reduce the role of market forces in determining wages and employment.

In addition to defining the market in which the forces of labour supply and demand can interact, unions, governments, and corporations can also directly affect the process of wage setting. The power of a union to raise wages partly derives from its threat of a strike. While a company may be able to replace an individual employee, if all workers walk off the job the company faces a serious loss of production and profit. The strike threat gives unions an institutional power to affect the level of pay. While this power originates outside of the market forces of supply and demand, it is not independent of these forces. For example, in times of recession when labour supply exceeds labour demand, the bargaining power of unions can be greatly diminished. Another important institutional factor in wage setting is the degree of centralization or decentralization of collective bargaining.[4] In Canada, the United States, and Great Britain, bargaining is relatively decentralized; it largely takes place at the firm or plant level. In the Scandinavian countries and in Austria, bargaining is extremely centralized; all unions bargain as a united whole with a single all-industry national employers' federation. In many other European countries, bargaining is nationally organized, but on an industry-by-industry basis. The more decentralized bargaining is, the more responsive unions are to supply and demand forces.

Large corporations and governments also have a direct institutional effect on wage rates. In highly competitive markets, a firm with labour costs higher than its competitors' will face losses and ultimately bankruptcy. Large corporations operating in regulated markets or having achieved a dominating role in their markets often face much less competition and, as a result, have much more discretion in setting wages. Governments affect wages through legislation, such as minimum wage and pay equity legislation, or through wage subsidies and payroll taxes.

Sociological Forces

A third set of forces affecting labour market outcomes is sociological factors such as social norms and customs.[5] Sociological factors affect the labour market process in two ways: through their influence on who can compete in a particular labour market, and through their direct impact on wage determination.

Family background, parents' occupation, and socioeconomic class may have an important effect on an individual's occupational choice and thus on an individual's earnings. The chances of becoming a doctor are likely to be lower for the sons or daughters of a construction worker than for the children of a doctor.

Changes in social norms can significantly affect labour market outcomes. As we will see in Chapter 4, the rise in the labour force participation of married women has greatly affected overall labour supply in Canada. Some of the rise can be explained by economic factors such as the increase of real wages for women. Among the noneconomic forces affecting the workforce participation of women has been the dramatic change in attitudes regarding the appropriateness of married women's working outside the home. Contrary to half a century ago, women working for pay is now widely accepted in Canadian society.

Cultural values are another factor affecting wage and employment determination. Cultural values are likely to affect occupational choices and earnings of different ethnic groups in the labour market as they shape the attitudes of individuals regarding the importance of education, entrepreneurial risk-taking, work ethic, and the desire to succeed financially and economically.

Custom is a social force that affects the labour market independently of labour demand and supply. A custom is a practice that has gained acceptance simply because it has been followed for a long time. Customs can have a strong influence, particularly on wage differences between different occupational groups.[6] Pay differences between firefighters and police officers, for example, reflect views long held by the two groups regarding social status and equity.

Each society has to decide which mix of market, institutional, and socio-logical forces it considers to be appropriate. Some societies choose a mix more heavily weighted toward institutional forces, while others rely more heavily on market forces.

Economists as Policymakers

Often, labour economists are asked to explain the causes of economic out-comes. For example, why are equally productive men and women paid dif-ferent wages? Why is the unemployment rate for teenagers higher than for adult workers? At times, labour economists are asked to recommend policies to improve labour market outcomes. What, for instance, should the govern-ment do to reduce the wage discrepancies between men and women? What should it do to reduce unemployment of certain groups in the labour market? When labour economists are trying to explain labour market events or out-comes, they act as scientists. When they are trying to improve outcomes, they are policymakers.

To help clarify the two roles that economists play, let us look at the example of minimum wage laws. An economist trying to explain teenage unemployment might come up with the following statement: "Minimum wage laws cause teenage unemployment." In a debate on how to improve the situation of the working poor, another economist might state: "The government should raise the minimum wage." Note what the two economists are trying to do. The first econ-omist is making a claim about what causes teenage unemployment, that is, about how the world works. That economist takes on the role of scientist. The second economist is making a claim about how to improve the situation of a particular group, that is, about how to change the world. This economist takes on the role of policymaker. Note also the differences in the language used by each econo-mist. The first statement is descriptive: it includes a claim about how the world *is*. We call this type of statement a **positive statement**. The second statement is prescriptive: it includes a claim about how the world *ought to be*. We call this statement a **normative statement**.

positive statement

a statement about how the world is

normative statement

a statement about how the world ought to be

Evaluating Positive and Normative Statements

The central difference between positive and normative statements is how we judge their validity. Positive statements might be right or wrong. They are for-mulated in such a way that they can be confirmed or rejected by examining evidence. There are many studies, for example, in which economists have tested the relationship between the minimum wage and teenage unemploy-ment by using data on changes in the minimum wage and unemployment over time or across different groups of teenagers. To find out whether a min-imum wage increases teenage unemployment does not involve a value judg-ment. The answer to the question carries no implication as to whether the government should go ahead with increasing the minimum wage.

In contrast, evaluating normative statements involves not only facts but also values. Deciding whether increasing the minimum wage is good or bad policy involves personal values. Some working poor may receive an increase in wages as a result of the minimum wage increase. Others may lose their jobs as a result of the minimum wage increase. How do we know if it is a good idea to increase the minimum wage when there will be winners as well as losers? If there were only winners, normative statements and the government policies to which they lead would not be controversial. Economic policies, however, very rarely involve only winners. They usually involve tradeoffs, and some people gain at the expense of others. If the gains made by the winners are greater than the losses of the losers, is it a good idea to proceed with a minimum wage increase? Should the winners compensate the losers to have an acceptable policy? Clearly, the answers to these questions involve value judgments. They depend on our personal ethical, religious, or philosophical views.

Links Between Positive and Normative Economics

The example of the minimum wage indicates that positive and normative statements are often related. Our positive views about how the world works affect our normative views about what policies are desirable. If economists establish that a minimum wage causes teenage unemployment, that might lead them to reject the view that governments should increase the minimum wage in order to ameliorate the situation of the poor. Yet, logically, the normative conclusion cannot be derived from the positive statement alone. A value judgment is required to come to the conclusion that the loss of those suffering unemployment outweighs the gain of those whose income increases because

Labour Market Issue 1.1

Efficiency Versus Distribution–A Matter of Value Judgment

Policies, as we saw in the example of the minimum wage, nearly always result in some people gaining and some losing. Whenever some groups win and others lose, value judgments must be made in assessing the policy. Immigration policy is a case in point.

Whose economic well-being should Canada try to improve when it sets immigration targets: the well-being of people born in Canada (native-born Canadians), or that of immigrants? Suppose that the objective of immigration policy is to improve the well-being of the native-born population. What aspect of well-being should be the focus of immigration policy: the income per person, or the distribution of income?

Immigration may increase the income per person in the native-born population, but that does not mean that all native-born Canadians will gain from increased immigration. Immigrants increase the number of people in an economy looking for work. Because of the increased competition for jobs, the wages of some native-born workers will fall. At the same time, however, Canadian firms gain, because they can hire workers at lower wages. Also, native-born consumers gain when they use the goods and services produced by immigrants, because lower labour costs lead to less expensive goods and services.

Immigration not only changes the size of the economic pie (which economists call "efficiency"), but also changes how the pie is sliced up (the distribution). Immigration policy, therefore, must be judged in terms of its impact on both dimensions: efficiency and distribution. The importance that Canadians attach to these two dimensions depends on their particular values. The science of economics provides no guidance on how to rank the two.

of an increase in the minimum wage. Policy recommendations, therefore, should not be presented as if they were the sole outcome of scientific analysis. Whenever economists make normative statements, they are crossing the line from science to policymaking.

The relation between positive statements and normative judgments does not run just one way. We have seen in the above example how the result of a scientific inquiry may lead to a particular value judgment. Normative views, however, also affect the way we do science. Facts do not organize themselves into concepts and theories just by being examined. Questions must be asked before answers can be given, and the questions are an expression of our interest in the world; they are essentially valuations. Economists are guided by moral, political, or ideological values in their selection of problems. When the nineteenth-century English economist David Ricardo stated that the principal problem in economics is to determine the laws that regulate the distribution of income, he expressed a personal value judgment about what he considered to be the most important subject to be researched by economists. Values are thus necessarily involved already at the stage when we observe facts and carry on analysis. They do not only come into play when we draw political conclusions from facts and valuations.

Summary

The employment relationship is essential to our daily lives. The majority of Canadians depend on income from employment. The employment relationship is studied in three related fields: human resources management, labour relations, and labour market analysis. Labour economics deals primarily with labour market analysis.

Scarcity is a central problem faced by every society. Because of scarcity, choices have to be made. In making choices, the opportunity cost of alternative uses of resources has to be considered.

There are two types of pure economies: command and free-market economies. In practice, all economies are mixed economies. Mixed economies combine elements of command and market economies. In market economies, firms and households largely make the decisions about what to produce and to consume. Economists analyze these decisions using a cost–benefit approach.

In markets, the decisions of firms and households are coordinated through the price mechanism. Labour markets coordinate the decisions of firms and households regarding the exchange of paid work. The operation of labour markets is determined by three forces: market forces, institutional forces, and sociological forces.

Positive economics uses theories to explain and to predict labour market behaviour. Normative economics is concerned with changing certain aspects of the labour market. Positive economics describes "what is" and normative economics describes "what should be." Claims about how the world works often affect our views of how the world ought to be. Likewise, normative views often affect the way we try to explain the world.

Key Terms

command economy (page 9)

free-market economy (page 10)

internal labour market (page 12)

invisible hand (page 12)

marginal benefit (page 10)

marginal cost (page 10)

mixed economy (page 10)

normative statement (page 14)

opportunity cost (page 9)

positive statement (page 14)

profit (page 10)

scarcity (page 9)

utility (page 10)

Weblinks

Certified Human Resources Professionals
www.chrp.ca

Canada Industrial Relations Board
www.cirb-ccri.gc.ca

Canadian Industrial Relations Association
www.cira-acri.ca

Canadian Labour Congress
www.clc-ctc.ca

Discussion Questions

1. There is ongoing debate in Canada whether the government should charge user fees for healthcare services or whether healthcare should be freely available to all individuals. Apply the concept of opportunity cost to this debate.

2. List two choices you made recently and explain whether, explicitly or implicitly, you made these choices in terms of marginal cost and marginal benefit.

3. One of the problems of command and/or centrally planned economies is that they are outperformed by market economies in terms of the incentives of workers to work reasonably hard and efficiently.
   a. Can you think of anything inherent in a command economy that would reduce the incentives for work?
   b. Can you think of anything inherent in a market economy that would lead to relatively stronger incentives for work?

4. Provide examples of custom significantly affecting the relative wages or salaries of occupational groups.

5. "A policy that redistributes income from one group to another always involves comparing the welfare loss of some people against the welfare gain of others. Whether the redistribution is equitable or just cannot be resolved with scientific methods but requires a value judgment." True or false? Explain.

Using the Internet

1. Use an online business magazine (for example, www.canadianbusiness.com or www.economist.com) to find two examples of social or legal forces acting in a market environment. You can choose either a labour, commodity, or financial market. Explain how these social or legal forces might prevent market forces from freely determining wages or prices in the market.

Exercises

1. For each of the following issues, determine whether it falls under the field of human resources management, labour relations, or labour market analysis:
   a. termination for just cause
   b. training and development
   c. causes of unemployment
   d. seniority rights
   e. pay equity
2. What is the difference between an internal and an external labour market? Can a firm decide on its own what wages to pay in the internal labour market, or do the market forces of supply and demand have some influence?
3. Calculate as best as you can:
   a. your opportunity cost of taking this course in labour economics
   b. your opportunity cost of going out on a Saturday night
4. Classify each of the following statements as positive or normative. Explain.
   a. Each Canadian family should have access to free childcare.
   b. Laws requiring equal pay for work of equal value will make women better off.
   c. Lower payroll taxes encourage firms to employ more people.
   d. An unemployment rate of 11% is too high.
   e. Employers should subsidize the work clothing of their employees.
   f. The deficit reduction of the federal government affects poor people unfairly.

References

[1]Meltz, N. (1989). "Industrial Relations: Balancing Efficiency and Equity." In J. Barbash and K. Barbash (Eds.), *Theories and Concepts in Comparative Industrial Relations.* Columbia: University of South Carolina Press, pp. 109–113. Also, Barbash, J. (1989). "Equity as Function: Its Rise and Attrition." In J. Barbash and K. Barbash (Eds.), *Theories and Concepts in Comparative Industrial Relations.* Columbia: University of South Carolina Press, pp. 114–122.

[2]Kaufman, B.E. (2006). *The Economics of Labor Markets* (7th ed.). Mason, OH: Thomson South-Western.

[3]Osterman, P. (1984). *Internal Labour Markets.* Cambridge, MA: MIT Press.

[4]Katz, H.C. (1993). "The Decentralization of Collective Bargaining. A Literature Review and Comparative Analysis." *Industrial and Labor Relations Review*, 47: 3–22.

[5]Solow, R. (1990). *The Labor Market as a Social Institution.* Oxford: Blackwell.

[6]Marsden, D. (1986). *The End of Economic Man? Custom and Competition in Labor Markets.* New York: St. Martin's Press.

Chapter 2

Overview of the Labour Market

Chapter Learning Objectives

After completing this chapter, you should be able to:

- describe the concept of a market
- describe the conditions under which both demand and supply curves are drawn
- explain how demand and supply curves can shift to a new position
- explain how the market eliminates shortages and surpluses
- describe what is meant by price elasticity of demand and of supply
- calculate the coefficient of price elasticity
- discuss the factors that influence price elasticity
- explain how the labour market differs from other markets
- contrast the stock and flow approaches to the analysis of the labour market
- explain the circular flow model of the economy
- discuss how globalization affects the Canadian labour market

GLOBALIZATION AND HUMAN RESOURCES MANAGEMENT

Intensified international competition and an accelerating pace of technological change have forced Canadian firms to be continuously innovative. Continuing innovation not only involves constant improvement in products, production processes, and materials, but also involves changes in organizational structures and human resources management. Organizational structures can no longer be rigid; they must adapt to a changing business world. Human resources managers need to help the organization bring about and adapt to change. Since knowledge is the key to success for companies in the global market, human resources managers need to facilitate the learning process and the acquisition of new skills.

This shift in emphasis toward constant acquisition of new skills has sometimes been termed the move from Fordism to Toyotism. **Fordism** generally describes a mass production system—the assembly line in car manufacturing is a typical example of mass production—that combines a small group of highly skilled managers and technically trained personnel with a workforce having relatively low educational attainment and vocational skills, organized in a vertical hierarchy. The Fordist organizational model resembles a military command model with layers of middle managers who pass information and commands up and down the hierarchy. Such an organization is relatively inflexible but well suited to mass production in capital-intensive sectors, where large-scale production is essential to competitiveness. Fordism is associated with gaining the loyalty of the workers through the payment of relatively high wage rates. In return, the employee relinquishes all participation in production decisions.

Toyotism denotes an organizational model involving more flexible management forms of semi-independent groups linked laterally rather than vertically. Employees have more autonomy and responsibility within the organization. As a result, Toyotism requires an increase in the competence of employees across the board, which is accomplished through continual training and upgrading. Problems in production are tackled through consultation among the various groups involved. Toyotism also puts pressure on union–management relations to change from an adversarial relationship to one of cooperation and consensus. Another feature of Toyotism is the division of the workforce into two groups: full-time, skilled employees and part-time, casual labourers.

Fordism

a mass production system that combines a small group of highly skilled managers and technically trained personnel with a workforce having relatively low educational attainment and vocational skills organized in a vertical hierarchy

Toyotism

an organizational model involving flexible management forms of semi-independent groups linked laterally rather than vertically

The Market Mechanism
(Or How the Market Works)

Approximately 17 million people in Canada are employed or are looking for a job. There are close to 2 million registered business establishments and a multitude of government and nonprofit agencies that provide employment for job seekers. The interaction between those looking for a job and those employers looking for workers takes place in the labour market. The outcomes of this interaction between employers and job seekers can be viewed in two ways: in terms of the number of people employed, either part-time or full-time; or in terms of the wage rate, or salary. How are employment levels and wage rates determined? Why do some people remain jobless in spite of their search for employment? Why do some workers earn a higher wage rate than others? The answers to these questions come from knowing how a market works. The workings of a market are discussed in this chapter.

The labour market is one of several markets in the economy. Generally, a **market** exists whenever there is a good or a service that buyers and sellers want to trade. The interaction between the buyers and the sellers results in an exchange of the good or service and in the establishment of a price. The market exchange is completed when both the buyer and the seller agree to the price and the quantity of the good or service to be exchanged. These exchanges can occur in geographically defined areas where buyers and sellers meet each other physically, as at farmers' markets or in retail stores. The locations of some other markets are not so easy to identify. For example, the markets for gold and crude oil are international in nature. The prices for these products are determined on a worldwide basis. Furthermore, the buyers and sellers in these markets are not likely to meet face to face.

In the **labour market**, labour services (such as those of carpenters or computer programmers) are exchanged. In these markets, the price agreed to by the buyers and the sellers is called the **wage rate**. Buyers in the labour market are employers who require employees to provide goods and services for their customers. Suppliers in the labour market are individuals who are working or seeking employment. As with product markets, some labour markets are local while others are national or international in scope. The market for retail clerks is likely of a local nature, while the market for airline pilots is national, and the market for those who can extinguish oil fires is worldwide.

Before studying the labour market in more detail, let us review how a market operates. In any market there is interaction between buyers and sellers. This interaction results in an exchange of a product or service and the determination of a price. The determination of a price is the primary function of a market. The price carries a different name in different markets. It may be called the interest rate, which is the price set in money markets. In the rental housing market, the price is called the rent. In the foreign exchange market, the foreign exchange rate is the price at which the Canadian dollar exchanges for another currency. This text deals with the labour market. The price established in this market is the wage rate.

market

the interaction of buyers and sellers, in which a price is established and a product or service exchanged

labour market

the interaction of buyers and sellers of labour services

wage rate

the price of an hour of work established in the labour market

The buyer's side of the market is called the demand side and the seller's side of the market is the supply side. For the purposes of analysis, we will discuss the two sides separately, starting with the demand side. Following our discussion of the supply side of the market, both sides will be joined and the process of price determination will be discussed.

The Demand Side

The demand for a product or service represents the willingness and ability of consumers to purchase that product or service. In order to analyze the demand for any product or service, the factors that influence demand must be taken into consideration. These factors are:

- the price of the product or service
- the price of related products or services
- income levels of consumers
- consumers' expectations about future prices and incomes
- tastes and preferences
- the number of buyers

It is difficult to analyze the demand for a product or service while attempting to consider all of the above factors at once. Therefore, to simplify our discussion, we will review the response of the quantity demanded to a change in the price, assuming that all other factors that influence demand remain constant. This assumption is temporary; once the relationship between the price and the quantity demanded is established, the other factors that influence demand will be allowed to vary.

As the price of the product decreases, the quantity demanded increases. There are two reasons for this. First, as the price falls, consumers are able to buy more of this product with their current income. This is referred to as the **income effect**. Second, as the price falls, this product may be substituted for more expensive products. This is referred to as the **substitution effect**. That is, one product is substituted for another. As the price of the product increases, the quantity demanded decreases. Income and substitution effects now work in the opposite direction. As prices increase, consumers can buy less of the product with their current income, and they substitute other products for this higher priced product.

The inverse relationship between the price and the quantity demanded is known as the **law of downward-sloping demand**. On a graph, this relationship is referred to as the **demand curve** (see Figure 2.1). The demand curve depicts the quantities demanded of the product at various prices. The relationship depicted by the demand curve will change if there are changes in any of the other factors that influence demand. For example, if consumer incomes are increasing, the quantity of a product demanded will likely increase at a given price. This change will shift the demand curve to the right (see Figure 2.2a). If the price of a substitute product falls, the demand curve will shift to the left (see Figure 2.2b). Shifts in the entire demand curve are referred to as changes

income effect (demand)

the effect of changes in price on how much a consumer can buy with a given income

substitution effect (demand)

changes in price encourage consumers to substitute one product for another

law of downward-sloping demand

there is an inverse relationship between the price and the quantity demanded

demand curve

a graph of the relationship between the price of a good and the quantity demanded

FIGURE 2.1

The Demand Curve

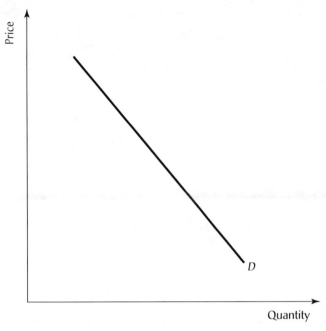

FIGURE 2.2

Influences on the Demand Curve

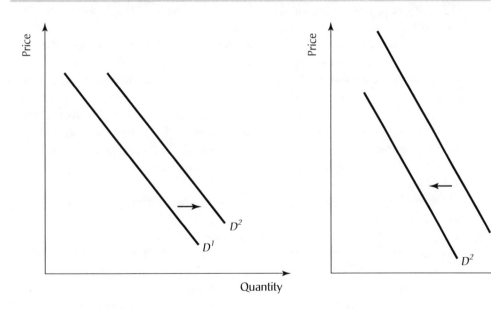

a. An increase in income shifts the demand curve to the right.

b. A decrease in the price of a substitute shifts the demand curve to the left.

change in demand

a shift in the demand curve resulting from a change in a factor, other than the price, that influences the demand for a product or service

change in the quantity demanded

a movement along the demand curve in response to a change in the price of the product or service

in demand. A **change in demand** results when one of the factors previously held constant in drawing the demand curve changes. If the price of the product or service changes, there is no shift in the demand curve as the curve reflects the quantity that would be purchased at all possible prices. If there is a change in the price, the quantity of the product demanded at the new price can be determined by identifying the quantity associated with the new price. In essence, there has been a movement along the curve to the new price. A movement along a demand curve in response to a change in the price is referred to as a **change in the quantity demanded**.

The Supply Side

Supply represents the willingness and ability of firms to sell a product or service. Those who want to analyze the supply side of the market must take several factors into consideration. These factors are:

- the price of the product
- production costs
- the prices of related products or services
- expected future prices
- the state of technology
- the number of suppliers
- government regulations
- weather conditions

As with the demand side, it is difficult to analyze the supply side of the market with all these factors constantly changing. Therefore, for the purposes of this discussion we assume that the factors affecting supply, other than the price, temporarily remain constant.

What happens to the quantity supplied as the price increases? If everything else remains the same, the quantity supplied increases as the price increases. In other words, the quantity supplied is positively related to the price. The positive relationship exists because of the relationship between output and costs. Economists define the **short run** as a period of time during which at least one factor of production is fixed and cannot be changed. The **long run** is defined as a period of time in which all factors of production can be changed. In this section, we will focus on the change in production costs in the short run.

short run

a period of time during which at least one factor of production remains fixed

long run

a period of time during which all factors of production can be changed

diminishing returns

additional output decreases as a result of hiring one more worker, when other factors are fixed

In the short run, if we assume there is fixed capital (given plant size, machinery, and tools), production can be increased by hiring more workers. Initially, this improves the efficiency of the operation. As workers are hired, jobs can be specialized and productivity improved. There will come a point, however, when the additional output created by adding one more worker is less than the addition to total output achieved by the hiring of the previous worker. The new workers have less capital to work with. Economists refer to the decrease in additional output gained from hiring one more worker as **diminishing returns**. When diminishing returns set in, costs of production go up. To produce an additional unit of a product or service, more hours of work or numbers of workers must be paid. To cover the increasing cost, firms only supply more goods or services if prices increase. In the case of natural resources, such as oil and gold, costs may increase if more of the product is to be supplied. Not all oil is easily accessible. It is more costly for the supplier to extract oil from some locations than from others. To supply more oil, costs increase and price increases follow. Similarly, some gold is close to the surface and easy to access. Some gold is not as close to the surface and is more expensive to extract.

The positive graphical relationship between the price and the quantity supplied is referred to as the **supply curve** (see Figure 2.3). If one of the factors influencing supply other than the price changes, the supply curve will shift. For example, if production costs increase because of an increase in wages paid to employees, the supply curve will shift to the left (see Figure 2.4, page 28). At the same price, quantity supplied will be less: there has been a decrease in supply. A **change in supply** occurs when there has been a change in one of the factors, other than the price, that influence the supply curve. A change in supply is associated with a shift in the supply curve. A change in the quantity supplied is associated with a response to a change in the price of the product or service. As with the demand curve, a **change in the quantity supplied** is associated with a movement along the supply curve.

supply curve

a graph of the relationship between the price of a good and the quantity supplied

change in supply

a shift in the supply curve resulting from a change in a factor, other than the price, that influences the supply of a product or service

change in the quantity supplied

a movement along the supply curve in response to a change in the price of the product or service

FIGURE 2.3

The Supply Curve

Since the axes for the demand and the supply curves are labelled the same, we can draw both curves on the same graph (see Figure 2.5). The combination of the demand and the supply curves is the representation of the market for a particular product or service. When we analyze the market, we refer to the graph with both curves.

It is easy to draw demand and supply curves on a page, but it is more difficult to determine the real demand and supply curves for a particular product or a service. In the real world, the demand and supply curves are forever changing, and pinning them down can be difficult. Nonetheless, we can use the concept of demand and supply to predict the result of changes in the marketplace.

Price Determination

Suppliers try to gather information on the demand for their products. Unfortunately, this information is rarely perfect. In light of what information is available, they must select a price for the product or the service. Assume that the suppliers charged a price represented by P_1 in Figure 2.5. At this price the quantity demanded by consumers is less than the quantity supplied by the producers. A **surplus** or excess supply exists. To get rid of the surplus, the

surplus

a situation in which the quantity demanded by consumers is less than the quantity supplied

FIGURE 2.4

Influences on the Supply Curve

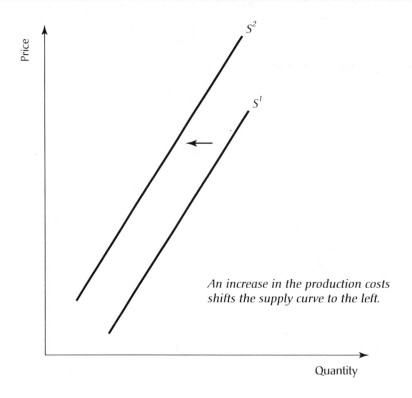

An increase in the production costs shifts the supply curve to the left.

FIGURE 2.5

The Market

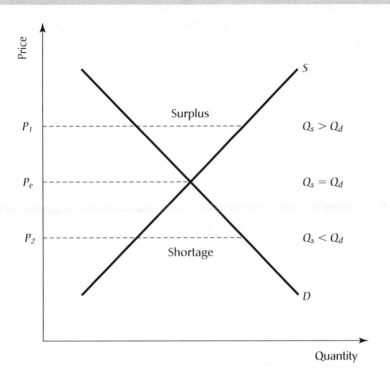

price is lowered. As the price falls, the quantity demanded increases and the quantity supplied decreases. As long as there is a surplus, the price will decline.

Assume that the suppliers initially charged a price represented by P_2 in Figure 2.5. At this price, the quantity supplied is less than the quantity demanded. There is a **shortage**. The price rises as a result of the shortage. As the price increases, the quantity supplied increases and the quantity demanded decreases.

What if the price charged is the one at P_e? At this price, the quantity demanded is equal to the quantity supplied. There is neither a surplus nor a shortage. Therefore, there is no reason for the price to change. The market is in a state of balance. The price determined by the intersection of the demand and supply curves is known as the **equilibrium price**. When something is in equilibrium, it is not likely to change. If the price is not at equilibrium, it will change and move toward equilibrium. When you see prices changing in the marketplace, you are seeing the mechanism that brings the market into balance.

The equilibrium price and quantity change when there is a change in either demand or supply. That is, a shift in either curve will result in a change in the equilibrium price and the corresponding equilibrium quantity. In Figure 2.6 (page 30), an increase in income has shifted the demand curve to

shortage

a situation in which quantity demanded is greater than quantity supplied

equilibrium price

the price at which the quantity demanded equals the quantity supplied the right. If we assume that the market was in equilibrium prior to the shift, the quantity demanded is now greater than the quantity supplied at the previous equilibrium price (P_1). The price increases until it reaches the intersection of the new demand curve and the supply curve: a new equilibrium price is established (P_2) as well as a new equilibrium quantity (Q_2). Similarly, a shift in the supply curve will result in a new equilibrium price.

Price Elasticity

This section expands on our knowledge of the demand for and the supply of a product or service. It is important to learn more about the demand for a product than to state simply that there is an inverse relationship between price and quantity demanded. How much does the quantity demanded increase when the price decreases? For some products, the price is an important factor in the decision to buy a product. If the price increases, the quantity demanded decreases significantly. For other products, the price is not an important factor in the buying decision; changes in the price of the product will have little impact on the quantity demanded. Economists use the term **price elasticity of demand** to describe the responsiveness of quantity demanded to a change in the price.

price elasticity of demand

the responsiveness of quantity demanded to a change in price

FIGURE 2.6

A Change in the Equilibrium Price

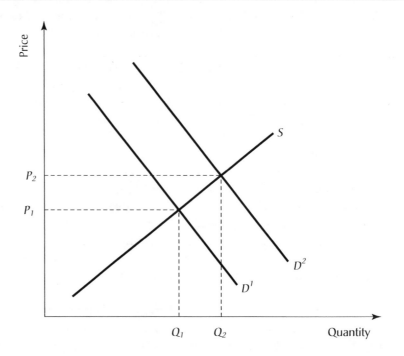

An increase in demand has raised the equilibrium price from P_1 to P_2.

If the percentage change in the quantity demanded is greater than the percentage change in the price, the demand is said to be elastic. For products with an elastic demand, the price is an important factor in the decision to purchase the product. For products with an elastic demand, consumers respond significantly to changes in the price. If the percentage change in the quantity demanded is less than the percentage change in the price, the demand is said to be inelastic. For products with an inelastic demand, the price is not an important factor in the decision to purchase the product. Economists compute the price elasticity of demand as the percentage change in the quantity demanded divided by the percentage change in the price.

The formula to determine the price elasticity of demand is:

$$Coefficient\ of\ price\ elasticity\ of\ demand = \frac{\%\ change\ in\ the\ quantity\ demanded}{\%\ change\ in\ the\ price}$$

The sign of the calculated value of the coefficient of price elasticity of demand will always be negative because of the inverse relationship between the price and the quantity demanded. When discussing the coefficient of price elasticity of demand, the general practice is to drop the negative sign and focus on the absolute value. If the absolute value of the above fraction is greater than 1, the demand is elastic. If the fraction is less than 1, the demand is inelastic.

For example, if a 10% increase in the price resulted in a 5% reduction in the quantity demanded, the coefficient of price elasticity is as follows:

$$Coefficient\ of\ price\ elasticity\ of\ demand = \frac{-5\%}{10\%}$$
$$= -0.5$$

Since the absolute value of the coefficient is less than 1, the price elasticity is said to be inelastic.

The concept of price elasticity is useful, for example, in calculating what happens to total revenue when the price changes. The total revenue is the price multiplied by the quantity purchased. If the demand is elastic, a price decrease will result in an increase in total revenue. The percentage drop in price is more than offset by the percentage increase in quantity demanded. A price increase results in a decrease in total revenue. The percentage increase in price is larger than the percentage decline in demand. If the demand is inelastic, a price decrease reduces total revenue. The percentage drop in price is larger than the percentage increase in quantity demanded. A price increase raises total revenue. The percentage increase in price exceeds the percentage fall in the quantity demanded.

Three main factors affect the elasticity of demand:

- *The number of substitutes*. For products with many substitutes (such as chocolate bars), the demand is more elastic. For products or services with few substitutes (such as cigarettes, haircuts, or gasoline), the demand is inelastic.

- *Luxury versus necessity*. Necessities tend to have an inelastic demand. Basic telephone service is considered a necessity in North America;

the elasticity is less than 1. Diabetics need insulin to survive; the demand for insulin is very inelastic. Luxuries such as exotic travel tend to have elastic demand curves.

- *Percentage of income spent on product.* If a product takes up a large percentage of consumers' income, the demand tends to be elastic. Purchases of cars, household appliances, and furniture constitute major household expenditures. The price elasticity of demand for these items is greater than 1. If only a small fraction of income is spent on a good, then a change in its price has little impact on the consumer's overall budget. The purchase of a pack of chewing gum does not have a significant impact on a household's budget. The demand for chewing gum is usually price inelastic.

price elasticity of supply

the responsiveness of quantity supplied to a change in price

The concept of price elasticity can also be applied to the supply side of the market, and is known as the **price elasticity of supply**. The terminology used on the supply side of the market is the same as on the demand side of the market. If the percentage change in the quantity supplied is greater than the percentage change in the price, the supply is said to be elastic. If the percentage change in the quantity supplied is less than the percentage change in the price, the supply is said to be inelastic.

The formula for the price elasticity of supply is:

$$\textit{Coefficient of price elasticity of supply} = \frac{\%\ \textit{change in the quantity supplied}}{\%\ \textit{change in the price}}$$

Since price and the quantity supplied have a positive, or direct, relationship on the supply side of the market, the sign for the coefficient of price elasticity of supply is always positive. If the above fraction is greater than 1, the supply is said to be elastic. If the fraction is less than 1, the supply is inelastic.

On the supply side of the market, a special case of elasticity sometimes occurs. A vertical supply curve indicates that the quantity supplied does not change in response to a change in price. This is a perfectly inelastic supply curve and carries a coefficient of zero. Examples of a perfectly inelastic supply are a limited edition of art prints or the amount of a crop available after harvest. Regardless of how high the price gets, no more art prints will be manufactured. Even if the price of an agricultural crop rises, no more will be produced until next year.

The main determining factor in the elasticity of supply is the time factor. The longer the period of time we are talking about, the more elastic the supply curve. Over a longer period of time, suppliers have more opportunities to adjust the quantity supplied in response to the change in price. Car manufacturers can build additional plants, farmers can increase or reduce their quantity of livestock, and banks can add or close branches or change office space.

In the theoretical chapters of this text, graphs will make reference to elastic and inelastic curves. You will notice that elastic curves are drawn as fairly flat curves and inelastic curves are drawn as steep curves. It should not be assumed that elasticity and slope of the line are identical. To determine the slope of a line, one looks at the absolute changes, whereas the determination of elasticity focuses on percentage changes. The slope of a straight line does not change regardless of the section of line chosen to make the slope calculations. The coefficient of price elasticity varies at different points and parts of the line. Even though it is not technically correct to say that an inelastic curve is a steep curve on a graph, it is a convention used by economists to explain various outcomes where elasticity is important.

Special Features of the Labour Market

Up to this point in our discussion, all markets have been treated in a similar manner. When we analyze the labour market using demand and supply curves, the labelling of the axes changes. The price on the vertical axis is replaced by the wage rate (the price of labour). The quantity of the product or service on the horizontal axis is replaced by either the number of workers or the number of hours of work. Both are measures of the quantity of labour. The labour market operates in a similar fashion as other markets. Nevertheless it differs from the commodity and other markets in several respects.

Labour Services Are Inseparable from People

The first feature that distinguishes the labour market from other markets is that the item being exchanged—labour services—is embodied in human beings. If one buys commodities (such as a suit, a car, or a dozen bagels), ownership and possession of the purchase are transferred from the seller to the buyer. In most societies, workers cannot be owned; their services can only be rented. The high degree of control that ownership generally entails does not exist in the labour market. Because workers cannot be owned, managers and business owners cannot use their employees as they please. The rise of trade unions and the presence of labour standards legislation are reactions to employers' attempts to gain control over workers. The legalization of collective bargaining between trade unions and management has allowed employees to have a voice in the nature of the employment relationship. Provinces have enacted minimum employment standards legislation primarily to improve employment relationships for workers not represented by a union in negotiations with management. For example, the number of hours of work per week is subject to rules regulated by legislation, or by negotiation between union and management. Other labour legislation guarantees a minimum wage rate, paid vacations, and regulations with respect to overtime pay. Some governments have enacted regulations requiring advance notice of employment termination and severance pay for job loss. Legislation regarding employment standards and union–management relations is discussed in Chapter 3.

Because the service provided by labour is inseparable from the person performing it, there is a direct, personal relationship between the supplier (the worker) and the purchaser (the employer). Generally, when a commodity is transferred, neither party has an interest in the personal characteristics of the other party. For example, if you purchase a chocolate bar at a convenience store, the store clerk is not concerned about whether the chocolate bar is going to a "good home" or whether it is being purchased by a "nice person." In contrast, workers have definite preferences with respect to their working conditions. Employers have preferences regarding the characteristics of their potential employees. The decisions made by both parties are based on a complex set of considerations, including not only the wage rate but also a host of nonmonetary factors associated with the job or worker. These factors include work environment and the personalities of co-workers and managers, and are often considered as important as the wage rate. The aspect of fairness is probably more important in the labour market than in any other market. Workers want fairness in hiring, promotion, and layoff procedures, and they want "just" or "fair" wages. Employers want a "fair day's work" from their workers and the freedom to earn a "fair return" on their capital investment. Employers' perceptions of fairness are likely to vary from employees' perceptions.

Employment Relations Last Longer

A second distinguishing feature is that employment relationships often last for a relatively long period of time. Many people have worked at the same company for more than 30 years. Exchanges of products are generally of short duration. People rarely own a car or an item of clothing for 30 years. Why does the employment relationship for many people last a long time? Employers find it to their advantage to maintain a stable core workforce, since they may have made substantial investments in workers in the form of hiring and training. Likewise, individual workers, as they get older, find it to their advantage to remain with one employer for a considerable time. The reason is partly economical, since wages and fringe benefits normally increase with tenure on the job. However, there are also psychological reasons for favouring a lengthier employment relationship: people generally place a value on security and familiar surroundings.

A significant implication of the long-term employment relationship is that it reduces the sensitivity of wages to changes in demand and supply. Prices rise and fall daily in certain commodity markets. In the barley market, for example, an excess supply quickly leads to a drop in price as sellers underbid each other to attract a buyer. Buyers, in turn, have little reason not to switch from one seller to another, since bushels of barley are much the same. In the labour market, however, an excess supply of labour typically does not quickly lead to a fall in wage rates. Although unemployed workers might offer to work for lower wages, most firms would find it unprofitable to hire them because the costs of hiring and training, as well as the potentially negative effect on morale, would far outweigh the savings in lower wages. Furthermore, the presence of a legislated minimum wage rate or a negotiated wage rate in a collective agreement may prevent the lowering of the wage rate for new, or existing, employees. Thus, while in many commodity markets prices fluctuate to restore a balance between demand and supply, wage rates in the labour market change more slowly. The change is particularly slow in a downward direction. Firms may find it costly to terminate employees and hire employees at lower wage rates. The resulting sluggishness creates an imbalance between the demand and supply of labour, which may persist for a considerable time before wage rates change enough to bring about the necessary adjustments in the labour market.

In those labour submarkets where the employment relationship is short-term and turnover costs are minimal—for example, in the market for day labourers—wage rates exhibit a flexibility similar to other markets.

Workers and Jobs Are Highly Diverse

The third special feature of the labour market is closely related to the first feature. Because labour services are embodied in human beings and because each person is unique, there is extreme diversity in the characteristics of the "good" being exchanged. Such diversity does not occur in other markets. For many items, such as agricultural products or semi-finished products such as steel, all units are fairly similar, if not identical, and the decision to buy or to sell is made predominantly on the basis of price. Consumer goods (such as dairy products, cars, or textiles) or final investment goods (such as metal stamping machines, construction cranes, or computer hardware systems) are more differentiated; the decisions to buy and sell these products are influenced by nonprice factors as well as by price. The differentiation in the characteristics of workers and jobs is greater than in other markets. Individual workers differ by age, gender, race, education, experience, and skills. They also differ in psychological and social traits, such as self-confidence, motivation, and congeniality. Employees are faced with a similar diversity in characteristics of potential employers; employers differ, for instance, in the type of work, health and safety standards, commuting distance, and their labour relations, as well as in wages and fringe benefits.

This differentiation complicates the search for and evaluation of information required by both buyers and sellers before an exchange can take place. Because all bushels of barley are alike, buyers need only to acquire information about the price demanded by various sellers. In the labour market, however, both buyers and sellers must invest much more time and effort in evaluating the many nonpecuniary, intangible characteristics that distinguish each worker and job. The exchange is more costly to undertake and less likely to result in the most efficient match of buyer and seller, compared to markets in which the product is more standardized. If the job or the worker turns out to be a disappointment, the employee and firm may look for more attractive opportunities. The result is turnover and search for new possibilities. In short, the labour market has more uncertainty and incomplete information than do other markets.

Labour Markets Are Highly Fragmented

A fourth distinctive characteristic of the labour market is the number of individual submarkets. There is not just one national or regional labour market: there are many individual labour markets characterized by geographical location, occupation, and skill level. When we analyze how wage rates are determined, we must distinguish between the labour markets for airline pilots, bricklayers, and corporate lawyers. Each occupation has different supply and demand conditions. Likewise, geographical location gives rise to distinct labour markets. The demand and supply for French-speaking high school teachers in Alberta is likely to be different from the demand and supply in New Brunswick. For some occupations, such as hockey players, computer analysts, or academics, the labour market may be national or even international. Few other markets are as fragmented as the labour market, in part because it is not always easy to move from one labour market to another. Movement among markets becomes more difficult the greater the geographic distance or the disparity in skills.

Of what significance are these special features of the labour market? Are the differences between the labour market and other markets so great that we cannot use demand and supply curves to analyze the market? Labour economists differ in their answers to this question.

One position taken by many labour economists is that the labour market should be treated like any other market. Economists should focus on the mechanism that balances supply and demand through the variations in wage rates, rather than study the sociological, institutional, and regulatory details of the labour market. They argue that one can understand the workings of a market without getting caught up in the details of the market. Do those who are studying the market for a product like fish need to understand all the ins and outs of the fish trade? One can comment on fluctuations in fish prices without knowing how to catch fish, or on trends in housing prices without knowing all the municipal construction bylaws. In fact, a market may be analyzed more effectively by someone detached from the details of the market.

The opposite position is held by other labour economists. They believe that one cannot equate the labour market with other markets. The idea that the labour market acts like a machine to equate the supply of labour and demand for labour by varying wage rates, in their view, is taking abstraction too far. These economists argue that regulatory and institutional elements are more important in the labour market than in other markets. Regulations imposed by governments and by collective bargaining between labour and management play a significant role in the determination of employment and wages, and institutions affect the balance of power between workers and management. Unions, work councils, quality circles, and other aspects of worker participation in the governance of companies fall into this category. Also, the fact that high unemployment persists over extended periods of time shows that the labour market does not readily equate supply and demand. If one treats the labour market like any other market, one is prone to misunderstand unemployment and other outcomes of the labour market.

Can the two positions be reconciled? Unfortunately, there is no ready answer. If we set the level of abstraction so high that institutional realities drop out of focus, important aspects of contemporary labour markets can easily move out of the picture. On the other hand, if we change the focus to highlight detailed institutional characteristics, we may end up with a newspaper account of economic life without any real understanding of how the market operates. The art of theorizing is to simplify the detailed complexity of daily life without losing the essential elements one wants to explain. The aim, therefore, is to set a middle level of abstraction that reflects the dominant institutional facts of the labour market. What does this mean for our analysis of the Canadian labour market? We will use the theory of supply and demand to explain earnings and employment levels in the labour market. We will also discuss important institutional aspects of the labour market and how they influence demand and supply.

The Labour Market and the National Economy

The millions of exchanges of labour services that occur daily in the labour market are not taking place in isolation from the rest of the economy. The labour market is but one of several markets interacting with each other. Figure 2.7 (page 38) offers an illustration of how the labour market fits into the overall economy. This diagram represents the **circular flow model** of the economy. In this model there are two types of decision makers: households, and firms. Firms produce goods and services using various inputs, such as labour, land, and capital (buildings, machines, or tools). These inputs are called **factors of production**. Households own the factors of production and they consume the goods and services produced by firms. The market in which the factors of production are exchanged is called the **factor market**. The labour market is a factor market in which labour services are offered in exchange for wages. The market in which goods and services are exchanged is called the **product market**, or the market for goods and services.

Households and firms interact in both the factor market and product market. In the market for goods and services, households are buyers and firms are sellers. In the factor market, households are sellers and firms are buyers. In the labour market, for example, households provide firms with the labour services that the firms use to produce goods and services.

The inside clockwise arrows of the diagram represent the flow of goods and services between households and firms. Let us start with the households at the top: they sell the use of their labour, land, and capital to firms in the factor markets. The inputs sold in the factor markets are then used by firms to produce goods and services, which are sold to households in the markets for goods and services. The services of factors of production flow from households to firms, and goods and services flow from firms to households.

The outside counterclockwise arrows represent the corresponding flow of money. Households spend money to buy goods and services from firms, which use some of that revenue to pay for the services of factors of production, such as the wages for their employees. Money not paid out for factors of production is the profits payable to the firms' owners. It should be noted that the owners of businesses are also members of households.

With every market transaction, goods and services move in one direction, and money moves in the other direction. When a household makes a purchase, money moves from the hands of households to the hands of firms, and goods move from firms to households. If a firm purchases the services of a factor of production, money moves from the business to the owners of these

circular flow model

a visual model of the economy that shows how goods and services and money flow between households and firms via markets

factors of production

the inputs used to produce goods and services (labour, land, and capital)

factor market

the market in which factors of production are exchanged

product market

the market in which goods and services are exchanged

FIGURE 2.7

The Circular Flow Model

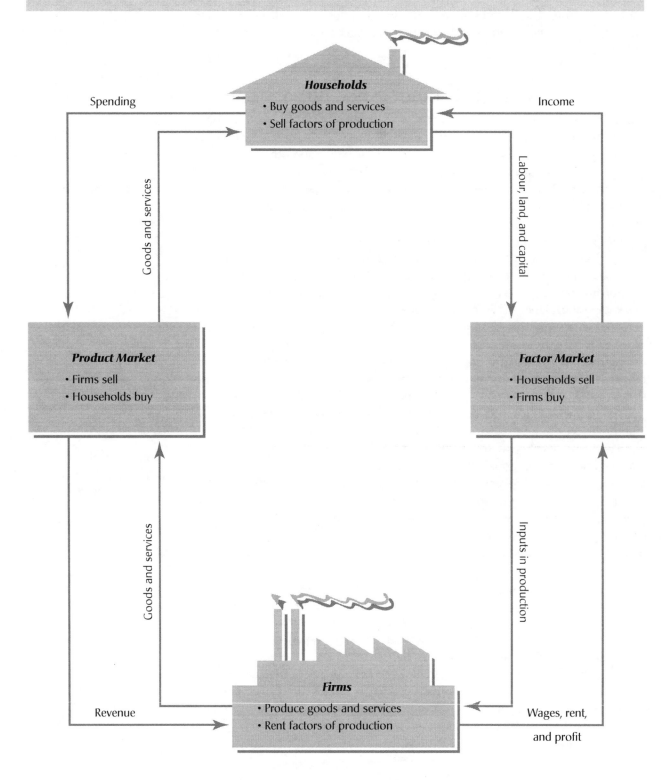

Spending

Households
- Buy goods and services
- Sell factors of production

Income

Goods and services

Labour, land, and capital

Product Market
- Firms sell
- Households buy

Factor Market
- Households sell
- Firms buy

Goods and services

Inputs in production

Firms
- Produce goods and services
- Rent factors of production

Revenue

Wages, rent, and profit

factors—wages and salaries to the owners of labour, rent to landowners, and profit or interest to owners of capital resources. Hence, the factor markets not only facilitate the exchange of production factors but they also organize the distribution of income.

Thus there is a link between the product markets and the factor markets: households represent the demand side in the product markets and the supply side in the factor markets, and firms represent the supply side in the product markets and the demand side in the factor markets. This link is a central point in understanding the operation of the labour market in the economy. For example, a sustained increase in the spending of households on goods and services—that is, a rising demand in the product markets—leads firms to increase their production. In order to do so, firms will hire more labour. So an increase in demand in the goods markets leads to an increase in demand in the labour market. The demand for teachers is linked to the demand for educational services, and the demand for car mechanics is related to the demand for automobiles. For this reason, the demand for labour, like the demand for other production factors, is called a **derived demand**. Changes in the demand for labour, in turn, will feed back into the product market. For example, if job vacancies increase and are filled with unemployed people, incomes increase and the demand of households for goods and services will rise.

Clearly, the circular flow model in Figure 2.7 is a simplified version of the economy. Several sectors in the economy have been omitted. In the diagram, the flow of goods, services, and payments that takes place between business firms is omitted. For example, automobile manufacturers buy hundreds of parts from other companies. The government sector of the economy (which sells services in the goods and services market and buys inputs in the factor markets) is also omitted, as is the international trade sector of our economy. Nevertheless, the circular flow model provides a first abstract view of the economy as a system of buyers and sellers interacting in different markets. It demonstrates how the labour market is linked with the rest of the economy.

derived demand

the demand for workers that is derived from the demand for goods and services

The Flow Approach to the Labour Market

Now let us take a closer look at the structure of the labour market. When we talk about the structure of the labour market, we are interested in the components of labour demand and labour supply and how changes in these components take place.

To begin, we must distinguish between two types of variables: **stock variables** and **flow variables**. A *stock* is a quantity measured at a given point in time; a *flow* is a quantity measured per unit of time. The bathtub is a typical example used to illustrate stocks and flows. The amount of water in the tub is the stock: it is the water in the tub at a given time. The water pouring from the faucet into the tub is the flow: it is the quantity of water being added to the tub per unit of time. Clearly, the measure of the stock and the measure of the flow of water differ. We say that the bathtub contains 100 litres of water, but that water is flowing from the faucet at 10 litres per minute. In this

stock variable

a variable whose quantity is measured at a given point in time

flow variable

a variable whose quantity is measured per unit of time

example, stocks and flows are related. The stock of water in the tub represents the accumulation of the flow out of the faucet. As the flow increases in volume so does the stock, assuming the drain is plugged. If the bathtub is unplugged, the stock of water depends on the volume of water flowing into the tub and the volume of water flowing out.

The image of the water in a bathtub can help us to visualize the labour market as a system of stocks and flows. At any given moment, a certain number of people are employed or unemployed and a certain number of job openings are available to be filled. The stocks of job vacancies and employed workers together constitute the **demand for labour**—workers would not be employed if there was no demand for them. The stocks of unemployed and employed workers constitute the **supply of labour**—there would be no employment if workers did not supply their services to employers.

The numbers of employed and unemployed people change according to the flows into and out of employment and unemployment. Workers enter the pool of the employed through recalls or by being matched in the labour market with job vacancies (new hires). Workers leave employment as a result of quits, layoffs, and retirements. If the flows out of employment exceed the flows into employment, the stock of employed people will decline. As people leave employment because of quits or layoffs, they enter the pool of the unemployed. Thus some outflows from employment become inflows into unemployment. Workers also move into the ranks of the unemployed as they graduate from school or give up full-time homemaking and cannot find jobs. Workers who are recalled or newly hired constitute outflows from unemployment. Workers may also withdraw from the labour market altogether because they may have become discouraged as a result of unsuccessful job searching, or they may have decided to go back to school full-time. If the flows into unemployment exceed the flows out, the stock of unemployed people will rise.

Although only relatively small changes in the stocks occur from month to month, the gross flows that account for these changes are much larger. On average, roughly a quarter-million people move from being unemployed to being employed each month. Approximately the same number of people move from not in the labour force to employed each month. Large numbers of Canadians leave employment and drop out of the labour force, or become unemployed each month as well. Similarly, each month people move between the categories of unemployed and not in the labour force. Some of the unemployed become discouraged and drop out of the labour force. Others, who were not in the labour force, start a search for employment.

Even when the size of a stock remains constant over time because the inflow is offset by the outflow, the composition of the stock changes. This is why the number of people who have experienced unemployment, or who have had employment during a particular period, is substantially larger than the total number who are employed or unemployed at a given time. The stocks of employed and unemployed people are measured at a particular moment. The flows of workers entering and leaving the state of unemployment are measured per unit of time (a week, a month, or a year).

demand for labour

the stocks of job vacancies and employed workers

supply of labour

the stocks of employed and unemployed workers

Until the early 1970s, labour economists predominantly applied a stock approach to the labour market. They were interested in measuring the number of employed and unemployed people at a given time and in explaining the changes in the stocks over time. Over the last three decades, labour economists have increasingly turned to a flow approach. Flow analysis has distinct advantages over stock analysis. It provides insights into movements between the different labour force states (employment, unemployment, and being outside of the labour market). The flow approach also offers much more detailed information on the causes of the net changes in the stocks. For example, in studying the reasons for changes in the flows (layoffs, quits, re-entrants, or new entrants to the labour market), economists gain a better understanding of the conditions that bring people into unemployment. Did unemployment increase in a particular year because more people were laid off or quit their jobs, or because a large cohort of school leavers entered the labour market for the first time? With a flow approach to the labour market, these and other questions can be tackled more effectively.

Labour Markets in a Global Economy

Previously, we discussed the labour market in the context of the national economy. National boundaries, however, are increasingly breaking down with respect to economic activities. Industrialized nations like Canada have become increasingly integrated through growth in foreign direct investment and foreign trade—a process known as **globalization**. In general, globalization is understood as the process by which markets and production in different countries are becoming more interdependent due to international trade in goods and services and the transfer of capital and technology. The spread of international production across national boundaries has been accelerating due to the rapid growth of multinational corporations—companies that operate production facilities in different countries. Much international trade involves the shipment of products between divisions of the same multinational corporation. Foreign-controlled businesses are an important component of the Canadian economy. A review of Canada's largest corporations reveals that most are completely, or partially, foreign-owned.

Globalization is facilitated by the move toward reducing trade barriers (customs duties, quotas, and regulations) between nations. Canada is a member of the World Trade Organization (WTO), which represents most of the nations in the world and is committed to reducing trade barriers. Canada, the United States, and Mexico have signed the North American Free Trade Agreement (NAFTA), an agreement that eliminates many barriers to trade among these countries. Canada has also signed trade deals with Israel and Chile. The activities of multinational corporations and freer international trade are having important effects on the Canadian labour market. They affect the levels of employment and unemployment in many industries and the types of skills demanded throughout the economy. They also influence organizational structure, human resources management, and employment standards of companies in Canada.

globalization

the integration of countries through growth in foreign trade and foreign investment

The impact of globalization on organizational structures and human resources management was the focus of the opening vignette to this chapter. The trend toward globalization also exposes differences in labour employment standards between countries. Workers in Canada work with more regulation and protection than their counterparts in the United States, but with much less protection than European workers. Differences in employment regulations are particularly large between Canada and developing countries in Latin America and Asia. Does increased economic integration imply that employment standards regulations in Canada must match those in the countries it trades with? Must Canadian governments relax labour standards in order to keep Canadian firms competitive in world markets?

Canada and the United States agreed that NAFTA would not be signed unless a side agreement were approved to guarantee Mexico's adherence to standards in areas such as minimum wages, child labour law, and occupational safety and health. Pressure for requiring Mexico to improve its labour market standards stemmed from at least two concerns: first, concern for the well-being of children and mainly low-skilled workers in Mexico, and second (and probably more important), concern for Canadian and U.S. workers whose jobs may be threatened because of lower wages and what some perceive as Mexico's cost advantage due to its lower labour standards.

Labour Market Issue 2.1

A Canadian-Made Automobile?

Globalization allows multinational corporations to compare the employment practices in various countries before deciding on production schedules. Often, the comparison is between employment practices in developed countries and those in developing countries. Production may be relocated to take advantage of labour cost savings.

The automobile industry provides a good example of globalization. Many Canadians in Southern Ontario are employed in the production of motor vehicles and parts for motor vehicles. In fact, on a dollar basis, cars and car parts are the largest export products for Canada. In spite of the fact that a great deal of automobile production takes place in Canada, there does not seem to be a Canadian car. Many of the parts used in Canadian-assembled automobiles come from other countries. Many of the automobile parts made in Canada are shipped to other countries. The Canadian content of cars assembled in Canada ranges anywhere from 15% to 25%. These percentages are for American- and Japanese-owned automobile manufacturers located in Southern Ontario. The

Canadian content does not depend on whether the assembly plant is owned by a company based in the United States or in Japan.

For cars assembled outside of Canada, there can be a significant amount of Canadian content. Canadian content represents about 10% of the value of cars produced in the United States. Canadian content is also high in vehicles built in the United States by foreign companies such as BMW. If a Canadian wanted to select an automobile to purchase based solely on the amount of Canadian content in the car, it would be a difficult choice.

What impact does the globalization of the car market have on the Canadian labour market? Even though labour costs do not represent the total costs of building an automobile, they represent a large proportion of the costs. Multinational corporations are clearly willing to have cars assembled and parts made for cars in a variety of countries. The employment relationships (wage rates and other labour standards) that exist in Canadian labour markets must be competitive.

Do differences in labour standards in fact lead to differences in labour costs? This question is more difficult to answer than it first appears. It is neither conceptually nor empirically clear that more stringent employment standards necessarily mean higher labour costs. Some regulations, such as health and safety regulations, may reduce costs or raise productivity. Other regulations may have the opposite impact; that is, they may increase costs or reduce productivity.

Even when more stringent labour standards lead to higher labour costs, it is often not clear from the outset who will bear these costs. Costs nominally placed on companies may partly or fully be shifted back to workers. For example, an increase in the cost of labour due to mandated employer-purchased health insurance decreases the demand for labour, which at existing wages would decrease employment. But if the provision of mandated employer-purchased health insurance makes work more attractive, that benefit will increase the supply of labour, so that the long-term cost will fall partly on workers as well as on employers. As long as employers do not carry the regulatory costs solely, these costs may not affect plant location and investment decisions negatively.

The threat, however, remains that companies will relocate in countries with less stringent employment standards and lower wages. Given freer trade and capital mobility, governments are under increasing pressure not to enact or enforce employment standards or labour relations laws. Do more stringent employment regulations increase labour costs? To what extent do labour costs affect plant location and investment decisions? Has the threat of companies relocating production outside of Canada influenced the willingness of governments to implement employment regulations and standards? Many questions still remain unresolved. Nonetheless, it is clear that increased globalization has an impact on the Canadian labour market.

Summary

In a market, buyers and sellers get together to exchange products or services. The buyer's side of the market is referred to as demand, and the seller's side is referred to as supply. The interaction of the demand and supply sides of the market leads to the setting of a price. In the labour market, the price is known as the wage rate.

The relationship between the quantity demanded of a good or service and its price is generally negative. This leads to a downward-sloping demand curve. On the supply side, there is a positive relationship between the price and the quantity supplied. The supply curve slopes upward to the right. The equilibrium price is determined by the intersection of the supply and demand curves. As the two curves shift, the equilibrium price changes.

It is important to know more about the demand curve for a product than the inverse relationship between price and quantity demanded. The price elasticity of demand measures the responsiveness of the quantity demanded to a change in the price. For some products and services, the price is an important factor in the decision to buy. For other products and services, it is not. The price elasticity of supply measures the degree of responsiveness that sellers can exhibit with respect to the quantity supplied when the price changes.

The labour market has several features that distinguish it from other markets. Employers buy the services of workers; they do not buy the workers. A great deal of legislation has been enacted to regulate the relationship between employers and employees. That employment relationship often lasts a long time, and its long-term nature implies that wages are less flexible than prices in other markets. Wages are particularly sticky in a downward direction. Because wages do not adjust quickly, imbalances in labour markets can persist over long periods of time. In the labour market, the services provided by individuals differ from one person to the next, whereas in many product markets the products being exchanged are identical. Exchanges in the labour market, therefore, involve a lot of uncertainty. The labour market is highly fragmented along geographical and occupational lines.

The labour market is just one market in the overall economy. It is a factor market in which labour is exchanged. In the labour market, households represent the supply side and businesses represent the demand side. In product markets, households represent the demand side and businesses represent the supply side. The links between the labour market and the rest of the economy can be illustrated in a circular flow model. In this model, labour services flow from households to firms and goods flow from firms to households. In exchange, money travels from businesses in the form of income to households and then back to businesses as households spend income on goods and services.

The flow approach to the labour market focuses on changes in the components of labour demand (numbers of job vacancies and employed workers) and labour supply (numbers of employed and unemployed workers). The number of employed people changes depending on the inflows to employment (new hires and recalls) and the outflows from employment (quits, layoffs, and withdrawals from the labour force). Quits, layoffs, and entrants to the labour force who cannot find jobs increase unemployment. Hires and withdrawals reduce unemployment.

The labour market is increasingly affected by the trend to globalization. The pressure to innovate requires more flexible forms of management and the constant acquisition of new skills. International competition also puts pressure on governments to adjust legislated labour standards to those of Canada's trading partners.

Key Terms

change in demand (page 26)

change in supply (page 27)

change in the quantity demanded (page 26)

change in the quantity supplied (page 27)

circular flow model (page 37)

demand curve (page 24)

demand for labour (page 40)

derived demand (page 39)

diminishing returns (page 26)

equilibrium price (page 29)

factor market (page 37)

factors of production (page 37)

flow variable (page 39)

Fordism (page 22)

globalization (page 41)

income effect (demand) (page 24)

labour market (page 23)

law of downward-sloping demand (page 24)

long run (page 26)

market (page 23)

price elasticity of demand (page 30)

price elasticity of supply (page 32)

product market (page 37)

shortage (page 29)

short run (page 26)

stock variable (page 39)

substitution effect (demand) (page 24)

supply curve (page 27)

supply of labour (page 40)

surplus (page 28)

Toyotism (page 22)

wage rate (page 23)

Weblinks

Toyotism and Fordism
www.marxists.org/glossary/terms

The Canadian National Economy
www.td.com/economics/analysis/canada/national-economy/national.jsp

Discussion Questions

1. If human beings could be bought or sold like commodities such as barley or gold, how would it change the operation of the labour market? Would the supply of labour become more or less sensitive to the non-monetary aspects of employment? Why?

2. Give examples of companies or industries that follow the organizational model of Fordism. Give examples of companies or industries that follow the organizational model of Toyotism.

3. Will economic integration through NAFTA force Canada, Mexico, and the United States to harmonize their labour standards, regulations, and payroll taxes? Discuss.

4. In any market, the price stops moving when it reaches the equilibrium point. Are both buyers and sellers equally pleased with the equilibrium price? Explain.

5. Some students encountering the concept of elasticity for the first time assume that it refers to the slope of the demand curve or the supply curve. Refer to the elasticity formula and explain why slope and elasticity are not identical.

Using the Internet

1. Access the website www.marxists.org/glossary/terms. Look up the discussion of Toyotism and Fordism. Also look up the discussion of Taylorism, and write a short summary of this approach to management.

Exercises

1. Describe the features of labour markets that distinguish them from other markets.
2. a. Where does the labour market belong in the circular flow model depicted in Figure 2.7 (page 38)? Can you draw it in?
   b. In the circular flow model, show the flows that correspond to the following activities:
      i. Nadja earns $7.50 as a rafting guide on the Ottawa River.
      ii. Daniel pays a car dealer $23 000 for a pick-up truck.
      iii. Agnes spends $12.75 on a meal in a fast food restaurant.
      iv. Paul earns $3000 in dividends from shares of Canadian companies.
3. Discuss the distinction between a stock variable and a flow measure of employment and unemployment.
4. Using demand and supply curves, draw a market diagram to illustrate the impact of the following:
   a. an increase in lumber prices on the market for new houses
   b. the aging of the baby-boom generation on the market for healthcare
   c. an increase in consumer incomes on the market for restaurant meals
   d. a freezing spell in Florida on the market for orange juice in Canada
5. Why is the equilibrium price the price at which the quantity supplied equals the quantity demanded?
6. Suppose that hamburgers and pizza are substitutes. What is the effect on the price of a hamburger and the quantity of hamburgers sold if:
   a. the price of a pizza increases
   b. the cost of producing a pizza increases
7. The cost of producing microchips has fallen dramatically over the years. Using a supply and demand diagram, show the effect of the cost decline on the equilibrium price in the market for computers.
8. The price of a product has increased by 3% over a period of time, while the quantity supplied has increased by 5%. Determine the coefficient of price elasticity of supply. Is the supply elastic or inelastic in this part of the supply curve? Explain.
9. The quantity demanded of a product fell by 2% in response to a 5% increase in the price. Determine the coefficient of price elasticity of demand. Is the demand elastic or inelastic in this part of the demand curve? Explain.
10. Assume that in a production process workers and robots are substitutes. If the price of a robot falls, what will happen to the demand curve for workers? If workers and robots are complementary in the production process (that is, they are employed together), and the price of a robot falls, what will happen to the demand curve for workers?

Chapter 3

Institutional Aspects of the Labour Market

Chapter Learning Objectives

After completing this chapter, you should be able to:

- outline the jurisdictional responsibilities of the federal and provincial governments with respect to the labour market
- list the labour standards that have been enacted by various levels of government
- describe the history of employment insurance in Canada
- discuss the trends in union membership in Canada
- discuss the characteristics of union membership in Canada

MATERNITY AND PARENTAL LEAVE

Labour relations and employment standards legislation is constantly changing. As society's views about the employment relationship change, legislators are pressured to change the labour laws. One of the most recent amendments to labour legislation in Canada is the provision for maternity and parental leave. Provincial legislation with respect to taking time off from work to have and care for a baby was introduced in the 1970s. Initially, mothers were allowed to take about 17 weeks off work (without pay) to have a child. Later, the length of the leave was extended, and provisions were also introduced for fathers to take unpaid time away from the job after the birth of the child.

Provincial labour laws provide for unpaid leave. Federal Employment Insurance (EI) legislation provides for financial benefits for those on maternity or parental leave. Maternity leave benefits under EI are for a maximum of 15 weeks and can be claimed by women only. Parental benefits are given for a maximum of 35 weeks and can be claimed entirely by one parent or divided between both parents provided that each qualifies for EI benefits.

What factors are important in determining the length of time one receives maternity or parental benefits? Since the benefit period has been extended under Employment Insurance, there has been an increase in the time that women take off of work, with their current median time away from the job being 10 months. Self-employed women return to work much earlier, with a median time away from the job of approximately one month; self-employed individuals are not eligible for EI benefits, however. Women who returned to work early also reported lower salaries on the job, suggesting that women with lower annual earnings may not be able to afford long absences from work even if they are receiving benefits amounting to 55% of their earnings. The length of time a woman stayed away from the job was also related to whether or not the father took time off from his job: if the father took time off, the mother was more likely to return to work earlier. Although fathers are less likely than mothers to take time off, the proportion of fathers opting for parental leave benefits has increased to approximately 10% since the parental leave benefits were extended.

The previous chapter indicated that regulatory and institutional elements are more prevalent in the labour market than in most other markets. The first part of this chapter discusses government intervention in the Canadian labour market, and the constitutional responsibilities of the federal and provincial governments are reviewed. The labour market regulations imposed by governments in Canada are discussed in the second part of the chapter. These regulations can be grouped into the following categories: employment standards, human rights, health and safety, workers' compensation, employment insurance, and union–management relations. The chapter ends with a discussion of trends in union membership in Canada.

Jurisdiction

Labour markets in Canada are heavily regulated by government, at both the federal and provincial levels. The powers and responsibilities associated with each level of government are outlined in the *Constitution Act, 1867*. With respect to the labour market, the federal government is responsible for labour legislation in certain industries and the provinces for the remaining industries.

The federal government has the authority to regulate and control those industries of an interprovincial, national, or international nature—such as interprovincial railways, bus lines, and trucking companies; airlines and air transport; banks; grain elevators; pipelines; canals; tunnels; bridges; ferries; shipping companies; radio and television stations; communication industries (including telephone and cable companies); uranium mining; and flour and feed companies. The federal government also regulates the working conditions of employees who work for the federal government and for Crown corporations such as the Canadian Broadcasting Corporation. Companies with operations that have been declared to be of general advantage for Canada, or for two or more provinces, also fall under federal jurisdiction.

The **Canada Labour Code** legislates employment standards and labour relations practices for industries that fall under federal jurisdiction, and for their employers and employees. Since the employees of federally regulated industries represent only a small percentage of all employees in Canada, the various provincial labour laws regulate the working conditions of most Canadians.

Canada Labour Code
labour standards and practices for industries that fall under federal jurisdiction, and for their employers and employees

According to the Canadian Constitution, the provinces are responsible for property matters and civil rights. This authority permits provincial governments to impose conditions on the relationship between employers and employees. This intervention varies by province and takes several forms. One form is legislation regulating labour relations, that is, union–management negotiations. Labour relations legislation covers the establishment of a union, negotiation of a collective agreement, certain aspects of a collective agreement, and the rules for the settlement of disputes. In addition to labour relations legislation, all provinces have legislation outlining basic employment standards such as minimum wage rates, vacations with pay, maximum hours of work, severance pay, and so on. Some provinces may have enacted certain employment standards that others have not. For example, not all provinces require employers to give advance notice to employees regarding termination of employment. Employment standards that are common to all provinces, such as a minimum wage rate and maximum hours of work, may also vary from province to province. Employment standards are also established for the three territories in Canada and may vary between territories. Parliament can pass legislation with respect to any employee in the territories.

Governments in Canada also affect the operation of labour markets by imposing payroll taxes on employers and employees. For example, Employment Insurance and the Canada Pension Plan are financed by employer and employee payroll deductions. Some provinces levy payroll taxes for other purposes. For example, in Ontario a payroll tax provides revenue for healthcare. The impact of payroll taxes on wages and employment is covered in Chapter 10.

Government Involvement in the Labour Market

Government regulation of the employment relationship falls into the following categories:

- Employment standards
- Human rights
- Health and safety
- Workers' compensation
- Employment insurance
- Union–management relationships

Employment Standards

All jurisdictions in Canada have enacted minimum employment standards. These standards are sometimes found in one piece of legislation, often called the *Employment Standards Act*; sometimes they are contained in several pieces of legislation. For example, there may be special legislation regulating hours of work, or there may be legislation specific to an industry such as construction or trucking. A discussion of the most common employment standards follows. The specifics of various employment standards regulations listed below were updated for the writing of the text, but since the legislation in each jurisdiction is under constant review, these standards may have recently been altered.

Minimum Age

All jurisdictions have general minimum age requirements. That is, the legislation specifies that an individual must be of a minimum age before he or she can be hired. In general, the minimum age applies to all industries in a jurisdiction but some provinces have special considerations for specific industries. The minimum age requirements range from a low of 14 in Nova Scotia and Quebec (if there is no parental consent) to a high of 17 for the federal government and the three territories. Six provinces have set the minimum age at 16. Alberta and British Columbia have set the minimum age at 15; in order to employ someone younger than 15 in British Columbia, parental consent is required. A province may have several minimum age regulations geared to different work environments. For example, in Ontario, the minimum age to work in an industrial establishment is 16, in a factory it is 15, and in a place other than a factory the minimum age is 14.

Hours of Work

All jurisdictions except New Brunswick place a statutory limit on the number of hours of work allowed in a day or in a week. (New Brunswick has a restriction only for those under 16 years of age.) Four provinces set only a weekly maximum: 40 hours in Newfoundland and Labrador and Quebec, and 48 hours in Nova Scotia and Prince Edward Island. The other jurisdictions specify both daily and weekly maximums, with the daily maximum set at eight hours and the weekly maximum again varying from 40 to 48 hours. In some situations, such as seasonal industries, the weekly maximum hours can be extended. Most jurisdictions also require that an employee be paid for a minimum number of hours per day.

Overtime Pay

All jurisdictions have legislated a requirement that employees receive a premium rate of pay for working an excessive number of hours in a day or a week, but the definition of this number of hours varies by province. Seven jurisdictions provide for a premium rate of pay after eight hours in a day in addition to having a weekly limit on hours before the overtime rate kicks in. Eight jurisdictions have legislated that overtime pay be earned after 40 hours in a week. Four jurisdictions have set 44 hours and two jurisdictions have set 48 hours as the weekly limit before the premium pay begins to apply. The

Labour Market Issue 3.1

Enforcing Employment Standards on Home Workers

The federal and provincial governments hire employment standards officers to investigate complaints that companies are not complying with the minimum standards in compensating their employees. In order to carry out investigations into alleged violations, officers have the authority to enter a company's premises and to inspect payroll records.

In some industries, employees do not work on the company premises but operate from home. For example, the garment industry is making increasing use of home workers. The capital equipment (sewing machine) can easily be installed at the worker's home, and the material is taken there. Workers need not travel to a factory to sew clothes.

Home workers are covered under employment standards legislation, but officers are not permitted to enter private homes unless invited. How do governments guarantee that employee compensation complies with the legislation? Home workers in the garment industry are paid a "piece rate"; that is, they are paid for each piece of clothing produced. The piece rate must be set so that it at least matches the minimum hourly wage rate in the province, but how can officers ensure that home workers are compensated fairly when the hours worked by home workers are not monitored?

Mandated weekly rest periods are also provided in most jurisdictions. For some provinces, at least 24 consecutive hours of rest must be given in a period of a week; in others, a longer consecutive rest period is prescribed. Most jurisdictions also mandate a meal break of one-half hour after five consecutive hours of work.

The drawback of home work for the individual worker is the lack of enforcement of employment standards.

Chapter 3: Institutional Aspects of the Labour Market

most common premium rate of pay is 1.5 times the regular rate of pay. Newfoundland and Labrador states that employees must receive at least $9.00 per hour for every hour worked in excess of 40 in a week. British Columbia has legislated that two times the hourly rate must be paid for hours worked in excess of 12 in a day in addition to the requirement that 1.5 times the hourly rate be paid for hours worked in excess of 40 per week.

Vacations with Pay

Granting employees an annual paid vacation is a relatively recent employment standard. After World War II, one week's paid vacation began appearing in collective agreements. Following the lead of provisions inserted in collective agreements, governments imposed annual paid vacation requirements. At present, all jurisdictions provide for at least two weeks of paid vacation after one year of employment. In addition to the two weeks' vacation time, employers are usually required to give the employee a minimum of 4% of the employee's annual earnings. Saskatchewan alone has legislated a minimum of three weeks' vacation and payment of 3/52 of one's annual earnings after one year of employment; the province has also legislated four weeks' annual vacation after 10 years of service with an employer. The following jurisdictions have provisions for three weeks' vacation: the federal government, the Northwest Territories, Nunavut, Quebec, New Brunswick, Newfoundland and Labrador, British Columbia, and Alberta.

Statutory Holidays

In addition to annual paid vacations, certain days are designated as statutory holidays. Employees are entitled to the day off and, in most cases, are entitled to be paid for the day as well. All jurisdictions have the following statutory holidays: New Year's Day, Good Friday, Canada Day (Memorial Day in Newfoundland and Labrador), Labour Day, and Christmas Day. The federal government and Ontario have declared Boxing Day to be a statutory holiday. Victoria Day is a statutory holiday in all jurisdictions except New Brunswick, Nova Scotia, Prince Edward Island, and Newfoundland and Labrador. In Quebec, the holiday associated with Victoria Day is referred to as Dollard Day. The first Monday in August is a holiday in British Columbia (British Columbia Day), New Brunswick (New Brunswick Day), Saskatchewan (Saskatchewan Day), the Northwest Territories, and Nunavut. Some provinces have designated Remembrance Day and Thanksgiving Day as statutory holidays. Alberta has a designated Family Day. Quebec has an additional holiday on June 24 and, in some cases, employees can substitute Easter Monday for Good Friday. The Yukon has Discovery Day (third Monday in August) and the Northwest Territories has National Aboriginal Day (June 21). Most provinces require that employees be paid 1.5 times the regular rate for work performed on a statutory holiday. Newfoundland and Labrador has established the premium rate at 2.0 times the regular rate. All provinces except Ontario, Nova Scotia, and Saskatchewan require that the employee be employed for a minimum number of days prior to receiving statutory holiday pay.

Minimum Wage Rate

All jurisdictions have legislated a minimum wage rate, although there are numerous exceptions and not all employees are entitled to receive a minimum hourly wage rate. For industries that fall under federal jurisdiction, the minimum wage rate is aligned with the equivalent in the province where the employees work.

Economic conditions vary by province. The industrial composition of the economy also varies by province. As a result, the minimum wage rates vary greatly by province and territory, from $9.75 per hour to $11.00 per hour (see Table 3.1). During poor economic times, the minimum wage rate is rarely adjusted; when the economy is expanding, the minimum wage rate is increased more frequently.

Pay Equity

Concern over the differences in wages that have existed between men and women has prompted governments to enact legislation that attempts to address the situation. Initially provinces simply stated that equal pay must be given for equal work. The legislation was altered to state that equal pay must be given for similar or substantially similar work. Since in many situations men and women do not do the same job, some jurisdictions have legislated that equal pay must be given for work of equal value; this is the concept of pay equity. In order to implement **pay equity**, an approach must be developed that

pay equity
equal pay for work of equal value

TABLE 3.1

Minimum Wage Rate by Province and Territory

Jurisdiction	Hourly Rate	Effective Date
Alberta	$9.75	Sept. 1, 2012
British Columbia	$10.25	May 1, 2012
Manitoba	$10.25	Oct. 1, 2012
New Brunswick	$10.00	Apr. 1, 2012
Newfoundland and Labrador	$10.00	Jul. 1, 2010
Northwest Territories	$10.00	Apr. 1, 2011
Nova Scotia	$10.15/$10.30	April 1, 2012/April 1, 2013
Nunavut	$11.00	Jan. 1, 2011
Ontario	$10.25	Mar. 31, 2010
Prince Edward Island	$10.00	Apr. 1, 2012
Quebec	$9.90/$10.15	May 1, 2012/May 1, 2013
Saskatchewan	$10.00	December 1, 2012
Yukon	$10.30	May 1, 2012

Source: Current and Forthcoming Minimum Hourly Wage Rates for Experienced Adult Workers in Canada, http://srv116.services.gc.ca/dimt-wid/sm-mw/rpt1.aspx?lang=eng, Human Resources and Skills Development Canada, 2012.Reproduced with the permission of the Minister of Public Works and Government Services Canada, 2013.

allows for the comparison of the values of different jobs. All provinces and territories have legislation that addresses the pay difference between men and women although the legislation varies among provinces.

The implementation of pay equity legislation relies on the complaint system. That is, if a worker believes that he or she is underpaid, the worker can file a complaint to have the situation investigated. Several provinces, however, are taking a proactive approach that shifts the burden of implementation from the employee to the employer, on the assumption that reasons for the male–female wage differential are deeply rooted in the economy and cannot be remedied by complaints alone. Employers must review their compensation procedures to ensure that their practices comply with the legislation. This compulsory review has been adopted in both the private and public sectors in Ontario and Quebec and in the public sectors in Manitoba, New Brunswick, Newfoundland and Labrador, Nova Scotia, and Prince Edward Island.

A discussion of the impact of pay equity legislation on the labour market appears in Chapter 11.

Other Standards

severance pay

a lump-sum payment to an employee upon termination of employment

Several other employment standards have been enacted across the country. These standards include pregnancy or maternity leave, parental leave, adoption leave, bereavement leave, **severance pay**, advance notice of termination, required rest periods, and payment of wages.

Labour Market Issue 3.2

The Rationale for Severance Pay

During the period of high unemployment in the 1980s, many unions negotiated severance pay clauses with their employers. Upon termination of employment, the employee received a lump-sum severance package, the size of which depended on the person's tenure with the company. As more collective agreements contained provisions for severance pay, and as unemployment persisted, pressure was put on governments to include some form of severance pay in employment standards legislation. Is there a valid argument for government-legislated severance pay? Upon termination should the employee receive a financial payment?

The first argument in favour of paying severance pay is based on the belief that employees earn ownership of their jobs. The longer an employee works at a job, the more the job belongs to the employee. If the employee is terminated from a job, the employee should be compensated. This argument parallels that of government confiscation of one's property. If your property is expropriated for a new highway or airport, you should be compensated for the loss of something that you own. Similarly, if your job is taken away from you, compensation should be forthcoming.

In collective agreements and legislation, employees with more seniority are entitled to more severance pay. It can be argued that seniority rules benefit the company as well as the employee. When benefits are provided to those with more seniority, there is less turnover in the labour force. Employees tend to remain with the company, knowing they are eligible for a severance package if their employment is terminated. Thus, hiring and training costs are reduced.

A second argument in favour of severance pay is that employees are usually paid less than they are worth in the first years of employment with a company. In their last years with the company, employees are usually paid more than would be warranted by their productivity. If an employee stays with a company until retirement, the years of underpayment are usually matched by the years of overpayment. If an employee is terminated before the age of retirement has been reached, there will be more years of underpayment that are not matched by years of overpayment. Therefore, employees should be compensated for those years of underpayment.

The counter-argument claims that many employees are overpaid in their initial years with a company. While learning a job, productivity is low. Employees are paid more than they are worth in order to attract good employees and establish a stable workforce. Overpaying new employees may be a characteristic of firms that promote from within the organization. The firm expects to get more productivity once the employee has experience with the firm. Therefore, if an employee is terminated before retirement, there is no need for further compensation since the years of overpayment have outnumbered the years of underpayment.

A third argument for severance pay is provided by the type of training received on the job. If the training is specific to the company, and only to that company, it may be difficult for the employee to find other employment upon termination. The employee has invested in learning this skill and the company has benefited, so the employee should be compensated for the loss of the job.

A counter-argument asserts that the return on any investment is uncertain. Some people lose money on their investments. Why should the same logic not apply to investing in a career? Maybe the career investment will pay off, and maybe it will not. If the terminated employee were highly trained in a company-specific skill, the salary previously earned by that employee may have been relatively high. The high salary would be a sufficient return gained on the investment in learning a skill. In addition, not all training given by companies is specific. If the training received by the employee is general in nature, it can be transferred to other companies so the likelihood of finding new employment is much improved. Under these circumstances, there may be no obligation for the company to give the employee a severance package.

In occupations with a high likelihood of termination, the wage rate often compensates for this unattractive feature. Employees in these jobs earn more than they would in jobs with a lower risk of termination. Under these circumstances, the argument in favour of severance pay is not strong. Conversely, those analysts who argue in favour of severance pay believe that one's weekly paycheque does not include payment for a possible loss of employment.

Arguments for severance pay can also be made on the basis of income distribution. Some employees may be terminated because of advances in technology; with the introduction of new technology, some benefit while others are harmed. For example, the public may benefit because the product is improved and available at a lower cost. The company may benefit from more sales and higher profits. Should those who benefit from the new technology compensate those who are hurt by that technology (by loss of employment)? Unfortunately, it may be difficult to identify the winners and losers in such situations. Furthermore, if all of society benefits from an innovation, should the company that introduces the innovation be expected to bear the entire burden of paying severance pay?

Should severance pay be awarded if worker termination comes from a change in government policy? For example, the Canadian government has pursued a policy of freer trade with other nations. Trade barriers have been dropped. Industries and workers once shielded from international competition are now forced to compete. Who should compensate these workers if they are terminated because of their company's inability to compete? If they were protected from international competition in the past, their earnings were probably higher than they otherwise would have been. Should the workers also be compensated for loss of employment? Some countries have established redundancy funds to pay those who have been terminated because of changes in government policy and technology. Other countries offer retraining, counselling, and assistance with mobility.

Human Rights

In 1948, the United Nations adopted the Universal Declaration of Human Rights, which advocates equal rights for all individuals regardless of race, religion, gender, or language. Canadian jurisdictions followed suit by passing legislation prohibiting discriminatory practices in employment. The legislation covers employers, employer and employee associations, and employment agencies. Employment discrimination is defined as any distinction, preference, or exclusion based on certain grounds, which nullifies or impairs equality of opportunity in employment or in conditions of employment. Legislation in all jurisdictions in Canada prohibits discrimination based on race; nationality, ethnicity, or place of origin; colour; religion or creed; marital status; physical or mental disability; or gender.

All jurisdictions forbid employment discrimination based on age, although not all jurisdictions apply the same age range. In Alberta, individuals 18 years of age and older are covered by human rights legislation; in New Brunswick, the age is 19. In British Columbia and Newfoundland and Labrador, those who are between 19 and 65 years of age are covered. In Ontario and Saskatchewan, the legislation covers individuals between 18 and 65 years of age. The other provinces make general references to age in terms of the minimum and maximum ages for employment.

Freedom of political belief, conviction, and opinion is covered in human rights legislation in British Columbia, Manitoba, Newfoundland and Labrador, Prince Edward Island, Quebec, and the Yukon. All provinces prohibit discrimination based on sexual orientation. In the jurisdictions of Ontario, Quebec, the Northwest Territories, and the federal government, discrimination against those who have been pardoned for an offence is forbidden. Discrimination against a person because of the source of that person's income is prohibited in Alberta, Manitoba, Nova Scotia, Prince Edward Island, Saskatchewan, and the Yukon Territory.

employment equity

all barriers to employment have been removed and equitable treatment of employees exists

Closely related to human rights is legislation aimed at achieving **employment equity**. The goal is to create a work environment in which all barriers to employment have been removed and equitable treatment of employees exists. The push for employment equity came from the concern over employment issues facing women, racial minorities, Aboriginal people, and people with disabilities. Human rights legislation deals with intentional discrimination. Employment equity regulations aim at both intentional and systemic discrimination, which can occur in human resources practices and policies that on the surface appear to be neutral. The regulations are proactive as opposed to dealing with complaints.

At present, only the federal government and Quebec have mandatory employment equity regulations. Ontario has a voluntary Equal Opportunity Plan whereby government will help employers diversify their workforces. The remaining provinces handle employment equity through affirmative action programs.

Health and Safety

All jurisdictions have a form of health and safety legislation for the workplace. The common practice is to give the government the right to enforce regulations regarding safety in the workplace. The regulations require employers to help ensure the safety of an employee. In all provinces except British Columbia, occupational health and safety legislation is separate from workers' compensation legislation. A common element of safety legislation is the right of an employee to refuse to perform unsafe work.

One outcome of governments' efforts in this area is the Workplace Hazardous Materials Information System (WHMIS). It is based on the belief that employees have the right to be informed about the handling, storage, and disposal of hazardous chemicals in the workplace.

Workers' Compensation

Ontario was the first jurisdiction to introduce workers' compensation, in 1915. All provinces now have workers' compensation, although Prince Edward Island did not introduce it until 1949 and Newfoundland until 1951. This legislation provides that workers who sustain personal injuries on the job or are disabled by industrial diseases are entitled to compensation. The compensation fund is financed by contributions from employers. In return, employees give up the right to take legal action against employers.

Employment Insurance

The introduction of employment insurance in Canada required a change to the Constitution. In 1935, the federal government introduced the *Employment and Social Insurance Act*, which was later found to be unconstitutional as it interfered with provincial jurisdiction in the areas of property and civil rights. The change to the Constitution, introduced in 1940, gave the federal government exclusive jurisdiction in the field of unemployment insurance legislation. The initial legislation was updated in 1955 and named the *Unemployment Insurance Act*. It provided income support for individuals during a temporary interruption of earnings, with an emphasis on returning to the ranks of the employed as soon as possible. Contributions to the unemployment insurance fund were paid by both employers and employees. Contributions and benefits were based on the individual's insurable earnings, with a ceiling on the amount that was insurable.

In 1971, the legislation was redrafted to cover more employees: 90% of the labour force was covered against loss of employment income. An individual could now receive up to two-thirds of his or her insurable earnings; however, benefits became taxable, so the net income gain from benefits was reduced. Eligibility requirements were reduced to as little as eight weeks of employment and the maximum benefit period increased. Benefits were provided to those whose employment was interrupted by illness or pregnancy. A lump-sum payment was made to individuals who retired from employment.

After 1971, more changes were made to the legislation, including basing eligibility requirements on the unemployment rate in the area, reducing benefits to 60% of earnings, and including pension income and severance pay as earnings. The changes also improved maternity leave, introduced adoption leave, and granted paternity leave to fathers in the event of the mother's death or incapacity.

Because the contributions from employers and employees were not enough to meet the obligations of the fund in the past, the federal government subsidized the unemployment insurance fund. In 1992, the government stated that it would no longer do so: the fund was now to be fully financed by employer and employee contributions. In addition, the number of weeks of employment to qualify for benefits was increased and no lump-sum payment was to be made to those 65 years of age and above. In 1993, quitters were disqualified from receiving benefits, and the benefits for new claimants were reduced to 57% of earnings.

Effective January 1, 1997, the *Unemployment Insurance Act* became the *Employment Insurance Act*, and a number of important changes were made.

- Employers were now required to withhold employment insurance premiums from all employees—full-time, part-time, and casual.

- Benefits were now based on hours of work rather than weeks of employment. The minimum number of hours ranged from 420 to 700 hours in the previous year, depending on the unemployment rate in the area; this was an increase from the minimum 15 hours per week previously required. The change from a system of eligibility based on weeks to one based on hours of work had two objectives: to discourage employers from hiring someone for less than 15 hours per week with the intention of avoiding EI premiums, and to allow individuals with non-standard employment patterns to qualify for EI if they met the hours criterion but could not meet the weeks criterion.

- New entrants into the labour force needed 910 hours of work to qualify for benefits. The lengthier qualifying period for new labour force entrants was aimed at their establishing a stronger attachment to the labour force before making an EI claim.

- Individuals who received less than $200 a week in benefits could earn up to $50 a week without a reduction in benefits, and benefits were increased for low-income individuals with children.

- Individuals who made frequent claims would receive reduced benefits (this change was repealed in 2001; all beneficiaries of EI receive the same proportion of insured earnings [55%]).

- The responsibility for the administration of the employment insurance program was given to the Department for Social Development.

Union–Management Relationships

All jurisdictions regulate the interaction between employers and the representatives of the employees, be they craft unions, industrial unions, or professional associations. Whereas individuals can negotiate employment conditions with employers based on existing human rights, employment standards, and safety legislation, groups of employees need special legislation for those negotiations. Once a worker's employment relationship is determined through union–management negotiations, he or she can no longer negotiate with the employer as an individual.

Union Membership

Many of the employment standards discussed in this chapter have been enacted only recently. Before these standards were legislated, employees relied on group pressure—mainly from trade unions—to force management to improve the working conditions. In fact, many standards were copied from the wording of collective agreements.

About 4.3 million Canadian employees are members of trade unions. Approximately one-third of full-time Canadian employees and one-quarter of part-time employees are represented by a union in negotiations with management with respect to working conditions. The percentage of the labour force represented by a union varies among occupations, industries, and provinces.

Labour Market Issue 3.3

A Comment on Government Intervention in the Labour Market

In this chapter, most of the legislation affecting the employer–employee relationship in Canada has been introduced. This legislation represents government intervention in the operation of the market. The buying and selling of an employee's services is regulated by legislation. The level of government intervention in the labour market is greater than in many other markets because the labour market is associated with the exchange of services provided by human beings. Employers do not own their employees; they contract with them to provide a service.

The level of government intervention in the labour market varies among provinces. The differences in legislation among provinces, however, are not as great as the differences in labour legislation among countries. For example, governments in the United States, Canada's major trading partner, are less interventionist in the labour market than are governments in Canada. The United States has a history of emphasizing individual freedoms and is not as quick to restrict these freedoms as governments in Canada are. Higher levels of government intervention in the labour market restrict the flexibility of employees in managing their operations. On the other

hand, Canada is less interventionist with respect to the labour market than governments in Europe are.

Is government intervention in the labour market a positive or a negative feature of the market? Some argue that government intervention in the labour market does not allow the markets to operate efficiently. It can be argued that policies such as the minimum wage rate and employment insurance lead to higher levels of unemployment than would otherwise be the case. Trade unions also prohibit the entry of workers into certain jobs, thus disrupting market flows.

Restrictions on hours of work and overtime limit the flexibility of employers. Larger companies may relocate to countries where their operations are not as restricted.

The argument in favour of government intervention centres around protection for the employee and establishing a level playing field for all employers. Employers are not allowed to gain a competitive advantage by paying very low wages and providing very poor working conditions. It also appears that legislated employment restrictions do not reduce the level of productivity in the workforce.

Table 3.2

Union Density Rate by Industry, First Half of 2011		

INDUSTRY	TOTAL EMPLOYEES (000s)	UNION DENSITY (%)
Goods-producing	3 062	26.9
Agriculture	114	4.5
Natural resources	292	19.3
Utilities	144	63.8
Construction	838	30.3
Manufacturing	1 675	24.9
Service-producing	11 445	30.4
Trade	2 371	12.2
Transportation and warehousing	690	41.1
Finance, insurance, real estate, and leasing	893	8.8
Professional, scientific, and technical	825	3.9
Management and administrative and support	512	16.0
Education	1 209	67.6
Healthcare and social assistance	1 831	52.7
Information, culture, and recreation	647	25.3
Accommodation and food	981	7.3
Other	519	9.9
Public administration	968	66.5

Source: Statistics Canada. *Perspectives on Labour and Incomes.* (Vol. 23, No. 4). Winter 2011. Catalogue no. 75-001-X.

union density

ratio of the number of employees belonging to a union to the total number of paid employees

Union density is the ratio of the number of employees who belong to a union to the total number of paid employees. In 1967, union density in Canada was 33.2%, with 40.9% for men and 15.9% for women. By the first half of 2011, union density had fallen overall to 29.7%, with 28.2% for men and 31.1% for women. Employees with a postsecondary certificate, diploma, or degree are more likely to be members of a union. For employees with some high school education, the union density was 19.6% in 2011; for employees with a university degree, it was 34.0%. These percentages may reflect the fact that many employees with a postsecondary education work in the public (as opposed to the private) sector in the economy. The union density for public-sector employees was 71.1% in 2011, while for private-sector employees it was 16.0%.

Union density by industry for the first half of 2011 is presented in Table 3.2. There are significant differences in union density by industry. Union density is highest in education, public administration, and utilities, and lowest in professional and scientific occupations, agriculture, and accommodation and food.

TABLE 3.3

Union Density by Province, First Half of 2011

PROVINCE	TOTAL EMPLOYEES (000s)	UNION DENSITY (%)
Newfoundland and Labrador	197	37.3
Prince Edward Island	59	30.3
Nova Scotia	392	28.4
New Brunswick	312	27.4
Quebec	3 369	36.0
Ontario	5 593	26.5
Manitoba	530	35.7
Saskatchewan	423	33.9
Alberta	1 674	22.6
British Columbia	1 824	30.0

Source: Statistics Canada. *Perspectives on Labour and Incomes.* (Vol. 23, No. 4). Winter 2011. Catalogue no. 75-001-X.

Union density also varies by occupation. Occupations with the highest union densities are teaching and nursing. Other occupations with high union densities include police and fire protection, and technical and support staff in the health industry. Occupations with high union densities tend to be public-sector occupations. Occupations with the lowest union densities include sales, management, and food and beverage-related jobs. Union densities also vary by province (see Table 3.3), which is, in part, a reflection of the types of industry in that province. Newfoundland and Labrador and Quebec have the highest union densities, while Alberta, Ontario, and New Brunswick have the lowest.

Summary

Both the federal and provincial governments have jurisdiction over working conditions in Canada. The federal government has the authority to regulate and control those industries of an interprovincial, national, or international nature. The provinces are responsible for civil and property rights in Canada, which allows them to impose conditions on the employment relationship.

Government regulation of the employment relationship falls into the following categories: employment standards, human rights, health and safety, workers' compensation, employment insurance, and union–management relationships.

Only about one-third of all employees in Canada belong to a labour union. Approximately 71.1% of public-sector employees belong to a union, compared to only 16% of private-sector employees. Since 1990, union membership has declined slightly. Union density in Canada is 29.7% in 2011.

Key Terms

Canada Labour Code (page 49)   severance pay (page 54)
employment equity (page 56)   union density (page 60)
pay equity (page 53)

Weblinks

Employment Standards

Manitoba
www.gov.mb.ca/labour/standards

British Columbia
www.labour.gov.bc.ca/esb/

Alberta
www.employment.alberta.ca/SFW/1224.html

Newfoundland and Labrador
www.gov.nl.ca/lra/faq/labourstandards.html

Prince Edward Island
www.gov.pe.ca/labour/index.php3

Nova Scotia
www.gov.ns.ca/lae/labourstandards/

New Brunswick
www.gnb.ca/acts/acts/e-07-2.htm

Quebec
www.cnt.gouv.qc.ca/en/index.html

Ontario
www.labour.gov.on.ca/english/es/

Saskatchewan
www.labour.gov.sk.ca/standards/

Pay Equity
www.payequity.gov.on.ca

Canadian Labour Congress
www.clc-ctc.ca

Employment Insurance
www.hrsdc.gc.ca/en/ei/legislation/ei_act_entry_page.shtml

International Labour Organization
www.ilo.org

Discussion Questions

1. Write a brief summary of a relatively unknown labour statute in your province or territory. You may come across legislation that applies only to certain industries. For example, students in Ontario may review the *Industrial Standards Act*.
2. Human rights legislation aims to prevent discrimination based on age, yet the Supreme Court has upheld the rights of employers to force employees to retire at age 65. In your opinion, is this practice discriminatory?
3. What industries other than the garment industry frequently use home workers?
4. Why would some industries and occupations have higher union densities than others?

Using the Internet

1. Access the pay equity site (www.payequity.gov.on.ca). Compare pay equity legislation in another province with that of the province in which you live. Compare pay equity legislation in another country with that of the province in which you live.

Exercises

1. List the labour legislation in your province or territory.
2. The number of weeks that an individual is permitted to receive employment insurance benefits varies according to the number of weeks of insured earnings and the region in which the individual resides. What are the maximum weeks of benefits in your area?
3. If you are currently employed, determine whether your working conditions are regulated by federal or provincial legislation.

Trends and Recent Developments in the Canadian Labour Market

4. TRENDS IN THE CANADIAN LABOUR FORCE

5. EMPLOYMENT

6. UNEMPLOYMENT

7. TRENDS IN LABOUR COMPENSATION

Trends and Recent Developments in the Canadian Labour Market

This text explores the operation and outcomes of the Canadian labour market. Before we study how the labour market works in detail, we will outline the major trends and developments in the Canadian labour market since World War II.[i] The purpose, at this point, is to establish the developments and labour market outcomes that will be explained in later chapters. It is preferable first to provide observations on the labour market before developing theories. As Sherlock Holmes says, "It is a capital mistake to theorize before all facts are in. Insensibly one begins to twist facts to suit theories, instead of theories to fit facts."

What kinds of information do labour economists use to develop and test their theories? Casual personal observation provides one source. For example, someone looking for a job learns whether, and under which conditions, firms are hiring. A member of a collective bargaining team gains particular insight into how wages are determined at the local level. Most of us work for pay at some time in our lives, so most of us have some sense of how the labour market operates. However, although our own experience may provide some insight, personal experience cannot cover all aspects of the labour market. We must therefore be careful not to rely solely on personal experience when analyzing the Canadian labour market.

Statistics provide a more systematic and objective source of information about the labour market than personal experiences. This information is mostly obtained from government-run surveys of households and businesses. The statistics are like a snapshot and summarize the state of the labour market at a particular point in time. When we look at this information over a number of years, we can identify trends in the Canadian labour market. Most of the data presented in the following chapters come from these surveys.

[i] Unfortunately, trends in several variables cannot be traced back to the mid- or late 1940s. This is due to a lack of appropriate surveys in earlier years or due to revisions in survey questionnaires that resulted in inconsistent data over time. For example, some of the time series considered in this text start in 1976 because the Labour Force Survey questionnaire was significantly changed in 1975.

Part II of the text is divided into four chapters, whose order of presentation is related to the concepts of demand and supply. To paraphrase the late British economist Alfred Marshall, it takes both demand and supply to determine market outcomes, as it takes two blades of a pair of scissors to cut cloth. In Canada, important structural changes on both the supply side and the demand side have been transforming the Canadian labour market and the nature of work.

Chapter 4 discusses the trends in the labour force, which represents the supply side of the labour market. Trends on the demand side are presented in Chapter 5 with the emphasis on employment, which is only part of the demand side; job vacancies are the other part. However, because we have no consistent data on vacancies, we use employment as a proxy for demand. Chapters 6 and 7 consider the outcomes of the interaction between demand and supply: long-run changes in unemployment and the level of compensation for those who are employed.

Chapter 4

Trends in the Canadian Labour Force

Chapter Learning Objectives

After completing this chapter, you should be able to:

- evaluate the factors that bring about changes in the labour force
- explain changes in domestic population
- evaluate the impact of the "baby boom" on the labour force
- describe the changing patterns of immigration
- discuss changes in the ethnic composition of the labour force
- explain changes in the labour force participation rates for men and women
- describe changes in the gender composition of the labour force

Brain Gain or Brain Waste?

Mark, after graduating from a Canadian university with a degree in mechanical engineering, saw a wider range of job opportunities in his field south of the border. He moved to California, where he has been working with a U.S. company for the last five years. Mark is an example of Canada's brain drain—the loss of knowledge workers from Canada especially to the United States. Laura received a degree in chemistry from a university in Argentina and worked for several years in a laboratory of a pharmaceutical company in her home country. When the political and economic crisis in Argentina worsened, she decided to emigrate to Canada. Laura is an example of Canada's brain gain—the admission of highly skilled immigrants to Canada from the rest of the world.

While the number of highly educated workers emigrating from Canada on a permanent or temporary basis appears to have increased during the 1990s, so too did the number of highly skilled immigrants to Canada. It is estimated, for example, that for every university degree holder migrating from Canada to the United States, there are four university degree holders migrating from the rest of the world to Canada.[1] While the number of highly educated professionals and skilled workers admitted to Canada has steadily increased over the years, a large number of them seem to end up in jobs in which their qualifications and skills are not adequately utilized. Laura could not find employment in her field. Since her arrival in Canada, she has been working as a salesclerk in a fashion boutique.

Underutilization of immigrants arises when formal education or skills gained through work experience in their home countries are not recognized in Canada or are discounted even though there is no objective evidence of their inferiority. For example, foreign professional or trade credentials may not be recognized by Canadian regulatory bodies even in cases where foreign standards are equivalent to Canadian standards. Alternatively, immigrant credentials that have been recognized by the relevant Canadian licensing bodies may not be accepted by employers because they believe that the immigrant's training is of lower quality than Canadian training. Also, employers may demand "Canadian experience" even though foreign experience is in fact applicable to the Canadian workplace. The returns on foreign work experience appear to be low for recent immigrants, in particular for immigrants from non-European countries.[2] Recent estimates of the income lost by immigrants due to non-recognition or discounting of their educational qualifications, professional credentials, and work experience are in the range of $2 billion annually.[3] While these are first, rough estimates, their magnitude indicates that the economic loss from the underutilization of immigrants' skills is substantial. Canada's brain gain appears to be turning into a brain waste.

The Labour Force

In order to determine the amount of labour available to the economy, it is necessary to distinguish between the quantity and the quality of labour supplied. The quantity depends on the size of the population, the proportion of the population that desires work, and the number of hours of work that individuals are willing to make available per year. The quality depends on such factors as the level of education, skills, and health of the workforce. The impact of education will be more fully discussed in Chapter 12. The total labour supply in an economy includes those who are working (the employed) and those who are not working but are seeking work (the unemployed). The sum of all employed and unemployed individuals in a country is called the **labour force**, which we use throughout this text to mean the total labour supply. That is:

Labour force = Total labour supply =
Number of employed + Number of unemployed

How is the size of the labour force determined? Each month, Statistics Canada releases statistics based on a survey of households, called the Labour Force Survey (LFS). For each survey, about 1 in every 200 Canadian households is asked a series of questions about the labour market status of its members. Based on the answers, each adult (aged 15 and older) in each surveyed household is placed into one of three categories:

- Employed
- Unemployed
- Not in the labour force

A person is considered **employed** if he or she did any work at all for pay or profit during the week prior to the week of the Labour Force Survey (the reference week). The definition also includes any household member who worked without pay in a family enterprise and people who are normally employed but are not working at the time of the survey because they are, for example, ill, on holidays, or on strike. To be counted as **unemployed**, a person must be without work, must be available for work, and must have actively looked for work within the past four weeks. Individuals who have not searched for work but who expect to start working soon, either because they are on temporary layoff or they are waiting to start a new job within four weeks, are also counted as unemployed. A person who is neither employed nor unemployed is **not in the labour force**. These are people who are retired, in school full-time, at home looking after their own children, or not looking for work for some other reason. Adding the total numbers of employed and unemployed people from the LFS, Statistics Canada computes the labour force for every month.

labour force
the number of people who are either employed or unemployed

employed
describes a person who works for pay or profit during the reference week of the Labour Force Survey

unemployed
describes a person without work, available for work, and looking for work

not in the labour force
describes a person who is neither employed nor unemployed

Over the last 60 years, three outstanding developments have affected labour supply, not only significantly altering the size of the Canadian labour force but also radically changing its composition. These trends are:

- the dramatic increase in the fertility rate during the baby-boom period and its subsequent, equally dramatic, decline, which largely accounts for the aging of the population and the workforce
- the increasing reliance on immigration as a source of labour force growth, which has led to a profound change of the ethnoracial composition of Canada's urban workforce
- the increase in the labour force participation of women, particularly of adult women, which has fundamentally changed the gender composition of the labour force

In the following, the trends and their associated structural changes are discussed separately.

Figure 4.1 shows the growth of the Canadian labour force over the last five decades. In 1947, 4.9 million people were members of the labour force. By 2012, the labour force had grown nearly 286% to 18.9 million people. From 1950 to 1980, the Canadian labour force experienced growth rates unsurpassed among western industrialized countries. Growth was particularly strong between 1966 and 1978, with annual growth rates varying from 3.3% to 3.7%. In the last two decades of the twentieth century, growth slowed down. Annual average growth rates were 1.8% in the 1980s; during the 1990s, the rates averaged only about 1%. Starting in the late 1990s, however, growth of the labour force picked up again: from 1999 to 2012 it averaged about 1.5% annually.

Part of the decline in the growth rate of the labour force can be attributed to the fact that growth is an exponential phenomenon. The growth rate is calculated based on the labour force of the previous year, which is constantly increasing. As the labour force grows each year, the number of entrants required to maintain a constant growth rate must also grow exponentially. The difference between annual growth rates of 3% and 1% becomes clear if one realizes that growth at 3% a year implies a doubling of the labour force in about 23 years.[ii] If the growth rate falls to 1%, the doubling time grows to 70 years.

To understand the growth pattern of the labour force, we have to look at the factors that determine changes in the labour force. Figure 4.2 (page 74) outlines these factors. Let us start with the population available for employment, that is, the **civilian working-age population**, also called the **labour force source population**. The LFS defines the civilian working-age population as the Canadian population aged 15 years or over, excluding full-time members of the Armed Forces, institutional residents such as inmates in prisons or psychiatric hospitals, persons living on Native reserves, and residents of the Yukon, Nunavut, and the Northwest Territories. The reason for excluding Aboriginal peoples living on reserves and the residents in Canada's North is that conducting an extensive, monthly survey in remote and sparsely populated areas would be extremely costly.

civilian working-age population (labour force source population)

the Canadian population aged 15 years and over excluding full-time members of the Armed Forces, institutional residents, persons living on Native reserves, and residents of the Yukon, Nunavut, and the Northwest Territories

---

[ii] The convenient way to calculate how long it takes for a quantity to double, if we know its exponential growth rate, is to divide the growth rate into the number 70.

FIGURE 4.1

Labour Force Growth, 1947–2012

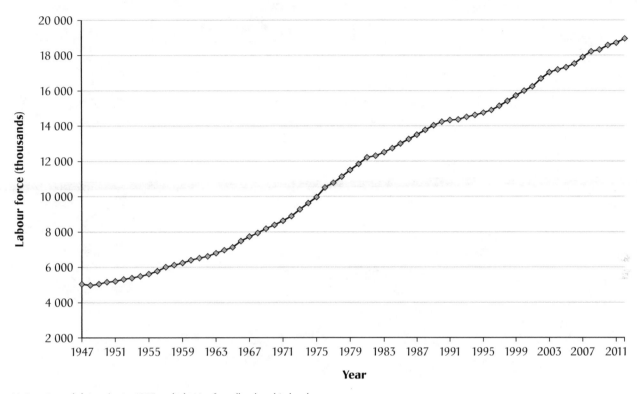

Notes: Annual data prior to 1950 exclude Newfoundland and Labrador.
Estimates prior to 1966 are based on persons aged 14 and over.
Estimates from 1966 include persons aged 15 and over.
Estimates from 1966 to 1974 have been adjusted to conform to current concepts.
Estimates prior to 1966 have not been revised.

Sources: For 1947–75, adapted from Statistics Canada. (1995). *Canadian Economic Observer,
Historical Statistical Supplement, 1994/5*. Catalogue no. 11-210 and
http://www.statcan.gc.ca/pub/11-516-x/sectiond/4057750-eng.htm; for 1976–2011, adapted from
Statistics Canada CANSIM, table 282-0002

The percentage of the working-age population participating in the labour force, through either employment or the search for employment, is called the **labour force participation rate** (LFPR):

$$Labour\ force\ participation\ rate = \frac{Labour\ force}{Working\text{-}age\ population} \times 100$$

For example, in 2012, the working-age population comprised nearly 28.31 million people, of whom 18.88 million were in the labour force (17.51 million employed and 1.37 million unemployed), resulting in a LFPR of 66.7% (18.88/28.31).

labour force participation rate

the percentage of the working-age population that is in the labour force

FIGURE 4.2

Labour Force (Supply of Labour)

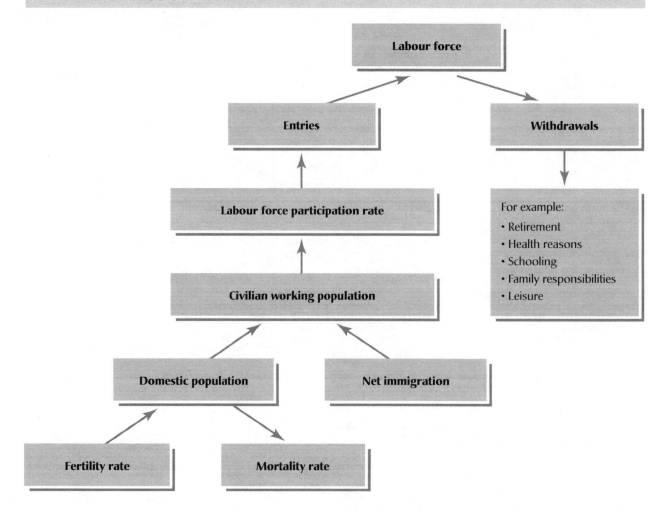

The labour force grows as the working-age population increases, provided that the labour force participation rate does not decline. As shown in Figure 4.2, the growth in the working-age population results from increases in the domestic population and changes in international migration. Changes in international migration are the net result of subtracting the number of emigrants from the total number of immigrants. The country's domestic population is affected by fertility and mortality rates. The right side of Figure 4.2 shows the withdrawals from the labour force, which includes people who have decided to retire or to return to school full-time. It also includes those who are forced to quit work for health or family reasons. The net change in the labour force is determined by subtracting the withdrawals from the entries into the labour force.

The Population Base

From 1947 to 2012, the working-age population in Canada grew from 9 million to 28.3 million, an increase of 214%. As mentioned above, the changes in the population base come from changes in the domestic population and from net migration. Each of these changes is discussed below.

Growth of the Domestic Population

Since the early 1960s, domestic or natural population growth in Canada declined almost without interruption from about 2% in 1961 to below 1% in 2012. **Natural population growth** is the balance between the total numbers of births and deaths. The **birth rate** (the number of births per 1000 of population) has steadily fallen from 28 in the late 1950s to approximately 11.3 in 2010. Part of the decline is attributable to the aging of the baby-boom generation born between 1947 and 1966. Over the 1980s, women of this generation moved through their prime childbearing years, creating an "echo" generation of boomer children that mitigated slower growth. By the mid-1990s, most women born during the baby boom had entered their lower fertility years. By 2005, women of the baby-boom generation had largely aged beyond their childbearing years. The other reason for the drop in the number of births can be found in the long-run changes in the reproductive behaviour of Canadians, which are reflected in the continuous decline in the **fertility rate**. The fertility rate measures the number of births per 1000 women aged 15 to 49 years. In 1959, at the height of the baby boom, there was an average of 3.9 births per woman. By the early 1970s, it had fallen below 2.1, the critical population replacement rate. Allowing for premature deaths, a fertility rate of 2.1 implies that each couple leaves at least two children behind to replace themselves. Between 2002 and 2005, the fertility rate had fallen to 1.5, the lowest rate ever recorded in Canada. By 2010, the fertility rate increased slightly to 1.7. Within 50 years, the fertility rate of Canadian women declined by 56.4%.

The decline in fertility rates is typical for most economically advanced countries. Canada now ranks among the group of industrialized countries with very low fertility. Only the United States stands out from other industrialized countries in that its fertility rate has been close to the replacement level for more than a decade.

The **mortality rate** is the number of deaths per 1000 persons. In the last 50 years, it has hardly deviated from the 7.0 mark (7.4 in the late 1960s, about 7.2 in 2003, and 7.5 in 2010). Preventive and curative medicine has made great inroads in fighting cardiovascular diseases, which had been rising steadily since the beginning of the twentieth century. As a result, mortality related to diseases of the circulatory system has continued to fall. Rates of deaths due to other diseases, such as cancer, however, have been rising.

The long-run decline in Canada's birth rate and the insignificant changes in the mortality rate have led to the continuous decrease in the net growth of Canada's domestic population. Since the aging of the population is accompanied

natural population growth
the difference between the numbers of births and deaths

birth rate
the number of births per 1000 of population

fertility rate
the number of births per 1000 women aged 15 to 49 years

mortality rate
the number of deaths per 1000 of population

The Fertility Gap Between Canada and the U.S.

For many years after World War II, fertility patterns in Canada paralleled those in the United States; by the early 1970s, the fertility rates in both countries had fallen below the replacement rate of 2.1. Since the mid-1970s, however, the countries' fertility rates have moved in opposite directions: while the U.S. rate has been rising and recently reached the replacement level, Canada's rate has continued its downward trend.

What accounts for the difference? In a recent study, Alain Belanger and Genevieve Ouellet of Statistics Canada explored some possible explanations.[4] The first and foremost reason can be found in ethnoracial differences. Hispanic and black women in the U.S. have fertility rates close to 3 and 2.2 per woman, respectively. Both groups constitute a much higher proportion of the population in the U.S. compared to Canada, and their share in the U.S. population has been growing. But even the rate for non-Hispanic white women in the U.S. is well above that for Canadian women. Differences in the ethnoracial composition of the two populations, therefore, cannot entirely explain the differences in fertility. At most, they account for approximately 40% of the Canada–U.S. gap.

Differences in birth control methods used provide another reason. Though more women in the U.S. use some form of contraception than Canadian women, Canadian women, especially teenagers, rely on more effective contraceptive methods, such as birth control pills, implants, injections, and intrauterine devices (IUDs). These methods are both less expensive and more accessible in Canada due to its universal healthcare system. As a result, unwanted births are less common in Canada, particularly for the 15–19 age group.

Canadian women also have a greater tendency than their American counterparts to marry later and to postpone childbearing. This may reflect the higher job insecurity of young people in Canada during the last two decades. The differences were substantial in the 1990s when the unemployment rate in Canada for those in their early 20s was half to two-thirds higher than the comparable U.S. rate. The result was lower income for young adults and likely a lower confidence in the future than is usually needed to take on the responsibility of family formation and parenthood.

Canada is also a more secular society than the United States. About 34% of American women of childbearing age practise their religion on a weekly basis, almost double the proportion of Canadian women (18%). Greater religious observance tends to go along with a higher marriage rate and a lower divorce rate, both of which have a positive effect on fertility.

by an increase in the number of deaths—even if mortality rates were reduced—and since the number of births is likely to continue to fall, domestic population growth is bound to decrease further.

Changes in the Age Composition of the Labour Force

Changes in the fertility rate not only affect the size of Canada's population but are also changing its age structure. A declining fertility rate narrows the base of the age pyramid and broadens its peak. Over the course of the twentieth century, the fertility rate decreased by half. The gradual aging of the population was interrupted for about 20 years by the baby boom. Between 1947 and 1966, fertility soared, resulting in an increase in births to levels that demographers had considered to be long in the past. Around 1970, fertility returned to the levels it would have reached had the secular trend continued unbroken, but the coming of age of those born in the baby boom fundamentally changed the age composition of the population and, with it, the labour force.

FIGURE 4.3

Age Pyramids of Canada for Selected Years

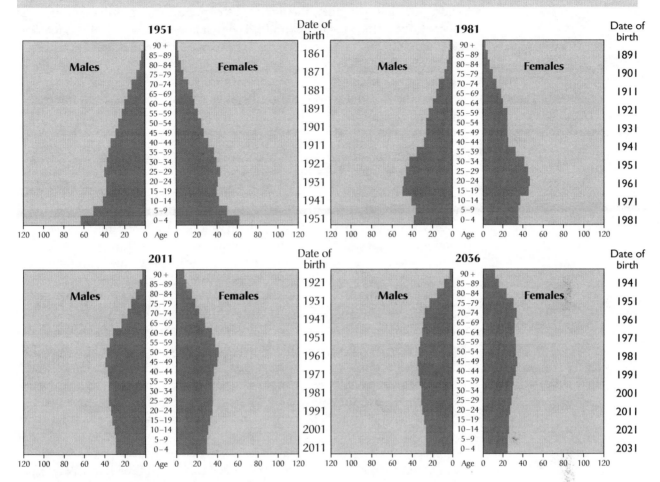

Note: Distribution in each age group for a total population of 1000.

Sources: For the eighteenth century, Coale, A.J., and Demeny, P. (1983). *Regional Model Life Tables and Stable Populations*. New York: Academic Press, pp. 86, 137. For 1861 and 1891, adapted from Census of Canada, 1931, vol. 1, Table 9 respectively; for 1921, 1951, and 1981, adapted from Censuses of Canada. For 2011 and 2036, adapted from Perreault, J. (1990). *Population Projections for Canada, Provinces and Territories, 1989–2011*. Ottawa: Statistics Canada (Catalogue no. 91-520), pp. 150, 177, 187.

Figure 4.3 depicts how the baby-boom generation is transforming the age structure of the Canadian population from the typical population pyramid in 1951 to a barrel-like shape in the first three decades of the twenty-first century. As the baby boomers entered the labour force in increasing numbers since the mid-1960s, the share of younger people in the labour force increased, reaching a peak in the mid-1970s. In 1975, the share of youth in the labour force stood at 27%. Since 1982, the growth rate of youth has become negative and the share of youth has declined below the mid-1950s level; in 2011, it was only 13%. The maturation of the baby-boom generation and the renewed downward trend in fertility since the early 1970s have resulted in the smallest proportion of the population under the age of 15, and the largest share accounted for by the elderly, in Canadian history. At the beginning of the twenty-first century, close to one-third of the labour force was aged 45 and older, compared to 21% in the mid-1980s. Barring a spectacular reversal in the secular trend of declining fertility, the aging of the population and the labour force will continue in the new millennium. The first boomers, born in 1947, reached age 55 in 2002. By the year 2031, the last baby-boom cohort will have passed the threshold of 65 years of age. By then, the age structure will be inverted and the elderly will account for one-quarter of the total population.

The aging of the workforce is affecting the labour market in many different ways:

Implications for Job Advancement and Corporate Organizational Structures

Among the influences on the employment relationship is, for example, the phenomenon called "plateauing." As the workforce grows older, more workers compete for fewer senior positions and in turn block the advancement of younger colleagues. Changes in the organizational structure of corporations are also directly related to the changing age structure of the workforce.[5] As long as there are more younger workers than older ones, corporations structure their organizations to have fewer positions at the top and the bulk at the bottom. In other words, triangular corporate structures correspond to the triangular shape of the population's age pyramid. As the pyramid starts to take the shape of a barrel, organizations that maintain a pyramidal structure find themselves in trouble, with too many middle-aged employees and not enough entry-level people. As a result, many start to lay off employees in their forties because there are not enough middle and upper management positions to accommodate the large baby-boom cohorts. Other corporations adopt a more constructive approach by flattening their corporate structure. Realizing that the only way to fit a barrel into a triangle is to flatten the triangle, corporations begin to reduce the number of organizational levels and broaden each occupational level. Changes in the organizational structure, in turn, necessitate changes in career paths. The traditional linear promotion path to the top is increasingly replaced by a mix of lateral and promotional moves. Since lateral moves are often associated with changes in occupation and required skills, employees need more frequent re-education and retraining. This example demonstrates how the aging of the workforce through changes of corporate organizational structures will deeply affect the whole field of human resources management. Changes in organizational structures brought about by the aging labour force parallel organizational changes resulting from globalization, some of which were outlined in Chapter 2.

Implications for Canada's Social Security System

Debate has particularly intensified over the extent to which the aging trend will increase the burden on the current and future labour forces to support social services—particularly eldercare, health services, and pension support—to the expanding number of non-working elderly. In the Canada Pension Plan

(CPP) and the Quebec Pension Plan (QPP) the pension contributions of the currently working generations are largely financing the benefits paid to the retirees. The system is sustainable as long as there are more workers than retirees, assuming premiums and benefits remain unchanged. Those who argue that the demographics of the baby boom will place an unbearable burden on the social security system point to the increasing **dependency rate**—the ratio of retired recipients to taxpaying workers. In 2001, there were 342 recipients to every 1000 contributors, compared with 122 in 1981.[6]

dependency rate

the ratio of retirees to taxpaying workers

Table 4.1 shows projections of the working-age to retirement-age population for Canada and six other industrialized countries. As the ratio declines from 7.7 in 1960 to an estimated 2.6 in 2040, the dependency rate will dramatically increase. The threat to the financial sustainability of the public pension system posed by the aging of the population is accentuated by the fact that people live longer and retire earlier. With longer lives and shorter careers, retirees draw benefits for a longer time while contributing to pension plans for a shorter time. Some actuarial estimates suggest that, in order to maintain the solvency of the pension system under the present rules, tax rates would have to be increased and/or benefits would have to be reduced.

One possible counter-argument is that the dependency rate or beneficiary/worker ratio is only one of two ratios on which the financing of much of the social security services depends; the other is the ratio of average workers' wages to average retirees' benefits. The beneficiary/worker ratio, for example, does not consider the effects of increasing productivity. As output per employed worker (called average labour productivity) increases, wages likely increase as well. Put differently, a rise in labour productivity means that it will take fewer workers to support each retiree. An increase in the wage/benefit ratio could offset the rise in the old age dependency burden. However, given the relatively modest productivity growth in Canada over the last 20 years, this does not seem to hold much promise. One option to reduce

TABLE 4.1

The Ratio of Working-Age Population to Retirement-Age Population, Selected Countries, 1960–2040

Year	Canada	France	Germany	Italy	Japan	United Kingdom	United States
1960	7.7	5.3	6.3	7.5	10.5	5.6	6.5
1990	5.9	4.7	4.5	4.7	5.8	4.3	5.3
2010	4.7	4.1	2.8	3.9	3.4	4.5	5.3
2030	3.5	3.3	3.0	3.4	3.0	3.9	4.9
2040	2.6	2.6	2.1	2.4	2.6	3.0	3.1

Source: Patricia S. Pollard, "How Will Demographics Affect Social Security?" Federal Reserve Bank of St. Louis, International Economic Trends, August 1996, based on OECD data. Reprinted with permission.

Chapter 4: Trends in the Canadian Labour Force

the financial burden put on the working population would involve more flexible work arrangements for older workers. Such arrangements would include continued employment on a part-time basis, or on-call employment, increased opportunities in home-based work, or the gradual exit of older workers from the labour market by working first five days a week, then four days, then three days until they retire "full-time."

Other Implications

The growing labour force population over age 45 will likely have other effects on the labour market. Part-time work can be expected to increase substantially, since older workers are more frequently engaged in part-time work than workers aged 25 to 44 years. Long-duration unemployment is prone to rise because employers are reluctant to hire unemployed older workers they believe to be less healthy, less flexible, and less trainable than younger workers. The number of days of work lost per worker is likely to increase because older workers tend to lose more time from work because of illness or disability. On the positive side, job and labour force turnover rates probably will decline as older workers constitute a more experienced, stable workforce with less turnover.

Labour Market Issue 4.2

Aging of the Labour Force and Absences from Work

A Statistics Canada study reported that, in 1998, 5.7% of all full-time workers were absent from work for all or part of a week because of illness, disability, or personal or family responsibilities. The cost to employers in terms of wages and benefits paid for work not done was estimated to be close to $10 billion. Absences from work have been on the rise in recent years. One of the reasons suggested in the study is the aging workforce. Workdays lost, for both men and women, tend to rise with age. In 2003, older workers (aged 55 to 64) missed on average 12 workdays, more than double the five days that young workers (aged 15 to 24) were absent from work. Most of the difference can be attributed to illness or disability. Absences due to personal or family responsibilities did not differ much across age groups; they remained at about one day per employee with the exception of women aged 25 to 44 who missed slightly more than 1.5 days.

As the first large cohorts of the baby-boom generation, now in their early fifties, move toward retirement age, the increase in absenteeism may continue for some years. It would, however, be too simplistic to attribute the higher absence from work only to the aging of the workforce. Days missed from work also vary by industry, union coverage, occupation, and province. Employees in the public sector miss more days than their counterparts in the private sector, professionals have much lower absenteeism rates than clerical workers, and workers in British Columbia lose more days than those in Alberta or Ontario. Since employment shifts occur among industries, occupations, and regions, these variations are prone to effect changes in absence from work over time.

The aging workforce is also likely to create shortages in certain occupations. Two examples are the health and educational sectors. As the proportion of older people grows, the demand for healthcare services increases. These services are provided by healthcare specialists and general practitioners who are older, on average, than the overall workforce. The relatively large share of educators in older age groups may also lead to bottlenecks at a time when knowledge-based industries are increasingly demanding workers with higher levels of education.[7] As a result of potential shortages, older professionals may come back into the labour force after retirement, possibly to work part-time.

Immigration

Net immigration is the difference between the number of immigrants and the number of emigrants. Net immigration has played a vital role in Canada's demographic, economic, social, and cultural development for more than a century. Immigrants have been an important source of labour supply. Their spending, which stimulates the demand for goods and services, has also contributed significantly to increases in the demand for labour. The level of immigration has varied considerably. It is estimated that over the last 100 years, net immigration has contributed one-fifth of total population growth. As is indicated by the data in Figure 4.4 (page 82), since World War II, immigration to Canada appears strongly related to the business cycle.[iii] The **business cycle** refers to the more or less regular pattern of expansion and contraction in economic activity. If the economy was booming and firms expanded their production, immigration was increasing. During the early and mid-1950s, when the resource sector of the economy was booming, one-half of the growth of Canada's labour force came from immigrants. In the peak year of 1957, 282 000 immigrants entered Canada. In the late 1950s, the contribution of immigration to the overall labour force growth started to decline. By 1966, immigration accounted for only 12% of labour force growth; by 1975, the contribution had dropped to 6%.

Reflecting the slowdown in economic growth, the peaks in immigration following 1957 were lower. In 1967 and 1974, the numbers peaked at about 220 000 immigrants. In 1980, the number of immigrants fell to 140 000. The severe recession in 1981–82, in combination with restrictive immigration policies in place since the end of 1982, resulted in a dramatic decline in immigration, which reached a low of 84 000 new arrivals in 1985. A period in which total production of goods and services in an economy falls for at least two consecutive quarters is called a **recession**. Recessions are associated with high unemployment as firms reduce hours of work and lay off workers to adjust their production levels to the declining demand for their products. As unemployment among domestic workers rises, the federal government generally reduces the annual target number of immigrants accepted to Canada. After reaching a trough in 1985, immigration rose sharply again, doubling in three years to almost 161 000 in 1988.

business cycle

the more or less regular pattern of expansion and contraction in economic activity around full employment output

recession

a period during which the total production of goods and services falls for at least two consecutive quarters

[iii] The right-hand axis of Figure 4.4 shows the absolute number of immigrants admitted each year, while the left-hand axis denotes the immigration rate, which is defined as the number of immigrants per 1000 of population.

FIGURE 4.4

Number of Immigrants, 1944–2012

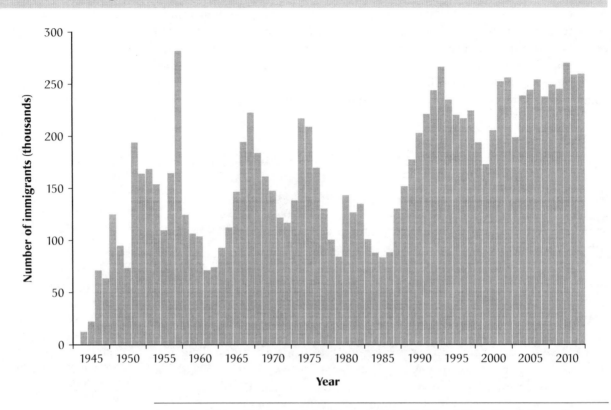

Source: For 1944 to 1971 data, Statistics Canada. Historical Statistics, Estimated Population and Immigration Arrivals (CANSIM Table 75-0001). Ottawa: Statistics Canada, 2010; and for 1972 to 2010 data, Statistics Canada. Components of population growth, Canada, provinces and territories, annual (CANSIM Table 051-0004). Ottawa: Statistics Canada, 2010.

Between 1991 and 2012, Canada received nearly 5.2 million immigrants, representing an annual average of about 235 142 people. Not since the settlement of the Prairies before the outbreak of World War I has there been such a sustained period of strong immigration. Although the deep recession of 1990–92 again led to a fall in the number of immigrants, the decline was less steep than in previous recessions. Only twice throughout the 1990s did immigration fall below 200 000 people per year. In 2010, Canada admitted 280 636 immigrants, the highest number of legal immigrants in more than 50 years.

As the rate of natural population growth is steadily declining, the total number of immigrants admitted annually appears to be determined less by the business cycle than by demographic considerations. Reflecting the government's population targets, immigration has once more become the driving force of population and labour force growth. Canada's total population increased by about 3.9 million between 2001 and 2012, a growth rate of 12.5% from 2001. An estimated 2 968 829 newcomers arrived in the country between

July 1, 2001, and June 30, 2012. They were responsible for more than two-thirds of this population growth. Only the remaining one-third is attributable to births.

During 1991 to 2001, the proportion of total growth in the Canadian labour force attributable to immigrants who landed in Canada during the 1990s and who were in the labour force in 2001 was equally large, almost 70%. Immigration continues to be a dominant force in labour force growth in Canada.

Origin of Immigrants

Canada is a country of immigrants. With the exception of Canada's Aboriginal peoples, Canadians are either descendants of earlier generations of immigrants or are newly arrived immigrants. Throughout most of the twentieth

FIGURE 4.5

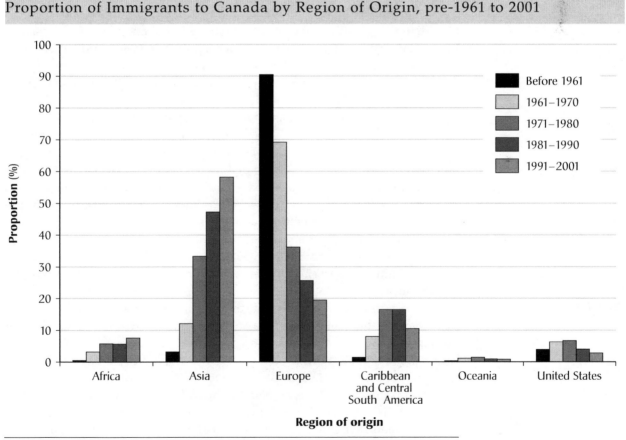

Proportion of Immigrants to Canada by Region of Origin, pre-1961 to 2001

Source: Adapted from Statistics Canada. (2003). Immigrant Status and Period of Immigration and Place of Birth of Respondent for Immigrants and Non-Permanent Residents for Canada, Provinces, Territories, CMAs. 2001 Census. Catalogue no. F0009XCB01002.

century, the majority of immigrants came from Europe. During the last 30 years, however, the ethnic composition of immigrants has dramatically changed, as can be seen from Figure 4.5. Prior to 1961, about 90% of all immigrants originated in Europe, with the United Kingdom, Italy, and Germany being the main source countries. In 2001, less than one-quarter (19%) came from Europe. Among the top 10 source countries of immigration in 2001, only two were European: Romania and Russia.

Since 1988, Asia has provided the largest share of Canadian immigration. In 2001, more than 62% of all immigrants admitted to Canada were from Asia, with most of them coming from China (including Hong Kong), India, Pakistan, and the Philippines. China has become the leading country of birth among immigrants. In 2001, China provided approximately one-fifth of Canada's total immigration. By opening the doors to immigrants from countries around the world, Canada has, over the last 40 years, been transformed from a predominantly European-based population to a multiracial society. In 2001, the visible minority population reached 4 million, a threefold increase over 1981.

Classes of Immigrants

Canadian immigration policy has been shaped by economic self-interest and humanitarian concerns. These two dimensions are reflected in the division of immigrants into two classes: the assessed and non-assessed classes.

The assessed classes include all immigrants admitted to Canada on the basis of their likely positive contribution to the Canadian economy. In 1967, Canada introduced a points-based selection system that assesses independent applicants on the basis of six factors: education; knowledge of one of the two official languages, English and French; work experience; age; arranged employment in Canada; and adaptability. The assessed classes are now referred to as economic classes, and include the traditional independent immigrants selected on the basis of the points system, the business immigrants (entrepreneurs, investors, and the self-employed), assisted relatives (evaluated according to the assessment unit system for their skill qualifications but awarded additional points for having relatives in Canada), and others (admitted under special occupational programs, for example, nannies and domestic services).

The non-assessed classes include immediate family members and refugees. Immigrants in the non-assessed classes are admitted on strictly humanitarian grounds without any consideration of their potential economic contribution. They are likely to face greater difficulties in being quickly integrated into the Canadian labour market. Changes in the admission criteria for the various categories appear on the Citizenship and Immigration Canada (CIC) website.

Each year, the federal government announces in its immigration plan the target numbers of immigrants to be admitted in each class. Table 4.2 shows the numbers for the three main classes under the immigration plan for 2011. The overall target range set out for that year was between 240 000 and 265 000 persons. The actual number admitted in 2011 was within the overall target range.

TABLE 4.2

Number of Immigrants Admitted and Number Planned by Class According to the Immigration Plan, Canada, 2011

CLASS	NUMBER PLANNED	OBSERVED NUMBER
Family	58 500–65 500	56 446
Economic	150 600–161 300	156 121
Other[1]	7 700–9 200	8 309
Total Immigrants	216 800–236 000	220 876
Total Refugees	23 200–29 000	27 872
Total	240 000–265 000	248 748

[1]Includes temporary resident permit holders, H. and C. cases. Other H. and C. cases outside the family class/public policy, and category are not stated.

Source: Annual Report to Parliament on Immigration, 2012, http://www.cic.gc.ca/english/resources/publications/annual-report-2012/section2.asp#a1. Citizenship and Immigration Canada, 2012. Reproduced with the permission of the Minister of Public Works and Government Services Canada, 2013.

Still, the number falls short of the current government's long-term objective to raise immigration to 1% of population per year, which would amount to about 300 000 people at present. Of the immigrants entering Canada in 2011, about 62.8% were admitted under the economic class, 22.7% as part of the family reunification program, and 11.2% under the refugee category.

Throughout the 1980s and up to the mid-1990s, immigrants in the family and refugee classes outnumbered those in the economic class. Starting in 1996, this pattern reversed. As the percentage of immigrants in the economic category rose, the percentage in the family and refugee category declined. This change in policy reflects the government's renewed focus on the employability and rapid economic integration of immigrants. The new *Immigration and Refugee Protection Act* (Bill C-11), which took effect in 2002, also contains provisions to tighten the refugee determination process, including more extensive screening of claimants and limitations in appeal processes. These provisions, introduced in response to the terrorist attacks of September 11, 2001, reduced the number of refugees admitted to Canada over the years.

The Rise in the Skill Level of Immigrants

As a result of changes in Canada's immigration policy, the skill profile of immigrants has undergone significant changes over the last 50 years. Immigration policy in the immediate postwar period largely focused on attracting unskilled labour required for urban industrial development. Many immigrants lacked any formal educational qualifications. With the transition from an industrial to a postindustrial society came the growing need for skilled workers and professionals.[8]

Chapter 4: Trends in the Canadian Labour Force

The points-based system for selecting economic immigrants was designed to ensure that the emerging need for skilled labour was met by immigration. Selection standards in the points system have been raised progressively over time. Initially the minimum number of points required for admittance was relatively low. By 1985, the required points for economic immigrants had increased from 50 to 70 out of 100 points. In 2002, the pass mark was raised further to 75 points. Achieving the two policy objectives of increasing the number of independent immigrants while at the same time raising the admittance requirements may, however, prove a difficult task. In late 2003, Citizenship and Immigration Canada announced that the pass mark for skilled workers had been lowered from 75 to 67.

Following the upgrading of the admission criteria over the years, the number of immigrants with higher educational qualifications and professional credentials increased considerably. Whereas most immigrants in the 1950s and 1960s averaged eight years of education or less, those arriving in 1991–96 averaged 14 years.[9] In 1980, 7.6% of the newly arrived immigrants held a university degree; in 2000, the percentage had increased to 34%.[10]

In stark contrast to the rising skill and educational level of newly arrived immigrants has been the recent deterioration in their labour market position. During the 1960s and 1970s the labour market outcomes for immigrants were largely positive. Immigrants had higher labour force participation rates and lower unemployment rates than native-born Canadians. A higher proportion of immigrants worked "year-round" than those born in Canada. Although most immigrants were at an economic disadvantage at the time of their arrival, their economic conditions improved rapidly over time; within a decade or two their earnings usually overtook the earnings of native-born Canadians of comparable socioeconomic backgrounds.

Since the early 1980s, however, most labour market indicators show that new arrivals to Canada have not performed as well as earlier immigrants. Several studies have found a decline in earnings of recent immigrants compared with those of earlier generations using the same number of years in Canada for both groups.[11] The reasons for this relative deterioration are not yet fully understood. It seemed, at first, that the relative decline in earnings was due to the recessions of the early 1980s and 1990s, which created particularly difficult labour markets for newly arriving immigrants. However, even with the economic recovery in the late 1990s, the employment and earnings prospects of recent immigrants do not seem to have improved relative to earlier immigrants or relative to the native-born.[12] One explanation points to the different growth patterns in the educational attainment of recent immigrants and native-born Canadians. Although recent immigrant cohorts have faced more stringent admission standards and have higher levels of education, educational attainment levels of the native-born population have risen even faster.[13] If the employment and earning success of immigrants in the 1970s was partly due to the educational advantage many immigrants held over the native-born, the recent rapid expansion of education (especially postsecondary education) in Canada has eroded the immigrants' earlier advantage.

Another reason why the increase in education and skills of immigrants has not led to better labour market performance may lie in the insufficient recognition of their educational qualifications and professional credentials by Canadian regulatory bodies and employers. While for most Canadians the returns to education are rising, for immigrants they appear to be declining. Changes in education and the increasing value given by employers to credentials received in Canada are undermining the earlier economic success of immigrants.

Destination of Immigrants

For many years, the large majority of immigrants have settled in Ontario, British Columbia, and Quebec. Among these three provinces, Ontario has long been the main destination: in 2010, it received 118 112 immigrants, or 42% of the Canadian total, followed by Quebec, British Columbia, and Alberta, attracting approximately 19%, 16%, and 12% of immigrants. The percentage of immigrants coming to Ontario between 2006 and 2010 decreased from 50 to 42.

The concentration of immigration in Canada's three most populous provinces largely reflects the choice of immigrants to settle in the three large metropolises of Toronto, Montreal, and Vancouver. Recently, Calgary and Ottawa–Hull have also emerged as urban centres attracting immigrants, but Toronto has increasingly become the first choice of immigrants. While in 1980, nearly one-quarter of all immigrants to Canada settled in Toronto, 30 years later, almost one third of them chose to live in the greater Toronto metropolitan area. Of the population in Canada's largest metropolis, which has grown to over 5.5 million, close to 50% is foreign-born. As immigrants are increasingly concentrating in a few large urban centres, the country's population and workforce is becoming more unevenly distributed, both within and across provinces.

Immigration is not only contributing to the rapid growth of Canada's major cities but is also profoundly changing the ethnoracial composition of the urban population and workforce. It is estimated that Toronto alone is home to over 100 different ethnoracial groups.[14] The growing ethnic and racial diversity of the population is having far-reaching repercussions on the labour market. For example, as the proportion of visible minority workers grows, equity issues are becoming a major concern. There is evidence that after account is taken of measured qualifications such as education, language knowledge, and work experience, immigrants of non-European origin earn substantially less than immigrants of European origin, and less than native-born workers. Racial discrimination may be part of the explanation for the disparity in earnings.[15]

Changes in the ethnoracial composition of the labour force also will affect organizational behaviour and human resources management in the workplace. Research on ethnic and racial diversity's impacts on work group effectiveness—including group cohesiveness, performance, and group goals—is still sparse in Canada. Studies in organizational behaviour indicate that, initially, communication is more difficult and cohesiveness is lessened the more diverse work teams are. Once communication and cohesiveness is established, however, they appear to be as productive as more homogeneous groups.[16] On the other hand, diverse groups appear to be relatively more effective when they perform cognitive, problem-solving, and creativity-demanding tasks.[17] Although the processes in which racial and cultural diversity contributes to task performance are not yet well understood, it seems that creativity is fostered when different cultures intersect. Workers with diverse cultural backgrounds can bring different approaches and ideas to these tasks. Canadian companies are starting to recognize the potential of a multiethnic workforce and are initiating strategies to manage diversity with the aim to raise productivity.

Changes in Labour Force Participation

Growth of a country's labour force depends not only on the growth of its working-age population, but also on the willingness of those of working age to participate in the labour force. From the definition of the labour force participation rate:

$$LFPR = \frac{Labour\ force}{Working\text{-}age\ population} \times 100$$

we can derive the expression

$$Labour\ force = LFPR \times Working\text{-}age\ population$$

or

Percentage change in the labour force = Percentage change in the LFPR × Percentage change in the working-age population

Making use of the chain rule we can write:

Percentage change in the labour force = Percentage change in the LFPR + Percentage change in the working-age population[iv]

Growth in the labour force thus depends on changes in the adult population and the LFPR.

Changes in the LFPR from 1947 to 2012 are shown in Figure 4.6. During this period, the LFPR increased by close to 12 percentage points, from 54.9% (1947) to 66.7% (2012). Three phases can be distinguished: no trend increase in the first 20 years from 1946 to 1966, a strong trend increase from the mid-1960s until the peak year of 1989, and a decline in the 1990s. Only toward the end of the 1990s did the LFPR start to increase again. In 2003, it had returned to the peak level reached in the late 1980s. In 2012, LFPR decreased slightly to 66.7%.

As demonstrated in Figure 4.6, the long-run net increase in the LFPR has been the result of two opposite trends: the decline in the male participation rate, and the increase in the female participation rate. For males, the participation rate dropped from 85.1% in 1947 to 71.3% in 2012, while the LFPR of

---

[iv] The chain rule from calculus is a useful arithmetic trick: The percentage change of a product of two variables is approximately the sum of the percentage changes in each of the two variables.

FIGURE 4.6

Labour Participation Rates, 1947–2012

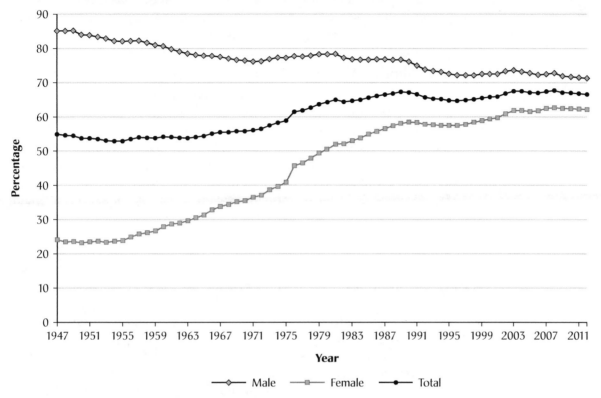

Notes: Annual data prior to 1950 exclude Newfoundland and Labrador.
Estimates prior to 1966 are based on persons aged 14 and over.
Estimates from 1966 include persons aged 15 and over.
Estimates from 1966 to 1974 have been adjusted to conform to current concepts. Estimates prior to 1966 have not been revised.

Sources: For 1947–75, adapted from Statistics Canada. (1995). *Canadian Economic Observer, Historical Statistical Supplement, 1994/5*. Catalogue no. 11–210 and http://www.statcan.gc.ca/pub/11-516-x/sectiond/4057750-eng.htm; for 1976–2012, adapted from Statistics Canada CANSIM, table 282-0002.

women increased from 24.1% to 62.2%. Over the last 60 years, the male–female gap in labour force participation rates narrowed from 61 percentage points in 1947 to 9.1 percentage points in 2012.

During the first two decades of Figure 4.6, from 1947 to 1966, the trends in the male and female LFPR offset each other, leaving the overall LFPR nearly unchanged. Beginning in 1966, however, the rise in the female LFPR was so strong that it dominated the fall in the male LFPR, resulting in the rise of the total LFPR until 1989. The upward trend in the LFPR came to an end in 1989. From 1990 until the end of 1996, the Canadian economy experienced the most prolonged downturn since the Great Depression in the 1930s. As a result, both female and male labour force participation rates declined. While weak market conditions played a major role in the decline of the LFPR, structural factors such as increased incidence of higher education, changes in the employment insurance (EI) program, and government downsizing were also important.

Starting in 1998, the LFPR resumed its upward trend, with the increase in the female LFPR accounting for most of the overall rise. After the financial crisis of 2008, LFPR slightly decreased. As the labour force participation rates of men and women have converged over most of the postwar period, women have gradually increased their share of the labour force. In 2012, women accounted for 47.3% of the total labour force.

Labour Force Activity of Men

The downward trend in the male labour force participation rate has resulted mainly from the decline in the participation rate of men aged 55 to 64 years. Initially, the percentage of men in this age group who were in the labour force declined slowly from 85% in the early 1950s to about 80% in the early 1970s. Since the mid-1970s, the decline in labour force participation was more rapid. In 1976, the participation rates of men aged 55–59 and 60–64 were 84.2% and 66.5%, respectively. By 2012, the respective rates had dropped to 78.9% and 58%. This decline has primarily come about because men are retiring from employment at an earlier age. The median retirement age for men was still close to 65 in the late 1970s. By 1999, it had fallen to just under 61. Recently, the median retirement age has been edging up; it remains to be seen whether early retirement patterns will change as the baby-boom generation starts to move into the age brackets of 55 years and older.

A number of factors may influence early retirement decisions, ranging from personal (such as deteriorating health or the wish to pursue leisure interests) to economic reasons (such as permanent layoff). With improvement in health across the population, illness and disability seem to have become a relatively less important factor. Labour Force Survey data indicate that the most frequently cited reason of older men for retiring early is job separation due to permanent layoff.[18] With the recessions in the early 1980s and 1990s and the restructuring of the economy leading to declines in relative employment in the goods-producing sector, older men seem to have been increasingly forced into retirement by job losses and bleak prospects for re-employment. Once laid off, older workers, especially those without postsecondary qualifications, face much greater difficulties in finding a new job compared to adults aged 35 to 54 years. Other reasons for early retirement have been the growth in real wages in the 1960s and 1970s, the appreciation in the value of homes over the last 30 years, and the growth of pension plans with relaxed criteria for retirement with full pension. These factors have increased the financial means for men to retire earlier.

The LFPR of men is also decreasing as the life expectancy of males increases. As men live longer, a greater percentage of men are classified as "not in the labour force." As the denominator of the LFPR ratio rises, the ratio declines.

Female Participation Trends

The decades-long growth in the labour force participation rate of women has been one of the most remarkable features of the Canadian labour market since World War II. The increase occurred among women of all working ages, with those between 25 and 54 years being the main contributors. As women have aged, their LFPR has moved like a wave through the age groups. While women aged 25 to 44 years increased their participation to the greatest extent during the 1970s, those aged 45 to 54 were the leading group during the 1980s with respect to labour force participation. The most significant change was for women in their childbearing years. Historically, women entered the labour force in two phases. The first phase was in the young adult period when they left school and were unmarried or were married without children; the second phase reflected women's return to the labour force once their children were older and in school or had graduated from school. This sequence created the traditional "double-peak" pattern resembling an inverted W, with labour force participation peaking in the 20–24 and 45–54 age groups.

FIGURE 4.7

Labour Force Participation Rates by Age and Gender, 1976 and 2012

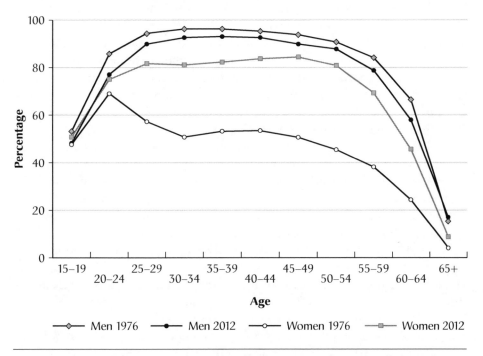

Source: Statistics Canada. Table 282-0002, Labour force survey estimates (LFS), by sex and detailed age group, annual (persons unless otherwise noted), CANSIM (database).

However, over the last two decades, the sharp dip and rebound in female participation rates have disappeared, reflecting the growing labour force attachment of women in their childbearing years. In the 1950s, 65% of women who interrupted their paid work for the birth of their first child returned to work, but only 8% did so within two years of the start of the interruption. The average interruption lasted 12 years. By the early 1990s, 78% of new mothers who interrupted their paid work returned after the birth of their child; 56% of the new mothers returned within two years of the interruption. The average interruption was only one year. Figure 4.7 shows that the pattern of age-specific participation rates for women now more closely resembles that of men, as the labour force participation rates of the two groups have converged.

Many factors, often classified as demand and supply factors, are cited for the growing presence of women in the workforce. When we summarize them, it becomes clear that any distinction between supply-related factors and demand-related factors is to some degree artificial. The long-term increase in women's participation in the workforce reflects the complex interaction of forces emanating from both sides of the market. The chief factors that have influenced the propensity of women, especially of married women, to seek work outside the home are discussed below.

The Change in Social Attitudes

Social attitudes concerning the appropriateness of women's working outside of the home, especially when married with small children, have undergone a remarkable transformation. Prior to World War II, strong social barriers, often in the form of social taboos, existed against women working outside of the home. Many social scientists consider World War II as the crucial event that changed attitudes about women's work in the labour market. With many men serving in the military, women replaced them on the factory floor. The fact that women filled "male jobs," and often performed extremely well in them, revealed the taboo as what it was—a social custom intended to exclude women from better paying jobs and thus from obtaining economic influence and power. Other researchers see the women's movement as the central social force that changed attitudes considering women's work.

There remains considerable debate, however, about whether the change in social attitudes has been the cause or the consequence of the movement of women into the workforce. Most labour economists tend to argue that the underlying determinants of the rise in female participation are economic in nature, and changing attitudes are simply the consequence of a process that has its roots in changes of the economy. Other social scientists, mainly sociologists and social psychologists, claim that social and cultural factors play a major role in determining the division of household and workplace activity along gender lines. A comparison of labour force participation trends across different countries may lend support to the latter position. For example, in Japan and the former West Germany, two of the most economically advanced countries in the world, the female LFPR declined from the late 1950s to the mid-1970s and early 1980s, and has shown only very modest increases since

FIGURE 4.8

Labour Force Participation Rates by Education and Gender, 2012

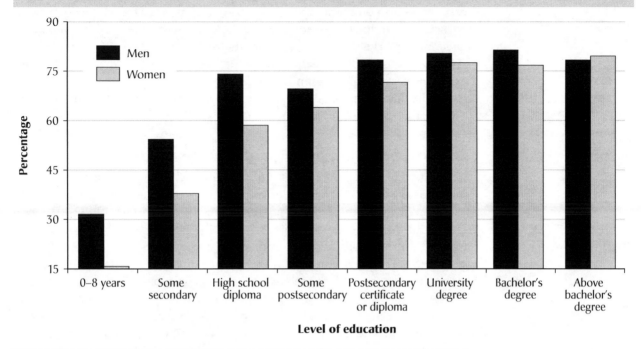

Source: Adapted from Statistics Canada. (2013) CANSIM, table 282-0004.

then. Meanwhile in Canada, Sweden, and the United States, the female LFPR increased rapidly throughout this period. In 2003, female labour force participation in comparable western economies ranged from a high of over 80% in Sweden to a low of 49% in Germany and 45% in the U.K.[19]

The Rising Educational Level of Women

More women than men complete secondary education, and women now constitute the majority of undergraduate students in Canadian universities. As Figure 4.8 indicates, there is a strong, positive relationship between years of education completed and the probability of participation in the labour force. In 2012, women with education above a bachelor's degree had participation rates that slightly exceeded those of men. Conversely, women with less than a postsecondary education had a much lower participation rate, both absolutely and relative to males.

There are several reasons why more education fosters labour force participation. First, higher education is often undertaken as an investment, in the sense that a person deliberately incurs the large direct cost (tuition fees, books, etc.) and opportunity cost (forgone earnings from work) of a postsecondary education with the expectation that these expenses will be recouped in the form of higher earnings and occupational attainment after graduation. To reap this return on higher education, however, requires a sustained period of participation in the labour force. Second, people with more education usually have more marketable skills and are, therefore, able to obtain higher paying and more stable jobs. As earnings rise progressively with educational attainment, the cost of time spent not working increases. Third, long-term improvements in education have shifted women's preferences in favour of work outside the home.

The Increase in Employment Opportunities for Women

While increased educational attainment widened job opportunities, employment possibilities improved independently of educational status. The increase in employment possibilities is reflected in the increase in the LFPR of women at all educational levels. Urbanization and the expansion of both the government and private service sectors of the economy have been especially conducive to participation of women in the workforce. Although women workers are still concentrated in relatively few occupational categories (clerical workers, nurses and health technicians, elementary and secondary school teachers, salesclerks in retail trade, and personal services such as hairdressers, waitresses, and dental hygienists), most of these occupational groups have grown overproportionately in size since World War II. Another source of job opportunities for women has been male-dominated occupations such as management positions in natural sciences, engineers, lawyers and notaries, accountants, optometrists, chiropractors, and architects. Some of the more recent advances may have been the result of employment equity legislation enacted in the mid-1980s.

The Increased Flexibility in Work Time Scheduling

As the service sector has grown, alternative work time arrangements—such as part-time work, flexible working hours, job sharing, compressed workweeks, and contracted work done in the home—have become more common. These changing workplace practices have facilitated women's integration into the labour market because they have allowed women to combine household work with contractual work for pay.

The Rise in Women's Real Hourly Earnings

The monetary value of an hour's time is measured by the hourly real wage a person could earn. As real earnings per hour have increased substantially for women over the last 50 years, the price per hour, or the opportunity cost of not participating in the labour market, has increased as well. The increased opportunity cost of not working convinces many women to substitute labour force work for non-paid work.

The Decline in the Number of Children per Family

For biological and cultural reasons, childbirth and child rearing have been the primary responsibility of the female parent. Given the strong negative relationship between the number of children in a family and the probability of labour force participation of women with children, the decline in fertility rates and family size and increased flexibility in childcare arrangements have had a powerful positive impact on the labour market participation for women. Several factors have been responsible for the decline in fertility rates. One factor is improved birth control techniques since the 1950s, which have permitted couples to plan the number and the timing of their children. A second factor is the growing cost of raising children: the cost includes the direct cost of food, clothing, and education, and the opportunity cost of the wife's time if she does not work for pay. The opportunity cost of raising children, in particular, has grown considerably as real earnings of women have increased, causing families to cut back on the number of children they desire. A third factor is the fact that many women delay childbearing until they have established their careers; this has allowed women to combine the role of wife and mother with a career and the accumulation of work experience.

The Development of Labour-Saving Household Technology and Substitutes for Household Products

Technical innovations, for example, in household appliances, and improvements in commercially prepared food and dry cleaning have greatly facilitated the entry of women into the workforce.

Advancement of Living Standards

Among the economic factors that have brought women into the labour force is the attempt of couples to maintain and advance their standard of living in the face of several economic squeezes. One squeeze stemmed from the large increase in labour supply as the baby-boom generation entered the labour market, which resulted in a relative decline in nominal wages and salaries, particularly for entry-level positions. Another squeeze was the high rate of inflation during the 1970s and 1980s, particularly for housing. As growth in nominal earnings was dampened by job competition, inflation eroded real income. Since the mid-1970s, real average annual labour income has made almost no gains. (Changes in real income are discussed in Chapter 7.)

The Rising Incidence of Marriage Break-Ups

Since World War II, divorce rates have increased, in particular since 1968, when the *Divorce Act* was amended to make divorces easier to obtain. From 1969 to the late 1980s, the number of divorces per 1000 married women more than doubled. During the 1990s, divorce rates stabilized at a slightly lower level compared to the peak in the late 1980s. In 2002, the divorce rate stood at 9.1 divorces per 1000 married women. With the long-term increase in the frequency of separation and divorce, more women have become sole supporters for themselves and often for their children. In order to reduce the negative financial impact of a divorce, they are often forced to seek employment in the labour market, or, in the case that they are already employed, to remain in the labour force.

Changes in the Gender Composition of the Labour Force

The increased involvement of women in the paid workforce has been one of the most profound economic and social changes in Canada over the last five decades. Long-run changes in demographic and labour force participation patterns account for the shift in the gender structure of the labour force. Women's share of the total population grew steadily over the course of the twentieth century. In 2001, females accounted for 50.9% of the total population, up from 48.7% in 1941. The rising demographic trend is largely attributed to the fact that mortality rates among women are lower than those among men. The dramatic increase in the labour force participation rate of women paralleled the demographic trend. As shown earlier, women have accounted for most of the growth in labour force participation since the mid-1970s and, as a result, women currently represent almost half of the Canadian workforce.

The rise in female labour force participation, in particular the marked increase in the labour force participation of married women, has had dramatic effects on family structure. Within 30 years, from the mid-1960s to the mid-1990s, the two-earner family changed from being the exception to being the rule. In a two-earner family, both spouses are engaged in paid work. In 1967, 33% of all husband–wife families were dual-earner families. By 1995, 62% of all husband–wife families were dual-earner families. While the predominance of the two-earner family has implications for men's labour market behaviour, the consequences are more serious for the labour market behaviour of women. Even when women are part of the paid workforce, they continue to spend considerably more time than their spouses on unpaid domestic work. This applies, in particular, to married women with children, whose labour force participation rate has increased most over the last decades. As a result, the provision of paid maternity leave and the availability of accessible, affordable childcare have become central demands for women and their advocacy groups. With the aging of the population, homecare for elderly family members will put additional demands particularly upon women. To alleviate some of the burden, the Ontario government, for example, has introduced into the *Employment Standards Act* 10 emergency days that workers can take in the form of job-protected leaves of absence in order to take care of sick and dying dependants.

The proliferation of two-earner families has had many economic ramifications. One is the negative effect on labour mobility, particularly geographical mobility. The costs of moving from one community to another are potentially much greater for the two-income family than for the family with only one working spouse. In the case of the single-earner family, the non-working spouse (traditionally the wife) sacrifices financially relatively little in making a move, while the husband may be able to considerably advance his career and income. For the two-earner family, however, the income and career gains from moving for one spouse may be largely offset if the relocation results in lower earnings and career prospects for the other spouse.

The growing proportion of women engaged in paid work and the accompanying changes in family structure also have had far-reaching implications for human resources management and public policy.[20] The changes have put pressure on employers to offer, for example, flexible work time arrangements and paid or unpaid maternity leaves to accommodate family responsibilities. Dual-earner families may want a full-time job for one earner and a part-time job for the other. Workers may also be more reluctant to take on extra tasks at work if they conflict with household responsibilities. Employers likely face greater difficulties in recruiting and moving employees if this conflicts with family responsibilities. The proximity of schools and the availability of accessible and affordable childcare have become important factors in employees' choices of jobs.

FIGURE 4.9

Labour Force Participation Rates of Youth, 1966–2012

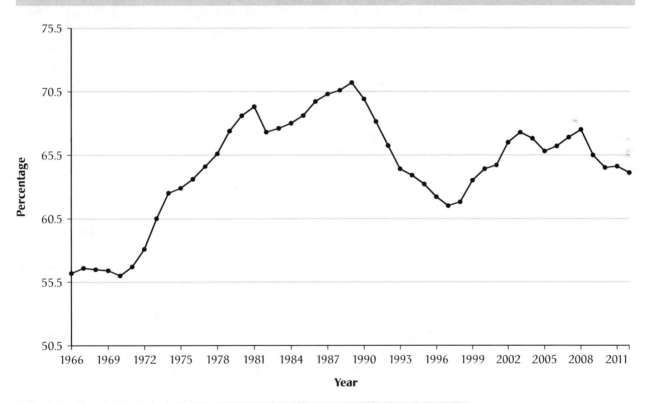

Sources: For 1966–75, adapted from Statistics Canada. (1995). *Canadian Economic Observer, Historical Statistical Supplement 1994/5.* Catalogue no. 11–210; for 1976–2012, adapted from Statistics Canada CANSIM, table 282-0002.

Labour Force Participation of Youth

As can be seen in Figure 4.9, participation rates of youth, that is 15- to 24-year-olds, showed a decline during the 1950s up to the mid-1960s. From the early 1970s until 1989, there was a continuous upward trend interrupted only during periods of recession. In 1969, the youth LFPR was 56%; by 1989, the peak year in the trend, it had increased to 71.2%. The rise in youth LFPR was attributable to two factors. The first factor was the increase in the overall proportion of students, especially those aged 15–19, holding part-time jobs while attending school. The second factor was the growing LFPR among young women.

With the onset of the 1990 recession, the overall participation rate of youth started to decline. Youth LFPR increased from 61.8% in 1998 to 67.5% in 2008. After the financial crisis, it declined again to 63.6% in 2012. The drop reflects the falling participation of both female and male youths. While a contraction of labour force activity is typical during recessions, particularly among young people, the magnitude of the decline in youth LFPR during the last economic downturn and its continuing fall during the earlier part of the recovery—a decline of almost 7.6 percentage points over 20 years (1989 to 2012)—has been unprecedented. Two factors are largely responsible for this dramatic shift: the poor job market for youth, and the continuous increase in school attendance. School attendance rates for 15- to 24-year-olds have risen steadily from 41% in 1979, to 48% in 1989, to 73% in 2001. Most of the increase reflects the tendency for young people to stay in school longer. Full-time students are historically less likely to work or look for work than their non-student counterparts. Also, during the 1990s it became much more common than in earlier decades for youth to stay out of the labour force while studying full-time, which was probably a reflection of the deteriorating labour market conditions for youths during that period.

With the expansion in the economy, labour force participation of young people started to increase. In 2012, however, their workforce participation still had not reached pre-financial crisis levels.

Provincial Labour Force Participation Rates

Workforce participation varies greatly across provinces, as is shown by the data in Figure 4.10. In 1976, the gap between Alberta, the province with the highest LFPR (67.4%), and Newfoundland and Labrador, which had the lowest LFPR (49.4%), was 18 percentage points. Participation rates overall were lowest in the Maritimes, followed by Quebec, and were highest in Alberta and Ontario. Over the last 40 years, provincial participation rates have been converging due to the relatively rapid rate increase in the Maritimes and a more sluggish growth in Ontario and British Columbia. Nevertheless, in 2012, the gap between Alberta and Newfoundland and Labrador was still 11.8 percentage points. Prince Edward Island, Canada's smallest province, experienced the most dramatic growth in workforce participation: in 2012, it ranked fourth-highest in the country in terms of labour force participation.

FIGURE 4.10

Labour Force Participation Rates by Province, 1976 and 2012

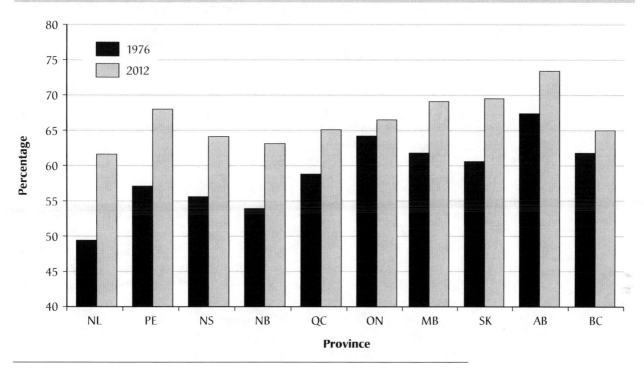

Source: Adapted from Statistics Canada CANSIM, table 282-0002.

Participation in the labour force reflects only part of the behavioural component of labour supply. Once people decide to become active participants in the workforce, they must determine the level of their labour supply, which could be measured by their preferred hours of work per week or per year. Unfortunately, no continuous data exist on Canadians' preferences regarding work time. To use the number of hours actually worked would confuse the hours preferred by labour force members with hours of work determined in collective bargaining agreements or set by companies. Clearly, the latter can deviate from the hours preferred. Trends in actual hours worked are described in Chapter 5, which deals with different aspects of labour demand.

Summary

The labour force is the sum of the employed and unemployed workers in our economy. Over the last 60 years, the labour force has more than tripled in size. The sources of this tremendous growth have been increases in the domestic population, net increases in the number of immigrants, and the rise in labour force participation. The relative contributions of these factors to the overall growth of the labour force have varied over the years. During the 1980s, increases in the labour force participation rate had the largest impact on labour force growth. During the last 35 years, immigration has been the main factor contributing to Canada's labour force growth.

Domestic or natural population growth has declined by more than half during the post–World War II period. The decline has been largely due to the fall in the fertility rate. Between 2000 and 2005, the fertility rate stood at 1.5, the lowest rate ever recorded in Canada. By 2010, it slightly increased to 1.7.

The coming of age of the baby-boom generation has led to a rapidly aging labour force. The changing age composition of the labour force has implications for job advancement, the organizational structure of companies, and the financing of Canada's social security system, as well as for other labour market variables.

The number of immigrants has generally followed the business cycle, increasing in times of economic expansion and contracting in recessions. In recent years, immigration has become the principal force of labour force growth. From 1991 to 2012, Canada received on average 235 142 immigrants per year. Prior to 1981, the majority of immigrants came from Western Europe. In the last two decades, Asia has provided the largest share of immigrants. Most immigrants settle in Toronto, Vancouver, and Montreal, with the Greater Toronto Metropolitan Area being the first choice of almost 50% of all new immigrants. The share of the assessed or economic class of immigrants has been increasing, while the proportion of immigrants entering Canada as part of the family reunification program or as refugees has been declining. This reflects the renewed focus of the government to attract skilled workers and professionals from around the world.

The participation rate refers to the percentage of the working-age population that is in the labour force. The participation rate for men has been declining mainly because of the tendency for men aged 55–64 to opt for early retirement. The labour force participation rate for women has been increasing for a variety of reasons, including changes in social attitudes, increases in educational levels and employment opportunities, changes in family structure, and the rise in real wages of women. The increase in the labour force participation of women has more than offset the decline in the labour force participation of men. The resulting change in the gender composition of the labour force has far-reaching consequences for human resources management and public policy. Labour force participation rates vary greatly across provinces. Traditionally, workforce participation has been lowest in Atlantic Canada and highest in Alberta and Ontario. Though provincial participation rates have been converging over the last 40 years, the regional gap is still significant.

Key Terms

birth rate (page 75)
business cycle (page 81)
civilian working-age population (page 72)
dependency rate (page 79)
employed (page 71)
fertility rate (page 75)
labour force (page 71)
labour force participation rate (page 73)
mortality rate (page 75)
natural population growth (page 75)
not in the labour force (page 71)
recession (page 81)
unemployed (page 71)

Weblinks

For latest releases from the Labour Force Survey
http://www.statcan.gc.ca/subjects-sujets/labour-travail/lfs-epa/
lfs-epa-eng.htm

For demographic data
www.canadabusiness.ca/eng/88/191/

For information on the Canada Pension Plan
www.servicecanada.gc.ca/eng/isp/cpp/cpptoc.shtml

For information on the business cycle
www.nber.org

For 2006 census data
www12.statcan.ca/census-recensement/2006/index-eng.cfm

For Citizenship and Immigration Canada
www.cic.gc.ca

For publications of the C.D. Howe Institute
www.cdhowe.org/pdf/backgrounder_81.pdf

Discussion Questions

1. Suppose you have to forecast the growth in the Canadian labour force over the next 20 years. Which factors would you consider to be essential? Discuss.

2. Explain how the aging of the baby-boom generation may affect the dependency rate and, as a result, may threaten the sustainability of the public pension system.

3. Suppose you are working as a human resources professional in a company. List and explain two ways in which the aging of the Canadian

labour force may affect the policies and practices in your organization.

4. Describe the major changes in the ethnic composition of immigration to Canada over the last 20 years. Discuss how the growing ethnic diversity in Canada's urban labour force may affect human resources policies.

5. The increase in the labour force participation rate of women was uninterrupted from the 1940s until 1990. Elaborate on some of the factors that played a role in this increase.

Using the Internet

Go the Statistics Canada website at www.statcan.gc.ca. Look under the links Canadian Statistics, Latest Indicators, Labour, Labour Force Statistics.

1. What are the latest monthly data on the Canadian labour force and the labour force participation rate? Calculate the Canadian working-age population.

2. What are the latest monthly data on the number of unemployed people? Compute the number of people who are employed.

3. Compute the change in the number of unemployed from the first available number to the most recent month in the table. Do the same for the number of employed workers. Is the decline in unemployment equal to the increase in employment? Explain your findings.

Exercises

1. In 2002, the Canadian working-age population was 24 945 100. Of these, 15 411 800 people had jobs. Of the remainder, 1 277 600 were looking for work, 415 800 wanted to work but did not actively look for work, and 7 839 900 did not want to work. Of those who wanted to work, 43 000 had given up looking for work because they thought there was no work available.
   a. Compute the Canadian labour force in 2003.
   b. Compute the number of people not in the labour force.
   c. Compute the labour force participation rate.
   d. Compute the employment rate.

2. When women have, on average, 2.1 children each, one generation replaces another. Over the last 30 years, Canada's fertility rate has been well below the replacement level. Why has domestic population not declined?

3. In discussing the contribution of immigrants to the Canadian economy, labour economists have focused on the labour market outcomes of immigrants compared to those born in Canada.
   a. State some of the labour market outcomes on which labour economists have focused.
   b. How have these labour market outcomes changed from the 1960s and 1970s to the most recent decade?

4. Labour force participation rates vary by province. For 2012, the rates

were:

Newfoundland and Labrador
61.6%

Prince Edward Island   68%

Nova Scotia
64.1%

New Brunswick
63.1%

Quebec
65.1%

Ontario
66.5%

Manitoba
69.1%

Saskatchewan
69.5%

Alberta
73.4%

British Columbia
65.0%

a. How would you explain the high participation rate for Alberta compared to other provinces?

b. How would you explain the low participation rate for Newfoundland and Labrador compared to other provinces?

References

[1]Drew, D., Murray, S., and Zhao, J. (June 2000). "Brain Drain and Brain Gain: Part II, The Migration of Knowledge Workers to Canada." *Canadian Economic Observer*. Ottawa: Statistics Canada (Catalogue no. 11-010), p. 313.

[2]Reitz, J.G., and Sklar, S. (1997). "Culture, Race, and the Economic Assimilation of Immigrants." *Sociological Forum*, 12(2): 233–277; Green, D., and Worswick, C. (2002). "Earnings of Immigrant Men in Canada: The Roles of Labour Market Entry Effects and Returns to Foreign Experience." Research paper, *Strategic Research and Review*. Ottawa: Citizenship and Immigration Canada.

[3]Reitz, J.G. (2001). "Immigrant Skill Utilization in the Canadian Labour Market: Implications of Human Capital Research." *Journal of International Migration and Integration*, 2(3): 347–378. Also, Watt, D., and Bloom, M. (2001). "Exploring the Learning Recognition Gap in Canada." Phase 1 Report. *Recognizing Learning: The Economic Cost of Not Recognizing Learning and Learning Credentials in Canada*. Ottawa: Conference Board of Canada.

[4]Belanger, A., and Ouellet, G. (2002). "A Comparative Study of Recent Trends in Canadian and American Fertility, 1988–1999." In Statistics Canada, *Report on the Demographic Situation in Canada 2001*. Ottawa: Minister of Industry (Catalogue no. 91-209 XPE), pp. 107–136.

[5]Foot, D.K., and Venne, R.A. (1990). "Population, Pyramids and Promotional Aspects." *Canadian Public Policy*, 16(4): 387–398. See also: Duchesne, D. (1994). "David Foot Discusses Career Paths." *Perspectives on Labour and Income*, 6(4). Ottawa: Statistics Canada (Catalogue no. 75-001-XPE), pp. 13–21.

[6]Chawla, R.K., and Wannell, T. (2004). "A C/QPP Overview." *Perspectives on Labour and Income*, 16(1). Ottawa: Statistics Canada (Catalogue no. 75-001-XPE), p. 52.

[7]Statistics Canada. (2003). *2001 Census: Analysis Series. The Changing Profile of Canada's Labour Force*. Ottawa: Minister of Industry (Catalogue no. 96F0030XIE2001009), p. 10.

[8]Green, A. (1995). "A Comparison of Canadian and U.S. Immigration Policy in the Twentieth Century." In D. DeVoretz (Ed.), *Diminishing Returns: The Economics of Canada's Recent Immigration Policy*. Toronto: C.D. Howe Institute, pp. 31–64.

[9]Reitz, J.G. (2001). "Immigrant Success in the Knowledge Economy: Institutional Change and the Immigrant Experience in Canada: 1970–1990." *Journal of Social Issues*, 75(3): 610.

[10]Worswick, C. (April 2004). "Immigrants' Declining Earnings: Reasons and Remedies." *Backgrounder*, 81. Toronto: C.D. Howe Institute, p. 4.

[11]Baker, M., and Benjamin, D. (1994). "The Performance of Immigrants in the Canadian Labour Market." *Journal of Labour Economics*, 12: 369–405; Grant, M.L. (1999). "Evidence of New Immigrant Assimilation in Canada." *Canadian Journal of Economics*, 32(4): 930–955.

[12]Statistics Canada. (2003). *Earnings of Canadians: Making a*

Living in a New Economy. Ottawa: Minister of Industry (Catalogue no. 96F0030XIE2001013).

[13]Reitz, J.G. (2001). "Immigrant Success in the Knowledge Economy: Institutional Change and the Immigrant Experience in Canada: 1970–1990." *Journal of Social Issues,* 75(3): 579–613.

[14]Troper, H. (March 2000). *History of Immigration Since the Second World War: From Toronto "The Good" to Toronto "The World in a City."* Toronto: Joint Centre of Excellence for Research on Immigration and Settlement, Working Paper No. 12.

[15]Baker, M., and Benjamin, D. (1997). "Ethnicity, Foreign Birth and Earnings: A Canada/U.S. Comparison." In M.G. Abbott, C.M. Beach, and R.P. Chaykowski (Eds.), *Transition and Structural Change in the North American Labour Market.* Kingston: John Deutsch Institute and Industrial Relations Centre, Queen's University.

[16]Johns, G., and Saks, A.M. (2001). *Organizational Behaviour* (5th ed.). Toronto: Addison Wesley Longman, p. 211.

[17]Guzzo, R.A., and Dickson, M.W. (1996). "Teams in Organizations: Recent Research on Performance and Effectiveness." *Annual Review of Psychology,* 47: 311, 331.

[18]Rowe, G., and Nguyen, H. (2003). "Older Workers and the Labour Market." *Perspectives on Labour and Income,* 15(1). Ottawa: Statistics Canada (Catalogue no. 75-001-XPE), p. 56.

[19]International Labour Office. (2003). *Yearbook of Labour Statistics,* 62nd issue. Geneva: ILO.

[20]Gunderson, M. (1998). *Women and the Canadian Labour Market: Transitions Towards the Future.* Scarborough: Statistics Canada in conjunction with ITP Nelson.

Chapter 5

Employment

Chapter Learning Objectives

After completing this chapter, you should be able to:

- describe the major trends in total employment over the last five decades
- explain the employment growth in the service sector relative to the other sectors of the economy
- describe the changes in the occupational distribution of the workforce
- evaluate the arguments in the debate over the deskilling or the up-skilling of the labour force
- discuss the trends in non-standard employment
- distinguish between different concepts of working hours
- describe and explain the trends in working hours

OUTSOURCING IN THE COMPUTER SERVICES INDUSTRY

A central trend on the demand side of the labour market has been the shift in employment toward employment in the service sector, away from resource and manufacturing industries. Another trend during the last 30 years has been the growth in self-employment. An example that illustrates the interrelation between both trends is the computer services industry, which has been one of the fastest-growing industries in the service sector. During the last decade, output growth in the computer services industry was about six times that of the overall economy.

Computer services can be divided into four subcategories: software publishers, online information services, electronic data processing services, and computer systems design and related services. Computer systems design services are by far the largest subgroup in the overall computer services industry. Annual job growth in computer systems design averaged 19% during the most recent decade, about 14 times the employment growth rate for the overall economy.

Among computer programmers and systems engineers, self-employment is very common. In computer systems design services, the self-employment rate is nearly double the rate for the service sector. One reason for the high self-employment rate is the growing practice of outsourcing, which describes the long-term contracting of a company's business processes to an outside service provider. Financial institutions offering home and Internet banking and insurance companies selling services online through specialized sites have been among the main customers of software services outsourced to service providers. The growth in outsourcing to computer services providers is the result of several factors:

- the increased strategic importance of computer systems to business
- the flexibility provided to companies by contracting out
- a shortage of skilled labour, which is compounded by the complexity of systems required to meet the customized information technology needs of companies

The most important change in outsourcing of computer services in recent years has been the growing use of offshoring. The move of firms in North America to offshore work to take advantage of low labour costs in developing countries is no longer restricted to manufacturing industries. India, Pakistan, and the Philippines, for example, have become major competitors in the global market for computer services providers. While initially companies in these countries focused on providing computer services for specific individual projects, they are now increasingly entering into long-term outsourcing contracts with their North American clients. The globalization of knowledge work and the ability or failure of Canadian computer services providers to adjust to the global restructuring of the industry will have far-reaching implications for future employment growth in the service sector.

Aggregate Labour Demand

As the number and characteristics of people wanting to work have changed significantly over the last 50 years, so have the number and characteristics of jobs that employers offer. The total number of jobs made available by firms and government agencies is called total labour demand, or **aggregate labour demand**. As indicated in the discussion of the flow approach to the labour market in Chapter 2, aggregate labour demand is measured by the number of employed workers plus the number of unfilled vacancies. Statistics on unfilled vacancies at the national level are unfortunately no longer available since the Job Vacancy Survey was discontinued in 1978. Therefore, this chapter will concentrate only on the long-run changes in employment as an indicator of aggregate labour demand.

aggregate labour demand
the total number of jobs made available by firms, government agencies, and non–governmental organizations

Two caveats seem appropriate at this point. First, to take employment as an approximation of aggregate labour demand is to some degree artificial, because the employed portion of the measured labour force reflects the continuous interaction of forces operating on both the supply and demand sides of the labour market. That is, the level of employment is determined by the interaction of demand and supply in the labour market. Second, care must be taken not to confuse employment with the number of jobs. Equating changes in employment with changes in jobs distorts the extent of job creation or loss. Since the Labour Force Survey (LFS) measures employment by counting employed workers rather than occupied jobs, a newly created job taken by someone already working does not increase employment. Likewise, the loss of a job previously held by a multiple jobholder (moonlighter) does not reduce the number of workers.

Changes in Level of Employment

Employment in an economy can be assessed by asking two questions: How many people are working, and how many hours are they working? Figure 5.1 (page 108) illustrates the dramatic expansion of employment in Canada from 4.8 million in 1947 to 17.5 million in 2012. This change represents an increase of 265%. Expressed in growth rates, employment increased during this period at an average annual rate of 2%. However, over the last three decades, average annual growth rates of employment have sharply declined. In the decade of 1970–80, employment grew on average 3.5% per year, but employment growth between 1980 and 1990 was much slower (1.8%), and during the 1990s it averaged 1.3% per year. Between 2001 and 2012, employment growth picked up at an average annual rate of 1.4%, even after it declined by 1.6% in 2009 during the financial crisis. The long-term decline in employment growth was largely due to the two deep recessions in the early 1980s and 1990s. As Figure 5.1 shows, in both recessions employment growth was negative and it took several years before the economy regained sufficient strength to generate growing employment.

Part of the long-term increase in employment can be explained by the increase in the number of people of working age. However, employment numbers overall have risen faster during the last half-century than the working-age population. This difference is illustrated in Figure 5.2, which shows the trend in the proportion of people 15 years of age and older who have at least some paid employment. The ratio of employment to working-age population is called the **employment rate**. In Figure 5.2, three main developments in the employment rate are discernible over the past 60 years. From 1947 to the early 1960s, the rate showed a downward trend, from about 54% to just a little over 50%. Upward movements in the employment rate of adult women failed to offset the rate decline of youths and adult men. Thereafter, the overall rate began an upward trend—driven mainly by increases in the women's employment rate—to reach 60.4% at the onset of the 1981–82 recession. Following a brief slide in 1982 and 1983, the ratio resumed its climb in

employment rate

the ratio of employment to working-age population

FIGURE 5.1

Employment Growth, 1947–2012

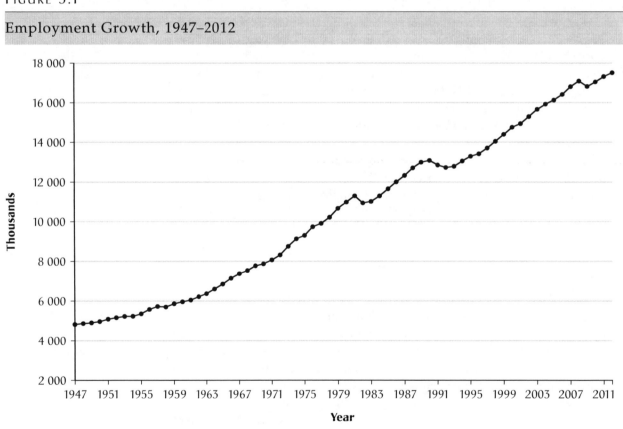

Sources: For 1947–75, adapted from Statistics Canada. (1995). *Canadian Economic Observer, Historical Statistical Supplement, 1994/5*. Catalogue no. 11–210; for 1976–2012, adapted from Statistics Canada CANSIM, table 282-0002.

FIGURE 5.2

Employment Rate, 1947–2012

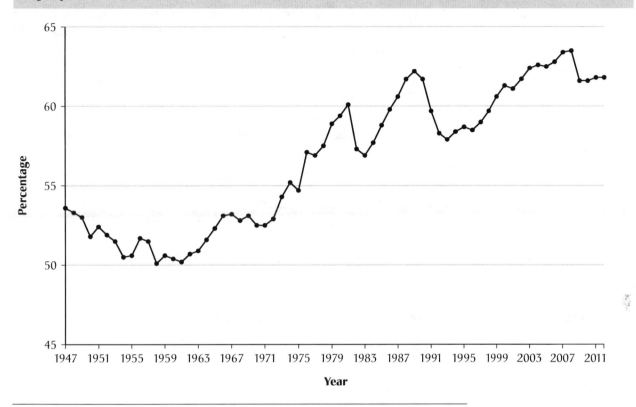

Sources: For 1947–75, adapted from Statistics Canada. (1995). *Canadian Economic Observer, Historical Statistical Supplement, 1994/5*. Catalogue no. 11-210; for 1976–2012, adapted from Statistics Canada CANSIM, table 282-0002.

1984, rising to its peak of 62.4% in 1989, just before the recession. With the onset of the 1990–92 recession, the ratio dropped once more, and remained fairly steady around 58.7% through the remaining years of the 1990s. By 1999, the employment rate started to increase again and in 2008 reached the earlier peak level of 63.5%. During a financial crisis, it dropped again to 61.6% in 2009, but very slightly increased to 61.8% in 2012.

The long-term trend increase suggests that the economy was able to generate more jobs than were required to keep up with the growth in the working-age population. Figure 5.2 shows that the decline of the employment rate during recessions is even more pronounced than the fall of total employment. This is because the change in the employment rate reflects the combined changes of the labour force participation rate and the unemployment rate. In a recession, the LFPR generally declines as workers leave the labour force, and the unemployment rate increases because fewer workers are needed as production is reduced. Both changes reduce the employment rate.

As discussed in Chapter 4, one of the most dramatic changes has been the growth in the labour force participation rate of women, in particular of adult women. The growth in the LFPR was paralleled by an increase in the female employment rate, which more than tripled over the last 60 years. In 1946, fewer than one in five (17.9%) adult women were working; since the late 1980s, more than one in two adult women have had jobs, and in 2012, their employment rate reached 58.4%. The employment rate of men displayed a starkly different trend. With few exceptions, men's employment rate decreased steadily while women's rate rose. In 1946, about 87% of adult men were employed; by 2012, their employment rate had declined to 68.3%. Most of the decline was due to the withdrawal—voluntary or otherwise—of older, poorly educated men from the employed labour force.

Compared to adult men and women, the employment rate of youths (both sexes combined) has shown the greatest sensitivity to the ups and downs in economic activity. Starting at 54.5% in 1946, it declined to roughly 44% in the first half of the 1960s. It shifted upward to 53% following the Labour Force Survey's exclusion of 14-year-olds from the working-age population in 1966, but then continued its decline until 1970 (50.3%). As can be seen in Figure 5.3, movements in the youth ratio over the last 35 years closely followed the business cycle. After hitting its peak in 1989 (63.4%), the ratio declined by more than 12 percentage points to 51.5% in 1997. The decline mirrors the drop in the youth

FIGURE 5.3

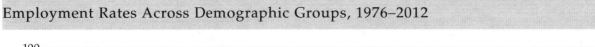

Employment Rates Across Demographic Groups, 1976–2012

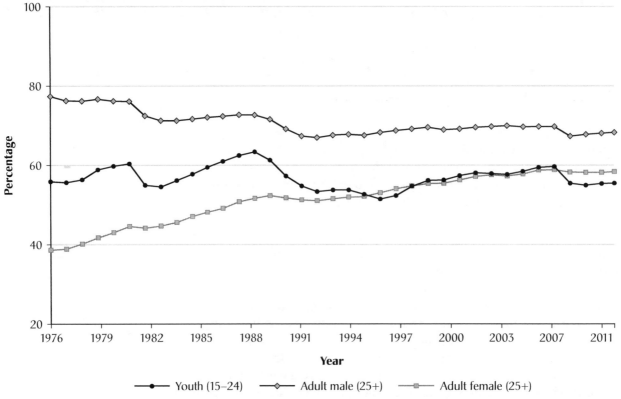

Source: Adapted from Statistics Canada CANSIM, table 282-0002.

Part II: Trends and Recent Developments in the Canadian Labour Market

labour force participation rate mentioned in Chapter 4. It is another indication of the declining employment opportunities for young people during the 1990s. Since the recent economic upturn, the employment rate for youth started to increase. In 2003, it stood at 58.1%, slightly exceeding the rate for adult women. Starting 2009, the employment rate for adult women exceeded the rate for youth. In 2012, it was 54.5% for youth and 58.4% for adult women.

Shifts in the Composition of Employment

Quantitative changes in the overall level of employment, or in the employment rate, hide many different features of labour demand. These features include the mix of jobs (for example, the percentage of full-time and part-time jobs), the quality of jobs (for example, in terms of job stability or working conditions), and the distribution of jobs (for example, by industry or occupation). As the demand for goods and services shifts over time, so does the demand for labour. While some industries and occupations expand, others contract, leading to changes in the skills required by employers and the geographic and industrial locations of employment. These compositional changes in labour demand are the focus of the next two sections.

The Shift to Service-Sector Employment

Historically in Canada, the most important change in the distribution of employment has been the shift in employment away from the goods-producing industries to the service-producing industries.[i] In the late nineteenth and early twentieth centuries, Canadians largely farmed and fished. After World War I, agriculture began to give way to manufacturing. The shift from primary-resource industries (particularly agriculture) to manufacturing industries has coincided with the rise of a modern industrial economy. The rise is reflected in the continuous decline in the proportion of employment in agriculture from roughly 33% of the employed labour force in 1921 to only 1.8% in 2011. The employment share not only of agriculture and other natural resource industries declined, but so did the share of manufacturing and construction. Over the last 50 years, their share in total employment dropped from 42.5% in 1961 to 17.5% in 2011. Currently, only 22% of total workers are employed in the goods-producing industries.

Until the 1950s, the employment gains in non-government services were very gradual. Major non-government services are listed in Table 5.1 (page 112) under "Dynamic Services" and "Traditional Services." Within 30 years, from 1921 to 1951, employment in these services rose from 25.2% to 35.1%, that is, by 10 percentage points. Since then the growth has accelerated. Between 1951 and 1991, service employment in the non-government sector increased by 24 percentage points, at an annual rate of about 1.3%. However, employment growth in government services (including municipal, provincial, and federal administrations) during the same period was relatively flat.

---

[i] Goods-producing industries include manufacturing, construction, utilities, logging and forestry, fishing, mining, oil and gas, and agriculture.

TABLE 5.1

The Structure of the Service Sector

DYNAMIC SERVICES

Transportation, communications, and utilities

Air, rail, and water transport

Ground transportation

Pipelines

Storage and warehousing

Broadcasting—radio, television, cable

Telephone systems

Postal and courier services

Utilities—electricity, gas, water, and sewage systems

Wholesale trade

Finance, insurance, and real estate

Banks and trust companies

Credit unions and mortgage companies

Insurance companies

Investment dealers

Real estate operators

Business services

Employment agencies

Advertising services

Architectural, scientific, engineering, and computing services

Legal services

Management consulting

TRADITIONAL SERVICES

Retail trade

Food stores

Drugstores and liquor stores

Shoe and clothing stores

Furniture, appliance, and auto repair shops

Department stores

Jewellery stores and photographic stores

Personal services

Hotels

Restaurants and bars

Film, audio, and video production and distribution

Movie houses and theatres

Barber and beauty shops

Laundries and cleaners

Funeral services

Machinery and car rental companies

Photographers

Repair shops (excluding auto)

Building security services

Travel agencies

NON-MARKET SERVICES

Education services

Schools, colleges, and universities

Libraries, museums, and archives

Health services

Hospitals

Nursing homes

Doctors and dentists

Medical laboratories

Social services

Daycare, meal services, and crisis centres

Psychologists and social workers

Religious organizations

Public administration

Note: For data-related reasons, this classification scheme has been organized within the framework of Statistics Canada's Standard Industrial Classification.

The shift to services is the outstanding feature on the demand side of the Canadian labour market. In 1967, the year of Canada's centennial, service-sector jobs overtook natural resource and manufacturing jobs for the first time. As the data in Table 5.2 (page 114) show, by 2011, nearly 78% of Canadian workers were employed in the service sector (non-government plus government services). The proportion of women working in service industries had reached 89.8% in that year and the share of men was close to 67.3%. The shift to services, however, is not unique to Canada; the transition has been one of the most consistent features of economic development in all major industrialized countries. The sectoral redistribution of employment over time was succinctly stated by Colin Clark some 40 years ago: "A wide, simple and far-reaching generalization in this field is to the effect that, as time goes on and communities become more economically advanced, the numbers engaged in agriculture tend to decline relative to the numbers in manufacture, which in their turn decline relative to the numbers engaged in services."[1] The shift from agriculture to services is sometimes described as the shift from the primary to the tertiary sector. Others who like to describe the present with the prefix "post" have called it the arrival of the "postindustrial" state. The relatively faster growth in service-sector employment is the result of several inter-related factors.

Differences in Productivity Growth Rates

Significant differences in productivity growth rates between the goods-producing industries and the service-sector industries have been cited as a major cause for the growth in the service sector. The level of output in any industry depends on its production factors, primarily labour and capital, and the production technology. The contribution of labour to growth in output depends on the increase in labour, measured as a percentage change in hours of work or number of employed workers, times the marginal productivity of labour. As we saw in Chapter 1, in economics, the word "marginal" means extra or additional; thus, the **marginal productivity of labour (MPL)** indicates the extra output obtained by adding one more worker or having a worker work one more hour. Similarly, the contribution of capital depends on changes in capital times the marginal productivity of capital. The marginal productivity of capital is calculated as the change in output over the change in capital by one unit. Even if the quantities of labour and capital remain constant, output still can change if technological progress takes place. For the same amount of inputs, we get more output today than we did in the past. This increase in output is attributed to a change in **total factor productivity**.

Primary-resource industries and most manufacturing industries saw much more rapid gains in productivity—individual factor or total factor productivity, or both—in the period 1947–1973 in comparison to the service industries. From 1973 onward, when productivity growth started to slow down in the goods-producing industries, the service sector showed an even greater decline in growth rates. Only since 1995 has labour productivity growth in the business-sector service industries exceeded that of manufacturing industries.[2]

marginal productivity of labour (MPL)

extra output obtained by adding one more worker or having a worker work one more hour

total factor productivity

the increase in output obtained from the same amount of inputs into the production process

TABLE 5.2

Employment by Industry and Sex, 2011

| | Number Employed | | | | | |
| | Both Sexes | | Men | | Women | |
	Thousands	%	Thousands	%	Thousands	%
All Industries	17 306.2	100.0	9 085.1	100.0	8 221.1	100.0
Goods-producing sector	3 804.9	22.0	2 969.8	32.7	835.1	10.2
Agriculture	337.2	1.9	215.5	2.4	90.1	1.1
Forestry, fishing, mining, oil and gas	337.2	1.9	275.7	3.0	61.5	0.7
Utilities	139.8	0.8	105.2	1.2	34.6	0.4
Construction	1 262.2	7.3	1 121.4	12.3	140.8	1.7
Manufacturing	1 760.2	10.2	1 252.1	13.8	508.1	6.2
Services-producing sector	13 501.3	78.0	6 115.3	67.3	7 386.1	89.8
Trade	2 669.9	15.4	1 369.8	15.1	1 300.2	15.8
Transportation and warehousing	843.4	4.9	640.6	7.1	202.8	2.5
Finance, insurance, real estate, and leasing	1 083.4	6.3	472.6	5.2	610.8	7.4
Professional, scientific, and technical services	1 309.2	7.6	757.6	8.3	551.6	6.7
Business, building, and other support services	677.0	3.9	378.4	4.2	298.6	3.6
Educational services	1 219.4	7.0	415.7	4.6	803.7	9.8
Healthcare and social assistance	2 091.5	12.1	371.9	4.1	1 719.6	20.9
Information, culture, and recreation	784.2	4.5	428.0	4.7	356.2	4.3
Accommodation and food services	1 093.4	6.3	455.5	5.0	637.9	7.8
Other services	758.7	4.4	351.7	3.9	407.0	5.0
Public administration	971.2	5.6	473.6	5.2	497.6	6.1

Source: Adapted from Statistics Canada CANSIM, table 282-0012.

In spite of recent acceleration in productivity growth, labour productivity in the service sector in 2001 was still well below the level of labour productivity in the manufacturing and primary-resource industries.[3]

Do productivity gains in an industry create jobs or destroy them? For the overall economy, productivity gains have generally been associated with positive effects on output and employment. Productivity gains lead to a rise in real wages or profits, or both, all other things being the same. Increases in real wages stimulate spending of households on consumption items, and increases in profits stimulate spending of firms on investment goods. Increased spending, in turn, has a positive effect on production and employment. What applies to the economy at large, however, may not apply for each industry that experiences productivity gains. For example, industries that experienced large productivity gains in the first decades after World War II—such as mining and oil, communication, and agriculture—channelled some of the gains into increasing the capital stock. Much of the increase in the capital stock has been in the form of labour-saving equipment. Considering the shift of employment to the service sector, one could argue that the relatively higher productivity growth in the goods-producing industries lowers employment opportunities in those industries relative to the service industries.

Increases in Real Income

How much people spend depends on their real income: as real income per person rises, expenditures rise. The increases in real income that occurred between the end of World War II and the late 1970s, however, are associated with an overproportionate growth in the demand for services. The demand for consumer services tends to grow faster than the demand for consumer goods. For example, as real income rises, people tend to eat more restaurant meals instead of buying food to prepare at home. The demand has increased particularly in the areas of medical care, education, recreation, communication, and transportation.

The relationship between an increase in real income and a more than proportional increase in the demand for services was established in the nineteenth century by the Prussian statistician Ernst Engel. **Engel's law** states that

Engel's law

expenditures on necessities such as food are a decreasing proportion of one's income as real income increases, while expenditures on rent and clothing remain constant and expenditures on luxuries increase in proportion

Labour Market Issue 5.1

Are All Industrial Nations Becoming Service Economies?

Are all industrial nations becoming service economies? The answer is yes. Employment data for the 10 leading industrial nations show that, in every country, the share of the labour force employed in services has increased significantly. During the last 30 years in countries such as Japan and Germany, which are associated with a strong manufacturing sector, the proportion of workers in service industries grew even more than in Canada.

Productivity plays a key role in explaining the similar development. Throughout the industrial world, productivity has grown much faster in manufacturing than it has in most services. Several service industries, such as telecommunications, use highly sophisticated equipment and their productivity has grown rapidly. But in most other services, productivity growth has been slow.

The role of productivity in the employment shift to the service industries can be made clear with a simple example. Assume that 5000 plant workers produce annually 5 million tonnes of steel. The average labour produc-

tivity would be 1000 tonnes per worker (5 000 000/5000 = 1000). Suppose productivity in the steel industry doubled to 2000 tonnes per worker as the result of mechanization and output rose by 50% to 7.5 million tonnes of steel. Since mechanization implies substitution of workers by machines, there must have been a reduction in the number of workers employed in that industry from 5000 to 3750, i.e. a reduction by 25% (7 500 000/3750 = 2000). If, over the same period, productivity in the real estate industry remained constant while sales volume rose by 50%, that industry must have employed 50% more workers than before. With both industries expanding their outputs by the same percentage, some workers must have moved out of the steel industry into the real estate industry. While the share of output produced in manufacturing generally has not declined, its share of employment has fallen. It is in this sense that all industrial countries are becoming service industries.

Chapter 5: Employment

income elasticity of demand

the relationship between changes in real income and changes in the quantity demanded

expenditures on necessities such as food take a decreasing proportion of income as real income increases, while expenditures on clothing and rent remain constant and expenditures on luxuries increase overproportionately. Many services are classified as luxuries. Economists define a luxury as a good or service with an income elasticity of demand greater than 1. The **income elasticity of demand** measures how the quantity demanded changes as consumer income changes. Like the price elasticity, which is discussed in Chapter 2, the income elasticity is a ratio of two percentage changes: the percentage change in quantity demanded divided by the percentage change in income. If income increases by 1% and the percentage change in the quantity demanded of a certain service—for example, the number of consultations with chiropractors—is greater than 1%, the income elasticity of demand for chiropractor services is greater than 1. The validity of Engel's law is clearly borne out by a comparison of estimates for the income elasticities of various goods and services. The income elasticity, for instance, for food items (mean value in Canada for the period 1926–1989) has been 0.39.[4] Beer has a very low income elasticity, 0.06. High income elasticities apply for many services, for example airline travel (5.82), movies (3.41), and restaurant meals (1.71). For medical services, the elasticity has been 1.95. An income elasticity of 1.95 implies that as real income increases by 1%, the demand for medical care increases by 1.95%.

Contracting Out of Company Internal Services

The shift to service-sector employment partly reflects the growing trend of companies in the manufacturing sector to contract out. Much of the business-services sector is devoted to providing services to goods producers: advertising services, accounting audits, legal advice, engineering expertise, etc. Firms in the manufacturing sector have increasingly turned to specialized firms for these services rather than using their own employees. When a manufacturer stops using in-house staff and hires a specialized firm to provide a service such as advertising, employment in the manufacturing sector falls and employment rises in the service sector. The shift may not affect the total number of people in an economy producing advertising services, however: advertisers were formerly counted as employees in the manufacturing sector and are now enumerated in the service sector.

International Competition

open economy

an economy in which imports and exports represent a large percentage of overall economic activity

Imported goods often compete with domestically produced goods on the basis of price, quality, and design. This competition, often from countries where wages are low, has been particularly strong in the Canadian manufacturing sector and has contributed to the rapid decline of that sector's share in total employment. Canada is a highly **open economy**, which means that imports and exports represent a large percentage of overall economic activity. Canadians spend almost 30% of total income on imports. In contrast, American spending on imports is just over 11%.

Increase in the Demand for Services as Inputs

The Betcherman report claims that all the factors we have discussed so far account for only a small part of the shift in employment to the service sector.[5] The report argues that the major force behind the transition has been the increase in the demand for services as inputs into the production of the goods-producing industries. The authors of the report claim that the stimulative influence of the goods-producing industries on services has been increasing over time. Of the 28 goods-producing industries, 25 had more stimulative power on the service sector in 1981 than in 1971. By 1985, most goods-producing industries had a significant influence on output in the service sector. Manufacturing and resource industries were important sources of demand for service inputs. In contrast, the stimulative power of the service industries on goods production was generally weak.

The report focuses on the relationship between the goods-producing industries and the dynamic services (see Table 5.1, page 112). Dynamic services are services with relatively high growth rates. Six service industries, which together make up the bulk of the dynamic-service subsector, were particularly dependent on demand from the goods industries for their output: finance and real estate, wholesale trade, business services, utilities, transportation, and communications. The links between the goods sector and the transportation, utilities, and wholesale trade industries have always been strong. One of the most striking changes in the overall structure of the economy, however, has involved business services, financial services, and communications. These industries have shown strong employment growth and significant increases in their links with the goods sector. Technological change has played an important role in these developments by increasing the demand for information and by providing the means for satisfying that demand through those information-based services.

Occupational Shifts

Given the extensive shifts in the industrial composition of employment, one would expect commensurate changes in the distribution of employment across occupations. Table 5.3 (page 118) shows the occupational distribution of the Canadian labour force for the period 1948–98. Major increases in employment occurred in white-collar jobs, with the managerial and professional group exhibiting the greatest change. Taken together, the share of the labour force in white-collar jobs (including managerial and professional, clerical, sales, and service) increased from 38.6% in 1948 to 70.7% in 1998.[ii] In contrast, the combined share of employment in the primary and processing occupations declined from 45.1% in 1948 to only 16.7% in 1998. According to the last census, the shift in the occupational distribution toward white-collar jobs has continued in recent years. By 2001, white-collar jobs comprised 74% of all occupations and the employment share of primary, processing, and manufacturing occupations had dropped further to 12%.

[ii] Due to recent changes in the occupational classifications in the Labour Force Survey, comparable data are not available beyond 1998.

TABLE 5.3

Occupational Distribution of the Canadian Civilian Labour Force, 1948–98

	1948	1951	1961	1971	1981	1991	1998
Managerial, professional	10.9%	14.9%	19.1%	23.9%	23.7%	31.6%	33.4%
Clerical	10.2	11.2	13.3	15.1	17.7	16.4	13.6
Sales	8.0	6.4	7.4	7.1	10.3	9.7	10.2
Service	9.5	9.7	11.8	13.2	13.4	13.3	13.5
Primary occupations	26.7	22.7	13.4	7.9	6.2	4.9	4.2
Processing	18.4	17.7	24.2	24.1	15.2	11.8	12.5
Construction	5.2	6.3	NA	NA	6.0	5.3	5.3
Transportation	6.8	6.5	5.8	4.5	3.8	3.6	3.8
Materials handling	4.1	4.6	5.0	4.3	3.8	3.3	3.4

Note: Data are derived from Statistics Canada's Labour Force Survey. Because of changes in survey frequency, questionnaire, and occupational classification, care should be exercised in making comparisons across time.

Sources: For 1948–51: Statistics Canada. (1983). *Historical Statistics of Canada* (2nd ed.). Ottawa: Statistics Canada (Series D355–382). The occupation categories have been adjusted as follows to fit the current breakdown as reported in Statistics Canada's *The Labour Force*: Communication, financial, and service workers are classified as "service"; manufacturing and mechanical trades workers are classified as "processing"; labourers and unskilled workers are classified as "materials handling"; agricultural, fishing, logging, and trapping workers are classified as "primary occupations." For 1961–71, Statistics Canada. (1983). *Historical Statistics of Canada* (2nd ed.). Ottawa: Statistics Canada (Series D383–412). Farmers and farm workers, loggers and related workers, fishers, trappers, hunters, and miners are classified as "primary occupations"; craftspeople are classified as "processing"; labourers and unskilled workers are classified as "materials handling." For 1981–91, Statistics Canada. (1987, 1992). *Historical Labour Force Statistics* (1987: pp. 143–147; 1992: pp. 161–171). Ottawa: Statistics Canada (Catalogue no. 71-201). For 1998, Statistics Canada. (1999). *Labour Force Update*. Ottawa: Statistics Canada (Catalogue no. 71-005-XPB).

The decline of primary and manufacturing jobs and the growth of service jobs have raised concern among those who believe that the decline of the manufacturing sector implies a decline in the availability of skilled, unionized, well-paid blue-collar jobs and that the new jobs provided by the expanding service industries are largely low-skilled, low-wage jobs. The claim of a "deindustrialization" or a "deskilling" of the labour force often conjures the image of a nation of hamburger flippers. For example, two leading exponents of this hypothesis describe in a study that "automobile workers who lose their jobs in this high productivity industry are found two years later to be in jobs that pay on average 43% less. Even six years after losing their jobs, these workers have recovered only five-sixths of the salaries they would have been earning had they not been laid off. Similar long-term losses are recorded for steelworkers, meat packers, aircraft employees, and those who refine petroleum, produce flat glass, and make men's clothing. These are not merely personal losses, for when a worker is forced out of a high productivity job into a low productivity job, all of society suffers. Real productivity goes down when an experienced, skilled autoworker ends up buffing cars in the local car wash."[6]

Even though there is a disproportionate number of well-paying blue-collar jobs in manufacturing industries, the decline in the employment share of the manufacturing sector as such does not allow us to draw conclusions about changes in the skill composition of the labour force. The link between sectoral shifts in employment and the skill level of the workforce is tenuous because most industries consist of high-skilled, high-paying jobs as well as low-skilled, low-paying jobs. Some service workers flip hamburgers, while others hold highly skilled, well-paid professional, managerial, or administrative jobs.

No clear conclusion about overall trends in the skill intensity of employment is possible at present. However, there is growing evidence that the skill level of the Canadian workforce is increasing rather than declining. Technological and organizational changes seem to have increased the literacy and numeracy requirements across the workforce. Employers look for an understanding of abstract principles, analytical and problem-solving abilities, and communication and interpersonal skills.

Some inferences about the changing skill structure of jobs can be drawn by looking at the demand shifts for more or less educated workers. Census data on educational qualifications show that the quantity of jobs requiring better educated workers (that is, workers who hold postsecondary degrees or certificates) has increased compared to the quantity of jobs employing less educated workers. To the extent that jobs filled by better educated workers require higher skills than jobs filled by less educated workers, the skill level of jobs has been increasing.

Between 1991 and 2001, employment in highly skilled occupations, defined as occupations that normally require a university education, increased by 33%. In 2001, about 2.5 million people were in highly skilled occupations, accounting for 16% of the total labour force, up from 13% a decade earlier.[7] Employment in skilled occupations, defined as occupations usually requiring a community college diploma or apprenticeship training, grew only by 3.3% from 1991 to 2001. With an estimated 4.7 million people in these occupations, their share of the total labour force amounted to 30%, down from 32% in 1991. The decline in the share of skilled occupations was largely caused by the fall in the number of occupations with apprenticeship training qualifications, such as skilled trades. The decline was particularly pronounced in certain construction trades. Occupations requiring a college education, on the other hand, increased by about 6% during the decade. The rate of growth in employment for low-skilled occupations, defined as those requiring at most a high school diploma, was 5.4%, considerably less than the overall labour force growth in that decade. With 6.8 million people occupying low-skilled jobs, their share in the labour force in 2001 was 43%, down from 45% a decade earlier. Managers were excluded from the education-based skill classification. This may reflect the differences in the types of work done by managers and the value placed on work experience rather than formal education in performing managerial tasks.[8] The number of managers increased 17.2% over the decade to 1.6 million.

One important factor contributing to the changing skill profile of the labour force is the growing emphasis on information-based work. The central role of information technology in today's economy is captured in phrases such as the "knowledge-based economy" or the "information economy." The industrial structure in Canada, as in most other developed economies, is becoming more knowledge based and information technology intensive. As Canada's industrial structure changes, so does the structure of its labour force. The proportion of knowledge workers has increased steadily over the last three decades.[iii] In 1971, about 14% of Canada's workforce were in what can be considered high-knowledge occupations; by 2001, this proportion had almost doubled to 25%.[9] The increase in knowledge-based occupations was particularly strong among professional occupations: their share in the labour force rose from 9% to 14% over the three decades. As the demand for knowledge workers increases, the skill level of the Canadian workforce is likely to increase as well. In 1971, for example, 34% of knowledge workers had a university-level or professional degree. By 2001, 52% of all workers in knowledge-intensive occupations had a university degree (see Table 5.4). In the computer and telecommunications (CT) industries, which are a sizeable subset of the information and communications technology (ICT) sector, the number of workers with a university degree increased three times as fast as the number in the rest of the economy over the last decade.[10] Workers with a postsecondary certificate (non-university) also made important gains in employment in the computer and telecommunications industries.

There is growing evidence that advances in information technology are changing workplace organization. The adoption of new information technologies leads to less hierarchical structures and to more decentralized decision making and broader job responsibilities.[11] These organizational changes will likely be reinforcing a trend toward an increase in the demand for skilled workers.

Another factor pointing to an increase in the skill structure of jobs is the fact that real wages of higher-skilled workers have increased relative to lower-skilled workers. The stronger growth of wages in high-skill occupations relative to low-skill occupations is not what one would expect if the skill level across the workforce were deteriorating. The decrease in the relative earnings of low-skilled workers—a topic covered in more detail in Chapter 7—would also indicate that changes in technology, trade patterns, and the ways in which work is organized bias employment in favour of the more skilled and educated worker.

The Growth of Non-Standard Employment

non-standard employment
employment that is not full-time for a full year

Linked to the relative growth of the service sector is another significant trend on the demand side of the labour market: the rise in **non-standard employment**. A non-standard job is one that is not a full-time, full-year, permanent paid job. The broadest measure of non-standard employment includes the following four types of employment: part-time employment, multiple jobholding, own-account self-employment, and temporary employment (which includes term or

---

[iii] The term "knowledge worker" is used in different interpretations in the literature. It refers here to three broad groups of knowledge-based occupations: management, professional, technical.

TABLE 5.4

Percentage of Employees in Knowledge-Based Occupations with University Degree, 1971–2001

	1971	1981	1991	2001
All knowledge-based occupations	34.3	42.4	47.7	51.6
Management occupations	37.4	31.3	37.8	42.0
Professional occupations	44.4	59.3	66.4	65.5
Technical occupations	7.7	10.5	14.2	19.9
All other occupations	2.7	4.5	6.5	9.1
All occupations	7.1	11.2	15.3	19.6

Note: Includes completion of bachelor's, professional, master's, or doctoral-level university degree.

Source: Adapted from Baldwin, J.R., and Beckstead, D. (2003). *Knowledge Workers in Canada's Economy, 1971–2001.* Statistics Canada. Ottawa: Minister of Industry (Catalogue no. 11-624-MIE- No. 004), Table 2.

contract, seasonal, casual, temporary agency, and all other jobs with a specific pre-determined end date). Although the majority of Canadian workers are still employed in full-year, full-time permanent jobs, rates of non-standard work arrangements increased from the 1970s up to the mid-1990s. Full-year full-time jobs are jobs that provide at least 49 weeks per year at 30 or more hours per week. Since the mid-1990s, the proportion of workers in a non-standard employment relationship appears to have stabilized. It is estimated that, in 2002, the share of the Canadian workforce engaged in one of the various forms of non-standard employment was 34%.[12] In the following, we will describe changes in each of the four—not mutually exclusive—types of non-standard work.

Part-Time Work

The most important category of non-standard work is **part-time employment**, defined as the number of workers who worked less than 30 hours per week on their main job. A worker's main job is the one with the greatest number of hours worked during the week referenced by the Labour Force Survey. Part-time work has been increasing since the mid-twentieth century, though the trend has accelerated since the mid-1970s. The proportion of part-time workers climbed from 12.5% of total employment in 1976 to 18.8% in 2012, or to a total of 3.3 million employees. Between 1976 and 2012, growth in part-time employment exceeded growth in full-time employment by a ratio of three to one. As Figure 5.4 (page 122) indicates, growth in part-time employment was particularly strong during the first years of the new millennium.

Who are the part-time workers? Part-time employment displays a strong gender bias. In 2012, 26.5% of all women with jobs worked part-time. In comparison, just 11.8% of employed men held part-time jobs. In the same year,

part-time employment
the number of people working less than 30 hours per week on their main job

FIGURE 5.4

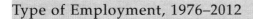

Type of Employment, 1976–2012

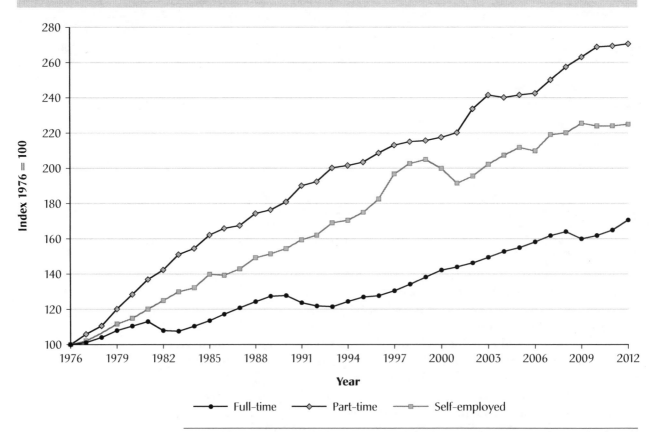

Sources: For full-time and part-time employment, adapted from Statistics Canada CANSIM, table 282-0002. For self-employment, adapted from Statistics Canada CANSIM, table 282-0012.

about 67% of all part-time workers were female, a figure that has changed little over the last 40 years.[13] While female part-time workers are roughly equally distributed across all age groups from 15 to 54, male part-timers are highly concentrated in the 15–24 age group. The different age profiles reflect the tendency of many women to work part-time throughout their work life as a means to supplement family income and to combine paid work with work at home. In contrast, part-time work for a large proportion of male part-timers is associated with school attendance and labour market entrance.[14]

Where are part-time jobs most likely to be found? Part-time work is mostly a service-sector phenomenon. As Table 5.5 shows, the rate of part-time employment is very low in the resource and manufacturing industries. The service industries with the highest proportion of part-time workers are retail trade and commercial services, which include accommodation, food, and beverage services. These industries experience uneven consumer demand, for instance, peak hours in shopping, entertainment, and restaurants and peak demand periods such as holidays and seasonal sales. The powerful fluctuations provide strong incentives to businesses for using part-time workers. The other service industries with a large share of part-time employees are education, healthcare, and real estate, rental, and leasing operations.

Sex differences in part-time work are pronounced across all industries. One-half of all male part-timers are working in the retail/commercial industries, which is consistent with the young age and lower educational attainment of men who work part-time. Women are more evenly distributed between the retail/commercial sector (41%) and education and health services (38%). The relatively high representation of women in education and healthcare conforms with the higher educational qualifications of female part-time workers.

The rise of part-time employment has raised concern among some labour market analysts who view changes in the proportion of part-time workers as evidence of a fundamental restructuring of the job market. They argue that part-time jobs are inferior to full-time jobs because they provide lower earnings, fewer fringe benefits, and less access to training and promotion. Also, because they are mostly non-unionized, part-time jobs offer diminished job

TABLE 5.5

Part-Time Employees by Sex and Industry, 1998–99

INDUSTRY SECTOR	PERCENTAGE OF EMPLOYEES WORKING PART-TIME		PERCENTAGE OF ALL PART-TIME WORKERS	
	WOMEN	MEN	WOMEN	MEN
Forestry, mining	7.4	/	0.2	/
Labour intensive tertiary manufacturing	5.1	1.3	1.0	0.9
Primary product manufacturing	5.3	/	0.3	/
Secondary product manufacturing	1.5	1.7	0.1	1.1
Capital intensive tertiary manufacturing	2.6	1.1	0.3	1.2
Construction	22.8	0.9	1.4	0.8
Transportation/storage, warehousing, wholesale trade	11.9	3.1	3.5	5.9
Communications and other utilities	11.5	2.1	0.8	0.8
Retail trade and commercial services	32.5	19.6	41.3	50.2
Finance and insurance	13.0	5.0	3.8	1.8
Real estate, rental, and leasing operations	24.3	12.9	1.8	2.9
Business services	13.9	5.8	5.8	7.1
Education and healthcare	26.8	16.0	37.8	23.8
Information and cultural industries	15.4	6.0	2.0	2.9

/ shows that data have been suppressed to protect respondent confidentiality

Sources: Adapted from Statistics Canada and Human Resources Development Canada. (2003). *Part-Time Work and Family-Friendly Practices in Canadian Workplaces*. Catalogue no. 71-584-M1E, Tables 1.1 and 1.5.

Chapter 5: Employment

security. Data from the 1999 Workplace and Employee Survey appear to support the argument. According to the survey, roughly one-third of part-time workers earned less than $9 per hour, and no more than one-quarter had access to non-wage benefits. Only 17% of part-timers reported a promotion while working with their current employer. This applies equally to men and women, even though the latter group has relatively higher educational achievement levels and almost half of the female part-time workers were with their employers for more than five years.[15]

underemployed

describes workers who are obliged to take part-time jobs although they prefer to work full-time

The concern over the growth in part-time employment and the generally lower quality of part-time jobs has received additional support due to the significant number of people who work part-time because they cannot find full-time jobs. The involuntary part-time workers are **underemployed** in that they are obliged to take part-time jobs although they would prefer to work full-time. In 2003, 27% of all female part-time employees indicated that they wanted full-time work but could not find it, slightly less than the 30% of men who worked part-time involuntarily.[16] Overall, this was double the proportion of underemployed workers compared to the mid-1970s.

When trying to reach a conclusion about trends in the rate of underemployment (which is defined as the number of involuntary part-time workers as a proportion of all part-time workers), one must keep in mind that any such conclusion depends on the years chosen as starting and cut-off points of the

Labour Market Issue 5.2

Four Young People and Ten Jobs

Adam, Daniel, Naomi, and Winston rent a small townhouse in Whistler, B.C. They came to this resort town to combine work with pleasure—that is, the outdoors. Since the cost of living in Whistler is very high, however, they find themselves working many more hours than they had anticipated. For most of them, little time is left for their favourite sports activities.

Adam, a history major from Quebec, rises every day during the week at 5:30 in the morning to start his shift as a bus driver. In the afternoon, he works with a landscaping company tending gardens in the summer and removing snow in the winter. Daniel, who did his undergraduate studies in physical geography, works during the winter as a ski instructor. Four times a week, after the ski lessons, he puts in several hours of work in a sports store fitting ski boots and repairing skis. In the summer he juggles jobs as a raft guide and safety kayaker with different rafting com-

panies. Naomi, a trained teacher from Ontario, holds two jobs throughout the year. During the day she is a cashier in a supermarket and four nights a week she works as a waitress in a pub. Winston, who holds a fine arts certificate from a college in Nova Scotia, is self-employed. He does freelance work as a photographer for receptions and tour groups. He runs his own little company producing and distributing photo cards of groups of nude, male ski bums chasing down the slopes of Whistler. In addition, he does layout work for a local magazine.

When asked whether they prefer this pattern of employment to holding a stable, full-time job, the answers are mixed. Adam and Naomi would like to pursue full-time careers but claim that there is no full-time work for them in Whistler. For Daniel and Winston, their work suits their preferences, at least at this point in their lives.

time series. Non-standard employment is highly cyclical. As with unemployment, involuntary part-time employment is tied to the business cycle. In times of recession, full-time employment generally decreases and involuntary part-time employment and unemployment increase. During economic recovery, the two measures are expected to fall. The rate of underemployment did indeed decline during the expansion years from the mid-1990s onward. Still, the involuntary part-time employment rate in 2003 hovered well above its 1980 level, revealing persistent underemployment. If one interprets changes in voluntary part-time employment to reflect changes in the relative supply of part-time workers and changes in involuntary part-time employment to reflect changes in the demand by firms for part-time workers, a rise in the rate of involuntary part-time employment could be seen as an indicator of the reduced availability of "good" jobs.

Multiple Jobholding

Growth in part-time work is only one dimension of a more extensive transformation of the labour market. Partly due to the rise in part-time employment, multiple jobholding, or **moonlighting**, has also become more common. During the mid-1970s, moonlighting was not very common: just one out of every 50 workers held more than one job. Over the following 25 years, the number of moonlighters more than tripled, by far outpacing the growth in employment in general over the same period. By 2002, about 779 000 workers, or 5% of working Canadians, were holding two or more jobs.

moonlighting
multiple jobholding

Who are the moonlighters? In 1977, moonlighting was much more prevalent among men than women. Barely one-quarter of all moonlighters were women. By 2002, women outnumbered men by a sizeable margin as multiple jobholders. The rising number of female moonlighters is not just a reflection of women's increasing participation in the workforce. The incidence of multiple jobholding has increased much more rapidly for women (from 1.7% in 1977 to 6.6% in 2002) than for men (2.8% to 5.4%).[iv] Among moonlighting women, one-half held part-time primary jobs, but only 20% of moonlighting men did so. Many women work in two part-time jobs to attain full-time weekly hours of work. Young adults (aged 20–24), both men and women, have the highest rate of moonlighting (7%). Although this is partly the result of the difficulties young people encounter in finding full-time jobs, it may also reflect their preferences for flexibility and for broadening their work experience. It has become increasingly common to stitch together several part-time jobs rather than supplement a full-time job with part-time work. The majority (51%) of moonlighters are well educated, holding either a postsecondary certificate or diploma or a university degree, compared to 45% of single-job holders. The proportion of highly educated moonlighters is particularly high among those holding several part-time jobs compared to part-timers holding only one job. The overrepresentation in this group of moonlighters indicates that some of our most highly trained people may be unable to secure suitable full-time jobs.

[iv] The rate of incidence of multiple jobholding shows the number of multiple jobs in a group as a percentage of all workers in that group.

Where are the second jobs mostly found? In 2002, more than 60% of women moonlighters had their main job in one of the following four broad industry categories: healthcare and social services (26%), wholesale and retail trade (15.8%), educational services (11.9%), and accommodation, food, and beverage services (8.4%). Moonlighting men held their main job mostly in trade (14.4%), manufacturing (12.5%), healthcare and social services (7.7%) and educational services (7.7%). Moonlighters in education, health and social services, or trade were most likely to have their second job in the same industry as their main job. In contrast, moonlighters with a main job in manufacturing rarely had their second jobs in the same industry.

Why do workers moonlight? Survey results from the Survey of Work Arrangements (SWA) as well as statistical evidence indicate that the majority of workers hold a second job for financial reasons.[17] They want to increase their earnings but are unable to do so by working more hours on their primary job. Other reasons for moonlighting, such as gaining different work experience or enjoying the work on the second job, are more frequently cited by men than by women. This may reflect the higher opportunity costs for women associated with work outside the home.

Own-Account Self-Employment

own-account self-employment

entrepreneurs without paid employees

More and more Canadians are starting a business on their own. Since the mid-1970s, year-over-year increases in self-employment have been higher than the average growth rate in paid employment. The exception was a brief period between 1998 and 2000, when the number of the self-employed as a proportion of all workers declined. Overall, self-employment grew from 10% of total employment in 1976 to about 15% in 2012. Over the last 35 years, the nature of self-employment has changed. From the mid-1970s throughout the 1980s, about 60% of the growth of self-employment involved entrepreneurs who engaged other employees. In sharp contrast, self-employed persons with paid help represented only about 10% of the net growth in self-employment between 1989 and 1997.[v] An overwhelming majority of the newly self-employed in the 1990s (nine-tenths of the growth in self-employment) were entrepreneurs working on their own without any paid help (**own-account self-employment**). Of the 2.7 million self-employed in 2012, well over half (68.8%) were their own boss without the additional help of employees.

While women are overrepresented in part-time work, men are more likely to be self-employed than women, though the gap has narrowed recently. The proportions of male and female workers self-employed in 2012 were 18.7% and 11.4%, respectively. The difference in the own-account form of self-employment was considerably smaller, 12% versus 8%. Close to 30% of own-account self-employed men as well as women worked in business services. Among men, own-account self-employment was also high in construction, distributive services, and agriculture, while a large proportion of own-account self-employed women worked in social services and "other consumer services," which include personal services such as laundry, haircare, and esthetic services.

[v] The decline in total self-employment from 1998 to 2000, shown in Figure 5.4 (page 122), was caused by the fall in the number of self-employed employers.

The tendency to be self-employed increases with age. Self-employment, in particular own-account self-employment, grew fastest among those over age 55, though the largest group of self-employed workers is found among the 35- to 44-year-olds. Older workers tend to have more of the experience, skills, capital, and contacts required to succeed in their own business. In some cases, older displaced workers may have more difficulty than younger individuals in finding paid employment, with self-employment the only alternative. As over the next decade the fastest-growing segment of the population will be those between 45 and 65, the trend increase in self-employment is likely to continue.

Different motives drive people to become self-employed. Some may be attracted by certain features of self-employment, for example the independence of being one's own boss or the ability to work flexible hours or from home. The Internet and e-commerce are powerful forces not only facilitating flexible work arrangements but also allowing the self-employed to find customers and to strike alliances with companies and other self-employed people offering complementary services. Others may be forced into self-employment because no other work is available. While both the "pull" and "push" factors are likely at work, recessions appear to have little effect on the self-employment rate. It may be, however, that long periods of slow growth (rather than recessions), as Canada experienced in the 1990s, encourage self-employment.[18] According to the Survey of Self Employment, one-quarter of all own-account self-employed in 2000 were self-employed because they could not find suitable paid employment.[19]

Temporary Work

Changes in the definition of what constitutes a permanent or a temporary job combined with the lack of surveys providing data in the past make it impossible to establish long-run trends on temporary work arrangements. The General Social Survey (GSS), conducted in 1989 and 1994, provides data on temporary or contract workers, defined as paid workers with a specified end-date for their job or completion of a task or project. The GSS included only employees because the concept of a temporary job is not particularly meaningful for the self-employed. In 1989, 8% of employees identified themselves as temporary workers. Five years later, almost 1 million or 9% of all employees were in temporary positions.

The 1995 SWA expanded the relatively narrow definition of non-permanent work used in the GSS by adding to term and contract work three other forms of non-permanent work: seasonal, casual and on-call jobs, and work done through a temporary help agency. These four types of temporary work arrangements are defined in the SWA as non-permanent jobs. Since 1997, the redesigned Labour Force Survey provides estimates of permanent and temporary (non-permanent) jobs. In 2003, 12.5% (1.6 million) of all Canadian paid workers described their main job as temporary.

The most common temporary work arrangements were term and contract jobs (48%), followed by casual and on-call jobs (26%), and seasonal jobs (24%). Other temporary jobs, such as temporary help agency workers, constituted the smallest segment (2%). Women made up the majority of casual and on-call workers, while men dominated seasonal forms of temporary paid work. Seasonal jobs are largely determined by the annual fluctuations in labour demand of such industries as agriculture, fisheries, forestry, construction, and tourism. For example, two out of three temporary jobs in primary industries were seasonal, as were nearly half (47%) in construction and 39% in transportation. Although seasonal jobs have been an important form of work in Canada for most of the twentieth century, the increased frequency of the other forms of temporary work is of more recent vintage.

As in the case of part-time work, the proportion of female and male temporary workers varies considerably across industries. Women temporary workers were highly concentrated in healthcare and social services, and educational services, followed by accommodation and food services and public administration. Together, public-sector services accounted for 35% of all female employees aged 15 and over but for 40% of all female temporary workers. The public sector appears to have become more reliant on this form of non-standard work conducted by women. Construction, trade, and manufacturing was the domain of male temporary workers. Together, these industries comprised 40% of all male temporary employees.

There is a common perception that workers in non-permanent jobs are young, low-skilled people in clerical, service, and manual jobs. In reality, however, the picture is much more diverse. Workers with non-permanent jobs include men and women of all ages and levels of education in many different occupations and industries. While one-third of paid workers with temporary jobs were between 15 and 24 years of age—compared to only 14% of permanent job holders—by far the majority (62%) were adults in the 25–54 age range. More than half held a postsecondary certificate or diploma or university degree, and more than one-third were working in professional, managerial, and technical occupations.

Rates of hourly pay in non-permanent jobs were lower than in permanent jobs and fewer fringe benefits (such as pension plans, supplementary healthcare plans, dental insurance, paid sick leave, and paid annual vacation leave) were provided by the employer. According to the SWA, 65% of permanent jobs in Canada boasted at least three of the five benefits, whereas 60% of the non-permanent positions offered none of them. To establish whether lower hourly pay and fringe benefits are causally linked to job permanency, however, would require statistical analyses that control for possible effects of other factors on the pay and benefit differential such as industry type, firm size, union membership and collective agreement coverage, region, and the age, sex, and occupation of workers in these two job categories.

Why Has Non-Standard Employment Been on the Rise?

The increase in the use of non-standard employment contracts reflects trends on both the supply and the demand sides of the labour market.

Demographic Changes

On the supply side, the demographic shifts toward larger labour force shares of younger people (until the late 1970s) and of women facilitated the growth of non-standard jobs. Many non-standard jobs correspond to the life-cycle needs of young people and adult women, in particular.

Young people often combine non-standard work with full-time or part-time education. They frequently consider the early phase of their labour market experience as an experimental phase. Many do not want to commit themselves to jobs that will lock them into long-run careers. Instead, they prefer job-hopping, which entails short work experiences on different jobs, in order to find out which career suits them better. Fringe benefits, such as health and life insurance or private pensions, do not rank very high on the priority list of young people. The flexible jobs offered in non-standard employment often fit the bill for younger workers.

For women, the picture is more varied. Many are committed to a long-term career and many have the educational background to pursue such a career. For them, disposable jobs are of little interest. Some women have been pushed into the workforce, perhaps owing to divorce or widowhood. For them, contingent employment may be the only alternative to welfare. At the same time there are many women with children at home who prefer part-time work or contracted work done at home because it allows them to strike a better balance between the demands of paid employment and family responsibilities.

Reducing Wage and Non-Wage Labour Costs

On the demand side, the shift to non-standard employment reflects one of the strategies of firms to reduce their wage and non-wage labour costs. In substituting lower paying, largely non-unionized, part-time and non-permanent jobs for higher pay, often unionized, full-time jobs, firms cut down overall wage costs. Non-wage labour costs include **payroll taxes** and **fringe benefits**. The three national payroll taxes are the employment insurance premiums, the Canada and Quebec Pension Plan contributions, and the workers' compensation premiums. In addition to the three national payroll taxes, there are currently six provincial/territorial payroll taxes, including Quebec's health services fund contributions and employer contributions to vocational training, and Ontario's employer health tax. As a cost factor in business, both payroll taxes and fringe benefits have increased in importance over time. The total effective payroll tax rate, for example, for the country as a whole more than doubled during the 1980s and 1990s, rising from $5.61 per $100.00 of wages and salaries to $12.23.[20]

Prior to 1997, employers were not obliged to deduct payroll taxes such as EI premiums if an employee worked less than 15 hours per week. The tax is also not applicable for self-employed workers and hence those hired on contract. These provisions provided a strong incentive to firms to offer part-time jobs of less than 15 hours and contract work. Only in January 1997 was the rule favouring "under 15 hours" jobs amended. Not surprisingly, part-time jobs of less than 15 hours per week started to decline in 1997.

payroll tax
a tax levied on employers, based on the level of employment, usually proportional to the firm's payroll

fringe benefits
job-related benefits paid by the employer

Not only payroll taxes but also fringe benefit contributions paid by firms differ dramatically according to job type. For example, employees in full-time permanent jobs are much more often entitled to occupational pensions, supplementary health benefits, dental benefits, and paid leave than are part-time and temporary contract workers.[21] The fact that part-time employees receive fewer non-wage benefits adds to the distortion in the relative costs of part-time versus full-time employees and of permanent versus contract workers.

Rising Uncertainty in the Business Environment

In addition to being a means of cutting labour costs, non-standard employment also allows firms to more readily adjust their workforce to changing market conditions. It is said that strategies such as the greater use of temporary employees, part-time employment, and the other forms of non-standard employment described earlier reflect the increase in the need for firms to have more flexible staffing arrangements. Long-run contracts that were preferred by employers in the stable 1950s and 1960s to assure themselves of a loyal and skilled workforce have become more risky since the 1970s.

One reason has been the increase in the scope and intensity of international and national competition due to liberalization in trade and the formation of larger trading blocs, as well as the large fluctuations in exchange rates. The exchange rate is the relative price of the currency of two countries. For example, if the exchange rate between the Canadian dollar and the U.S. dollar is U.S. $0.83 per Canadian dollar, one can exchange one Canadian dollar for U.S. $0.83 in foreign currency markets. An American who wants to obtain Canadian dollars would pay U.S. $0.83 for each dollar. A Canadian who wants to obtain U.S. dollars would pay $1.20 for each U.S. dollar. When people refer to the exchange rate between two countries, they usually mean the *nominal* exchange rate, which is the relative price of two currencies. Liberalization in trade with large fluctuations in exchange rates has led to increasing uncertainties regarding production cost. A declining value of the Canadian dollar against the U.S. dollar, for example, makes imports from the United States more expensive. If the Canadian dollar declines from U.S. $0.83 to U.S. $0.77, the price of a U.S. dollar in Canadian funds rises from $1.20 to $1.30. If U.S. imports, such as machines or computer software programs, are used by Canadian firms in the production of goods and services, production costs will rise. To compensate for increases in production costs caused by unpredictable exchange rate changes, firms often reduce their labour costs by replacing permanent employment contracts with more flexible work arrangements.

In particular, rising imports from East Asian countries have led firms in North America to seek ways to reduce labour costs and to achieve higher flexibility to react to overseas competition. East Asian countries generally produce goods with significantly lower labour cost per unit—lower wages or higher productivity, or both—and a traditionally high share of contingent workers. Canadian firms in the goods-producing sector are increasingly imitating the two-tier workforce of Japan and other East Asian countries, in which a core of workers possesses the polyvalent skills required to ensure functional flexibility in labour deployment. **Functional flexibility** refers to internal labour market rules that give employers greater freedom to move employees from one job to another within the firm. Traditionally, well-defined job ladders produce employees who are well qualified for higher level positions in their specialties, but these same employees may be less qualified to assume a different set of positions. Providing employees with a variety of experiences may prove to be functional when the company's needs are more difficult to predict in advance. In the two-tier system, the core workforce is supplemented by a pool of "just-in-time" workers who provide the numerical flexibility required to meet the unforeseen changes in sales or demand. **Numerical flexibility** refers to a company's practice of contracting out and making greater use of temporary or part-time workers to improve flexibility in its workforce.

Another reason for increased uncertainty is that technological developments are changing in shorter and shorter intervals. Among these changes are developments in new production materials (for example, ceramics and plastics replacing metals), production technologies (such as laser techniques, electronically guided machinery, and tools or robotics), and new products. These rapid changes shorten production cycles and the life cycle of products, which makes any long-term planning in production and sales more and more difficult.

A third reason, until the 1990–92 recession, was relatively high inflation, especially in the mid- and late 1970s and in the late 1980s, which locked many employers into expensive wage contracts because of COLA (cost of living allowance) clauses. COLA clauses generally require companies to raise their nominal wages in line with rising price levels, normally measured by the Consumer Price Index. Also, accounting techniques designed for periods of basically stable prices were unable to cope with the added tax liability imposed through inflation. After-tax profits fell sharply, depleting the reserves that were often used to cover labour cost in downturns. Starting in 1988, the Bank of Canada embarked on a zero-inflation policy using tighter monetary policy. The inflation rate has since dropped sharply, eliminating most of the uncertainties arising from rising price levels.

While non-standard forms of employment increase companies' numerical flexibility, for workers they mostly entail unstable employment, low wages, lack of fringe benefits, and minimal opportunities for training and promotion. The growth in non-standard jobs is seen by some analysts as a major contributor to the creation of a large group of second-class workers mired in low-paying, unstable jobs, and a resulting wage polarization. In an analysis of the labour market of the 1980s, the Economic Council of Canada stated: "Two quite distinct growth poles account for virtually all of the employment expansion in the 1980s: one includes highly skilled, well-compensated, stable jobs while the other consists of non-standard jobs with relatively low levels of compensation and stability."[22]

The growth of the polar ends of the occupational and earnings distribution and the decline of middle-wage jobs are often described as the "disappearance of the middle class." This notion will be covered in more detail in the next chapter.

functional flexibility

internal labour market rules that give employers greater freedom to move employees from one job to another within the firm

numerical flexibility

a company's practice of contracting out and making greater use of temporary or part-time workers to improve flexibility in its workforce

Also, since investment in training is discouraged by workers and employers alike due to the transient nature of the employment relationship, long-term productivity growth may be hampered. As a result, this type of employment may lead to the inability to compete in high technologies in the long run.

Hours of Work

Measuring employment by the number of workers reflects only one component of labour demand. The other component is the hours worked on a job. The volume of employment in an economy is defined as the product of the number of employed workers times the hours of work per employed person. Adjustments in employment can thus occur as a result of changing the number of people employed, that is, through hiring and firing, or through changes in hours of work. The recurrent debate over shortening the hours of work as a possible means to reduce unemployment is just one example illustrating the importance of this labour demand aspect.

To trace the long-term trend of working hours in Canada, one must decide between different dimensions of work time, for example, hours per day or week, days per week, or weeks per year. To complicate matters, there is a set of at least three quite distinct measures of hours to choose from: standard or usual hours, actual hours worked, and hours paid. Taking one week as reference period, a count of **standard working hours** is based on the notion of a standard workweek as established through law, collective agreement, or company policy. This measure is not affected by *temporary* changes in work schedules due to factors such as overtime, vacations, illness, or other absences from work. The total number of hours actually worked (**actual working hours**) reflects increases or decreases in work hours due to factors just mentioned. The total as well as average actual hours worked per week are usually slightly lower than total or average standard hours because net time lost from work is normally greater than net hours worked in excess of the regular schedule. The number of **hours paid** is the hours for which workers are paid regardless of whether they are working or not. Each of these three measures may exhibit a different trend, since each responds to a somewhat differing set of determining factors. Since the concepts of these three measures have changed over time, as has the coverage, no consistent data set is available to track weekly work hours for the Canadian economy as a whole over the last four decades.[vi]

The longest consistent data on hours worked covering the period 1901–81 pertains to the manufacturing sector (see Figure 5.5).[vii] This information reflects the widespread declining trend in the standard hours of work in

standard working hours

the number of hours in a standard workweek as established by law, collective agreement, or company policy

actual working hours

total hours actually worked

hours paid

hours for which workers are paid regardless of whether they were working or not

[vi] The most recent example of a redefinition of standard, or usual hours of work is the revision introduced by the Labour Force Survey in 1997. Between 1976 and 1996, usual hours referred to hours worked in a typical week. Thus, if paid overtime or unpaid extra hours were typical of the worker's schedule, they would be included in the estimates of usual hours. Since 1997, usual hours for employees are defined as those normally worked in a week for regular pay rates. Information on overtime hours, paid or unpaid, is now collected separately. The change was introduced to improve understanding of standard work schedules and overtime behaviour.

[vii] The series covering the period 1901–71 was put together from different data sources by Ostry and Zaidi (1979). Most of their primary data came from the Survey of Working Conditions, from which the figures for 1981 were added. Unfortunately, the series could not be updated to more recent years since the survey was discontinued in the early 1980s.

Canada. At the beginning of the twentieth century, workers in manufacturing typically put in 59 hours per week spread over six days. By 1957, the standard workweek was reduced to 40 hours over five days. Compared to the dramatic decline in normal work hours that occurred during the first six decades of the last century, Canadian workers have not seen much reduction in standard work time since then. As Figure 5.5 illustrates, the decline in standard weekly hours in manufacturing was not a steady one, as the sharpest drops occurred in the first 20 years of the century and from 1946 to 1957. Between 1901 and 1921, the standard manufacturing workweek fell by eight hours, that is, each year by half an hour. From 1921 to 1946, the trend continued downward but at a much slower pace. In fact, over the more than 20 years the workweek fell by only 1.5 hours. The period between 1946 and 1957 saw a dramatic change of nine hours, a drop of more than three-quarters of an hour a year. Since the early 1960s, the decline levelled off. From 1961 to 1981, weekly manufacturing hours fell by just slightly more than an hour to approximately 39 hours per week. Since then the length of the standard workweek in manufacturing

FIGURE 5.5

Standard Weekly Working Hours in Manufacturing, 1901–81

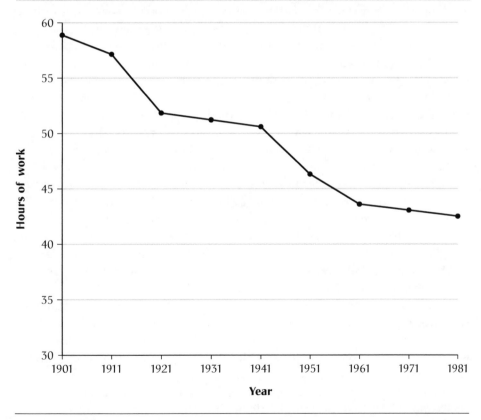

Sources: For 1901–71, Ostry, S., and Zaidi, M. (1979). *Labour Economics in Canada* (3rd ed.). Toronto: Macmillan, pp. 80–81; for 1981, Canadian Department of Labour, Wage Rates, Salaries, and Hours of Labour.

appears to have changed very little. According to the Labour Force Survey, the average number of hours usually worked on the main job in manufacturing was 39.6 in 2003, compared to 34.8 in the service-producing industries.

For the economy as a whole, the average hours usually worked on all jobs per week declined during 1976–2003 by two hours, from 39 to 37 hours.

What Caused the Changes in Standard Working Hours?

The decline in the length of the standard workweek during the first 60 years of the twentieth century was largely due to increased productivity and growth in real wages. As technology advanced, workers produced the same amount in less time. Both employers and employees enjoyed the benefits of growing productivity in the form of higher profits and higher real wages. Rapidly rising real wages allowed workers to trade some of the real wage gains for more leisure and still experience an increase in their standard of living. As long as productivity grew fast enough to keep reduced hours cost-neutral, it was in the employers' interest to accommodate worker and union demands for more free time.

After 1960, the length of the standard workweek "stabilized" despite strong growth in productivity (which lasted until the late 1960s) and continued growth in real wages (which lasted until the mid-1970s). These had been the very conditions that had led to the decline of the standard weekly working hours in the first half of the century. Labour economists offer a variety of supply and demand explanations for this levelling-off.

On the supply side, workers were investing in more years of education. Once they were employed, the pressure to recoup the cost of schooling and forgone wages as quickly as possible made them less likely to trade wage gains for shorter hours. At the same time, the trend to earlier retirement shortened the portion of the life cycle devoted to paid work. This left fewer earning-years during which workers could save for comfortable retirement. Also, workers increasingly opted to take their share of increased productivity in the form of more vacations and other non-wage benefits, rather than further shortening the standard workweek. For example, the average annual vacation in manufacturing rose from 2.7 weeks in 1959 to 3.6 weeks in 1979. Improvements were made in other non-wage benefits as well. Employers' payroll contributions to healthcare, dental care, and pension plans and to mandatory programs such as unemployment insurance, the Canada and Quebec Pension Plans, and workers' compensation almost doubled from 4.6% of labour income in 1961 to 8.7% in 1979.

On the demand side, employers had little incentive to reduce the standard workweek below 38 to 40 hours, since further reductions were unlikely to yield a proportional increase in productivity. Shorter hours could even have a negative effect on productivity as daily "gearing up" and "gearing down" would take a greater proportion of paid work hours.

Many of the factors underlying the stability of the standard hours in the 1960s and 1970s persisted into the 1980s and 1990s. Fringe benefits have continued to increase as a share of labour income, educational attainment has continued to rise, and early retirement has become even more common. Most importantly, however, real wages of full-time, full-year workers have increased only very modestly. Thus workers have had no major wage gains to trade for added leisure. Employers were also unlikely to support a reduction in work hours without a proportional reduction in wages, since the growth in productivity continued to be slow throughout the 1980s. Furthermore, with rapid technological change, employers have increased their investment in job-specific training of full-time staff. Shorter hours of work for these workers would mean a smaller return on that investment.

Changes in the Distribution of Standard Working Hours

While the average workweek, measured in standard or actual hours, has not changed significantly over the last three decades, substantial changes have occurred in the underlying distribution of hours worked. As the proportion of workers with standard workweeks (35 to 40 hours) declined, the proportions working short hours (less than 35) and long hours (more than 40) increased. This shift away from the middle is known as "hours polarization." Between 1976 and 2003, the share of workers who actually worked between 35 and 40 hours per week fell by about 10 percentage points down to 34.7%. The share of workers with shorter actual hours, on the other hand, increased from 34% to 41.5%, and those with longer hours rose from 22% to 23.8%.

More years in school may account for some of the increase in below-standard hours. Part-time employment is usually more feasible than longer work schedules for people attending school. The rise in women's labour force participation and their overrepresentation in part-time and temporary work are also likely to have contributed to the increase in the share of shorter hours. Women outnumber men at the short hours end of the distribution. Although the rise in the frequency of shorter workweeks may partly reflect the response of firms to rising costs and competition, the increasing incidence of above-standard workweeks may be part of the same response. Part-timers and casual workers enable an enterprise to meet shifting levels of demand with minimal current and future costs, but not all tasks are easily divisible and not all workers are substitutable. Long workweeks may be required of those with special skills or management responsibilities. As the proportion of men and women working in professional and managerial occupations has grown, so has the tendency for this group to work above-standard hours. In 2002, 31% of managers worked more than 40 hours per week, with 22% putting in more than 50 hours per week. For professionals, long hours are also quite common. In the case of skilled blue-collar occupations, given administrative and over-head considerations, firms may find it more cost-efficient to offer paid over-time than to hire and train new workers. For example, in 2002, 15% of trades and production workers put in an average of nine overtime hours per week.

The polarization in the distribution of working hours is related to the growing inequality in earnings. Empirical evidence suggests that the growing earnings inequality in Canada is strongly affected by growing inequality in the distribution of working time, as highly paid workers are working more weekly hours while low-paid employees have been working less weekly hours.[23] Differences in working hours between men and women, which we referred to earlier in this chapter, are also central in explaining the male–female earnings gap. At a given wage rate, fewer hours of work translate into lower annual earnings. Fewer hours also mean less opportunity to accumulate work experience and on-the-job training, which will negatively affect labour productivity and earnings.

Summary

The number of employed Canadians has almost tripled over the last five decades. The employment rate is affected by changes in the population and by economic conditions. The rapid growth in the employment rate of women has been a major characteristic of the Canadian job scene. In contrast, the employment rate of men has been steadily declining since the 1940s.

There has been a major shift in the composition of employment toward the service sector, away from resource and manufacturing industries. The relatively faster growth in the service sector can be attributed to a variety of factors, including differences in productivity growth in the goods- and services-producing industries, increases in real income, contracting out of services, intensified international competition, and the increased demand for services by firms in the goods-producing industries.

There have also been shifts in the occupational composition of the labour force, with the greatest employment gains being made in professional, management, and technical occupations. There are some indications that the skill structure of the labour force is becoming more polarized between higher-skilled and lower-skilled workers.

Growth in non-standard employment—that is, part-time work, moonlighting, self-employment, and non-permanent work—has been accelerating in relation to full-time permanent work. The rise in non-standard employment reflects demographic changes in the Canadian labour force as well as changes on the demand side. Firms are increasingly replacing long-term employment contracts with more flexible staffing arrangements to compensate for uncertainties caused by increased foreign and domestic competition and rapid technological change.

Standard hours of work declined up to the early 1960s. Since then, the decline has levelled off, largely due to the slowdown in productivity and the decline in real wages. Recently, the distribution of hours worked has been changing, with the proportion of workers working standard hours declining and the proportion of workers working shorter and longer hours rising.

Key Terms

actual working hours (page 132)

aggregate labour demand (page 107)

employment rate (page 108)

Engel's law (page 115)

fringe benefits (page 129)

functional flexibility (page 131)

hours paid (page 132)

income elasticity of demand (page 116)

marginal productivity of labour (page 113)
moonlighting (page 125)
non-standard employment (page 120)
numerical flexibility (page 131)
open economy (page 116)
own-account self-employment (page 126)

part-time employment (page 121)
payroll tax (page 129)
standard working hours (page 132)
total factor productivity (page 113)
underemployed (page 124)

Weblinks

For Industry Canada, research papers and statistics
www.strategis.ic.gc.ca/sc_ecnmy/engdoc/homepage.html

For research on knowledge workers
www.statcan.gc.ca/pub/11-624-m/11-624-m2003004-eng.pdf

For Statistics Canada Workplace and Employee Survey
www.statcan.gc.ca/survey-enquete/business-entreprise/8104208-eng.htm

For Social Development Canada
www.servicecanada.gc.ca/eng/isp/cpp/cpptoc.shtml

For Association of Workers' Compensation Boards of Canada
www.awcbc.org/en/

Discussion Questions

1. The decline of jobs in the primary and manufacturing sectors and the growth of service jobs have led to the claim that the skill level of the labour force is declining. Assess the validity of the "deskilling" hypothesis.
2. How is the emergence of a knowledge-based economy likely to affect the skill level of the Canadian workforce? Support your position with some examples.
3. Work time arrangements are often the outcome of historical developments. The spread of mass production of manufactured goods made standardized working and machine hours the most appropriate form of work organization. But the trend toward a service economy, the growth in female labour force participation, and the new technologies have increasingly made this model of work organization obsolete. Discuss how each of these three factors has increased the need for more flexible work time.
4. In what way do non-standard forms of employment increase the numerical flexibility of firms?
5. Why has the need for numerical flexibility increased over time?
6. The decline in standard weekly working hours has slowed down over the last 30 years. Evaluate some of the factors that may have contributed to the slowdown.

7. While the proportion of employees working standard hours (35 to 40 hours per week) is declining, the proportion working short hours (fewer than 35) and long hours (41 and over) is increasing. What factors may have contributed to the rising polarization in work hours?

Using the Internet

Access Statistics Canada's website (www.statcan.gc.ca). Search for 56F0004M and click on the Connectedness series. From the Other Issues in This Series menu, click Free and view under "A Profile of Employment in Computer and Telecommunication Industries." Click the link — "A Profile of Employment in Computer and Telecommunications Industries" and download the file 56f0004m2003009-eng.pdf. From the publication, extract the following information:

1. The proportion of university graduates in the computer and telecommunication (CT) workforce in 1990 and 2002, as compared to all other industries
2. The average age of the CT workforce compared to other industries
3. The proportion of part-time employment and self-employment in CT industries compared to the rest of the economy

Which profile of employment in CT industries emerges from the information you collected in Questions 1 to 3? How does this profile compare with the one in other industries?

Exercises

1. Suppose the labour force participation rates in three consecutive years are 65.6%, 66.0%, and 66.9%, and the unemployment rates are 7.5%, 6.8%, and 7.3%. Calculate the corresponding employment rates for the three years.
2. The most important change in the distribution of employment in Canada has been the shift in employment away from the goods-producing industries to the service-producing industries. Explain how Engel's law might apply to this shift.
3. According to Statistics Canada data, over the last 20 years, part-time employment increased by approximately 120% while full-time employment grew by only 36%. Why does the increase in part-time employment of 120% understate the growth of part-time jobs? Why does the increase in full-time employment of 36% overstate the growth of full-time jobs?
4. One of the reasons provided for the shift in employment has been the difference in productivity gains between the manufacturing and service sectors. If productivity rose more in the manufacturing sector than in the service sector, what effect would this have on employment in the manufacturing sector?

5. What is meant by "non-standard employment"? Describe some of the changes in non-standard employment over the last 25 years.
6. It is claimed that the growth in non-standard employment reflects the need for firms to have more flexible staffing arrangements. Why would the need for these arrangements be greater in recent years than in earlier years?

References

[1]Clark, C. (1957). *The Conditions of Economic Progress*. London: St. Martin's Press, p. 492.

[2]Rao, S., Sharpe, A., and Tang, J. (2004). *Productivity Growth in Service Industries: A Canadian Success Story*. Ottawa: Centre for the Study of Living Standards, p. 20.

[3]Ibidem, p. 15.

[4]Theil, H., Cheung, C.-F., and Seale Jr., J.L. (1989). *Advances in Econometrics. Supplement 1, International Evidence on Consumer Patterns*. Greenwich, CT: JAI Press.

[5]Economic Council of Canada. (1991). *Employment in the Service Economy (The Betcherman Report)*. Ottawa: Minister of Supply and Services.

[6]Bluestone, B., and Harrison, B. (1982). *The Deindustrialization of America: Plant Closings, Community Abandonment and the Dismantling of Basic Industries*. New York: Basic Books, p. 111.

[7]Statistics Canada. (2003). 2001 Census: Analysis Series. *The Changing Profile of Canada's Labour Force*. Ottawa: Minister of Industry (Catalogue no. 96F0030XIE2001009), p. 7.

[8]Lavoie, M., and Roy, R. (1998). *Employment in the Knowledge-Based Economy. A Growth Accounting Exercise for Canada*. Applied Research Branch Research Paper R-98-8E. Ottawa: Human Resources Development Canada.

[9]Baldwin, J.R., and Beckstead, D. (2003). *Knowledge Workers in Canada's Economy, 1971–2001*. Statistics Canada. Ottawa: Minister of Industry (Catalogue no. 11-624-MIE-No. 004), p. 5.

[10]Vaillancourt, C. (2003). *A Profile of Employment in Computer and Telecommunications Industries*. Statistics Canada. Connectedness Series, No. 9. Ottawa: Minister of Industry (Catalogue no. 56F00004MIE), p. 8, Table 2.

[11]Brynjolfsson, E., and Hitt, L. (2000). "Beyond Computation: Information Technology, Organizational Transformation and Business Performance." *Journal of Economic Perspectives*, 14: 23–48.

[12]Vosko, L.F., Zukewich, N., and Cranford, C. (2003). "Precarious Jobs: A New Typology of Employment." *Perspectives on Labour and Income*, 15(4): 41.

[13]Statistics Canada. (2000). *Women in Canada*. Ottawa: Minister of Industry (Catalogue no. 89-503-XPE).

[14]Comfort, D., Johnson, K., and Wallace, D. (2003). *Part-Time Work and Family-Friendly Practices in Canadian Workplaces*. Statistics Canada and Human Resources Development Canada, The Evolving Workplace Series. Ottawa: Minister of Industry (Catalogue no. 71-584-MIE), p. 15.

[15]Ibidem, p. 18.

[16]Statistics Canada. (2003). *Women in Canada: Work Chapter Updates*. Ottawa: Minister of Industry (Catalogue no. 89F0133), p. 8.

[17]Kimmel, J., and Powell, L.M. (1999). "Moonlighting Trends and Related Policy Issues in Canada and the United States." *Canadian Public Policy*, 25(2): 207–230.

[18]Manser, M.E., and Picot, G. (1999). "Self-Employment in Canada and the United States." *Perspectives on Labour and Income*, 11(3): 43.

[19]Vosko, L.F., Zukewich, N., and Cranford, C. (2003). "Precarious Jobs: A New Typology of Employment." *Perspectives on Labour and Income*, 15(4): 39.

[20]Lin, Z. (2000). "Payroll Taxes—Recent Trends." *Perspectives on Labour and Income*, 12(3): 25.

[21]Lipsett, B., and Reesor, M. (1997). *Flexible Work Arrangements*. Research paper. Ottawa: Human Resources Development Canada.

[22]Economic Council of Canada. (1990). *Good Jobs, Bad Jobs: Employment in the Service Economy*. Ottawa: Minister of Supply and Services, p. 17.

[23]Morissette, R., Myles, J., and Picot, G. (1994). "Earnings Inequality and the Distribution of Working Time in Canada." *Canadian Business Economics*, 2(3): 3–16.

6

Unemployment

Chapter Learning Objectives

After completing this chapter, you should be able to:

- describe how the amount of unemployment is measured
- discuss the problems that arise in interpreting the official unemployment rate
- distinguish between the frequency of unemployment and the duration of unemployment
- describe the main features of unemployment in Canada
- discuss the gap in unemployment rates between Canada and the U.S.
- distinguish between various types of unemployment and policy initiatives to reduce it
- discuss the factors that may have led to the increase in the natural rate of unemployment

DISCOURAGED WORKERS IN NEWFOUNDLAND

Mary, aged 47, lives in Freshwater, NL. She worked for several years as a fishplant weigher in the local fish plant. She liked her job. Not only did it provide a steady income but it also strengthened her ties to the community. The plant was like an extended family. Everybody knew everybody. Shortly after the federal government declared a two-year moratorium on northern cod fishing, the plant closed and Mary was permanently laid off. Her husband, Patrick, a 49-year-old fish cutter, was also among the 210 workers who lost their jobs.

Mary considered taking a retraining course, but her age and knowledge of the regional labour market, in the end, made her decide against it. If young people with degrees could not find jobs, she reasoned, how would she be able to find employment? After one year of unsuccessful job searching, she gave up. Patrick also left the labour force because he believed that no jobs were available.

Mary and Patrick are classified in Statistics Canada's Labour Force Survey as discouraged workers. Although they are without jobs and would like to work, they are no longer counted as unemployed because they have given up looking for work. In 2003, Newfoundland had an unemployment rate of almost 17%, the highest in the country. If the number of discouraged workers had been added to the official unemployment figure, the jobless rate would have increased to 21%.

In Chapters 4 and 5, the steady increases in both the labour force and the level of employment over the last 50 years were described. If we compare the development of the labour force (labour supply) and employment (labour demand) in Figure 6.1, we notice that the overall trend increase in employment has been lower than the trend increase in the labour force. One reason can be found in the fact that recessions have a relatively larger negative impact on labour demand than on labour supply. While labour demand is greatly reduced in recessions due to layoffs, labour supply is less affected since most of the unemployed seeking work remain part of the labour force. Note the large declines in employment during the last two recessions in 1981–82 and 1990–91 as compared to the relatively minor changes in labour supply.

Since unemployment is the difference between the quantity of labour supplied and the quantity of labour demanded, differences in the growth of the labour force and employment must affect the level of unemployment. Before looking at unemployment in Canada and the reasons behind the phenomenon, we consider how unemployment is measured and what problems arise in interpreting unemployment statistics.

FIGURE 6.1

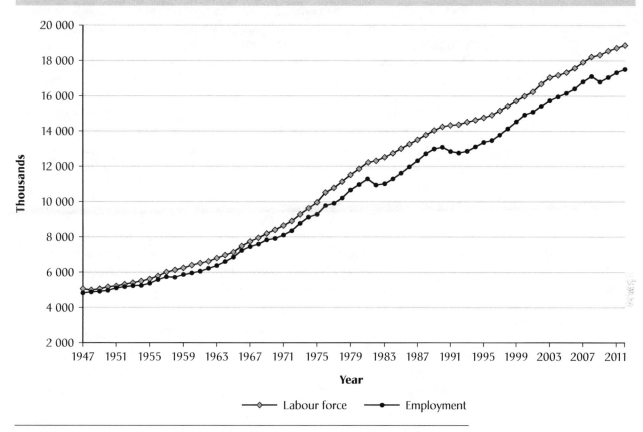

Labour Force and Employment Growth, 1947–2012

Sources: For 1947–75, adapted from Statistics Canada. (1995). *Canadian Economic Observer, Historical Statistical Supplement 1994/5*. Catalogue no. 11–210; for 1976–2012, adapted from Statistics Canada CANSIM, table 282-0002.

How Is Unemployment Measured?

Different countries use different methods for estimating the number of unemployed. For example, in France, Germany, and the United Kingdom, a person is recorded as unemployed if he or she is registered with one of the employment offices as a claimant for unemployment insurance benefits. This method of measuring unemployment can lead to serious underestimation of unemployment rates. For example, young people or adult women who enter the labour force for the first time and cannot find employment would not be registered as unemployed because they are not eligible for employment (or unemployment) insurance benefits. Likewise, long-term unemployed individuals who have exhausted their claims and are not receiving benefits are not included in this count.

Canada and the United States use the survey method to collect unemployment data.[i] As mentioned in Chapter 4, the Canadian unemployment statistics released each month are based on the Labour Force Survey conducted by Statistics Canada. To be counted as unemployed a person must be without work, must be available for work, and must have actively looked for work within the past four weeks. The criterion "actively looking for work" is defined as making some effort to find work, for example, answering a want ad, going for a job interview, or asking friends for job leads. The condition of active job search is waived for persons on temporary layoff and for people with a new job scheduled to start in four weeks or less. In both cases, it is assumed that the only reason these people are not looking for work is that they already have a job and would have worked in the reference week had work been available. As noted, a person must be available for work in order to be classified as unemployed. One would naturally expect that most people looking for work are in fact available for work, but although this is generally true, there are exceptions. For example, students looking for full-time summer jobs during the spring months are not currently available for work. Until they are free to take a full-time job, they are not part of the labour supply and are accordingly counted as not in the labour force.

unemployment rate

percentage of the labour force that is unemployed

The **unemployment rate** is the percentage of the labour force that is unemployed:

$$Unemployment\ rate = \frac{Number\ of\ unemployed\ people}{Labour\ force} \times 100$$

In 2012, the labour force included 18.876 million people, of whom 17.508 million were employed and 1.368 million were unemployed. The unemployment rate was thus 7.2%:

$$\left(\frac{1.368}{18.876}\right) \times 100 = 7.2\%$$

Do the Official Unemployment Figures Measure What They Ought To?

Measuring the amount of unemployment in the economy appears to be a straightforward task. In fact, it is not. There are several reasons why the official statistics may not accurately reflect the true amount of unemployment.

Inactive Job Seekers

The unemployment rate may overstate the extent of unemployment by including individuals who have only a weak attachment to the labour force. For example, some of those who report being unemployed may, in fact, not have been engaged in serious job search; when asked directly if they looked

[i] The different ways unemployment data are collected make international comparisons difficult.

for work, they might give a positive answer even though they may have at best answered one newspaper ad during the survey month, or gone for one interview to tender an application. They may be calling themselves unemployed in order to qualify for one of the government programs that provide financial assistance to the unemployed. It may be more realistic to view some of these people as out of the labour force.

Discouraged Workers

The officially reported unemployment rate may understate the true unemployment level in the labour force because it excludes the **discouraged workers**. These are people who are available and willing to work but have given up looking for work because they believe nothing suitable is available. People who decide to stop looking for work are classified as having dropped out of the labour force rather than as unemployed. Discouraged workers are not counted in the official unemployment statistics, even though they are interested in working, and are referred to as the **hidden unemployed**.

A simple example shows how the discouraged-worker effect lowers the unemployment rate. Assume there are 1.5 million unemployed out of a labour force of 17 million. This would mean an unemployment rate of $1.5/17 = 0.088$ or 8.8%. If 100 000 of these 1.5 million unemployed people simply stopped looking for work and dropped out of the labour force, there would be 1.4 million unemployed out of a labour force of 16.9 million. The unemployment rate would have dropped to $1.4/16.9 = 0.082$ or 8.2%.

Statistics Canada produces data on the discouraged worker from two sources. The first is the Labour Force Survey; the second is an annual supplement to the Labour Force Survey called the Survey of Job Opportunities. Discouragement in the labour force is measured through a series of questions. The survey asks willing and available workers who are not searching for work why they are not actively looking. One possible response is that the respondent believes no work is available. In 1997, 108 000 individuals chose this response. If these discouraged workers had been counted as unemployed instead of as being outside of the labour force, the officially recorded unemployment rate would have increased from 9.2% to 9.9%. In 2012, if discouraged workers had been included in the unemployment count (see R_5 in Table 6.1, page 148) the official unemployment rate would have increased from 7.2% to 7.4%.

The discouraged-worker effect is generally larger in times of recession, when unemployed people often become so discouraged that they stop looking for work. They are then classified as having dropped out of the labour force rather than as being unemployed. As a consequence, the increase in the official unemployment rate during a recession is smaller than would have been the case had the discouraged workers been counted as unemployed. Similarly, during expansions, people become encouraged about their job prospects. Once they begin looking for jobs they are considered part of the

discouraged workers
persons who want a job but have given up looking for work

hidden unemployed
discouraged workers who do not show up as unemployed on the Labour Force Survey

labour force. As a result, the decline in the unemployment rate, particularly in the early stage of a recovery, is smaller than it would have been had these people remained outside the labour force.

Underemployed Workers

The official unemployment account may also understate the true unemployment situation because those involuntarily employed part-time are recorded as employed rather than partly unemployed. "Unemployed" includes only those who did not work at all during the reference week. The group of those who work up to 30 hours in total regardless of the number of jobs, but who would prefer to work full-time (i.e., the involuntary part-time worker), can be large. This group is referred to as underemployed workers. As stated in Chapter 5, involuntary part-time employment has shown a marked increase over the last 20 years.

When sales decline, employers often react by reducing the hours of work before beginning to lay off workers. This reduction can take various forms; one form is to change full-time jobs into part-time jobs. Involuntary part-time employment tends to follow the business cycle. In times of recession, the number of full-time jobs decreases, while involuntary part-time work increases. Faced with the prospect of unemployment, workers often have no choice but to accept part-time positions, even when they would prefer full-time work. Thus labour hoarding, or the underutilization of employed labour, can imply a loss of millions of work hours that does not show up in the official unemployment statistics because these record only head counts. The unemployment rate and the rate of involuntary part-time employment are generally moving in the same direction. While the unemployment rate has declined significantly in recent years, the involuntary part-time employment rate has remained well above what it was in the early 1980s. Despite the overall improvement in the labour market as shown by the declining unemployment rate, the involuntary part-time rate revealed persistent underemployment. As the data in Table 6.1 (page 148) indicate, if the full-time equivalent of the involuntary part-timers had been included in the unemployment count (R_7), the unemployment rate would have been 9.6 rather than 7.2.

Marginal Workers

marginal workers

workers with a weak attachment to the labour force

Marginal workers are workers with a weak labour force attachment. Typically, young people (aged 15 to 24) belong to the group of marginal workers. Their tenuous attachment to the labour force is reflected in their frequent moves into and out of the labour force. Of those who are still in school, some may work sporadically during the school year; others seek employment only during the summer months. Among those not in school, many are not interested in, or cannot find, longer-term employment, and change frequently between casual jobs and non-market activities.

The ever-changing balance between market and non-market activities among marginal workers makes it difficult to draw lines around the three categories of employed, unemployed, and not in the labour force. The behaviour

Part II: Trends and Recent Developments in the Canadian Labour Market

of marginal workers severely complicates the interpretation of standard labour market statistics. Several labour economists have adopted the viewpoint that the distinction between a person who is unemployed and a person who is not in the labour force becomes meaningless for marginal workers because the behaviour of most of the unemployed and many persons outside the labour force is functionally indistinguishable. They suggest combining the unemployed with those not in the labour force in a category of non-employed or jobless and focusing, for example, in the case of youths, on the analysis of youth non-employment rather than merely on youth unemployment. Similar proposals replaced the old classification with two new categories: economically active (employed, those engaged in household work, and enrolled students), and the economically inactive (unemployed and all others). Whether the categories "unemployed" and "not in the labour force" are behaviourally distinct labour force states is ultimately an empirical question. Some tests have rejected the idea that the two categories are meaningless in terms of behaviour.[1] They conclude that the marginally attached are a distinct group behaving differently from the unemployed and those outside of the labour force. It would seem that our understanding of the group of marginal workers is still too limited to justify a revision of the conventional classification of labour market status. Nevertheless, the discussion reflects some doubts that the unemployment rate is a useful measure of unused labour for certain groups in the labour force.

The conclusion we can draw is that one single measure of unemployment, such as the official unemployment rate, cannot capture the complexity of the labour market. To complement the official unemployment rate, Statistics Canada has developed several additional measures. Table 6.1 shows these supplementary measures of unemployment for the year 2012, in which the official unemployment rate was 7.2%.

Using some of the supplementary measures in conjunction with the official unemployment rate provides a more complete picture of the underutilization of labour in the economy.

The Unemployment Rate as a Measure of Economic Hardship

The unemployment rate is used not only to measure the extent of unused labour but also as an indicator of economic hardship. Economic hardship occurs when the level of income is not enough to provide for minimum consumption requirements. An unemployed person does not receive any income from work. The larger the number of unemployed people in an economy, the greater the loss of earnings. There are several reasons, however, to suggest that hardship associated with unemployment has weakened over the last decades.

One reason is the change from the single-earner family to the dual-earner or multi-earner family, a change we described in Chapter 4. In earlier times, when the single-earner family dominated, the family's economic well-being depended on the employment of the single breadwinner, usually the man in

TABLE 6.1

Supplementary Measures of Unemployment and Percentage Point Change from the Official Unemployment Rate, 2012

		%	% POINT CHANGE FROM THE OFFICIAL UNEMPLOYMENT RATE
R_1	Counting only those unemployed one year or more	0.9	−6.3
R_2	Counting only those unemployed three months or more	2.6	−4.6
R_3	Made comparable to the U.S. official rate	6.3	−0.9
R_4	**Official unemployment rate**	**7.2**	
R_5	Official rate plus discouraged workers	7.4	0.2
R_6	Official rate plus those waiting for recall, replies, and long-term future starts	7.9	0.7
R_7	Official rate plus involuntary part-timers (in full-time equivalents)	9.6	2.4
R_8	Official rate plus discouraged searchers, waiting group and portion of involuntary part-timers	10.0	2.8

Source: Statistics Canada CANSIM, table 282-0086.

the family. As more and more women enter the labour force on a permanent basis, the family relies less on the employment income of any one member. In recent times, the majority of families with one member unemployed have at least one employed member, and many have two or more employed. Another reason has been the increase in income transfer programs, in particular the availability of employment insurance benefits. In the absence of such programs, the standard of living depends on the availability of employment and the adequacy of earnings. With the creation of the unemployment insurance system in the early 1940s and the growth of payments and coverage, particularly since 1971–72, families became more protected against loss of income due to unemployment. Although the level of benefits and the eligibility period have been reduced in recent years, the system still provides a substantial buffer against financial hardship caused by unemployment.

The degree of financial hardship caused by unemployment depends on many factors. Whether, for example, a person is unemployed for 4 weeks or for 40 weeks, or whether a family experiencing unemployment has no children or several children significantly affects the economic strain caused by unemployment. An aggregate figure, such as the official unemployment rate, clearly cannot reveal all these factors. In Table 6.1, two of the measures in the list of supplementary unemployment rates, R_1 and R_2, are more indicative of possible hardship associated with unemployment. R_1 relates to long-term unemployment. The underlying assumption is that those out of work for prolonged periods of time are more likely to suffer financial loss and will have a harder time finding a new job than those unemployed for short spells.

An Alternative Measure of the Utilization of Labour

The unemployment rate is supposed to measure the proportion of people who are without work and are actively seeking work. It measures the degree of *underutilization* of labour. An alternative way to assess the tightness or slack in the labour market is to focus on the utilization of labour. One measure is the employment rate or the employment–population ratio (E/P). The employment rate measures the proportion of the civilian population of working age that is employed:

$$Employment\ rate = \frac{Total\ number\ of\ employed}{Population\ of\ working\ age} \times 100$$

The employment rate has at least two important advantages over the unemployment rate. One is that employment figures in the numerator represent a more reliable statistic than the unemployment figures in the numerator of the unemployment rate. It is easier to establish whether a person is employed than whether a person is unemployed.

The other advantage of using the employment rate is that it makes redundant the sometimes hazy distinction between being in the labour force and not being in the labour force. The unemployment rate uses the labour force as its base, whereas the employment rate uses the total civilian population, excluding certain age groups and people in institutions. In this way, the sometimes difficult distinction between being in or out of the labour force need not be made. Also, the employment rate is a more consistent measure to compare over time. The population as a denominator is a more stable base than the labour force, because the working-age population hardly changes over the business cycle. In contrast, the labour force expands or contracts over the business cycle as people drop out of and move back into the labour force in response to changes in employment opportunities. As a result, unemployment rates change significantly due to changes in the denominator, thus giving a possibly wrong picture of the labour market situation. Take the case of an economic recovery during which the labour force participation rate increases significantly, and the unemployment rate declines. Focusing on the unemployment rate would understate the strength of the recovery if the employment gain exceeds the unemployment reduction.

Although the employment rate is undisturbed by the shifts of workers into or out of the labour force, the measure is not without its own problems. Estimates of unemployment focus on a problem, similarly to statistics on illness, crime, and poverty. The unemployment rate reports the number of people who cannot find work. For them, the economy has failed since it has not provided a job. The employment rate stresses a strength in the economy, namely its capacity to create jobs. Labour economists are divided over the question of whether the employment rate is a better indicator of the state of the labour market than the unemployment rate. An increase in the labour force participation rate (LFPR), for example, can be associated with simultaneous increases in employment and unemployment:

$$LFPR = \frac{Number\ of\ employed + Number\ of\ unemployed}{Working\text{-}age\ population}$$

In this case, the increases in the employment rate and the unemployment rate give very different pictures of the strength in the labour market. The increase in the employment rate captures only the employment effect and ignores the unemployment effect, thereby understating the weakness in the labour market. If one adopts the view that the strength of a labour market should be measured by the ability of job seekers to find jobs, then a rising unemployment rate would indicate that the labour market is not strong enough to provide jobs to all who look for work. If both indicators increase simultaneously, there is clearly some ambiguity as to whether or not the economy is doing well in providing jobs.

There is growing awareness that the unemployment rate and the employment rate should be used in conjunction with each other. For instance, if the employment rate and the labour force participation rate increase simultaneously and the unemployment rate is stable or even declines, this would indicate that the labour market is creating a sufficient number of jobs. If, however, the employment rate and the unemployment rate both increase, a look at the size of the increase in the LFPR would be necessary to assess the strength in the labour market.

Characteristics of Canadian Unemployment

Figure 6.2 shows the postwar history of the unemployment rate. Three features stand out.

First, since World War II, the unemployment rate has been on an upward trend. Unemployment seems to fluctuate around an increasing average rate: 4% in the 1950s, 5% in the 1960s, close to 7% in the 1970s, about 9% in the 1980s, and 9.5% in the 1990s. From 2000 to 2008, however, the average rate fell to 6.9%. The unemployment rate increased to 8.3% in 2009, during the financial crisis. It dropped to 7.2% in 2012 as economic recovery took place.

Second, there are large fluctuations in the unemployment rate; the unemployment rate has fluctuated between 2% and 12% since 1947. These fluctuations are closely related with recessions and expansions. Note that the increases in unemployment were much steeper in the last two recessions than in earlier recessions: unemployment peaked at 11.9% in the recession of the early 1980s, and at 11.3% in the recession of the early 1990s. Unemployment during the recession after the financial crisis increased to 8.3% in 2009 from 6.1% in 2008.

Third, unemployment rates exhibit some persistence over time; once high, they tend to remain high for some period. During the 1990s, for example, Canada experienced a sustained period of high unemployment. Starting in 1991, the unemployment rate remained within the 11% to 9% range for seven years.

The unemployment rate officially published by Statistics Canada represents a snapshot of only limited information. Looking at the unemployment rate tells us little about how people become unemployed, or how long they stay unemployed. As we pointed out in the discussion of the flow approach

FIGURE 6.2

Unemployment Rate, 1947–2012

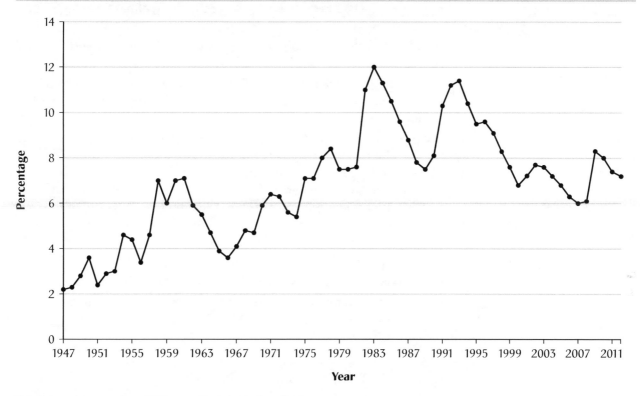

Notes: Annual averages from 1950 onward include Newfoundland.
Population aged 15 and over from 1966. Data prior to 1966 are based on population aged 14 and over.
Estimates prior to 1966 have not been adjusted to conform to current concepts.

Sources: For 1947–65, adapted from Statistics Canada. (1985, November). *The Labour Force.* Ottawa:
Statistics Canada (Catalogue no. 71-001); for 1966–75, adapted from Statistics Canada. (1999). *Historical
Labour Force Statistics, 1966–1998.* Ottawa: Statistics Canada (Catalogue no. 71-201); for 1976–2012,
adapted from Statistics Canada CANSIM, table 282-0002.

in Chapter 2, we can learn a lot from an analysis of labour market dynamics.
Figure 6.3 (page 152) shows the flows among the three labour market states of
employment (E), unemployment (U), and not in the labour force (N).

The Incidence of Unemployment

In any month, many people become unemployed and many others leave the
state of unemployment. Figure 6.3 illustrates the flows among the three labour
market states that affect the number of unemployed people at any given time.
There are two flows into unemployment (U): one from the pool of the
employed (E), and one from outside of the labour force (N). The two flows
include four groups of people:

- Workers who have been laid off (a layoff means that the person was not fired and may return to the old job if demand for the firm's product recovers)
- Workers who have lost their job permanently, either by being fired or because the firm closed down
- Workers who quit a job in order to look for alternative work
- Persons who are new entrants into the labour force (individuals looking for work for the first time) or who are re-entrants (individuals returning to the labour force after not having looked for work for more than four weeks)

incidence of unemployment

the proportion of people in the labour force entering the state of unemployment in a given period

The proportion of people in the labour force who become unemployed in a given period is called the **incidence of unemployment**. The incidence varies with the size of the flows into unemployment.

As people constantly enter unemployment, others leave unemployment. The two flows into unemployment are matched by two flows out of the state of unemployment: one from U to E, and one from U to N. The two flows include the following three groups of people:

- Persons who are hired into a new job
- Workers who have been laid off and are recalled by their employer
- Unemployed people who stop looking for work and thus, by definition, leave the labour force

FIGURE 6.3

Flows Among the Three Labour Market States

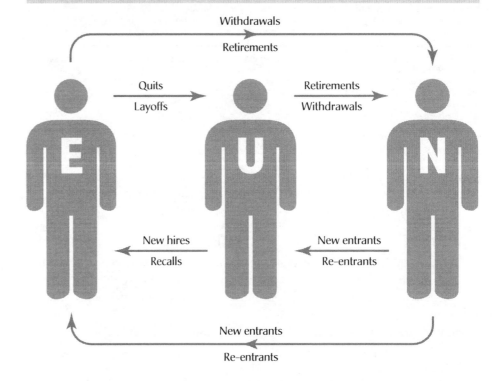

Part II: Trends and Recent Developments in the Canadian Labour Market

Flow analysis of unemployment is an instructive way of thinking about changes in unemployment. Unemployment rises when more people enter the pool of unemployed than are leaving. When we break down unemployment into the various flows, we can see that job losers—that is, people who are laid off either permanently or temporarily—are the biggest source in the incidence of unemployment. Over the last 30 years, they accounted for 40% to 60% of all unemployment.[2] Their number fluctuates greatly over the business cycle, increasing in recessions and contracting when the economy expands. In the recession of 1990–92, on any given day in Canada, almost 1 million of the 1.6 million unemployed people were job losers. In contrast, in the business cycle peak year of 1989, fewer than 500 000 of the 1 million unemployed were job losers. New entrants and re-entrants constitute the second-largest component of the unemployed. They account for one-quarter to one-third of unemployment. On any given day, around 300 000 unemployed people are entrants or re-entrants. Job leavers—that is, people who have voluntarily quit their jobs—are the smallest and most stable group among the unemployed. Their contribution to total unemployment varies between 10% and 15%. On any given day, around 200 000 people are job leavers. Although this number is relatively constant, it fluctuates slightly according to the business cycle: a larger number of people quit their jobs in good economic times than in bad times.

The Duration of Unemployment

The unemployment rate depends not only on the proportion of people becoming unemployed but also on the average time each person spends unemployed (the **duration of unemployment**). The simplest way to calculate the duration of unemployment is to look at the average duration of unemployment for those currently unemployed. Since these spells are in progress rather than completed, this duration measure is only an approximation.

duration of unemployment
the average time each person spends unemployed

It is essential to distinguish between the relative contributions of duration and incidence to the overall unemployment rate in order to assess the economic and social impacts of unemployment. A yearly unemployment rate of 9%, for example, may indicate that 9% of all members of the labour force are unemployed for one year. The unemployment rate (UR) can be approximated by the product of the incidence of unemployment (I) and the average duration of unemployment (D):

$$UR = I \times D$$

In our example, 9% would be the incidence and 52 weeks would be the average duration, so the product is $0.09 \times 52/52$. A 9% unemployment rate, however, could also describe a situation in which 80% of the labour force experiences unemployment once a year for six weeks ($0.80 \times 6/52$). An overall unemployment rate of 9% is thus consistent with considerably different durations and incidences of unemployment.

If turnover among the unemployed is rapid and an increase in unemployment occurs because more people are experiencing brief spells of unemployment, this situation poses a less serious problem than one in which the burden of unemployment is borne mainly by people experiencing longer spells of unemployment. Workers unemployed for many months or even longer than a year are more likely to suffer economic hardship, diminished social status, and lasting physical and psychological harm. Prolonged unemployment saps the will and initiative of the unemployed and furthermore leads to loss of valuable work experience. Employers tend to use the unemployment record as a screening device, eliminating job applicants with longer spells of unemployment. As an individual's duration of unemployment grows, the probability of finding employment declines.

From the mid-1970s to the mid-1990s the average duration of unemployment almost doubled: from 14 weeks in 1976 to 26 weeks in 1994. Since 1994, the average duration has gradually declined. In 2002, it was 16 weeks. The incidence of unemployment rose between 1976 and 2002 from 2.2 to 2.6.

Although the average duration of unemployment did increase, most people who become unemployed in any given month nevertheless remain unemployed for only a short time. In 2002, for example, 63% of unemployed people in Canada were unemployed for fewer than 14 weeks.[ii] Approximately one-third of the unemployed leave unemployment within one month. The observation that most unemployment spells are short, however, does not imply that most unemployment is due to short spells. The mean duration of unemployment spells does not indicate the fraction of overall unemployment attributable to unemployment spells of different durations. Both measures tell very different stories.

Consider the following example. Assume that 20 spells of unemployment begin each week, each lasting three weeks, and that one spell begins each week lasting 30 weeks. The mean duration of unemployment is approximately four weeks (90 weeks divided by 21 spells). However, one-third of total unemployment is due to one spell. While the majority of unemployment spells in Canada are still of relatively short duration, the relative importance of long-term unemployment in total unemployment has increased significantly.

From 1976 to 2002, the proportion of unemployed people without work for one year or longer more than doubled, from 4% to 9.3%. An increase also occurred for those unemployed for six months or more. Taken together, the share of long-term unemployment rose from 14.5% to 18%. Unemployment became more concentrated among a subset of workers in the labour force. Who are generally the long-term unemployed? The unskilled members of racial minorities, workers nearing retirement age, and people who live in economically depressed areas most frequently have problems finding employment.

The overall unemployment rate not only conceals how long people are unemployed but also conceals large differences in unemployment rates among various groups and regions.

[ii] To measure the duration of unemployment by the mean length of unemployment spells may be misleading. For example, many of the discouraged workers withdrawing from the labour force will re-enter the labour force at a later point when economic circumstances appear to have improved. If we count the time outside the labour force as unemployed, the average duration of unemployment clearly would increase.

Demographic Differences in Unemployment

The English political economist Thomas R. Malthus once referred to the unemployed as "those unhappy persons who in the great lottery of life draw a blank." The reference to a lottery might evoke the idea that all participants have the same chance of drawing a blank. The conception of a random draw, however, would be wrong. The lottery of unemployment is heavily biased. As Figure 6.4 (page 156) shows, some groups in our society are much more prone to unemployment than others.

Youth Unemployment

Unemployment of youths (people aged 15 to 24 years), particularly of teenagers, is always much higher than for the other age groups. In 2012, for example, the youth unemployment rate of 14.3% was over twice the adult rate of 6.0%, with the unemployment rate of teenagers at 20.1% being more than three times the adult rate. Although young people constitute only about 15% of the labour force, they make up nearly 30% of all unemployed.

As mentioned in earlier chapters, there are several reasons why young people experience consistently higher unemployment. First, movement from job to job is particularly common for young workers as they try to find out what kind of work is best suited for them.

Second, movement into and out of the labour force is also much more frequent as young people alternate between work, schooling, and other non-market activities. Many young people are not ready to settle into permanent employment immediately after leaving school. To interpret the higher job and labour force turnover of youth as a reflection of weaker work attachment, however, only tells part of the story. Many firms that offer stable employment, higher wages, and good working conditions are reluctant to hire youth. Young people are, therefore, often forced into jobs that involve low wages, poor working conditions, and little opportunity for skill acquisition and advancement within firms. From the worker's viewpoint these types of jobs are very much alike; changing between them does not entail noticeable advantages or disadvantages. Whatever the reasons for the frequent job changes and movements into and out of the labour force are, they often are associated with spells of unemployment.

A third reason for relatively high youth unemployment is that firms often hire young people on a short-term trial basis. Consequently, the rate of job loss is higher for youths than for adult workers. In cases of temporary or permanent layoffs in which the seniority principle is applied, young people who have little seniority are the first laid off.

Last, young people also have more difficulty finding jobs because they often lack training or work experience.

The relatively high unemployment of teens and young adults raises particular concern because frequent or long-duration unemployment experienced at an early age may have long-term "scarring effects." Early unemployment may set off a recurrent cycle of unemployment. With each

FIGURE 6.4

Unemployment Rates Across Demographic Groups, 1976–2012

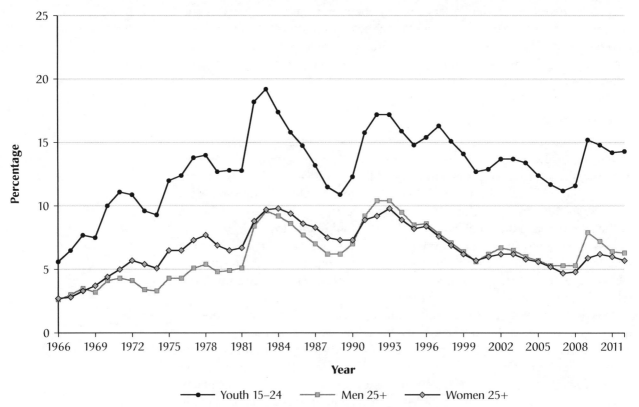

Notes: Annual data prior to 1950 exclude Newfoundland and Labrador.
Estimates prior to 1966 are based on persons aged 14 and over.
Estimates from 1966 include persons aged 15 and over.
Estimates from 1966 to 1974 have been adjusted to conform to current concepts. Estimates prior to 1966 have not been revised.

Source: Adapted from Statistics Canada CANSIM, table 282-0002.

spell of unemployment, poor work habits and discouragement may intensify, leading to further bouts of unemployment or to total withdrawal from the labour force. Related to this vicious cycle of unemployment is the notion of tracking. Young people face a limited number of entry-level jobs that lead to better jobs. Those who miss the good jobs are permanently tracked onto dead-end jobs characterized by high turnover rates. One possible way to break the cycle of recurrent unemployment at a young age is general and vocational training. The European apprenticeship system, in which young people receive extensive on-the-job training, is often credited not only with easing the school-to-work transition but also with making young people productive workers in the long term.

While youth unemployment rates have been persistently higher than adult rates, their ratio has varied considerably over time. As Figure 6.4 indicates, unemployment of youths relative to adults tends to worsen during recessions and improves in times of economic expansion. Throughout the 1990s, the labour market for young people deteriorated markedly, as is shown by the wide gap between youth and adult unemployment rates. The relative rise in youth unemployment in recent years reflects largely the increasing unemployment of full-time students looking for part-time work.[3] A possible explanation of more students seeking work may be the rapid rise of postsecondary tuition fees. From 1990–91 to 2004–05, university tuition rose by 185%.

Female Unemployment

Throughout the 1970s and 1980s, adult women had higher unemployment rates than men. As Figure 6.4 indicates, the gap generally narrows during recessions. The service sector, where most women are employed, is generally less sensitive to business cycle influences than is the manufacturing sector. During the 1990–92 recession, which hit the manufacturing sector particularly hard, the unemployment rate for adult men exceeded that for adult women. Since then, the unemployment rate for adult women has stayed slightly below the one for men.

It is not yet clear whether the reversal is a temporary phenomenon or whether male–female differences in unemployment rates are a thing of the past. One of the reasons cited for the relatively higher unemployment of youth also applies for adult women: the relatively high proportion of re-entrants to the labour force. Among unemployed adult females, an average of roughly one-third are re-entrants who had been out of the workforce for longer than one year. Female re-entrants typically have had work experience interrupted by family responsibilities, especially child rearing. Aside from this structural factor, the proportion of entrants and re-entrants always rises with the rate of increase of the labour force participation rate. A certain amount of female unemployment, therefore, is the result of the rapidly expanding female workforce.

Other Factors

Factors other than age and gender bias the unemployment lottery. Members of visible minorities are much more likely to be out of work than the rest of the population. According to the 2001 Census, Canada's Aboriginal peoples suffer unemployment nearly three times as high as non-Aboriginal Canadians. Foreign-born Blacks in their prime working age (persons aged 25–54) had an unemployment rate of 9.6%, compared with 6.2% for all Canadians in this age group.[4] There are also significant variations in unemployment across occupations. Workers categorized as unskilled or semi-skilled experience unemployment rates four to five times as high as those of managerial and professional workers. Relatedly, differences in educational attainment level affect the incidence and duration of unemployment.

Unemployment rates are lowest for those with university degrees, followed by those who hold other postsecondary diplomas and certificates. High school dropouts experience unemployment rates 2.5 times higher than their age counterparts with a completed high school certificate.

Regional Differences in Unemployment

Unemployment rates also differ across regions of the country, as can be seen in Figure 6.5. These differences have persisted over the last 50 years. Unemployment tends to be highest in the Atlantic region, followed by Quebec and British Columbia. The lowest unemployment rates are found in Ontario and on the Prairies. Although the unemployment rate in the Atlantic region has been consistently higher than in the rest of the country, the difference has grown since the 1970s. In 2012, the unemployment rate ranged from a low of 4.6% in Alberta to a high of 12.5% in Newfoundland and Labrador. Even within provinces, there can be significant variation by area. Ontario, for example, had an overall unemployment rate of 7.8% in 2011; this rate included unemployment of 8.4% in Toronto, 6.3% in Ottawa and 7.1% in the Hamilton-Niagara Peninsula. Nova Scotia's unemployment rate was 8.8%, but in Halifax it was 6.0%.

In the Atlantic provinces and Quebec, with the exception of the few metropolitan areas, labour markets are relatively small. The range of jobs available to job seekers is limited, and employers have a less varied pool of skills to draw from. The recent collapse of the fishing industry in the Atlantic provinces has limited the number of available jobs even further. In addition to the limited size of the labour market, higher job and labour force turnover in these regions results in a higher incidence of unemployment. These higher rates stem from at least two related sources. Many people are accustomed to pursuing a way of life that involves employment in several, often seasonal, industries such as fishing, small farming, and logging during the course of a year, with a relatively high chance of experiencing unemployment in between. At the same time, low-paying casual jobs are in relatively greater supply than regular, more stable employment, making continuous attachment to the labour force more difficult.

Although migration from the Maritime provinces to Central and Western Canada has been occurring, migration has been insufficient to alleviate the problem of regional differences in unemployment. Workers often cannot, or will not, move to take advantage of job opportunities in other parts of Canada. Migration patterns sometimes reinforce unemployment in the high-unemployment regions. When unemployment increases across the country, and people who have migrated in previous years lose a job, they often return to their province of origin (known as return migration). Unemployment is often easier to endure in a familiar environment. As return migration increases during recessions, the rate of migration in the other direction (out-migration) often drops because the pull factor of higher wages is outweighed by the higher risk of not finding a job in the new province.

FIGURE 6.5

Regional Unemployment Rates, 1976–2011

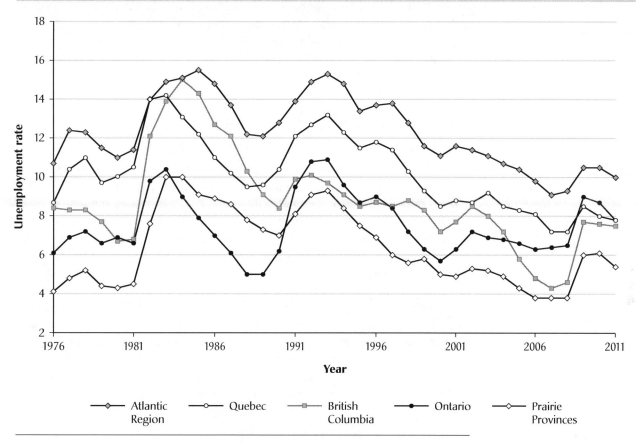

Source: Adapted from Statistics Canada CANSIM, table 282-0002.

The economy in British Columbia has largely been dependent on natural resource industries and relies heavily on exports. Since these industries are very sensitive to the business cycle, British Columbia generally experiences larger fluctuations in economic activity than most other provinces, and accordingly reports relatively large fluctuations in unemployment. The Asian economic crisis in 1997–98 and the financial crisis in the late 2000s, for example, hit the B.C. economy and its labour market particularly hard.

Ontario has the most diversified economy, with a large manufacturing and service sector. While many manufacturing industries (in particular the auto sector) are highly cyclical, most service industries are less dependent on the business cycle. The 1990–92 and late 2000s recessions very severely affected Ontario's manufacturing sector, causing large layoffs. Between 1989 and 1992, the unemployment rate more than doubled from 5.1% to 10.9%. From 1993 to 2000, the unemployment rate decreased and dropped to 5.7% in 2000. During the financial crisis, the unemployment rate jumped to 9% in 2009 from 6.5% in 2008. As economic recovery took place, unemployment decreased to 8.7% in 2010 and 7.8% in 2011. In 2012, it stayed at 7.8%. The last two recessions had a bigger impact on Ontario than on any other province.

Unemployment generally tends to be lower in agricultural regions. Canada is no exception. The largely agricultural provinces of Manitoba and Saskatchewan traditionally have experienced the lowest unemployment rates in the country. When Alberta—with its heavy reliance on the gas and oil industry—is added, a stronger cyclical unemployment pattern emerges in the Prairie provinces. Production and employment in the gas and oil industry follows the business cycle much more closely, compared to production and employment in agriculture.

Unemployment in Canada and the United States Compared

An important labour market development in the past 20 years has been the growing gap between the Canadian and U.S. unemployment rates. As Figure 6.6 shows, from 1947 to the beginning of the 1980s, the unemployment rates in Canada and the United States were remarkably similar, both in their levels and in the timing of their rises and falls. Economists are divided over whether to date the beginning of the divergence in 1977 or in 1982. In the 1980s, the Canada–U.S. unemployment rate gap was about 2 percentage points. During the 1990s, the gap averaged almost 4 percentage points. Starting 2009, the US employment rate was well above the level in Canada as the US was hit hardest during the financial crisis. The unemployment differential has affected both men and women, all regions, all age groups, all industries and occupations, and all educational attainment groups.

Why has Canada historically experienced unemployment well above the level in the United States? A number of key points have emerged from recent research.[5]

Macroeconomic Performance

Both countries experienced recessions in the early 1980s and 1990s but, for the first time, the recessions were deeper in Canada than in the United States. It therefore seems reasonable to attribute the relative increase in Canadian unemployment to the greater severity of the two recessions in Canada. The economic recovery and expansion in the latter part of the 1980s, however, was stronger in Canada than in the United States. The simultaneous increase in the labour force participation rate and the employment–population ratio throughout the 1980s also indicates a strong employment performance in Canada. It is, therefore, difficult to explain the persistent unemployment gap during the 1980s as simply a weaker performance by the Canadian economy.

The situation in the 1990s was markedly different. Between 1989 and 1996, the performance in terms of real output growth was much weaker in Canada compared to the United States, and both the participation rate and the employment–population ratio dropped significantly compared to the United States. All three measures of economic activity indicate a substantial deterioration in the Canadian economy. Thus, in contrast to the 1980s, the further widening in the Canada–U.S. unemployment differential during the 1990s can be explained mainly, if not entirely, by the very poor performance of the Canadian economy and labour market.

FIGURE 6.6

Unemployment Rates, Canada and U.S., 1947–2012

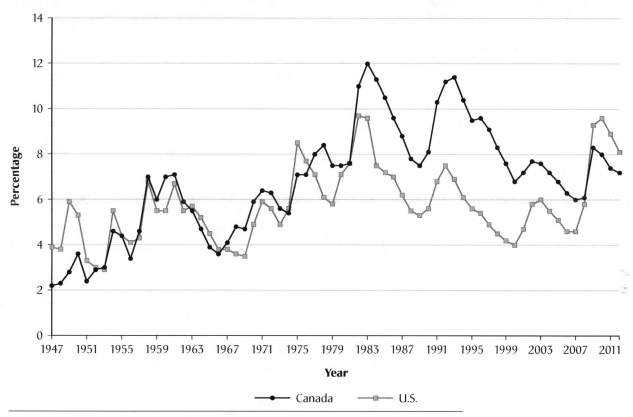

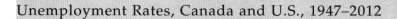

Sources: For 1947–65, adapted from Statistics Canada. (1985, November). *The Labour Force.* Ottawa: Statistics Canada (Catalogue no. 71-001); for 1966–75, adapted from Statistics Canada. (1999). *Historical Labour Force Statistics, 1966–1998.* Ottawa: Statistics Canada (Catalogue no. 71-201); for 1976–2012, adapted from Statistics Canada CANSIM, table 282-0002. For United States, adapted from U.S. Bureau of Labor Statistics (http://www.bls.gov/cps/cpssat1.pdf and http://www.bls.gov/cps/prev_yrs.htm).

Employment Insurance

Because a relatively weaker economic performance is not a convincing explanation for the persistence of the unemployment gap between Canada and the United States during the years of economic expansion that occurred in the 1980s, other reasons must account for it. One reason frequently pointed to is Canada's more generous employment insurance (EI) program, which was known as unemployment insurance until 1996.[6] Differences between the systems in Canada and the U.S. date back to the 1971–72 revisions in the Canadian program and the tightening of the U.S. program in the early 1980s. Amendments to the *Unemployment Insurance Act* in 1971 significantly reduced the qualifying period and increased benefits and eligibility periods. These changes could have led to an increase in the Canadian unemployment rate by increasing the duration as well as the incidence of unemployment.

More generous EI benefits and longer eligibility periods make searching for a job while being unemployed less costly. As a result, recipients of EI benefits may prolong their job search, thereby increasing the duration of unemployment.

The EI system is also likely to affect the number of layoffs. In seasonal and cyclically sensitive industries such as construction, forestry, and steel, firms frequently have slack periods when they have more workers than they need; as a result they might lay off part of their workforce, recalling them when sales and production pick up again. Two costs of a temporary layoff policy, however, limit its use. One is that firms must pay higher wages to attract workers to the industry given the higher risk of layoffs. The second is that some workers with valuable transferable skills may take jobs elsewhere, resulting in higher training costs for the firm. With an employment insurance system, both costs of layoffs are reduced. Since laid-off workers qualify for benefits, firms with a layoff policy need not pay such high wages to attract workers. Benefits allow laid-off workers to more easily sit out a spell of unemployment until the firm recalls them. A relatively generous EI system, therefore, may contribute to higher layoff rates, thereby increasing the incidence of unemployment.

Furthermore, the EI program can increase unemployment by attracting additional persons into the labour force, especially from demographic groups that have traditionally experienced higher unemployment rates. For young people or adult women, for example, the availability of employment insurance benefits may increase the attractiveness of market work over non-market activities. As more people join the labour force, the incidence of unemployment is likely to increase.

Several specific features of the Canadian employment insurance system may have been particularly important in explaining the emergence of the unemployment gap in the 1980s. For one, it was much easier for Canadians who voluntarily left their jobs to receive insurance benefits. This may explain why the share of unemployment attributed to people who quit their previous job or were recently out of the labour force was significantly higher in Canada than in the United States. Another feature relates to the regional provisions introduced to the Canadian program in 1978; these tied the maximum number of weeks a person can collect benefits and the minimum hours a claimant must work in order to become eligible for any benefits in part to the unemployment rate in the area of residence. Workers who live in a region where the unemployment rate exceeds the national average need fewer hours of work to qualify, and receive benefits for more weeks than workers who live in a region where the unemployment rate falls below the national average. As a result, when a recession increases the unemployment rate across regions, the employment insurance program becomes more generous. This encourages prolonged job searching and, by increasing unemployment duration, may raise the overall unemployment rate.

The regionally extended benefits and shorter qualification periods in regions of higher unemployment may also reduce labour mobility among regions. As the costs of remaining in high-unemployment regions are reduced by more generous EI provisions, there is less economic incentive to move from regions of high unemployment to regions of low unemployment—a process that should reduce overall unemployment. Empirical evidence indeed indicates that regional extended benefits have a substantial effect on sustaining high unemployment.[7]

As the unemployment gap between Canada and the U.S. appears to have emerged shortly after the introduction of these regional provisions and around the same time as the 1981–82 recession, this regional feature of the Canadian EI system seems particularly relevant.

The increase in the unemployment gap in the 1980s is accounted for almost equally by an increase in the average duration of completed spells of unemployment and a relative increase in the incidence of unemployment in Canada.[8] The longer spells of unemployment, in particular, suggest that Canada's relatively more generous EI program may play some part in explaining the differential. On the other hand, the average spell durations of new entrants and re-entrants to the labour force are also longer in Canada than in the U.S. Both groups are less likely to be covered by EI. This indicates that there may be other forces at work. For example, temporary layoffs are more common in the United States, while permanent layoffs are more important in Canada. Unemployment spells caused by permanent job loss tend to be longer on average.

Differences in the Measurement of Unemployment

Although both Canada and the United States use the same concepts and ask very similar questions in their labour force surveys, some differences in the measurement of unemployment exist that can affect the unemployment gap. In both countries, a person who is classified as unemployed is without work, is available for work, and has actively looked for work. The difference lies in the way active job search is measured. In Canada, people satisfy the requirement of active job search if they are just looking at want ads in the newspaper or listings on the Internet, picking up job applications (even if they do not return them), or placing the occasional call to friends to inquire about job vacancies. These people are counted as unemployed. In the United States, these search methods are classified as "passive methods." People who use only passive search methods are excluded from the U.S. unemployment count. In the United States, a person is classified as unemployed only if he or she uses "active methods" such as answering ads or placing calls to employment agencies or companies. These are search efforts that actually could lead to a job offer. It is estimated that the differences in measuring active job search account for about 0.7 percentage points of the unemployment gap in the 1990s.[9] Obviously, this leaves much of the gap of 4 percentage points to be explained by other factors.

Another difference exists in the measurement of the working-age population. In the United States, this population includes people aged 16 and over. In Canada, the cutoff is 15 years of age. Fifteen-year-olds who are in the labour force and unemployed are included in the Canadian unemployment count; in the United States, they are excluded. Removing this group from the labour force, however, reduces the unemployment gap by less than 0.1 percentage point, as most 15-year-olds attend school full-time.[10]

The unemployment gap is likely the result of several factors operating at the same time. A definitive quantification of their respective contributions has yet to emerge.

Types of Unemployment

We have described how unemployment is measured in Canada and have discussed some of the problems related to interpreting unemployment statistics. We have also presented some of the distinctive features and contributing factors of unemployment in Canada. None of this, however, systematically explains why economies experience unemployment. In most markets in the economy, prices adjust to bring the quantity supplied and the quantity demanded into balance. There is neither a shortage nor a surplus. In an ideal labour market, wages would adjust to balance the quantity of labour supplied and the quantity of labour demanded. This adjustment would ensure that all workers were employed. Why does reality differ so much from this ideal?

As Figure 6.2 (page 151) revealed, the unemployment rate is never zero even in boom times. For example, in 1989, when the economy was in the seventh year of the expansion that followed the 1981–82 recession, and overall production was close to maximum capacity, the unemployment rate never fell below 7.4%. The first step in finding out why there always exists some unemployment in an economy is to distinguish among four main types of unemployment:

- frictional unemployment
- seasonal unemployment
- structural unemployment
- cyclical unemployment

Frictional Unemployment

Labour turnover is a normal feature of the labour market. People are constantly entering the labour force—people graduate from school, mothers return to the labour force, and formerly discouraged workers try once more to find a job. At the same time, other people retire and create job vacancies for new entrants and re-entrants. Also, there is the constant change of businesses offering jobs. Some firms reduce production or close down for good, laying off workers; others expand or start up and hire workers. The constant flow of workers into and out of the labour force as well as the constant creation and destruction of jobs require people to search for jobs and firms to search for workers. Firms do not usually hire the first person who applies for a job, and unemployed people do not usually take the first job offered to them. Instead, both firms and workers spend time searching for what they believe will be the best match available. Unemployment that occurs as the result of this constant churning in the labour market is called **frictional unemployment** or search unemployment. One can think of frictional unemployment as unemployment resulting from short-run job-matching prob-

frictional unemployment
unemployment associated with the normal turnover of labour that is inevitable in a well-functioning labour market

lems: suitable job vacancies exist, but it takes time to match jobs and job searchers appropriately. Usually, frictional unemployment is of relatively short duration. The time spent looking for work is frequently a month or less.

In contrast to other types of unemployment, frictional unemployment entails some economic benefits. For the individual worker, a short spell of unemployment allows a more intensive and wide-ranging job search. For the economy, a certain amount of frictional unemployment is necessary for the job-matching process to allocate workers to jobs efficiently. Not all frictional unemployment is beneficial, however. Moving from one dead-end job to another, for example, can be highly demoralizing for the individual involved.

There are several ways that public policy can reduce frictional unemployment. One is to improve the information on available jobs, their rates of pay, location, etc. This could be done through computerized nationwide or regional job banks, an improved public employment service, and job fairs. Another way is to eliminate undesirable causes of job and labour force turnover by reforming those features of the employment insurance system that lead to increased frequency of unemployment.

With the advance of the Internet and the creation of websites by employment agencies, the exchange of information regarding job openings has been greatly facilitated. These websites range from general to very specific job classifications and either cover the whole country or focus on small geographic areas. It remains to be seen what impact the Internet employment agencies will have on frictional unemployment.

Labour Market Issue 6.1

Commercial Employment Agencies

WWW One of the functions of the labour market is to match job seekers with employment opportunities. Matching vacant jobs with qualified and willing workers is not always done quickly because information is not perfect. That is, workers do not always know what jobs are available, and employers do not always know where to find the workers to fill job vacancies. The role of the employment agency is to bridge the information gap and bring workers and employers together. The employment agency is a labour market intermediary.

The federal government operates a no-cost employment referral service. Its goal is to facilitate the matching process and reduce frictional unemployment. Yet many Canadians find employment through commercial employment agencies. Why do workers and employers use commercial agencies when a no-cost agency exists? Perhaps it is because commercial agencies are often specialized both on an occupational basis and on a geographic basis. For example, an agency might specialize in placing accountants or might operate in a defined geographic area.

Also, commercial employment agencies often assist firms that contract out some of their tasks. Firms may find it expensive to hire full-time workers to perform certain functions and it may be easier to contract out these services on a temporary basis. Temporary workers can be found through a commercial employment agency. It may be cheaper, in the long run, for firms to use a specialized employment service rather than rely on the no-cost federal service, which does not specialize in temporary placements. Some cost savings may be achieved by using employment agencies that specialize in a certain type of job. Even though the agency may charge the employer a fee, the quick results provided by the firm may reduce costly bottlenecks in human resources within the firm.

Seasonal Unemployment

seasonal unemployment

unemployment resulting from the decline in the number of jobs at certain times of the year

Some jobs are only available during certain seasons of the year. In most parts of Canada, construction, fishing, and farming generally stop during the winter months. Unemployment that arises because the number of jobs has declined due to the season is called **seasonal unemployment**. We have seen earlier that the Atlantic provinces have unemployment rates above the national average. Part of the problem in this region is the high seasonal unemployment. For people working in tourism, farming, and fishing during the summer months, it is very hard to find seasonal work during the winter. For example, in Prince Edward Island, the unemployment rate during the winter months is generally twice as high as in summer.

Seasonal unemployment has been important in Canada because natural resource industries traditionally have played a major role in its economy and because it is a northern country. In recent decades, however, seasonal variations in unemployment have become less pronounced. This is in part because some sectors that are significantly affected by weather—like agriculture and fishing—are now much smaller than they used to be. Another reason is that industries, such as the construction industry, have developed technologies that allow them to operate throughout the winter months.

Official unemployment rates compiled by Statistics Canada are defined as seasonally adjusted or unadjusted. The seasonally unadjusted figures report the actual unemployment rate in a particular month. The seasonally adjusted figures show the unemployment rate that would have existed had there not been high or low seasonal demand conditions in a particular month. The seasonally adjusted rates permit comparisons of unemployment rates from month to month since the fluctuations associated with seasonal factors are averaged in over the year.

Structural Unemployment

Another reason for substantial unemployment even in an economy operating at full capacity is that not all labour submarkets are in equilibrium at the same time. As we saw in Chapter 2, instead of a single labour market, there are a great number of submarkets for particular jobs with specialized skills and qualifications. As a result of structural changes in the economy, there will be more vacancies than unemployed workers (excess demand) in some markets coexisting with an excess of workers over vacancies (excess supply) in others. The markets with excess supply of labour contribute positive amounts of unemployment. In contrast, those with excess demand cannot have negative unemployment. The average unemployment rate must always be positive. Vacancies and unemployment do not simply cancel each other out: they coexist.

Structural changes refer to changes in the industrial and occupational mix of an economy as well as to changes in its workforce. Employers may be having trouble finding software engineers, but construction workers may be out of work in large numbers. When technological changes such as the introduction of robotics in the automotive industry or budget cuts in healthcare lead to job losses in these sectors, there may be other industries, such as electronics or fibre optics, that are rapidly growing and creating new jobs. Job vacancies in these industries may not be filled by unemployed job searchers over an extended period of time because the workers lack the right skills or live in the wrong location. Unemployment due to the matching problems that arise from such structural changes in the economy is called **structural unemployment**. Since it arises from long-run adjustment problems, it can last for many months and as such is a more serious problem than frictional unemployment.

It is often not easy to establish a clear distinction between frictional and structural unemployment. In both cases, a sufficient number of jobs exist in the economy, and both involve job search. The main difference is the speed with which the job-matching process is completed—relatively quickly in the case of frictional unemployment, but slowly for structural unemployment.

There are several ways in which public policy might reduce structural unemployment. One way is for governments to provide training programs or subsidize training in private companies through direct payments or tax incentives. Recent reforms to the employment insurance program have allocated funds away from the payments of benefits to the unemployed and toward the funding of training. A second way would be to improve communication between schools, colleges, and universities and the business community in developing co-op programs that will provide a better match between the skills of graduates and the skills required by employers. A third possibility is to facilitate the movement of unemployed workers out of depressed regions through payments of reallocation allowances. A fourth possibility could be for the government to act as employer of last resort by offering employment in the public sector to people who suffer persistent unemployment.

Economists describe the unemployment rate that prevails under normal conditions (i.e., when the economy is operating at full capacity) as the **natural rate of unemployment**. The term appears rather misleading as there is nothing natural about unemployment. Economists chose the term to remind us that friction in the labour market and structural changes in the economy are unavoidable. Since there is always some unemployment, what do we mean then by "full employment"? **Full employment** occurs when the actual unemployment rate equals the natural rate of unemployment. At full employment, all unemployment is frictional, structural, or seasonal.

The natural rate of unemployment is not a fixed number. It changes over time as the structures of the labour market and the labour force change. Since the natural rate of unemployment cannot be observed directly, there is some dispute about its level at any time. Estimates of the natural rate of unemployment for the late 1980s varied between 6.5% and 8%; for the 1990s, the estimates ranged from 7.5% to 9%. However, there is a general consensus among economists that the natural rate of unemployment has followed an upward long-run trend, more than doubling over the last 30 years. Some of the reasons for the increase are discussed in the next section.

structural unemployment
unemployment resulting from a mismatching of workers and job opportunities based either on skills or on geography

natural rate of unemployment
the unemployment rate that exists when the economy is functioning at full capacity

full employment
when the actual rate of unemployment equals the natural rate of unemployment

Cyclical Unemployment

cyclical unemployment (demand-deficient unemployment)

unemployment that arises because the economy does not generate enough jobs for those seeking one

Often, the observed unemployment rate deviates from the natural rate. The difference between actual unemployment and the natural rate of unemployment is generally defined as **cyclical unemployment**. The sharp peaks in unemployment in Figure 6.7 reflect the cyclical unemployment that occurs in recessions. When the observed unemployment rate equals the natural rate, the economy is operating at full employment and cyclical unemployment is zero. Since cyclical unemployment frequently arises from inadequate demand in an economy, it is also called **demand-deficient unemployment**. Since the demand for labour depends on the demand for goods and services, declining demand for output leads to declining demand for labour. As an economy moves into a recession, sales decline and, as a result, firms cut back on production. When production levels decline, fewer hours of work are needed and fewer workers are employed. Frictional unemployment and structural unemployment arise because of job-matching problems. Cyclical unemployment occurs because the economy does not generate enough jobs for all who want to work. Famous British economist John Maynard Keynes was the first economist to show in a systematic way how a decline in overall demand creates unemployment.

fiscal policy

changes in government spending and taxation

Public policy might reduce cyclical unemployment in several ways. The most widely used approach is to use fiscal and monetary policy to stimulate economic growth. **Fiscal policy** refers to the government's decision regarding the level of government spending or taxes. When the economy slows down, the government can increase its own spending on goods and services: it can build new schools or hospitals, repair roads, or expand its own research facilities. It can also cut taxes to increase the spending of households or companies. Increased spending leads to increased production. As production increases, more employees are hired, resulting in a reduction of unemployment. **Monetary policy** refers to changes in the supply of money by the Bank of Canada, which affect the interest rates in the economy. If a recession looms, the Bank of Canada can increase the money supply in order to reduce interest rates. As interest rates decline, bank loans become less expensive. This consequently stimulates spending by households and firms. Government intervention in the form of fiscal or monetary policy, or both, can limit the severity of an economic downturn and the resulting cyclical unemployment.

monetary policy

changes in money supply by the Bank of Canada

To break total unemployment down into frictional/structural and cyclical unemployment is an attractive method for distinguishing the effects of the business cycle from those associated with frictional and structural changes in the labour market. Nonetheless, the actual breakdown of unemployment into these categories is often not as straightforward because the sources are not independent of each other. An increase in cyclical unemployment can, over time, lead to increased frictional and/or structural unemployment. We will discuss the possible impact of a rise in cyclical unemployment on the natural rate of unemployment in more detail in Labour Market Issue 6.2 (page 172).

Why Has the Natural Rate of Unemployment Shifted Upward?

Figure 6.7 shows that the natural rate of unemployment increased from the 1950s until the 1990s, when it started to decline. In the remainder of this chapter, we explore the question of why the rates of frictional and structural unemployment have increased.

Demographic Shifts

Labour turnover is a major source of unemployment. One factor that may have led to higher labour turnover is the changing composition of the labour force. As mentioned earlier, two labour force groups with above-average job

FIGURE 6.7

Actual Unemployment Rate and Estimated Natural Rate of Unemployment, 1953–2003

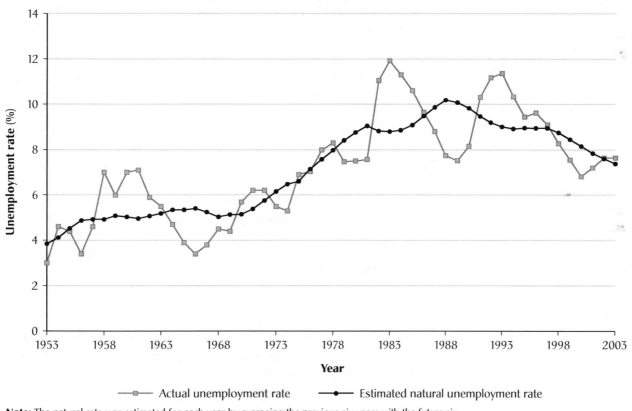

Note: The natural rate was estimated for each year by averaging the previous six years with the future six years of the unemployment rate. After 2003, the actual unemployment rate was set at 7%.

Sources: For 1947–65, adapted from Statistics Canada. (1985, November). *The Labour Force*. Ottawa: Statistics Canada (Catalogue no. 71-001); for 1966–75, adapted from Statistics Canada. (1999). *Historical Labour Force Statistics, 1966–1998*. Ottawa: Statistics Canada (Catalogue no. 71-201); for 1976–2003, adapted from Statistics Canada CANSIM II database http://cansim2.statcan.ca, series V2062815.

and labour force turnover rates are youth and women. As a result of the baby boom and rising labour force participation, the share of young people, 15–24 years of age, in the labour force increased from 22% in 1960 to a peak of 27% in 1975. Since the mid-1970s, their labour force share has dramatically declined. The increase in the proportion of adult women in the labour force was even more dramatic and, in contrast to young people, has continued throughout the last decades. It rose from 22% in 1947 to 47% in 2011.

These demographic shifts can have increased the natural rate of unemployment in two ways. The first is referred to as the *weights effect* of demographic changes on unemployment. The overall unemployment rate is a weighted average of the unemployment rates of the various demographic subgroups. Unemployment can be expected to rise if the groups with relatively high unemployment rates, such as youth and women, increase their share (weight) in the labour force.[iii]

Another possibility is that the entrance of large numbers of young people and women into the labour force can lead to crowding in the labour market of these two groups. If relative wages were flexible, the increase in supply of youth and women would decrease their wages relative to adult men, making it profitable for firms to provide employment for them. Because relative wages do not fall easily, the result is a relatively higher rate of unemployment for young people and women as scarce jobs are rationed among a large pool of job seekers. This effect has been termed the *cohort overcrowding effect*. The weight effect is based on the relatively higher rates of labour turnover in the two groups, and the crowding effect refers to a more serious structural problem, namely an imbalance between the supply of young and adult female workers and the number of jobs available for these two groups.

Empirical studies indicate that demographic changes working through the weight effect have had a minimal impact on overall unemployment. In contrast, the cohort overcrowding effect seems to have contributed to the increase in the natural rate of unemployment, at least during the 1960s and early 1970s. Since the mid-1970s, however, the explanation of higher unemployment relying on demographic shifts has lost much of its force. In 1976, the share of youth in the labour force started to decline and by 2011 it had fallen to 15%, seven percentage points less than the level in 1960. The share of adult women in the labour force is still rising but the corresponding unemployment rate has been below that of adult men since 1991.

Another observation that casts doubts on the demographic explanation is that the average unemployment rate even of prime-aged males (men aged 25–54)—a group with a very stable labour force share—rose until the late 1990s.

Employment Insurance

Considerable attention has focused on the growth of income-transfer programs in Canada as a cause of increased frictional unemployment. To the extent that most people prefer leisure to work, it is the pressure of financial

---

[iii] As noted earlier, the unemployment rates of women have been lower than those of men since 1991.

necessity that encourages job acceptance and discourages excessive turnover. Government transfer payments reduce the incentive to work, leading to an increase in both unemployment and non-participation in the labour force.

The transfer program that has received the most attention is employment insurance. As the discussion of the unemployment gap between Canada and the United States earlier in this chapter has shown, the relatively greater generosity of the Canadian employment insurance system can have raised the natural rate of unemployment by increasing the duration and incidence of unemployment.

Over the last 25 years, a large number of studies have been conducted examining the sizes of the various effects of employment insurance on unemployment. Findings confirm the links established in theory between features of the employment insurance system, length of job search, and unemployment duration. Several studies found large "spikes" in the number of unemployed re-entering employment at the point when EI benefits are exhausted.[11] These "spikes" reflect the incentive for individuals to remain unemployed as long as EI benefits last.

Empirical research also has shown that the availability and generosity of benefits have a positive effect on the incidence of unemployment. A more generous EI system increases the number of those who newly enter or re-enter the labour force in order to build eligibility for EI benefits. This holds especially for individuals with relatively low labour force attachment. For example, in Atlantic Canada young people frequently drop out of school in part to get short-term jobs that enable them to collect EI.[12] "Spikes" are found not only in unemployment duration but also in the incidence of unemployment. A significant number of employed people enter unemployment at the 10-week period required to be eligible for 42 weeks of regionally extended benefits.[13]

The 1996 EI reforms, outlined in Chapter 3, have tightened the conditions for eligibility and duration of benefits. As a result, one should expect the natural rate of unemployment to decline, all other things remaining the same. Annual EI monitoring and assessment reports published by Human Resources Development Canada and several recent studies indicate that the reforms may in fact have contributed to a decline in frequent use of the EI system as well as to shorter average benefit periods.[14]

The fact that there are strong indications that employment insurance affects the level of unemployment does not imply that employment insurance should be eliminated. The primary objective of the program is to provide insurance against the loss of income resulting from unemployment. As such, it eases the financial burden of those who find themselves unemployed. Also, employment insurance allows people to conduct a more thorough job search, thereby increasing the chances of a better job match and of receiving a higher wage than would otherwise have been the case. Furthermore, employment insurance benefits enable the unemployed to maintain a certain spending level. As such, EI transfers provide a significant boost to the economy in times of recession when overall consumption is generally down. As often happens in cases of economic tradeoffs, economists disagree on whether the benefits of

Labour Market Issue 6.2

Unemployment Hysteresis

Figure 6.7 (page 169) indicates that the natural unemployment rate may not be independent of the actual unemployment rate. Both tended to increase from the 1950s onwards. It has been suggested that the natural rate itself depends in part on the history of actual unemployment. In particular, a long period of high unemployment may lead to an increase in the natural rate. Economists use the term **unemployment hysteresis** to describe the long-lasting impact of the history of actual unemployment on the natural rate. Why should actual unemployment affect the natural rate over time? There are several reasons why sustained periods of high unemployment might alter frictional and structural unemployment.

First, a recession can have permanent effects if it alters the people who become unemployed. As time spent unemployed increases, skills, work attitudes, and habits deteriorate, which results in increased matching problems. The unemployed also may lose self-confidence. As confidence in one's own abilities declines, job search may become less intensive. The problem is reinforced by the hiring process of firms. Employers use employment records as a screening device and shy away from hiring the long-term unemployed. The longer a person has been unemployed, the lower the chances of being hired even after the recession has ended. The result is a vicious cycle in which employers become reluctant to hire the long-term unemployed who then give up job search. The final result is that a recession, by affecting job search and hiring, can lead to a permanent loss of employment.

Second, a recession can permanently affect unemployment by changing the wage bargaining process. Unemployed workers may become *outsiders* to labour negotiations. For example, they may lose their status as union members. If the workers who remain employed, the *insiders*, care more about higher wages and less about the employment of the outsiders, wages are likely to rise at the expense of jobs. The more successful the insiders are in pushing wages up, the longer unemployment will persist.

Third, regional dimensions of the employment insurance system could raise natural unemployment. As described in the text, the Canadian EI program has been much more generous in the high-unemployment regions of the country. More generous EI provisions tend to reduce work incentives in the high-unemployment regions. As overall unemployment increases, regional unemployment disparities are exacerbated by discouraging the migration of unemployed workers from high- to low-unemployment regions, thereby increasing structural unemployment.

There is no agreement on the importance of hysteresis in explaining the upward drift of natural unemployment in Canada.[15] There is also little agreement on whether hysteresis can explain why unemployment in the European Union (EU) has been so high for so long. The European unemployment rate was much lower than the U.S. and Canadian rates until the early 1970s. All three rates increased in the 1970s and early 1980s. Since then, however, the U.S. rate has declined while the unemployment rate in many European countries—especially in France, Germany, Italy, and Spain—has remained very high. The hysteresis argument holds that policies in these European countries aimed to reduce inflation created high unemployment that in turn led to a high proportion of long-term unemployment. Policies to reduce long-term unemployment have not met with much success.

unemployment hysteresis

the dependency of the natural rate of unemployment on the actual unemployment rate

employment insurance in terms of providing income support, potentially improving job matching, and stabilizing the overall economy outweigh the cost in terms of higher unemployment.

Industrial Restructuring

A factor often cited as contributing to greater structural unemployment is the industrial restructuring from manufacturing to services, or more broadly from an industrial economy to an information- and knowledge-based economy. This transformation has been associated with other interrelated changes: increased outsourcing of work to "downstream" parts suppliers and subcontractors for components and services, mergers and acquisitions, deregulation, and heightened foreign competition. These changes have led to the displacement of blue-collar, industrial jobs. Older workers in heavily unionized industries such as steel, car manufacturing, and machinery were particularly hard hit by industrial restructuring. For many of these displaced workers, the long duration of unemployment was due to several factors, including the lack of jobs in the local labour market, the reluctance to uproot their families to move to different parts of the country with better employment opportunities, and the unwillingness of many of the unemployed to accept low-paying jobs in alternative occupations.

Technological Change

Technological change is a major force in the process of structural change. Since the beginning of the Industrial Revolution, workers have worried that technological change will destroy their jobs. Every major wave of technological innovation, from the steam engine to the automobile to the microchip, has raised fears of permanent mass unemployment. In his essay "Economic Possibilities for Our Grandchildren," published in 1930, the English economist John Maynard Keynes reflected on the implications of the tremendous productivity increases brought about by technological progress: "In quite a few years—in our lifetimes I mean—we may be able to perform all the operations of agriculture, mining, and manufacture with a quarter of the human effort to which we have been accustomed." For Keynes, the advances in productivity raised the spectre of **technological unemployment**, which he defined as "unemployment due to our discovery of means of economizing the use of labour outrunning the pace at which we can find new uses of labour."

technological unemployment

unemployment due to advances in technical and organizational know-how occurring at a faster pace than the ability to find new uses for labour

In order to analyze the relationship between technological change and unemployment, it is useful to distinguish between two related but separate dimensions of technological progress.

First, technological progress allows the production of more goods and services with the same number of workers. Alternatively formulated, technological change allows the economy to produce the same amount of output with fewer workers; when expressed in this manner, it reflects the fear of those who worry about technological unemployment. Since technological change increases labour productivity, a given output level requires fewer workers. The critical question then is this: As technological change increases productivity over time, does it also increase unemployment? If we look at the overall economy over longer periods, the answer is no. Periods of high productivity growth, such as the 1950s and 1960s, were associated with a lower

Chapter 6: Unemployment

unemployment rate; periods of low productivity growth, such as the 1980s and 1990s, were associated with a higher unemployment rate. Instead of causing more unemployment, technological change seems to decrease unemployment. It should be noted that what applies to the economy at large does not necessarily hold for the individual. At the individual level, technological change often leads to the displacement of workers.

Second, technological progress leads to the rise of new industries and occupations and the disappearance of old ones. This structural dimension of technology seems to be at the heart of the fears of technological unemployment. Technological change implies a constant process of job destruction and job creation. New goods are developed; old ones disappear. New production techniques are invented, requiring new skills and making old ones obsolete. The mechanical loom, for example, largely wiped out the jobs of the weavers during the nineteenth century but created many new jobs in the emerging textile industry. When the automobile replaced the horse and buggy, many occupations (such as harness maker and blacksmith) were all but destroyed, but many more new ones were generated, creating large numbers of new jobs. The petroleum and rubber industry, the car insurance industry, and road construction, to mention only a few, are industries that evolved as spin-offs. With the increased use of computers in large parts of the economy today, we are witnessing the latest example of what the Austrian economist Joseph Schumpeter called the process of "creative destruction." Although, historically, technological change has not created massive unemployment in the economy, technological unemployment is a serious problem for those groups of workers left with insufficient skills to fill the newly created jobs. The decline, both relative and absolute, in the wages of low-skill workers during the last 15 to 20 years reflects a decline in the demand for less skilled workers, and technological progress appears to be the main cause. Whether the wage decline will be sufficient to preserve a minimum number of jobs for low-skill workers remains to be seen. We still know very little, quantitatively speaking, about to what degree technological change is contributing to structural unemployment.

Summary

An unemployed person is someone who is not working but is looking for work. The unemployment rate is computed by Statistics Canada using data from the monthly Labour Force Survey. The official unemployment rate may not be an accurate indicator of unemployment because of the presence of discouraged workers, underemployed workers, and marginal workers. The validity of the unemployment rate as an indicator of economic hardship is increasingly questioned. While the unemployment rate measures the underutilization of labour in the economy, the employment rate measures the extent to which labour is utilized.

The proportion of people in the labour force entering unemployment in a given period is called the incidence of unemployment. Job losers represent the biggest group of those entering the ranks of the unemployed, followed by the group of new entrants and re-entrants to the labour force. Job leavers are the smallest group among the unemployed. The average time a person remains unemployed is called the duration of unemployment; the duration of unemployment increased during most of the 1980s and 1990s. The product of the incidence and the duration of unemployment determines overall unemployment.

Since World War II, the average level of unemployment in the economy has been on an upward trend. The increase in the unemployment rate also has been much steeper in the last two recessions. Not all labour force groups suffer equally from unemployment; youth and, until recently, female workers were more likely to be unemployed. Workers in the Atlantic provinces and Quebec are more affected by unemployment than individuals in other provinces. During the last 20 years, the unemployment rate in Canada has consistently been higher than the rate in the United States. The unemployment gap can be traced to differences in macroeconomic performance, the employment insurance system, and differences in the measurement of unemployment.

Economists distinguish among four types of unemployment: frictional, seasonal, structural, and cyclical (or demand-deficient). Frictional unemployment is associated with turnover in the labour market, and structural unemployment stems from a mismatch between workers and jobs. Seasonal unemployment is caused by seasonal fluctuations on the demand or supply side of the labour market. Cyclical unemployment, or demand-deficient unemployment, is related to fluctuations in aggregate demand for goods and services. The natural rate of unemployment is a combination of frictional and structural unemployment, and describes the unemployment that exists when the economy operates at full capacity. The natural rate of unemployment has increased over most of the post–World War II period. The increase has been attributed to demographic shifts in the labour force, changes in the employment insurance system, industrial restructuring, technological change, and unemployment hysteresis.

Key Terms

cyclical unemployment (page 168)
demand–deficient unemployment (page 168)
discouraged workers (page 145)
duration of unemployment (page 153)
fiscal policy (page 168)
frictional unemployment (page 164)
full employment (page 167)
hidden unemployed (page 145)
incidence of unemployment (page 152)

marginal workers (page 146)
monetary policy (page 168)
natural rate of unemployment (page 167)
seasonal unemployment (page 166)
structural unemployment (page 167)
technological unemployment (page 173)
unemployment hysteresis (page 172)
unemployment rate (page 144)

Weblinks

For Women in Canada updates
http://www.statcan.gc.ca/bsolc/olc-cel/olc-cel?catno=89-503-XPE&lang=eng

For 2001 Census data
http://www.12.statcan.ca/english/census01/home/index.cfm

For U.S. Bureau of Labor Statistics
http://www.bls.gov/home.htm

For commercial employment agencies
http://www.jobs.com; www.workopolis.ca

For Federal Department of Finance
http://www.fin.gc.ca

For Bank of Canada
http://www.bankofcanada.ca

Discussion Questions

1. What is the difference between being unemployed and not working? Give some examples of people not at work who are not unemployed.
2. In 2002, the Canadian economy generated approximately 560 000 new jobs, the largest number since the 1950s. Yet the unemployment rate declined by only a small amount. How is this possible? Explain.
3. The frequency of unemployment is high and the majority of unemployment spells are short. Based on these observations, several labour economists have drawn the conclusion that the burden of unemployment is equally shared. Discuss.
4. Unemployment differs greatly among Canada's regions. Evaluate some of the factors that may affect the regional unemployment differential and the problems this raises for Canada's policymakers as they try to reduce unemployment.
5. An important trend in the Canadian labour market has been the rise in non-standard employment. Discuss some of the possible connections between the rise in non-standard employment and the trend increase in unemployment in Canada.
6. Unemployment rates between Canada and the United States have differed substantially over the last 20 years. Evaluate some of the factors that may have contributed to the unemployment gap between the two countries.
7. Why is frictional unemployment inevitable? How might the government reduce it?
8. Are simultaneous increases in unemployment and job vacancies a sign of growing frictional, structural, or cyclical unemployment? Explain.

9. Over most of the postwar period, the natural rate of unemployment has gradually increased. Evaluate some of the factors that may have contributed to the increase.

10. Some economists have associated the increase in the natural rate of unemployment in Canada with the amendments made to the *Unemployment Insurance Act* in 1971, which made the insurance system much more generous compared to earlier years. Explain how these changes could have affected the incidence and the duration of unemployment in Canada.

11. "Historically, technological progress has been accompanied by higher overall employment."

"Historically, technological progress has been labour saving (machines have been replacing workers)."

Can both statements be true at the same time? Explain.

Using the Internet

Go to the Statistics Canada website at www.statcan.ca. Follow the links Canadian Statistics, Economic Conditions, Labour Market, and Labour Force Characteristics.

1. State the changes in the employment rate, labour force participation rate, and unemployment rate from 2001 to 2004. Based on these three indicators, how would you assess the labour market conditions in each of the three years?

2. State the changes in the same three labour market indicators for 2002 to 2003. Comparing the changes with those of the previous year, would you say that the labour market conditions have improved or worsened overall? Explain.

Exercises

1. Suppose you are a member of the Labour Force Survey Team and you have collected the following information: There were 8500 people in the families surveyed by you, 1000 of them children and teenagers under 15, and 500 retired; 3700 people had full-time jobs, and 1400 had part-time jobs. There were 500 full-time homemakers, 500 full-time students aged 15 and over who were not looking for work, and 200 people who were ill and could not work. The remaining people did not have jobs but all said they would like to have one; 100 of these people had not looked actively for work for several months, however. Calculate the labour force, the labour force participation rate, and the unemployment rate based on your survey data.

2. In 1975, the total working-age population was 16.323 million, the labour force participation rate was 61.1%, and the unemployment rate was 6.9%. In 2003, the working-age population was 25.2 million and the

labour force participation rate had risen to 67.5%. How quickly would total employment have had to grow from 1975 to 2003 to keep the unemployment rate at 6.9%?

3. Assume that the unemployment rates in three consecutive years are 7.5%, 8.6%, and 9.5%. Suppose that the employment/population ratios for the same three years are 56.7%, 57.5%, and 58.3%. Judging by the two measures of labour utilization, is the economy gaining or losing strength?

4. Suppose that, over the course of a year, 100 people are unemployed for four weeks each (the short-term unemployed), while 10 people are unemployed for 52 weeks each (the long-term unemployed). Approximately what percentage of the total spells of unemployment were attributable to the long-term unemployed?

5. Suppose that the unemployment rate of young people is 14% and the share of youth in the labour force is 16%. Suppose further that the unemployment rate of adults is 7% and their share in the labour force is 84%.
   a. Calculate the total unemployment rate.
   b. What if the labour force share of youth declines from 16% to 12%? How will this affect the total unemployment rate?

6. There are two flows from employment to unemployment.
   a. State the flows.
   b. How are the two flows likely to change over the business cycle?

7. Evidence shows that women and young people have more frequent spells of unemployment than adult men, but that unemployment of these two groups is of shorter duration than men's. What does this suggest as possible causes of unemployment for youth and women?

8. What type of unemployment are the following workers experiencing? Explain.
   a. Workers in a fish plant in Newfoundland and Labrador lose their jobs when the cod fishery closes down.
   b. Ski lift attendants in British Columbia are laid off due to the lack of snow.
   c. A salesclerk in a video store loses her job when a new video store opens around the corner.
   d. Bank tellers lose their jobs as banks install automated teller machines.
   e. Lack of consumer confidence and growing pessimism among Canadian business leaders leads to wide-scale layoffs in the natural resource and manufacturing industries.

References

[1] Jones, S., and Riddell, W.C. (1999). "The Measurement of Unemployment: An Empirical Approach." *Econometrica,* 67 (January): 147–161.

[2] Benjamin, D., Gunderson, M., and Riddell, W.C. (2002). *Labour Market Economics: Theory, Evidence, and Policy in Canada.* Toronto: McGraw-Hill Ryerson, p. 516.

[3] Gunderson, M., Sharpe, A., and Wald, S. (2000). "Youth Unemployment in Canada, 1976–1998." *Canadian Public Policy*, 25 Supplement: S85–S100.

[4] Milan, A., and Tran, K. (Spring 2004). "Blacks in Canada: A Long History." *Canadian Social Trends,* 72. Ottawa: Minister of Industry (Catalogue no. 11-008 XIF), p. 7.

[5] Riddell, W.C., and Sharpe, A. (1998). "The Canada–U.S. Unemployment Rate Gap: An Introduction and Overview." Special Issue. *Canadian Public Policy*, 24: 1–37.

[6] Keil, M.W., and Simons, J.S.V. (1990). "An Analysis of Canadian Unemployment." *Canadian Public Policy*, 16(1): 1–16.

[7] Card, D., and Riddell, C.W. (1993). "A Comparative Analysis of Unemployment in Canada and the United States." In D. Card and R. Freeman (Eds.), *Small Differences That Matter: Labour Markets and Income Maintenance in Canada and the United States.* Chicago: University of Chicago Press, pp. 149–189.

[8] Baker, M., Corak, M., and Heisz, A. (1996). *Unemployment in the Stock and Flow.* Ottawa: Statistics Canada. Research Paper Series, No. 97 (Catalogue no. 11F0019MPE).

[9] Riddell, C.W. (1999). "Canadian Labour Market Performance: An International Perspective." *Canadian Journal of Economics*, 32 (November): 1097–1134.

[10] Statistics Canada. (1998). *Labour Force Update. Canada–U.S. Labour Market Comparisons*, 2(4). Ottawa: Minister of Industry (Catalogue no. 71-005-XPB), p. 30.

[11] Belzil, C. (1995). "Unemployment Duration Stigma and Re-employment Earnings." *Canadian Journal of Economics*, 28 (August): 568–585.

[12] May, D., and Hollett, A. (1995). *The Rock in a Hard Place: Atlantic Canada and the UI Trap.* Toronto: C.D. Howe Institute.

[13] Baker, M., and Rea, S. Jr. (1998). "Employment Spells and Unemployment Insurance Eligibility Requirements." *Review of Economics and Statistics*, 80 (February): 80–94; Green, D.A., and Riddell, W.C. (1997). "Qualifying for Unemployment Insurance: An Empirical Analysis." *Economic Journal*, 107: 67–84.

[14] Gray, D. (April 2004). "Employment Insurance: What Reform Delivered." *Backgrounder*, 82. Toronto: C.D. Howe Institute.

[15] Jones, S.R.G. (1995). *The Persistence of Unemployment: Hysteresis in Canadian Labour Markets.* Montreal and Kingston: McGill-Queen's University Press; Fortin, P. (1996). "The Unbearable Lightness of Zero-Inflation Optimism." In B.K. MacLean and L. Osberg (Eds.), *The Unemployment Crisis: All for Nought?* Montreal and Kingston: McGill-Queen's University Press, pp. 13–38.

Chapter 7

Trends in Labour Compensation

Chapter Learning Objectives

After completing this chapter, you should be able to:

- distinguish between wages, earnings, labour income, and total income
- describe the trends in total labour income and labour's share in national income
- evaluate the changes in average labour income
- describe the changes in weekly earnings and nominal and real hourly wages
- describe the changes in the gender and age wage gap
- discuss the growing wage differential between skilled and unskilled workers

CANADA'S LOW WAGE EARNERS

Anne is 28 years old and a single mother with one child. She works full-year, full-time, as a salesclerk in Saskatoon. Her annual earnings are $18 643. Anne is one of approximately 6.6 million people in Canada who, according to the 2001 Census, were making less than $20 000 in 2000. More than one-fifth, or about 1.5 million, of the low wage earners were working on a full-year, full-time basis.

Earnings of $20 000 are the equivalent of a wage of $10 an hour for an individual working 50 weeks a year, and 40 hours each week. A wage income of $20 000 represents less than one-half of the average earnings ($43 231) of all Canadians working full-year, full-time in 2000.

Who are the 1.5 million low pay earners working full-year, full-time? The conventional wisdom is that people who work for low pay are young people, high school dropouts without skills, second earners in the family, or people who live alone without family responsibilities. The reality, however, is more complicated.

The majority of the low wage earners are women; close to one-third are the only earners in their families. More than 60% of all low pay earners are over the age of 35. Most surprisingly, 27% have a college diploma or university degree, and another 14% have a certificate from a trade school.

Of the female low wage earners who worked full-year, full-time, the majority worked in just 17 occupational categories. Retail salespersons and salesclerks, retail trade managers, cashiers, and food and beverage servers were the top-ranking categories in which women with low earnings were employed. The fastest employment growth among female low wage earners occurred in the job category of early childhood educators and assistants.

Retail trade managers, retail salespersons, and salesclerks also ranked high among the occupational categories in which male low wage earners are working. Other jobs in which a large number of male low wage earners are found are truck drivers, cooks, janitors, caretakers, and superintendents. Truck drivers were the occupational category experiencing the fastest employment growth among men with low earnings.

Introduction

The determination of wage rates is at the core of labour economics. It is through changes in wage rates that labour services are allocated to their various uses and that a balance between demand and supply is maintained in the market. Employers are concerned with wage rates because they, together with labour productivity, largely determine labour cost. Workers are concerned with wage rates because, for the majority of them, earnings from employment are the most important source of income. Their paycheques determine how much they actually can purchase in a given period in relation to the prices of goods and services. Workers are not only interested in their own wages, but they also are particularly concerned with how their wages compare with those of their fellow workers.

Few economic variables are as controversial and as hotly debated as the wage rate. At the centre of the debate is often the notion of a "fair" wage. Is a bank CEO's contribution to the economy so much more than that of a chemist in a cancer research laboratory that it should justify the tremendous difference in their compensation? Is it "fair" that a cashier in a supermarket in Toronto earns significantly more than a cashier with similar work experience in a supermarket in Montreal? Is it "just" that female lawyers graduating from the same law school at the same time earn initially about 9% less than their male peers? These are difficult questions for which economists do not offer any answer. From the perspective of economic theory there is no "just" wage. A wage reflects the price an employer is willing to pay for a specified labour service in a particular location at a certain point in time. This does not imply, however, that a society has to accept wage levels and structures as determined by markets. Government labour regulations, taxation laws, and social programs are intended to redistribute earnings as determined in the market.

In this chapter we are interested in the broad trends of labour income in Canada, labour's share in total national income, wage levels, and the growing polarization between high and low earnings. Before examining these trends, it is useful to discuss briefly the meaning of wages and other components of labour compensation. To economists, the meaning of the term *wage rate* is intuitively obvious—it is the price of labour per hour of work. Measuring the actual wage rate, however, proves to be quite difficult. Also, labour compensation does not consist only of wages.

Concepts and Measures

There are essentially two ways to compute wages. One is on the basis of time (time wages), and the other is per unit of output (production wages or piecework). The great majority of Canadian workers are paid by the hour, day, week, month, or year. That is, they are paid in relation to the amount of time spent on the job. Workers paid by the hour or the day are usually referred to as **wage earners**, while those paid by the week or longer time periods are commonly referred to as **salaried workers**. In Canada, wage earners generally outnumber salaried workers. Wages and salaries include bonuses, commissions, tips and gratuities, taxable allowances, and retroactive wage payments, in addition to basic pay. Estimates are usually calculated on a "gross" basis, that is, before deductions for income tax, employment insurance premiums, pension contributions, etc. **Net wages** or take-home pay is gross wages minus the deductions just referred to. While the term "wages" or "wage rate" refers to the payment for a unit of time, "earnings" refers to wages multiplied by the number of time units (typically hours or weeks) worked. Thus, earnings

wage earner
worker paid by the hour or the day

salaried worker
worker paid by the week or longer time period

net wages
gross wages minus taxes and other payroll deductions

Chapter 7: Trends in Labour Compensation

depend on both wages and the length of time the employee works. In the case of piecework, earnings refer to wages multiplied by the number of units of output produced by the worker. Earnings in that case depend on wages and the worker's production level.

Labour Income

Both wages and earnings are defined and measured in terms of direct monetary payments to employees. In addition to wages, workers receive non-wage benefits as compensation for their labour, benefits that are mostly payments in kind or deferred. Examples of payments in kind are employer-provided extended healthcare benefits such as dental and pharmaceutical insurance, for which the employee receives a service or an insurance policy rather than money, and paid vacation time, since employees are given days off instead of cash. Deferred payments can take the form of employer-financed retirement benefits for which employers set aside money now to enable their employees to receive pensions later. Other non-wage benefits are the percentages of workers' salaries that employers must set aside so that staff is properly covered by employment insurance, the Canada or Quebec pension plan, and workers' compensation. Stock options are another example of non-wage benefits often awarded to senior managers. All these different non-wage components are termed **supplementary labour income**. Total labour compensation or **labour income** then comprises earnings (wages and salaries) and supplementary labour income.[i] The individual's **total income** is the total command over resources of that person during a particular period (usually a year), including both labour compensation and unearned income. The latter can include income from stocks, bonds, debentures and other investments, transfer payments received from the government in the form of welfare payments, employment insurance benefits, and the like. Figure 7.1 illustrates the relation between labour income, non-labour income, and total individual income.

Nominal Wages Versus Real Wages

Another important distinction in any study of wages or earnings is that between money or nominal wages and real wages. The **nominal wage** denotes the rate of payment to workers in current dollars, e.g., $15 per hour or $550 per week. Nominal wages are most useful in comparing the pay of various workers at a given time. Compared over time, however, nominal wages lose much of their meaning as an indicator of the standard of living if the price level changes during the particular period. For example, a worker who earned $12 per hour in 1985 and $15 an hour 10 years later would have received a nominal wage increase of 25%. The worker would be better off in real terms only if the price level had increased by less than 25%. If the price level increased by more than 25%, the worker would clearly be worse off.

supplementary labour income

non-wage benefits received by an employee

labour income

earnings and supplementary labour income combined

total income

the total of labour compensation and unearned income

nominal wage

the rate of payment to workers in current dollars

---

[i] Ideally, labour compensation should also include the monetary value of fringe benefits such as subsidized meals, uniforms and clothing, low-cost loans and housing, discounts on merchandise, and recreational, athletic, and daycare facilities. However, no survey currently provides these data.

FIGURE 7.1

Calculating Total Income

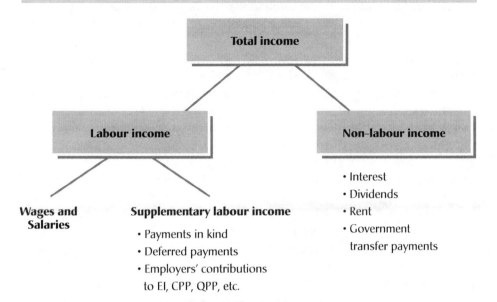

The relative changes in nominal wages and the price level are measured by real wages, which are nominal wages divided by some measure of prices. A rise in real wages suggests that more can be purchased with workers' nominal wages and vice versa. For example, if a worker earns $120 a day and a summer dress costs $60, one could say the worker earns the equivalent of two summer dresses a day (real wage = $120/$60 = 2). If the worker's daily pay rose to $150 over a period of 10 years and the price per dress increased to $70, the real wage would have increased to 2.14 (real wage $150/$70 = 2.14), that is, by 7%. The **real wage**, thus, measures the quantity of goods and services that can be bought with nominal wages.

Calculations of real wages are especially useful in comparing the purchasing power of workers' earnings over a period of time when both nominal wages and product prices are changing. Thus, real wages are normally expressed as an index number, which compares the purchasing power of an hour of work to some base period (the base is set equal to 100). The base year in Table 7.1 (page 187), for example, is 1992. In the next-to-last column, the index of real hourly wages in 2003 is listed as 104.7. This means that hourly real wages were 4.7% higher in 2003 than in the base year 1992:

$$[(104.7 - 100)/100] \times 100$$

To arrive at the index of real hourly wages requires the calculation of an index of nominal wages and an index of prices. An index of nominal wages can be constructed for each year (with 1992 as a base) by dividing the wage in each year by $15.38 (the hourly wage in 1992) and multiplying by 100. For the base year, 1992, the nominal wage index is 100:

$$(\$15.38/\$15.38) \times 100$$

real wage
the quantity of goods and services that can be bought with the nominal wage

For 2003, the index is 128.09:

$$(\$19.70/\$15.38) \times 100$$

The nominal wage index is reported in the sixth column of Table 7.1. Nominal wages in the Canadian manufacturing sector increased from 1992 to 2003 by 28.1%.

Changes in prices of goods and services can be measured by the **Consumer Price Index (CPI)**. The CPI measures the retail price of a basket of goods and services bought by a typical family. It is used to monitor changes over time in the cost of living of a typical family. If the CPI rises, the typical family must earn higher nominal wages in order to maintain the same standard of living. As the fifth column in Table 7.1 indicates, the CPI in 2003 was 122.3. The cost of living between 1992 and 2003 thus increased by 22.3%. If we divide the index for nominal wages in 2003 by the CPI and multiply by 100, we get the index of real hourly wages, as indicated in the seventh column [(128.09/122.3) × 100 = 104.7]. While the nominal hourly wages increased by 28.1%, real hourly wages rose by only 4.7%. The difference between nominal and real wage changes is due to the increase in the price level measured by changes in the CPI. The increase in the overall level of prices is called **inflation**. We can write the relationship between changes in the nominal wage rate, the real wage rate, and inflation in general as follows:

Change in the real wage rate = Change in the nominal wage rate − Inflation rate

For example, nominal wages and inflation increased between 2002 and 2003 by 3.1% and 2.8%, respectively. As a result, the real wage rose by 0.3%.

So far we have focused attention on the worker, for whom wages are income. For the majority of the workforce, wages are the single largest determinant of living standards; however, for most employers, they are the single largest cost component in the production process. Yet the crucial item for the company is not the amount of wages or compensation paid per hour but the labour cost per unit of output. Choosing an hour as the time reference, unit labour cost is defined as the hourly wage rate divided by average labour productivity, which is measured by the units of output a worker produces in an hour:

$$Labour\ cost\ per\ unit\ of\ output = \frac{Wage\ rate}{Output\ per\ worker\ (labour\ productivity)}$$

For example, a company paying an hourly wage of $15 to workers producing 60 units of output per hour would have a lower labour unit cost than a company paying $13 to employees who produce only 40 units per hour. In the former case, the labour cost per unit is 25 cents ($15/60), while in the latter it is 33 cents ($13/40).

When it comes to tracking the long-term changes in earnings and labour compensation in Canada, as in the case of work hours, there is a mix of data series, many of which are discontinued, scattered over different industrial sectors or labour force groups, and varying in definitions and coverage. Ideally, one would like to find a consistent time series on total labour compensation derived from a broadly based survey of well-defined occupations in specific

Consumer Price Index (CPI)

a measure of the price of a basket of goods and services bought by a typical family

inflation

an increase in the overall level of prices in the economy

Table 7.1

Average Wages and Earnings of Production Workers in Canadian Manufacturing, 1945–2003

Year	Weekly Earnings (Current Dollars)	Average Weekly Hours Paid For	Average Hourly Wage (Current Dollars)	Consumer Price Index (1992 = 100)	Index of Nominal Hourly Wages (1992 = 100)	Index of Real Hourly Wages (1992 = 100)	Annual Percentage Change in Real Hourly Wages Over Previous 10 Years
1945	30.98	44.1	0.67				
1950	45.94	42.1	1.06	14.9	6.89	46.2	
1955	60.53	41.0	1.44	16.8	9.36	55.7	
1960	72.39	40.4	1.77	18.5	11.50	62.2	3.5
1965	89.30	41.1	2.14	20.0	13.91	69.6	
1970	132.75	39.7	3.01	24.2	19.57	80.9	3.0
1975	213.43	38.6	5.06	34.5	32.90	95.3	
1980	342.19	38.5	8.19	52.4	53.25	101.6	2.6
1985	486.97	38.6	11.59	75.0	75.36	100.5	
1990	599.37	38.3	14.19	93.5	92.26	98.7	−0.3
1992	652.92	38.3	15.38	100.0	100.0	100.0	
1995	694.58	38.5	16.19	104.2	105.27	101.0	
1998	755.92	38.6	17.59	108.6	114.37	105.3	
2000	796.89	38.9	18.29	113.5	118.92	104.8	0.6
2001	808.10	38.9	18.59	116.4	120.87	103.8	
2002	830.14	39.1	19.10	119.0	124.19	104.4	0.5
2003	842.00	38.9	19.70	122.3	128.09	104.7	

Note: The weekly earnings include overtime. The figures in this table are derived from several sources. Since definitions of earnings and industrial classification systems have changed over time, caution should be exercised in making comparisons over time.

Sources: For 1945–65, Statistics Canada. (1983). *Historical Statistics of Canada, 1945–1965* (2nd ed.). Ottawa: Statistics Canada (Catalogue no. 11-516, Series E61-62, E131); for 1970–80, Statistics Canada (1973–80, March issues). *Employment Earnings and Hours*, Vols. 51–58, Tables 14, 15, and 18. Ottawa: Statistics Canada (Catalogue no. 72-002); for 1985–98, Statistics Canada. (2000). *Canadian Economic Observer, Historical Statistical Supplement 1999/2000*, Table 9. Ottawa: Statistics Canada (Catalogue no. 11-210); for 2000–2002, Statistics Canada. (2002). *Canadian Economic Observer, Historical Statistical Supplement 2002/03*; for 2003, Statistics Canada. (2004, May). *Canadian Economic Observer* (Catalogue no. 11-010); for Consumer Price Index, Statistics Canada. (1999, July). *Canadian Economic Observer, Historical Statistical Supplement 1998/99*, Vol. 7, Table 12. Ottawa: Statistics Canada (Catalogue no. 11-210); and for 1999–2003, Statistics Canada CANSIM database, Table 326-0002.

industries and geographic regions. Unfortunately, no such source is available in Canada. Information on various components of labour income must be pieced together from various data sources. The following sections present three data sources to provide a picture of the main developments of various aspects of labour compensation over the last decades.

Changes in Total Labour Income and Labour's Share

The first source is Statistics Canada's National Income and Expenditure Accounts. Estimates of wages and salaries and supplementary labour income in the national accounts are primarily based on income tax records. At the end of the calendar year, all employers are required to submit T–4 forms to the Canada Revenue Agency (CRA). These forms provide information on company payrolls and personal income tax deductions that were remitted from employees regularly throughout the year. Quarterly and monthly estimates of labour income are derived by linking the annual tax data to related series generated from the Labour Force Survey or the Survey of Employment, Payrolls, and Hours.

Figure 7.2 describes the annual percentage changes in total labour income, adjusted for inflation, from 1948 to 2003.[ii] Over those 50 years, the trend in annual growth rates has been declining. Labour income showed strong growth throughout the 1950s and 1960s, in both decades averaging 6% per year. Since the mid-1970s, largely due to the three recessions in 1974–75, 1981–82, and 1990–92, growth rates dipped. Throughout the 1980s growth rates dropped by more than half to an average of 2.2%, and in the 1990s they declined further to an annual rate of 1.8%.

gross national product (GNP)

the total income earned by Canadians in a given year

labour's share

labour income as a ratio of total income (GNP)

Growth in labour income closely followed the total income earned by Canadians, commonly defined as Canada's **gross national product (GNP)**.[iii] As a result, labour income as a ratio of total income (GNP), called **labour's share**, has fluctuated within a narrow band over the last five decades (see Figure 7.3, page 190). In 1947, labour's share was 0.49; 64 years later it was 0.53. In other words, as the output of the economy has grown, employees (whose income is represented in labour's share) and owners of capital (who receive the remaining portion of total income) have shared equally in the growth of total income. Labour's share noticeably increased during recessions, starting with the 1953–54 recession and continuing the same pattern in the last three recessions of 1974–75, 1981–82, and 1990–92. Were it not for the cyclical movement of labour's share, the near constancy of the ratio over a long period would be more pronounced.

The approximate constancy of labour's share in national income is not unique to Canada. In fact, it has been observed in many other industrialized countries, such as Germany, Japan, and the United States. As long ago as 1927, the American economist Paul Douglas noticed to his surprise that the division of national income between capital and labour had been roughly constant in the U.S. over a long period.

[ii] In the National Income Accounting System, labour income is defined as all compensation paid to employees residing in Canada. This includes Canadians employed abroad, if their residence is listed as being in Canada. Not included are earnings received by self-employed people such as independent professionals, proprietors of unincorporated businesses, and farmers.

[iii] As a measure of total Canadian income, GNP is preferable to gross domestic product (GDP), which is total income earned domestically. Suppose a resident of Hong Kong works temporarily in Vancouver. The income that person earns is part of Canadian GDP because it is earned in Canada, but the income is not part of GNP because the worker is not a Canadian national. While GNP excludes the income earned by foreigners in Canada, it includes the income that Canadians earn abroad. The use of GNP as a benchmark is consistent with the definition of labour income, which includes the earnings of Canadians working abroad. GNP is generally about 4% lower than GDP.

FIGURE 7.2

Annual Changes in Real Labour Income, 1948–2003

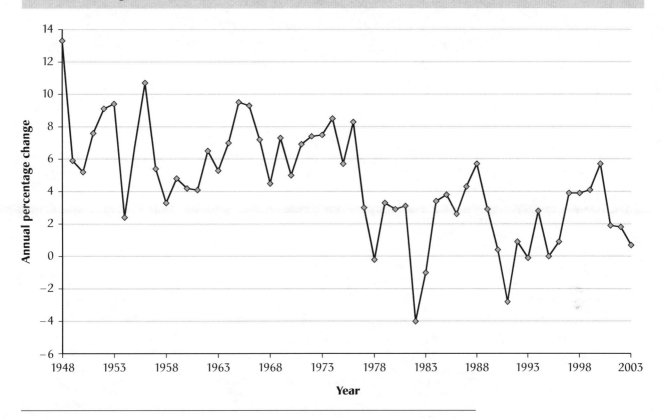

Sources: For 1947–94, adapted from Statistics Canada. (1995). *Canadian Economic Observer, Historical Statistical Supplement 1994/5*. Catalogue no. 11–210; for 1995–2003, adapted from Statistics Canada CANSIM II database http://cansim2.statcan.ca, series V1996534.

The observed constancy of labour's share allows us to draw an interesting conclusion from the following simple equation.

$$Labour's\ share = \frac{L}{Y} = \frac{W \times E}{P \times y} = \frac{\frac{W}{P}}{\frac{y}{E}}$$

In this formula, L stands for labour income and Y for total income measured in current prices, or nominal GNP. Labour income is the average nominal labour income per worker (W) multiplied by the number of employed workers (E). Total income can be decomposed into its real component; that is, the quantity of goods and services actually produced (y), and the price level (P).

The second ratio in the formula is just a different way of expressing the first ratio. The numerator (W/P) now denotes the average nominal labour income divided by the price level—the real average labour income. The denominator (y/E) is the real output produced in an economy divided by the

FIGURE 7.3

Share of Labour Income in Gross National Product, 1947–2011

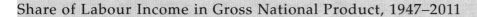

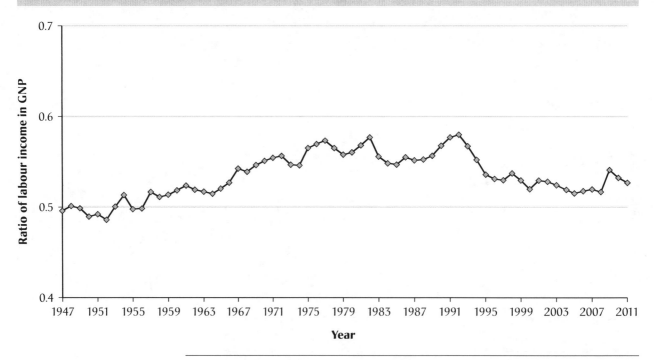

Sources: For 1947–94, adapted from Statistics Canada. (1995). *Canadian Economic Observer, Historical Statistical Supplement 1994/5*. Catalogue no. 11–210; for 1995–2003, adapted from Statistics Canada CANSIM II database http://cansim2.statcan.ca, series V19996534 (labour income) and V647785 (GNP); for 1997–2011, adapted from Statistics Canada, Estimates of Labour Income: Data Tables, catalogue number 13–021–X.

average labour productivity

the output produced per worker in a given period

number of employed workers. We call this ratio **average labour productivity**; it tells us how much, on average, an employed worker has produced within a certain period.[iv]

A constant labour's share implies that nominal earnings and supplemental labour income rose over time in line with inflation plus average labour productivity. Put differently, real average labour income fully absorbed the gains in labour productivity made over the years. If workers had been paid less in real terms than what they had contributed to overall production—that is, if real average labour income were less than labour productivity—the share of labour income in national income would have declined.

When interpreting the constancy of labour's share, one must keep in mind that national accounts define labour income broadly, including cash compensation, the realized value of stock options, and the value of taxable fringe benefits such as the personal use of a company car. Likewise, as a factor of production labour includes a heterogeneous group of people: anyone who draws a wage or salary from a business is counted as an employee, from dish-

[iv] Labour productivity is also defined as output produced per hour rather than per employed worker. Both definitions of average labour productivity are used in the literature. The former definition is more precise because it avoids possible biases in labour productivity caused by changes in hours of work and thus allows comparisons of labour productivity over time. The latter definition is more practical, since the number of employed workers is easier to establish than the number of hours actually worked.

In a recession, total output produced declines and unemployment rises. Why then does labour's share in total output rise during a recession? One reason is that in a cyclical downturn firms tend first to adjust their labour input by reducing hours of work. Initially, they try to hold on to their workforce, especially if they have invested substantial amounts in hiring and training. This investment would be lost if workers who were temporarily laid off were not available for recall when production returned to normal. This strategy is called **labour hoarding**. As firms retain workers who have little work to do, labour productivity falls. Only if a recession is deep and prolonged will firms lay off workers on a larger scale.

The other reason for the increase in labour's share is that firms cannot easily cut wage rates to adjust their labour cost to falling demand. They are often bound by collective agreements that specify the wage rates to be paid. Even if a wage contract were to expire during a recession, unions or individual employers would strongly resist wage cuts.

Rigid wages and falling labour productivity explain the rise of labour's share in recessions. In our formula for labour's share, we can see that if wages (W) and employment (E) remain constant while real output ($P \times y$) declines, labour's share (L/Y) must increase. Or using the second expression, as labour productivity (y/E) declines relative to the real wage rate (W/P), labour's share rises.

---

washers paid minimum wage to car mechanics, doctors, lawyers, and chief executive officers of corporations earning several million dollars a year. Furthermore, the meaning of labour's share becomes less clear in light of certain arbitrary legal definitions in the national accounts regarding the classification of income of business owners. For example, if two doctors are partners in an unincorporated medical practice, their income is counted as proprietor's income, but if they incorporate their business and draw a salary from their corporations (which, given the tax advantages, is likely), their income is counted as employee compensation. Because corporate officers control the firm's capital and in many cases are the owners of the firm, their compensation should be classified as capital income. Attributing the income of business owners to labour income may partly explain the long-run stability of labour's share.

Some people are simultaneously members of the workforce and owner of capital: that is, they derive income both from their labour services and from owning capital. The income distribution by factors of production, also called factoral or functional income distribution, therefore, should not be confused with personal income distribution. **Functional income distribution** refers to the shares of total income owned by the factors of production, labour, and capital. **Personal income distribution** is concerned with how national income is distributed among groups of individuals or families ranked by the size of their annual incomes.

Changes in Average Labour Income

While aggregated data on labour income can give a picture of how workers as a group fared over time, they convey little information about the compensation of individual workers. Changes in total labour income reflect changes in

labour hoarding

practice of firms to retain workers during a downturn in the economy in order to avoid the possibility of temporarily laid off workers' no longer being available when the economy returns to normal levels

functional income distribution

the share of national income going to the owners of the factors of production, labour, and capital

personal income distribution

the share of national income going to groups of families or individuals

real average labour income

total annual labour income, adjusted for inflation, divided by average annual number of paid workers

the number of employed persons as well as compensation levels. To obtain a measure, albeit imperfect, of the compensation received by a worker, we divide total annual labour income by the average annual number of paid workers. Adjusted for inflation, this is called the **real average labour income**.

From the late 1940s throughout the 1950s, real average labour income grew at an average annual rate of about 4%. These significant income gains continued until the mid-1970s at an only slightly reduced average annual rate of 3.5%. From 1976 on, however, the picture started to change dramatically. With high inflation rates outpacing growth in average nominal labour income, changes in real average annual labour income became negative in 1978. In 10 of the following 20 years, 1979–1998, growth rates remained negative. In years when growth was positive, the advances were not significant enough to out-weigh negative growth. During the last five years, 1999–2003, the picture did not improve, leaving annual growth rates at just 0.5%. The overall result is that over the last 25 years no gains were made in real average labour income.

Also of interest are the differences in labour income changes by sector. While average labour income increased in the goods-producing sector, it declined in the services-producing sector. The increase in the goods-producing sector resulted from a substantial increase in the supplementary income component, which more than compensated for the slight loss in wages and salaries. In contrast, the labour income loss in the services-producing sector resulted from the large decline in real wages and salaries, surpassing the modest growth in supplementary labour income. Several factors may account for the different patterns in the two sectors: the higher rate of union-ization, the large share of adult men, and the slower employment growth in the goods-producing sector, versus the high levels of youth and female employment and the higher rate of part-time employment in the services-producing sector.

These factors point to a main difficulty in interpreting changes in average annual labour income figures: this measure of compensation does not distin-guish between factors that influence an individual worker's labour income and those that do not. Factors such as the number of hours worked, changes in labour statutes (such as regulations governing minimum wages and over-time premiums), and the hourly, weekly, or monthly wage rate can affect the labour income of individual workers. Further, a change in legislation may extend coverage of various components of supplementary labour income to new groups of workers or increase supplementary labour income contribu-tions made on behalf of existing workers.

On the other hand, there are factors that have no effect on an individual worker's labour income but may affect average labour income overall. These relate to the distributional aspects of employment in the labour market. One example of distributional factors is shifts in the composition of employment within and among industries, regions, and occupational groups, or shifts between full-time and part-time workers or persons holding more than one job. Substantial employment growth in low-wage service industries would be reflected in a decline of average labour income, although an individual worker's labour income might remain constant (assuming no job change).

To understand how shifts between industries affect the annual income per employee, suppose that there are only two industries in the economy: one that might be called the "goods" industry, and the other the "services" industry. Half of the employees work in the goods industry and the other half work in the services industry. Suppose also that all employees working in the goods industry receive a labour income of $35 000 per year regardless of their occupation or the region they work in, and that all employees in the services industry receive $29 000 per year. The average annual income in the economy would be $32 000 [($35 000 × 0.5) + ($29 000 × 0.5)]. Now suppose that labour income in both industries remains constant but that employment in the goods industry falls by 15% over a particular period, while employment in the services industry rises by 15%. The average annual income would fall to $31 550 [($35 000 × 0.425) + ($29 000 × 0.575)] or by 1.4%, even though workers' labour income in both industries did not change. Similar effects would be observed if employment growth in part-time jobs was relatively higher than in full-time jobs.

Changes in Average Weekly Earnings and Hourly Wages

The Survey on Employment, Payrolls, and Hours (SEPH) collects data on labour compensation. Although SEPH does not collect data on actual wage rates, the information it gathers can be used to calculate measures of average weekly earnings and hourly wages by dividing total earnings by total paid weeks or hours. The average hourly wage data from the SEPH have the advantage of being directly derived from a survey, but they are limited when compared to labour income estimates from the System of National Accounts. The information is available only from March 1983 on and is less comprehensive because it excludes compensation elements not directly reflected in the payrolls of firms, such as employers' contributions to pension funds, health, and insurance programs.

In 1983, Canadian employees in all industries were paid an average of $383 per week, including overtime premiums. Twenty years later, in 2003, average weekly earnings had risen to $690, that is, by 80%. Although weekly earnings increased at about 4% annually between 1983 and 1990, their growth dropped off sharply after the 1990–91 recession. If inflation is taken into account, real weekly earnings stagnated over the entire period of 1983–2003.

The weekly earnings figures for all industries hide marked differences in the earning levels between the goods- and services-producing industries. In 1983, average weekly earnings in the goods-producing industries were $471, compared to $351 in the services-producing industries. In other words, employees in services-producing industries earned 75 cents for every dollar earned per week by their counterparts in the goods-producing industries. By 2003, weekly earnings in the two sectors had grown to $864 and $638, respectively. That is, at 74 cents, the gap had changed very little over the last 20 years.

Because average weekly earnings are the product of average hourly earnings times average usual hours worked per week, an increase in nominal weekly earnings may not reflect any gain in the reward for labour services but may just result from Canadians' working longer hours compared to earlier years. Average hourly wages, therefore, is a preferable indicator. Average hourly wages computed for all industries grew from $9.83 in 1983 to $17.20 in 2003. On an hourly basis, the wage gap between the services- and goods-producing industries in 1983 was very much the same as the difference in weekly earnings, namely 74 cents for every dollar earned in an hour. A similar gap applied in 2003: $15.48 in the services-producing industries as compared to $20.43 in the goods-producing industries, or 76 cents for every dollar.

These earnings estimates share a problem with the National Accounts estimates of labour income, namely that they are subject to the effects of compositional changes in employment that do not reflect changes in employees' hourly earnings. To correct partly for these problems, Statistics Canada constructed a series of average hourly earnings with fixed weights. Overtime compensation is omitted because it is an important source of income differences between industries. All employees are included on the assumption that salaried employees work their "standard workweek."[v] The fixed weights are calculated using employee paid hours data for 1986, the base year for the series. Separate weights are applied for 258 three-digit industry categories to exclude the effects of shifts in the employment composition between these industries. Fixed weights are also applied separately within each of the provinces and territories, so that differential employment growth rates among these regions will not be a source of compositional variation in the earnings series. Finally, fixed weights are also used for employees paid by the hour and salaried employees. Significant shifts between these two employee groups, for example, can occur over the business cycle. Employers tend to retain highly qualified salaried employees during recessions partly because the hiring and termination costs for this group of employees are higher than for hourly paid workers.

Figure 7.4 shows the annual growth rates in the fixed-weighted nominal and real average hourly wages and the inflation rate (as measured by the CPI) from 1984 to 2003. Over the 20-year period, nominal wages and the inflation rate followed a similar path, with the exceptions of the years 1991–92 and 1993–94, when the inflation rate dropped more than nominal wages, raising real wages in these years by 2.3% and 1.3%, respectively. From 1997 to 1998, the growth rate in nominal wages increased while the inflation rate dropped further, leading to a modest positive increase in real hourly wages. In 10 of the 20 years, the growth rate in real wages was negative or zero, which offset most of the small gains made in the other years; as a result, over the entire period real hourly wages remained largely stagnant.

Changes in Nominal and Real Wage Rates

base wage rate

the wage rate that applies to the lowest-paid classification for workers in a bargaining unit

The direct data source for wage rates is Labour Canada's series in base wage rates as negotiated in collective agreements. The **base wage rate** in a contract applies to the lowest-paid classification for workers in the bargaining unit.

[v] The SEPH questionnaire defines a standard workweek as the "average number of hours of work normally scheduled in a workweek."

FIGURE 7.4

Nominal and Real Average Hourly Wages, 1984–2003

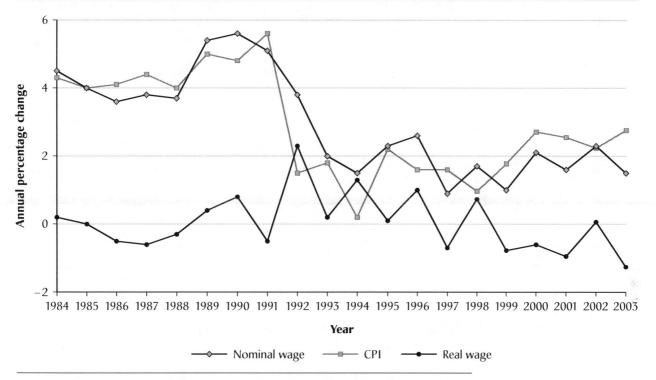

Source: Authors' tabulations, for 1984–99, based on Statistics Canada. (2000). *Canadian Economic Observer, Historical Statistical Supplement, 1999/2000*, Tables 9 and 12. Ottawa: Statistics Canada (Catalogue no. 11-210). For 2000–03, based on Statistics Canada. (May 2002/May 2004). *Canadian Economic Observer*, Tables 9 and 12. Ottawa: Statistics Canada (Catalogue no. 11-010).

The data are available on a consistent basis over a relatively long period of time. However, they are only available for unionized workers. Figure 7.5 (page 196) shows the year-to-year changes in the nominal wage rate, the inflation rate, and the real wage rate (the rate of change of nominal wages minus the inflation rate) for the period 1967–2003. Nominal wage rate changes are the compound annual average percentage increase in base wage rates in major collective agreements over the duration of the contract. Major wage settlements refer to agreements involving 500 or more employees. Only those collective agreements are included that do not contain COLA clauses. As we saw in Chapter 5, COLA clauses tie nominal wage changes to changes in the inflation rate.

The picture that emerges from Figure 7.5 is similar to the one reported in Figure 7.4. Between 1967 and 1976, unions were able to obtain wage concessions that substantially exceeded the inflation rate. Real wage growth, as a result, was very high during this period, averaging 4.5% per year. By 1975, nominal wage increases exceeded 19% and inflation had reached almost 11%, leading to the largest increase in real wages in the past three decades.

FIGURE 7.5

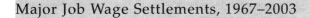

Major Job Wage Settlements, 1967–2003

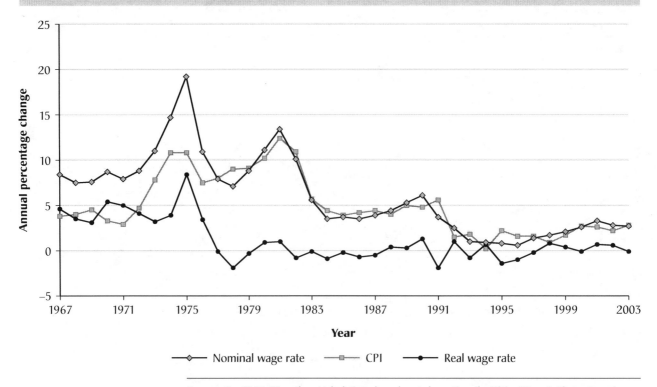

Sources: For 1967–77, authors' tabulations based on Labour Canada. *Major Wage Settlements*, various issues. Ottawa: Bureau of Labour Information. For 1978–2003, Statistics Canada CANSIM II database http://cansim2.statcan.ca, series V4327082.

Responding to the acceleration in wages and prices, the federal government introduced the Anti-Inflation Program (AIP) in October 1975. As a result of the wage and price controls of the AIP, wage settlements and prices declined substantially during the three years of the AIP, although prices declined less than wage settlements did. In 1977, for the first time, real wage change was negative.

The lifting of the controls and the second major increase in OPEC oil prices in 1979 led to another round of wage and price increases, which reached two-digit levels in 1980. In contrast to the earlier wage and price escalation, however, nominal wage and price changes followed so closely that real wage growth remained below 1%. This time, the Bank of Canada responded with a forceful anti-inflation policy. As we mentioned in Chapter 6, the Bank of Canada can affect the overall level of economic activity through monetary policy. By reducing the supply of money, the central bank can raise interest rates, which discourages households and firms from spending money on goods and services. As overall demand declines, firms reduce their prices in order to sell their products or services.

When it raised nominal interest rates above 16%, the Bank of Canada created a severe recession in 1981–82. As economic activity drastically slowed down, inflation and nominal wage growth declined dramatically. Throughout most of the 1980s real annual wage change remained negative. Only toward the end of the decade did real wage growth become marginally positive when nominal wages and prices started to edge up again, with contract settlements surpassing inflation. Average annual growth in real wages over the whole decade, however, remained in the negative range.

In 1988, the governor of the Bank of Canada announced that he was determined not only to prevent inflation from rising but also to reduce the inflation rate permanently to near zero. Later, in February 1991, the governor and the minister of finance agreed to set an inflation target of 2% by the end of 1995. The target was in fact reached by 1992. In its pursuit of the zero-inflation policy, the Bank of Canada was the main contributor to the 1990–91 recession, arguably the worst recession Canada has experienced since the Great Depression. By tightening monetary conditions, the central bank raised real short-term interest rates to close to 10%. The increase, together with the Canadian–U.S. exchange rate appreciation of almost 20%, caused annual real growth in the gross domestic product to decline sharply from a positive rate of 5% to a negative rate of 2%. The drastic decline in GDP and employment put such pressure on prices and nominal wages that both grew during the early and mid-1990s at the lowest rates experienced over the last 30 years. Since increases in wages were slightly below the inflation rate for most of the period 1990–1997, average annual growth in real wage rates was –0.2%. Over the last six years, 1998–2003, real wage growth remained flat, averaging just 0.4% annually.

In conclusion, the various measures of worker compensation—whether total or average real labour income, average real hourly wages, or real hourly wage rates negotiated in major wage settlements—all show that compensation has grown very little over the last 27 years. Important differences, however, have appeared in the pattern of wages for different labour force groups.

Earnings Gaps

So far, we have focused on the trends in levels or percentage changes of various earnings or compensation measures. Changes in average levels or percentages, however, do not tell us much about the structure of wages, namely the relationship of one wage rate to another. Wage differences can be analyzed with different focuses: regional, industrial, occupational, gender, age, and so on.

The Gender Gap

Men and women have fared very differently since the early 1970s. Earnings have remained largely stagnant for men, whereas for women they have increased steadily in each of the last three decades. The pattern was very consistent no matter whether all female and male earners were considered or only men and women who worked full-time, full-year. Despite substantial gains women have made in earnings, however, the gap was still around 30 percentage points in 2002. In the late 1960s, women who worked full-time, full-year, made on average 58 cents for every dollar earned by their male counterparts. In 2002, the gap was 71 cents to each dollar earned by men.[vi] In absolute terms, full-time, full-year female workers earned on average $36 000 compared to $50 500 earned by men.

Historically, women have earned less than men because they were concentrated in lower-paying occupations, averaged fewer hours of market work per week, had lower job tenure and less work experience, and received lower wage rates.

Some of the gains women have made over the last decades have been due to their large investments in postsecondary education. The number of women earners with a university degree has almost tripled since 1980. According to the 2001 Census, the share of women earners with a university degree now exceeds the share of men. As a result, women have advanced into higher-paying occupations in which traditionally they have not been highly represented. In 2000, almost one-third of women (31.7%) worked in occupations paying more than the national average; 20 years ago, only 23.4% did so.[1]

However, as Table 7.2 illustrates, women still are underrepresented in higher-paying occupations, such as management (especially senior management positions) and professional occupations in the natural sciences and engineering. They are overrepresented in lower-paying occupations such as clerical/administrative and sales and service occupations.

While women nowadays work longer hours compared to earlier decades, within the same occupation, they still tend to work on average fewer hours per week than men. Disregarding the relatively high concentration of women in part-time employment and concentrating on men and women who work full-time, full-year, and who have recently entered the labour market with a bachelor's degree, women work on average 5% to 8% fewer hours than men.[2] Since gender differences in hours of work among new labour force entrants are likely to fan out with age, differences in hours of work remain an important contributing factor to the gender earnings gap.

The Age Gap

While earnings differentials between men and women have declined, substantial differences in earnings have emerged based on age. In Canada, the gap between younger and older workers has widened considerably. From 1972 to 1980, the rate of growth of real earnings for both sexes did not vary much with age. Since 1980, however, young workers have fared much more poorly. For men, the generational divide occurs at the age of 40, with those younger than 40 experiencing earnings losses, and those over 40 (particularly over 50) experiencing gains.[3] For men in their mid- and late thirties who worked full-time, full-year, earnings fell by about 7% between 1980 and 1990

[vi] Data on the male–female wage gap before 1996 are drawn from the Survey of Consumer Finances (SCF) and after 1996 are taken from the Survey of Labour and Income Dynamics (SLID). For conceptual differences between the SCF and the SLID, see Drolet, M. (2003). "The Male–Female Wage Gap." *Perspectives of Labour and Income*, 14(1): 29–35.

TABLE 7.2

Distribution of Female Employment by Occupation, 1987–2003

| | YEAR | | |
OCCUPATIONAL GROUP	1987	1994	2003
Management	28.9	35.1	35.4
Senior management	16.9	19.8	24.2
Other management	30.6	36.9	36.1
Professional	49.8	52.2	53.4
Natural sciences/engineering/mathematics	16.7	17.0	22.0
Teaching	57.3	59.4	62.9
Doctors/dentists/other health	44.1	48.7	52.1
Nursing/therapy/other health-related	87.3	87.1	87.7
Clerical/administrative	74.4	74.9	75.1
Sales/service	55.7	56.4	58.7
Trades/transport/construction	5.3	5.4	6.6
Processing/manufacturing/utilities	30.2	29.2	28.9

Source: Adapted from Statistics Canada. (2003). *Women in Canada: Work Chapter Updates.* Catalogue no. 89F0133, p. 20, Table 11.

and rose only by 1.5% during the 1990s. The drop in earnings was worse for all younger groups, with those in their twenties experiencing declines in each of the last two decades.

The dividing line between gainers and losers for women appears to be at age 30. Women aged 30–34 faced a 1.4% decline in earnings between 1980 and 1990, but a 6% gain in the following decade. All older age groups experienced back-to-back gains in earnings in each decade. Women under the age of 30 regardless of education lost ground during the 1980s and 1990s.

Occupational Earnings Polarization

One of the most important changes in the Canadian labour market has been the widening of the earnings distribution. The debate on the growing polarization of occupational earnings and the consequent shrinkage of jobs paying middle-class wages is sometimes referred to as the "declining middle class" or the "decline of middle-class wage jobs."

When we discuss issues of inequality, we must be careful how we specify the variable we choose to compare earnings or incomes of groups. If we choose family income, this measure includes incomes of all family members and, as we saw earlier, includes income from other sources—for example, government transfer payments, dividends, or interest from bonds—in addition to labour earnings. A widening dispersion in earnings does not necessarily imply an increase in inequality of family income, especially if changes in spouses' incomes offset each other. In a study of the 1970s and 1980s, Beach and Slotsve concluded that overall inequality in family income did not change significantly during these two decades, although the inequality in men's earnings widened sharply.[4] The proportion of middle-class men (those with earnings between 50% and 150% of the median) declined over the last 25 years. At the same time, the proportions of both rich men (with earnings above 150% of the median) and poor men (with earnings below 50% of the median) increased. Among women, however, there was no evidence of a widening dispersion. The proportion of women in the middle class remained unchanged, while the proportion of poor women declined and that of rich women increased slightly.

Why has the distribution of men's earnings become more unequal? Because earnings are the product of wages and hours, perhaps the main reason is related to changes in hours rather than to wages. We noted in Chapter 5 that hours of work have polarized and that more people work more as well as less than the number of hours in the standard workweek. Morissette et al., for example, report that, while real earnings among men in the bottom fifth of wage earners declined by 16% between 1973 and 1989, about half of this decline can be attributed to the decline in the number of hours worked.[5] Still, among men who worked full-time for a full year, the real annual earnings of the bottom fifth fell by 7% over this period.

Where are the sources for the increasing inequality in wages? Do we have to look for explanations primarily on the supply or the demand side, or to institutional changes in the labour market? There is no consensus yet among economists. The various explanations can best be contrasted within the supply and demand framework of two labour markets: the market for skilled labour, and the market for unskilled labour. Wages of unskilled workers might decline in relation to those of skilled workers because the relative demand for unskilled workers has declined or because the relative demand for skilled workers has increased. Alternatively, the skill differential could have grown due to a decline in the supply of skilled workers relative to the supply of unskilled workers.

One of the explanations advanced is that changes in skill differentials over time have been driven by changes in the growth of the supply of higher-educated workers. The dramatic increase in higher-educated workers in the 1970s led to the narrowing of the skill differential in that decade. The supply increase was mainly due to the large baby-boom cohorts and the large expansion of secondary and postsecondary education. In the subsequent decade, the relative supply growth decelerated significantly and the wage differential widened. The slowdown in the growth of graduates from the postsecondary sector was larger in the U.S. than in Canada. This may be one of the reasons why the widening in the skill differential has been smaller in Canada than in the U.S.[6]

An alternative account is that the growing inequality of the earnings of skilled and unskilled workers has been driven by relative shifts in labour demand. Possible factors working on the demand side are industrial restructuring favouring the employment of more-skilled workers and increased international competition, especially from low-wage countries. Increased imports from these countries have reduced the demand for less-skilled labour in Canada, causing wages to fall relative to skilled workers.

Another explanation attributes the demand shifts to technological change. Many economists believe that the most important force at work in shaping the relative compensation of skilled and unskilled workers has been skill-biased technological progress. New machines and new methods of production require skilled workers, today more so than in the past. Several recent studies point to the computer revolution as the main source of skill-biased technological change.[7] Office automation has become inseparable from the computer. Robotics is growing on the shop floor and the assembly line. Computer-assisted technology is rapidly advancing in every manufacturing or service industry. The advent of computer technology, and the design and manufacturing applications it has spawned, puts more demands on workers. The new methods of production require workers to be more flexible and do a variety of tasks. Firms have responded to the need for higher-skilled workers by upgrading the skill level of their employees, displacing low-skilled workers in the process.

Yet another possibility, frequently advanced in the literature, hinges on the decline in labour market institutions mainly in the United States, such as union representation, minimum wage laws, employment insurance provisions, etc.[8] Traditionally, these institutions have compressed the wage structure or prevented the relative decline of workers at the bottom of the wage distribution.

Which of these various explanations is the more relevant is a matter of controversy. Although much of the literature treats changes in labour market institutions, foreign trade, and technological progress as separate factors, it should be stressed that they are likely interrelated processes. For example, in a context of stronger international competition, firms may come under

Labour Market Issue 7.2

Bargaining Structure and the Relative Wage Decline Among Unskilled Workers

Unions tend to protect or even raise wages of less-skilled workers relative to those of skilled workers. Workers in the United States are less unionized than those in most other industrialized nations. This fact is, therefore, often cited as an explanation of why the level of wage inequality in the United States is higher than in comparable economies. In Canada, unionization rates have changed much less and the wage gap between skilled and less-skilled workers has grown less sharply.

In France, union membership has also fallen drastically but declining unionization has not been associated with relative wage declines for low-skilled workers. One reason may be differences in the bargaining structure.

Collective bargaining in France is highly centralized. It takes place at the industry level and provisions bargained for by unions are often extended to non-union workers. In the United States and Canada, bargaining is decentralized. It takes place mostly at the firm or plant level where competitive forces are felt more directly.

Not only did the rate of unionization fall in the United States, but bargaining also became even more decentralized. As unionization declined and collective bargaining agreements increasingly had to respond to market forces at the firm or plant level, unions' power to prevent the widening of the wage gap between skilled and unskilled workers weakened.

increasing pressure to adopt new technologies quickly. Improved technologies, in turn, can make firms more competitive internationally, which can lead to an expansion of international trade.

Will the polarization of earnings between skilled and unskilled workers continue to increase? Nobody knows for sure. Most predictions point in the direction of a worsening of the earnings gap, yet one can think of reasons that would show in an opposite direction. First, the relative increase in demand for skilled workers may simply slow down. For example, one could think of computers in the future as becoming more and more user friendly, even for unskilled workers. One can even think of computers as replacing skilled workers, those whose skills involve primarily the ability to compute or to memorize. Second, how much firms spend on research and development and in what directions they direct their research efforts in developing new technologies depend on expected profits. The low relative wage of unskilled workers may lead firms to explore new technologies that take advantage of unskilled, low-wage workers. Market forces may cause technological progress to become less skill-biased in the future. Third, the large increase in the relative wages of more educated or skilled workers implies that the return to acquiring more education and training is higher than it was several decades ago. Higher returns to education and training may induce people to further their education, thus increasing the relative supply of skilled workers. This would stabilize relative wages.

Summary

In analyzing changes in labour compensation, one must distinguish among different concepts: nominal wages and real wages, earnings, labour income, and total income. Over the last 50 years, labour income has followed very much the same trend as total national income. Labour's share in national income has changed very little, suggesting that workers as a group have been paid according to their productivity. While real labour income per worker grew rapidly in the three decades following World War II, average real labour income has stagnated since the mid-1970s.

Average real weekly earnings and real hourly wages showed a similar picture in that there have been no gains over the last two decades. The gap in weekly earnings and hourly wages between the goods-producing industries and the services-producing industries has hardly changed since the early 1980s.

While earnings differentials between men and women have declined, differences in earnings between older and younger workers have increased considerably. The gap between the earnings of male skilled and unskilled workers has also been increasing. Explanations for the widening skill differential range from increased competition from low-wage countries, to skill-biased technological progress, to a weakening of labour market institutions.

Key Terms

average labour productivity (page 190)

base wage rate (page 194)

Consumer Price Index (CPI) (page 186)

functional income distribution (page 191)

gross national product (GNP) (page 188)

inflation (page 186)

labour hoarding (page 191)

labour income (page 184)

labour's share (page 188)

net wages (page 183)

nominal wage (page 184)

personal income distribution (page 191)

real average labour income (page 192)

real wage (page 185)

salaried worker (page 183)

supplementary labour income (page 184)

total income (page 184)

wage earner (page 183)

Weblinks

For Consumer Price Index (inflation)
www.bankofcanada.ca/about/backgrounders/consumer-price-index/

For how monetary policy works
www.bankofcanada.ca/monetary-policy-introduction/

For inflation targeting in Canada
www.imf.org/external/pubs/ft/seminar/2000/targets/freedmn2.htm

For average earnings by sex
www.statcan.ca/english/Pgdb/labor01a.htm

For analysis of earnings based on the 2001 census
www12.statcan.ca/english/census01/Products/Analytic/companion/earn/pdf/96F0030XIE2001013.pdf

Discussion Questions

1. Does the market distinguish between a "fair" and an "unfair" wage? Explain.
2. What is the difference between a person's labour income and total income?
3. a. Labour's share in national income has remained fairly constant over the last 50 years. What are the implications for the relationship between real average labour income and labour productivity?

   b. Labour's share in total output generally rises in a recession. Why is this so?
4. Does an increase in the average annual labour income suggest that the individual worker's labour income has increased? Explain.
5. Real base wage rates negotiated in collective agreements changed little in Canada during the period 1975–2003. How could one explain the stagnation in real wages?

6. Average labour income increased in the manufacturing sector and declined in the service sector during the 1970s and 1980s. Provide an explanation for the different changes of average labour income in these two sectors.

7. One of the most striking changes in the personal distribution of income has been the widening gap in the earnings between skilled and unskilled workers. Discuss some of the factors that could explain the growing inequality between these two groups.

Using the Internet

1. Many of the data used in this text come from Statistics Canada's CANSIM II database, to which most colleges and universities in Canada have access. Each data series in CANSIM II has a CANSIM II number. For example, the consumer price index series that we used in this chapter has CANSIM II number V735319. In this exercise, you will generate the real wage data (1967–2003) underlying Figure 7.5 (page 196). First, retrieve the data on effective wage increases in base rates for agreements without cost of living allowance (COLA), all industries (V4327083). You will need to average the quarterly data to get the annual values. In a second step, retrieve the consumer price index series (V735319). Average the monthly data to get the annual values and calculate the annual percentage change in prices, that is, the inflation rate. In a third step, subtract in each year the inflation rate from the corresponding nominal wage increase. The result is a time series on real wages.

Exercises

1. a. You are given the following data on hourly wage rates for the Canadian manufacturing sector and on the consumer price index (CPI):

Year	Average hourly rate	CPI
1985	$11.59	75.0
1990	$14.19	93.3
1992	$15.38	100.0
1995	$16.19	104.2
2000	$18.29	113.6
2003	$19.70	122.3

    Construct the index of real hourly wages for the years given, starting with 1985 and ending with 2003. Use 1992 as the base year. What is the percentage change in the average hourly nominal wage between 1985 and 2003? What is the percentage change in the average hourly real wage?

b. From 1950 to 1960 and from 1960 to 1970, the percentage changes in average hourly real wages in Canadian manufacturing were 3.5% and 3.0%, respectively. Comparing the percentage changes in average hourly real wages from 1985 to 2003 (see your answer in part (a)), why do you think real wage growth has declined so drastically?

2. The consumer price index for the period 1999–2003 was as follows:

1999	110.5
2000	113.5
2001	116.4
2002	119.0
2003	122.3

a. Calculate the rate of inflation, according to the CPI.

b. Suppose that the hourly wage rate for a group of workers that sign an employment contract for the three-year period starting in 2000 is indexed to the CPI according to the formula

$$\Delta W/W = 0.03 + 0.5\ \Delta CPI/CPI$$

(Note: ΔW denotes the change in the nominal wage rate from one year to the other and ΔCPI denotes the change in the CPI from one year to the other.)

Calculate the actual increase in the wage during each year of the contract period. If the wage was $18.00 in 1999, what was it in 2000, 2001, and 2002? What happened to the real wage in terms of the CPI during those years?

c. Repeat your calculation with 0.03 reduced to 0 and 0.5 increased to 1. What indexing formula would the employer have preferred?

3. What is the difference between a craft union and an industrial union? Which of the two types of unions is likely to have a stronger equalizing effect on the wage structure of workers? Explain.

4. The wage gap between skilled and unskilled workers is larger in the U.S. than in Canada. In trying to explain the difference in the wage gap, labour economists have pointed to the fact that the degree of unionization in the U.S. is significantly lower than in Canada. How could the difference in unionization explain the difference in the wage gap?

References

[1]Statistics Canada. (2003). *2001 Census: Analysis Series. Earnings of Canadians: Making a Living in the New Economy.* Ottawa: Minister of Industry (Catalogue no. 96F0030XIE2001013), p. 10.

[2]Finnie, R., and Wannell, T. (1999). "The Gender Earnings Gap Amongst Recent Bachelor's Graduates." In R. Chaykowski and L. Powell (Eds.), *Women and Work.* Montreal and Kingston: McGill–Queen's University Press, p. 17, Table 4a.

[3]Statistics Canada. (2003). *2001 Census: Analysis Series. Earnings of Canadians: Making a Living in the New Economy.* Ottawa: Minister of Industry (Catalogue no. 96F0030XIE2001013), p. 11.

[4]Beach, C., and Slotsve, G. (1996). "Are We Becoming Two Societies? Income Polarization and the Myth of the Disappearing Middle Class." *Social Policy Challenge,* Vol. 12. Toronto: C.D. Howe Institute.

[5]Morissette, R., Myles, J., and Picot, G. (1995). "Earnings Polarization in Canada, 1969–1991." In K. Banting and C. Beach (Eds.), *Labour Market Polarization and Social Policy Reform*. Kingston: Queen's University School of Policy Studies.

[6]Murphy, L.M., Riddell, W.C., and Romer, P.M. (1998). "Wages, Skills, and Technology in the United States and Canada." In E. Helpman (Ed.), *General Purpose Technologies and Economic Growth*. Cambridge and London: MIT Press.

[7]Krueger, A.B. (1993). "How Computers Have Changed the Wage Structure: Evidence from Microdata 1984–89." *Quarterly Journal of Economics*, 108: 33–60. Also, Berman, E., Bound, J., and Griliches, Z. (1994). "Changes in the Demand for Skilled Labor Within U.S. Manufacturing Industries: Evidence from the Annual Survey of Manufacturing." *Quarterly Journal of Economics*, 109: 367–397.

[8]Di Nardo, J., and Lemieux, T. (1997). "Diverging Male Wage Inequality in the United States and Canada, 1981–88. Do Institutions Explain the Difference?" *Industrial and Labor Relations Review*, 50: 629–651.

Microeconomic Theory of the Labour Market

8. LABOUR MARKET DECISIONS OF HOUSEHOLDS

   APPENDIX 8A: INDIFFERENCE CURVE ANALYSIS OF LABOUR SUPPLY

9. LABOUR MARKET DECISIONS OF FIRMS

10. WAGE RATE AND EMPLOYMENT DETERMINATION

    APPENDIX 10A: WAGE RATE CHANGES AND UNEMPLOYMENT

11. WAGE RATE DIFFERENTIALS

12. EDUCATION, TRAINING, AND EARNINGS DIFFERENTIALS

PART III

Microeconomic Theory of the Labour Market

This part of the text applies the principles of demand and supply introduced in Chapter 2 to the labour market. The goal is to understand how wage rates and employment levels are determined. The reasons for wage rate differences between occupations are also examined.

Chapter 8 introduces the supply side of the labour market. The influences on an individual's willingness to participate in the labour force, and on the number of hours that someone is willing to commit to work, are discussed in this chapter. These influences include government social assistance programs, changes in tax rates, the desire for more education, mandatory retirement, and the decision about whether or not to migrate to a new geographic location. The discussion in Chapter 8 assumes that individuals can only do two things with their time: work for pay, or enjoy leisure.

The demand side of the labour market is represented by employers' need for employees. The factors that influence the employer's demand for labour are introduced in Chapter 9. An important topic in this chapter is productivity, or the output per worker.

In Chapter 10, the interaction of the demand and supply sides of the labour market is discussed. The result is an equilibrium wage rate and an equilibrium level of employment. The impact of government initiatives such as minimum wage rates and payroll taxes on the equilibrium position is reviewed, as is the impact of unions on the equilibrium wage rate and employment levels. In addition to setting wage rates, the interaction of demand and supply in the labour market determines the level of employment. Not all individuals who would like to work are able to find a job. The causes of unemployment are discussed in Chapter 10, expanding on the discussion of unemployment in Chapter 6.

Not all workers earn the same wage rate. The reasons for these differences are explained in Chapter 11. The reasons can be categorized into three groups: adjustment lags, compensating wage differentials, and labour market barriers. The presence of discrimination—a labour market barrier—has prompted governments to enact pay equity legislation, which is discussed in this chapter.

As an individual's skill level also affects his or her compensation in the marketplace, training and education are discussed in Chapter 12. The chapter focuses on the investment aspects of education. Do the returns to an investment in education exceed the costs of such an investment?

Chapter 8

Labour Market Decisions of Households

Chapter Learning Objectives

After completing this chapter, you should be able to:

- define and describe the following terms: normal good, income effect, substitution effect (supply), reservation wage rate, marginal tax rate, economic rent, human capital, and demogrant
- discuss the factors that influence an individual's decision to participate in the labour force
- derive the individual's labour supply curve and the market supply curve for labour
- distinguish between a change in supply and a change in the quantity supplied
- explain the conditions under which the individual labour supply curve bends backward
- use income and substitution effects to analyze the work disincentives associated with sources of non–employment income
- explain the impacts of immigration and emigration on the supply curve for labour
- discuss the factors that influence an individual's decision to migrate

PART-TIME WORK

As pointed out in Chapter 5, more and more members of the labour force have a part-time job: they comprise about 20% of the number of Canadians who have a job. Some of those who are employed part-time are underemployed; they are working part-time but would prefer to work full-time. The majority of part-time workers, however, have chosen to work part-time. Who are the part-time employees in the labour force? The largest component of the part-time labour force is between 15 and 24 years of age, mainly students. In fact, about 90% of part-time employees are students, both postsecondary and secondary school students.

Women between the ages of 24 and 54 make up the second-biggest group of voluntary part-time workers. Their decision to seek part-time work is influenced by the presence of children under the age of 16 in the family. Approximately 61% of the women voluntarily working part-time have children under 16 years of age. Some of those who choose to work part-time are over 55 years of age; many in this group of employees are using part-time employment as a means of making an easier transition from full-time employment to retirement.

Researchers have pointed out some negative aspects of part-time employment for the employee. Part-timers often do not have the same access to training and development. Part-time work can be scheduled at "off hours" when the full-time employees do not want to work. Part-time employees likely receive a lower hourly wage rate and are more vulnerable to job loss than other employees.

Many individuals only want to offer their services to employers on a part-time basis. On the demand side of the market, many employers are seeking individuals who want to work part-time. For employers, hiring people on a part-time basis can be attractive. They can be hired to increase staffing at peak periods in the business day, week, or year. Often, they are not included in the bargaining unit and may not accumulate such benefits as seniority. Finally, part-time employees are often less expensive from the firm's point of view. Research has also indicated that employers may experience some drawbacks if they opt to hire many part-time employees. In some instances, part-time employees are less skilled and less productive. It may be difficult to retain able part-time workers, especially those who seek full-time employment. If part-time employees are working shorter shifts than full-time employees, there may be a loss of flow in the organization.

Introduction

All markets have a demand side and a supply side. The labour market is no exception. In order to analyze the workings of the labour market, it is necessary to study the two sides of the market separately. This chapter focuses on the theory behind the supply side of the labour market, with the aim of deriving the supply curve of labour. The supply curve derived in this chapter is similar to the supply curve introduced in Chapter 2. The difference between the supply curves in the two chapters is the labelling of the axes. The vertical axis for the labour supply curve measures the wage rate (the price of labour) while the horizontal axis measures either the number of hours of work or the number of workers (an indicator of the quantity of labour). Other concepts introduced in Chapter 2, such as opportunity cost and elasticity, will also be referred to in this chapter.

For an individual, the quantity of labour supplied to the labour market depends on the decision to work, the amount of time that an individual is willing to devote to work, and for how long one is willing to work. For a society, the total supply of labour depends on the participation rate (the proportion of the working-age population who have made the decision to look for work) and the number of hours that people are willing to work. This chapter begins with a discussion of the work/leisure tradeoff. That is, it analyzes the decision to allocate one's time between work and leisure. The chapter then reviews the factors that influence one's decision to participate in the labour force. Next, the chapter discusses how the number of hours that one is willing to work varies with the wage rate. Finally, the chapter discusses the development of the market supply curve for labour.

The Work/Leisure Tradeoff

The theory about the decision to work relates to the use of one's time. It assumes that individuals can do only two things with their time: work for pay in the marketplace, or participate in leisure activity. The definition of a leisure activity is very broad. It can range from participating in hobbies and sports to doing household chores. The definition also includes the time spent attending school. Activities such as sleeping and eating can also be considered leisure activities for the purposes of our discussion. Basically, any activity that is not classified as work for pay is a leisure activity.

Some textbooks subdivide leisure activities into a number of categories. *Non-market work* would include the time allocated to household chores for which no compensation is received. It also includes work done on a volunteer basis. *Consumption time* refers to the time spent enjoying the purchases made in the marketplace such as watching television or playing golf. *Idleness* refers to the time allocated for rest and reflection during which no production or consumption is undertaken. The discussion of leisure in this text lumps the various categories of leisure together. There is no need to distinguish between the types of leisure in order to develop a workable theory of labour supply.

Further, the theory of labour supply developed in this chapter assumes that individuals see work solely as an activity that takes them away from the pursuit of leisure activities. It assumes that individuals do not see work as an activity that provides satisfaction or pleasure, although many individuals do enjoy their occupation or profession and would choose to allocate many hours to work rather than to a leisure activity. For the purposes of establishing a theory of labour supply, the non-pecuniary benefits of working will not be considered.

A number of factors, both monetary and psychological, influence an individual's decision to work. One of these factors is the individual's demand for leisure. Leisure can be treated as a good that people desire; as such, the demand for leisure depends on the price of leisure, one's income and wealth, and one's preferences for leisure as opposed to working for pay.

What is the price of leisure? In order to take an hour of leisure, one must take an hour off work. The wage rate for that hour of work is the price of leisure. In other words, the price of leisure is the opportunity cost of not working. As the wage rate increases, the opportunity cost of not working (the price of leisure) increases. You will recall from the review of economic principles that as the price of a product increases, the quantity demanded of that product decreases. Therefore, as the wage rate increases, and the price of leisure increases, the individual will demand fewer leisure hours and will be encouraged to have less leisure time and to work more hours. This assumes that all other factors influencing the demand for leisure (such as one's preference for leisure) remain constant. The fact that individuals substitute work for leisure as the wage rate increases is known as the **substitution effect (supply)**. The word "supply" is added to the substitution effect to distinguish it from the substitution effect discussed in the next chapter. For the remainder of this chapter, we will simply refer to the substitution effect.

The demand for leisure also depends on one's income and wealth. If leisure is a normal good, the demand for leisure will increase with an increase in income. The definition of a **normal good** is one for which demand increases with increases in consumer incomes. The ability to purchase more of all products, including leisure, in light of increases in income is referred to as the **income effect (supply)**.

When the wage rate increases, the income and substitution effects have opposing influences on an individual's decision to work. The substitution effect encourages the individual to work more hours because the price of leisure has increased. The income effect encourages the individual to work fewer hours and purchase more leisure. Economists say that the income effect has a negative impact on the decision to work, while the substitution effect has a positive impact. If the substitution effect outweighs the income effect, an individual will decide to work more hours in response to a wage rate increase; if the income effect outweighs the substitution effect, an individual will decide to work fewer hours. If the two effects offset each other, there will be no change in the quantity of labour supplied.

The previous section assumed that an individual could work as many, or as few, hours as desired. For many individuals, there may be no opportunity to change the hours of work in response to changes in the wage rate.

substitution effect (supply)

leisure and work hours are substituted for each other as the wage rate changes

normal good

a good for which demand increases as one's income increases

income effect (supply)

the change in hours of work caused by a change in income

Employers may have established hours of work and employees must work those hours in order to remain employed with the firm. That is, if the company is open from 9:00 a.m. to 5:00 p.m. each day from Monday to Friday, those are the hours that the employee must work. It is not possible to choose to work fewer hours at this place of employment. In spite of certain institutional restrictions on hours of work, some employees may have more control over their hours of work than do others. Part-time employees may have the option of working more hours. The decision to work overtime for some workers may be voluntary. Commission salespeople may be flexible with respect to scheduling holidays and, if so, will likely schedule them during a time of the year when sales are low as opposed to times of the year when sales are high. Some flexibility in terms of the number of hours of work is also obtained through moonlighting. If it is impossible to acquire more hours of work at one's current job, a second job may be obtained.

Changes in the wage rate not only affect the number of hours that an individual, already in the labour force, is willing to work, but may also encourage some individuals to enter the labour force and begin the job search. The decision to look for work is the topic of the next section.

The Decision to Work

The decision to participate in the labour market is influenced by a number of factors, which are discussed in this section.

Age

The decision to participate in the labour force and the number of hours of work supplied to the labour force are related to one's age. Youths are often too young to participate in the labour force. Mandatory retirement programs may mean others are too old to participate in the labour force.

An individual's productivity in the labour market varies with age. When someone is young and inexperienced, he or she is often not a highly productive employee. As one gets older, employment productivity increases before eventually levelling off. As one ages and continues to work, his or her employment productivity may start to decline. Older workers may not be able to handle physical jobs as easily as they once did. Older workers may take more time off work because of health problems. If it can be assumed that a worker's wage rate is linked to his or her productivity on the job, we can refer to the substitution effect to investigate changes in labour force participation over one's life. Young workers command relatively low wages because of low levels of employment productivity. With the prospect of only being able to receive a low wage rate, their opportunity cost of not working is low. Young people may therefore choose to stay out of the labour force and remain in school or pursue other leisure activities such as travel. If employment productivity declines for older workers, and consequently earnings are lower, older workers may also determine that the opportunity cost of not working is low; they may leave the labour force. For productive workers who are neither young nor old, the opportunity cost of not working will be high. These individuals, especially males, are likely to remain in the labour force.

reservation wage rate
the lowest wage rate an individual is willing to work for

Most individuals will not agree to work for just any wage rate. The wage rate needs to be at a certain level before an individual will agree to look for work. The minimum wage that an individual would accept is referred to as the **reservation wage rate**. The reservation wage rate is influenced by factors outside the labour market such as the presence of children in the family, the availability of income from sources other than work, and a person's preference for leisure.

The income and substitution effects of a wage rate change may also influence the decision to retire. If a pension is available before the commonly accepted retirement age, an individual may find that the income effect dominates the work/leisure decision. The individual may choose to purchase more leisure and retire. For a person with the opportunity of collecting a pension, the decision to retire may be reinforced if his or her wage rate has been reduced. A lower wage rate will reduce the price of leisure. Conversely, if the wage rate continues to increase in one's later years, the price of leisure increases. The substitution effect may override the income effect and the individual may remain in the labour force.

The retirement decision has been the focus of much research in recent years. It affects an individual financially and psychologically. It also affects the national unemployment rate and government income support plans. If employed individuals retire, job openings may become available to younger unemployed individuals. If unemployed older workers leave the labour force, the unemployment rate will drop. If employed older workers continue to work, they will not be receiving Canada Pension Plan payments, and it appears that there will be less strain on government finances. On the other hand, if older workers retire, there may be less strain on the public finances if fewer people are unemployed. The decision to retire does not depend solely on economic factors, such as the wage rate and other sources of income. One's health, family, and leisure pursuits also influence the decision.

The decision to retire may not be in the hands of the individual: many companies have mandatory retirement policies. This topic is discussed in Labour Market Issue 8.1.

Fertility and Family Size

The presence of children affects the labour force participation of family members. The presence of preschool children in the family increases the reservation wage rate of at least one family member, thus making one family member less likely to be in the labour force. What factors influence the decision to have children? The decision to start a family is not solely based on economic variables, yet economic variables do play a part in it.

The decision to have children is based to some degree on the costs associated with having children. Some are direct, in the sense that children must be fed and clothed. In order to raise children, certain goods and services must be purchased, such as childcare, education, sports and entertainment, and medical care. The prices associated with these goods and services are part of the cost of raising a child. There are also indirect or opportunity costs if one fam-

Labour Market Issue 8.1

Mandatory Retirement

Many companies have mandatory retirement policies; employees who reach the mandatory retirement age are required to retire from the company. Are such policies a violation of the *Charter of Rights and Freedoms*? Do they contravene provincial human rights legislation, which prevents discrimination on the basis of age? These questions were put to the Supreme Court of Canada, which ruled that mandatory retirement is discriminatory; nonetheless, it also ruled that the objectives of mandatory retirement were justified on other grounds. Are there any economic arguments that support mandatory retirement policies?

One argument for mandatory retirement centres on the belief that an employee's productivity declines with age. Faced with declining productivity from an employee, the employer has two options: reduce the employee's wage rate, or terminate the employment relationship. Since it may be impossible to reduce the wage rate of an older employee, the employer may terminate the employment relationship. If the company has a mandatory retirement policy, an end date is established for the relationship: the employee knows that he or she will not be fired or have to accept reduced earnings, and the employer knows that the payment of a wage rate in excess of productivity will not last forever.

It can also be argued that mandatory retirement policies open up opportunities for younger workers. This argument often assumes that there are a fixed number of jobs in the marketplace. By forcing older workers to retire, younger workers can find employment and advancement opportunities. The number of jobs in the labour market is not fixed, however; jobs can be created through more spending. If older workers continued on with their employment, they would have more money to spend, which would create new jobs. On the other hand, if the way is paved for young workers to get the employment opportunities, their earnings will increase and they will have more money to spend.

After retirement, a person need not drop out of the labour force, but can continue to seek employment after reaching the mandatory retirement age with one company. People today live longer and may want to continue working past the mandatory retirement age. In the future, mandatory retirement policies may not substantially reduce the size of the labour force.

Human resources management within a company may benefit from a policy of mandatory retirement. The policy may assist in determining staffing and training requirements if it is known that employees who reach the mandatory retirement age will be leaving the company.

The main argument against mandatory retirement focuses on the discriminatory nature of the policy. As such, some jurisdictions in Canada prohibit mandatory retirement policies. From a financial viewpoint, a ban on mandatory retirement may ease the financial pressure on company and government pension plans; if individuals were permitted to work for more years, they would contribute more to pension plans and would collect from the plans for fewer years.

ily member, usually the woman, decides to stay at home to raise the children and forgoes an income. In terms of the forgone income, the opportunity costs are often higher than the direct costs. The opportunity cost will be even higher for women with greater earnings potential. This suggests that those women with greater earnings potential are less likely to have children, or are less likely to have a large family.

Does the number of children in a family depend on the income of the family? The income effect would indicate that higher-income families have more children or spend more money on the children they have. However, not all high-income families are large families, so variables other than income must be more important in determining family size.

Attitudes toward family size have changed considerably over the years. These attitudes are influenced by culture, religion, the women's movement, and the increased educational levels in the population. Changes in birth control technology have also had an impact.

On the basis of empirical evidence, which of these factors are the most important determinants of family size? Research into the factors that affect fertility is complicated by the fact that some of the factors can be interrelated. For example, family income can be related to the level of education of the adults in the family: the higher the level of education, the higher the level of income. If one partner has a high level of education, it is likely that the other is also well educated. For research purposes, it may be difficult to separate the family income factor from the educational level of the mother, who is likely to forgo income while raising children. If she is well educated, the opportunity cost is high. Nonetheless, empirical evidence indicates that as a woman's potential earnings increase, she has fewer children. There is also some evidence that the availability of government financial assistance to families in the form of tax credits, maternity benefits, and so on has a small positive correlation to the number of children in the family. That is, for some families, the increased income obtained through government assistance may result in more children.

Investment in Education

The overall supply of labour to the economy is affected by the number of individuals who decide to pursue further education and training. As more individuals enroll in postsecondary educational programs, the supply of hours for work is reduced. Some individuals may leave the labour force entirely while they pursue an education; others may switch to part-time work. Because individuals with higher levels of education stay in the labour force for a longer period of time, the reduction in the labour force that occurs while they are receiving an education is only temporary. The decision to further one's education will also have an impact on the supply of labour to individual occupations. More people will ultimately be qualified to do certain jobs and fewer workers will be available for other jobs.

human capital

human resources considered in terms of their contributions to the economy, as in skills, education, etc.

When individuals undertake expenses to acquire a skill, further their education, or relocate to a new job, they are investing in themselves. Economists refer to this spending as investment in **human capital**. If the investment results in the individual's acquiring new skills, these skills can be rented to employers just as other types of capital (such as machinery and equipment) can be rented out. The decision to undertake further education and training is an important one for analysts of the labour market. For this reason, Chapter 12 is devoted to the topic of education and training.

Non-Employment Income

The decision to participate in the labour force also depends on whether the individual has access to non-employment income. Examples of non-employment income include interest received from bonds and bank deposits, income from government social assistance programs, and allowances received from other family members. The theoretical concepts of the income and substitution effects can be used to analyze how various government social assistance programs influence the decision to work.

DEMOGRANT A **demogrant** is a lump sum payment to an individual based on membership in a certain demographic group, such as being a senior. The current old age security benefit paid to all Canadians 65 years of age and over is a demogrant. The sole criterion for receiving it is age, not income or any other characteristic. All those who qualify receive the same lump sum payment, although the net amount of this payment will vary between individuals since it is taxed at an individual's marginal tax rate. This program may not continue to operate as Canada is embarking on a plan to replace the current programs of old age security and guaranteed income supplement with a senior's benefit. This benefit will be tax-free and will be tied to income; individuals with higher incomes will receive less government money than those individuals with lower incomes.

demogrant

a lump sum payment to an individual based on membership in a particular demographic group

The family allowance program (1944–1993) in Canada was another example of a demogrant. Initially mothers received a monthly non-taxable lump sum payment for each child under 16 years of age. The size of the payment varied with the ages of the children but was the same for all mothers regardless of family income. The family allowance program experienced several changes over its life. It was extended to include 16- and 17-year-old children who were still in school or who were disabled. In 1973, the family allowance benefit was indexed to the rate of inflation and became taxable. The benefits were added to the income of the higher-income earner in the household for taxation purposes. In 1993, this program was replaced by an income-tested child tax benefit, which provides more assistance to families with lower incomes.

What impact does a demogrant have on the decision to work? There is an income effect since one's income has increased. The individual can afford to purchase more leisure. There is no substitution effect associated with a demogrant since the price of leisure (the wage rate) has not changed. Thus, demogrants (that is, income from not working) would have a negative impact on the decision to work.

WELFARE ASSISTANCE Governments pay welfare assistance to low-income individuals who are temporarily without work or who require financial assistance. Those who receive welfare must establish a need for that assistance. Policymakers are concerned that such assistance reduces the incentive to look for work; that is, there is an income effect associated with receiving welfare assistance. With more income, an individual can purchase more leisure. Individuals who decline to look for work while receiving welfare assistance are not getting the work experience and training necessary to obtain long-term employment. The longer an individual remains out of the employed labour force, the more difficult it will be to obtain a job. In recent years, provincial governments have reduced the amount of welfare assistance benefits in an effort to improve the incentive to work. There is a negative income effect associated with lower benefits; lower benefits mean lower incomes and a reduced ability to purchase leisure.

Is there a substitution effect associated with welfare benefits? The substitution effect refers to the opportunity cost of not working. If there is no work available, the opportunity cost is zero; the price of leisure is zero. If employment is available, the opportunity cost of not working and relying on welfare benefits for one's income is the wage rate that is sacrificed. The structure of the welfare program can have an impact on the opportunity cost of not working. If the amount of one's welfare benefit is reduced by the full amount of any income from employment, there is no financial gain from accepting employment. The opportunity cost of not working, or the price of leisure, is zero. If the welfare program is structured so that an individual can keep most of the earnings from employment, the price of leisure increases. For example, assume that one's welfare benefit was reduced by 25% of one's employment earnings. In effect, an individual would keep 75% of any employment earnings. There would be an opportunity cost associated with not working. The higher the opportunity cost, the greater the incentive to seek employment.

The price of leisure depends on the wage rate an individual can command in the labour force. The higher the wage rate, the more expensive leisure becomes. In order to encourage labour force participation, governments have been insisting that individuals who receive welfare assistance continue to develop their labour market skills. If skill training can lead to higher-paying jobs, there will be less incentive to continue receiving welfare benefits. In Ontario, welfare assistance is part of the Ontario Works program, which emphasizes providing work experience and upgrading the skills of those individuals receiving welfare assistance. They must agree to do community service jobs as a condition for receiving benefits. Single teenage mothers must attend school in order to receive welfare benefits.

EMPLOYMENT INSURANCE The federal government regulates the employment insurance program in Canada. Benefits are based on the number of weeks worked prior to unemployment and on the regional unemployment rate. Most recipients of employment insurance receive 55% of their insurable earnings for 14 to 45 weeks in a 52-week period. Individuals need a certain number of hours of work to qualify for benefits and must wait two weeks after applying before the benefits begin.

As mentioned in Chapter 3, the employment insurance program has undergone several changes since its introduction in 1941. Since 1971, changes have focused on reducing the work disincentives associated with the program by reducing benefits. There is an income effect associated with EI payments because high benefits increase the demand for leisure and reduce hours of work. Empirical evidence indicates that a positive correlation exists between the duration of unemployment and the size of the employment insurance benefits: that is, the higher the benefit, the longer individuals remain unemployed.

Employment Earnings and Welfare Benefits

The strength of the substitution effect for those receiving welfare assistance depends in part on how much of one's employment earnings can be kept while continuing to receive assistance. The following examples and calculations are taken from the Ontario Support To Employment Program (STEP).

Example 1

A single person could be entitled to $520 per month under the Ontario Works program. Assume the person has $500 in employment income during the month. The monthly entitlement under the Ontario Works program will be reduced because of the presence of employment earnings. The individual is allowed a basic exemption of $143. The individual is also allowed an exemption of 25% of the remaining employment income ($500 − $143 = $357). This amounts to $89.25 ($357 × 0.25).

$$\$500 - \$143 - \$89.25 = \$267.75$$

The amount of $267.75 is the amount deducted from the monthly entitlement. The monthly entitlement from Ontario Works is $520 − $267.75 = $252.25. The total monthly income including earnings and entitlement is $500 + $252.25 = $752.25. Earnings are up from $520 per month to $752.25 per month, an increase of $232.25. In effect, the individual keeps 46.45% of the $500 earned through employment.

Example 2

A family of two adults and two children under 12 years of age could receive a monthly entitlement of $1178. Assume the family earns $1000 of employment income in a month. The basic exemption of $346 is deducted from employment earnings. The family also has an exemption of 25% of the remaining employment income ($1000 − $346 = $654). This amounts to $163.50 ($654 × 0.25). The family may also be eligible for an exemption related to approved childcare expenses ($200). The amount to be deducted from the entitlement is:

$$\$1000 - \$346 - \$163.50 - \$200 = \$290.50$$

The monthly entitlement is $1178 − $290.50 = $887.50. Total monthly income from employment and from Ontario Works is $1000 + $887.50 = $1887.50, an increase of $1887.50 − $1178 = $709.50. Thus the family keeps 70.95% of the employment earnings.

Is there a substitution effect associated with employment insurance? In order to answer this question, we look at the price of leisure. Until recently, individuals who received benefits were not permitted to work and receive benefits simultaneously. As a result, the price of leisure was zero. The current program allows individuals to earn some money while continuing to receive benefits. The price of leisure is the wage rate sacrificed. It may also include the expenses associated with looking for a job, as a condition of EI is that individuals must look for employment. If good job opportunities are passed up while receiving benefits, the individual may be faced with a large drop in income when employment insurance benefits run out. The financial loss associated with not being able to find work in the future could also be part of the price of leisure.

Most studies on the impact of employment insurance on the labour market focus on the impact on the labour supply; however, there is also a labour demand aspect. Employment insurance is paid by employer and employee contributions. As such, it is a payroll tax and increases the cost of hiring a new worker. The increased cost of labour may reduce the demand for labour. On the other hand, employment insurance benefits can also increase overall labour demand, because they provide money for unemployed individuals to spend. The increased spending may prop up the demand for goods and services and the demand for workers.

The federal government has made an effort to provide EI recipients with access to skill training and upgrading. If training increases the potential wage rate for the individual, the opportunity cost of not working increases. The substitution effect would lead to more hours of work being supplied.

SUBSIDIZED CHILDCARE As more women decide to enter or re-enter the labour force, the demand for childcare facilities increases. Accompanying the increased demand is an increase in the price of daycare or childcare services. Governments are pressured to provide financial assistance to families requiring childcare. What is the impact on the labour force of government financial assistance to those with children? Will this assistance be provided only to those families that have more than one person in the labour force, or will it be provided to all families?

We can treat daycare expenses as a fixed cost. That is, assume that daycare expenses remain the same regardless of the number of hours an individual is employed during the week. Earnings from employment must be high enough to cover this fixed cost in order to make employment worthwhile. An individual's reservation wage rate is influenced by daycare expenses. The more expensive daycare becomes, the more money an individual must command in the labour market. If daycare is subsidized, the cost to the individual is reduced. The reservation wage rate will be lowered because less money will be required to meet daycare expenses. As a result, labour force participation is likely to increase.

The impact of subsidized daycare on parents' hours of work offered to the labour market depends on whether the assistance is available to all families or only to those with both parents employed (or the only parent employed, in the case of single-parent families). If daycare assistance is given to all families with children, it will be a demogrant; the income effect will encourage the purchase of more leisure. If daycare assistance is provided only to families with employed parents, the possible presence of an income effect encouraging the purchase of leisure is more complicated. If the subsidy is given as a lump sum, it may encourage some individuals to work fewer hours. If the subsidy is tied to hours of work, there will be less incentive to reduce hours of work. The impact of subsidized daycare on total labour supply is ambiguous. On the one hand, it tends to increase labour force participation, but, on the other hand, it tends to reduce the number of hours that individuals are willing to work.

The Individual Supply Curve

Not all individuals who have decided to participate in the labour force are willing to work the same number of hours per week. An important factor in the determination of weekly hours is the wage rate. The relationship between the wage rate and the number of hours that an individual is willing to work is rep-

Tax Laws and Childcare Decisions

It is likely that Canada's income tax legislation has an impact on the parents' decision about the type of childcare their child receives. Under Canada's current legislation, a family that decides to have one parent stay at home pays more income tax than a two-income family earning the same income. For families in which both parents work outside the home, the income tax legislation provides for a childcare expense deduction if costs are incurred while others look after their children. This deduction, which results in less income tax being paid, is not available to parents that do not work outside the home. Thus, if a parent stays home to look after the children, that family is punished financially in two ways. First, there is the opportunity cost of lost income that could be made if the parent were to enter the labour force. Second, the family is denied the tax deduction available to other families.

The tax legislation could be amended to provide all families with the same tax deduction for children. Such a change would make the legislation more neutral. That is, the legislation would not influence the parents' decision about childcare. Parents would be able to decide which option was best for their child: a stay-at-home parent, or a childcare facility. Some families would decide to take the financial benefit from the change in the legislation and have a parent stay at home. Other families would take the financial benefit and seek out the best possible childcare facility.

---

resented by the individual's **labour supply curve** (see Figure 8.1, page 224). The shape of this curve can be explained with reference to the income and substitution effects. At low wage rates, individuals are not willing to offer many hours of work and the price of leisure is also low. As the wage rate increases, the substitution effect dominates the income effect. As the wage rate increases, the opportunity cost of not working increases. The individual wants to work more hours. The desire to work more hours gives a positive slope to the labour supply curve, as shown in the figure.

Figure 8.1 also identifies the reservation wage rate. As mentioned earlier in the chapter, this is the lowest wage rate that an individual is willing to work for. Below this wage rate, the individual will not participate in the labour force. There is no supply curve below this wage rate.

As one's wage rate increases, one's income increases. The income may reach such a level that the individual decides to purchase more leisure; if so, the income effect will begin to dominate the substitution effect. With fewer hours of work, the slope of the supply curve will be negative. The switch in the dominance of the substitution effect to the income effect results in a **backward-bending supply curve for labour** (see Figure 8.2, page 225). The wage rate at which the income effect begins to dominate varies from individual to individual. Some may be willing to increase their hours of work at relatively high wage rates, while others in the same situation will opt for more leisure.

As discussed in Chapter 3, there are legislated requirements for payment of a premium wage rate for hours of work beyond a daily, or weekly, maximum. Many companies establish their own maximum hours of work beyond which a premium rate, or overtime rate, will be paid. What impact does a premium wage rate have on the number of hours offered for work by an individual, if we

labour supply curve

a graph showing the number of hours of work offered in relation to the wage rate

backward-bending supply curve for labour

a supply curve for labour that switches from a positive slope at lower wage rates to a negative slope at higher wage rates, with the substitution effect dominating at low wage rates and the income effect dominating at high wage rates

FIGURE 8.1

Labour Supply Curve

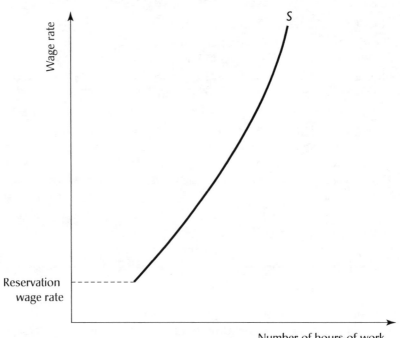

assume that working overtime is voluntary and not compulsory? Can employers encourage their employees to work more hours by offering a premium rate of pay for overtime? With a premium wage rate, the price of leisure will increase. Since the premium wage rate is likely to be at least 50% more than the regular wage rate, the price of leisure will increase substantially. The result is a strong substitution effect on the worker's behalf. Since, in most cases, the number of overtime hours is limited, the income effect is likely to be small. The substitution effect will dominate and encourage the individual to work more hours.

Does empirical evidence support the existence of a backward-bending supply curve? The results from a variety of studies indicate that men and women react differently to wage rate increases beyond a certain level. For men, higher wage rates may induce a slight income effect. That is, at higher wage rates the labour supply curve may bend backwards. For women, the substitution effect seems to dominate even at higher wage rates, maintaining a positive slope to the labour supply curve.

To this point we have been discussing the individual's decision to participate in the labour force. We have ignored the fact that most adults marry and start families. Decisions about work and leisure are often made as a family and not by individual members of the family acting alone. Family income as opposed to individual income influences the work/leisure tradeoff. Furthermore, family responsibilities for such things as household chores are

FIGURE 8.2

The Backward-Bending Supply Curve for Labour

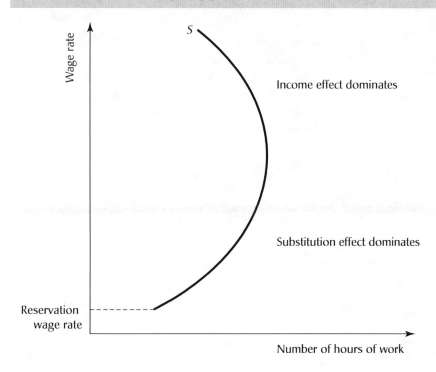

allocated to the various family members, keeping some members of the family from participating more in the labour market while allowing other members to devote more time to it. The spouse with the higher earnings potential may allocate more hours to the labour market.

Wage Rate Elasticity of Labour Supply

The impact of an increased wage rate on hours of work can be assessed by looking at the wage rate elasticity of supply. The term "price elasticity of supply" refers to the responsiveness of the quantity supplied to a change in the price. In reference to the labour supply, wage rate elasticity of supply refers to the percentage change in the quantity of labour supplied in response to a 1% increase in the wage rate. A knowledge of the wage rate elasticity provides us with more information about the impact of wage rate increases on the quantity of labour supplied. Specifically, wage rate elasticity tells us the impact that wage rate increases have on the hours that individuals are willing to work.

The **wage rate elasticity of labour supply** is determined by dividing the percentage change in the quantity of labour supplied by the percentage change in the wage rate.

wage rate elasticity of labour supply

the responsiveness of quantity supplied to changes in the wage rate

$$\text{Coefficient of wage rate elasticity of supply} = \frac{\textit{Percentage change in quantity of labour supplied}}{\textit{Percentage change in the wage rate}}$$

Chapter 8: Labour Market Decisions of Households

Marginal Tax Rates and the Decision to Work

Canada has a progressive income tax system whereby individuals with higher incomes pay a higher proportion of that income in tax. The progressive nature of the income tax system increases the importance of marginal tax rates. The word "marginal" means extra, or additional. The **marginal tax rate** is the proportion of any additional income earned that is paid in taxes. With a progressive income tax system, marginal tax rates increase as income increases.

The following hypothetical example outlines how the marginal tax rate is calculated.

Income	Tax Rate	Taxes Paid	Marginal Tax Rate
$40 000	20%	$8000	
			4500/10 000 = 45%
$50 000	25%	$12 500	
			5500/10 000 = 55%
$60 000	30%	$18 000	

If one's income increases from $40 000 to $50 000 in one year, income taxes for that year increase from $8000 to $12 500, an increase of $4500. Therefore, 45% of the $10 000 increase in income was paid in taxes even though the individual is in the 25% tax bracket. Why is the marginal tax rate 45% when the individual is in the 25% tax bracket? When an individual moves from a 20% tax bracket to a 25% tax bracket, the $40 000 income that was previously taxed at 20% must now be taxed at 25%. Thus, when an individual receives an increase in salary and moves into a new tax bracket, any earnings to that point must be taxed at the higher rate.

Can the marginal tax rate influence one's decision to work? Assume that an individual is provided with the opportunity to work overtime at one and one-half times the regular hourly wage rate. The price of leisure has increased since the hourly wage rate has increased. The substitution effect would predict that the individual would work more hours. However, when one considers the marginal tax rate on extra income, leisure is not as expensive as it would be without the tax. An individual will always bring home more money by working more hours. However, the individual may refuse overtime because the tax system has decreased the price of leisure.

---

marginal tax rate

the proportion of any additional income earned that is paid in taxes

If the coefficient of wage rate elasticity of supply is positive, increases in the wage rate result in increases in the number of hours that an individual is willing to work. In other words, if the coefficient of wage rate elasticity of supply is positive, the substitution effect and the resulting increase in the price of leisure have encouraged the individual to work more hours. If the coefficient of wage rate elasticity of supply is negative, increases in the wage rate result in fewer hours of work being offered; the income effect dominates the substitution effect in this section of the supply curve. The closer the coefficient is to zero, the smaller the impact of wage rate changes on the labour supply. As the coefficient moves further away from zero, either in a positive or a negative direction, wage rate changes have a greater impact on the quantity of labour supplied.

No two studies arrive at identical wage rate elasticities of supply. In general, the estimates of labour supply elasticity for women are positive. The estimates of labour supply elasticity for men are generally close to zero and some studies have indicated that the wage rate elasticity of supply is slightly negative. Overall, the positive wage elasticity of supply for women outweighs the low negative wage rate elasticity for men. Thus, any increase in the wage rate is likely to result in an overall increase in the quantity of labour supplied.

Market Supply Curve for Labour

So far, we have been discussing the individual labour supply curve. We now shift our discussion to the market supply curve for labour for an occupation. To get the labour supply curve for an occupation, it is necessary to find the sum of all the individual supply curves for people willing to work at that occupation. Since labour supply curves for individuals are normally positively sloped, the market supply curve is also positively sloped. The difference between the individual and market supply curves appears on the horizontal axis. For the individual supply curve, the horizontal axis refers to hours of work (see Figure 8.1, page 224). For the market supply curve, the horizontal axis usually refers to the number of workers.

It is important to distinguish between a change in the quantity of labour supplied and a change in the supply of labour. A change in the quantity of labour supplied is the change in the amount of labour supplied in response to a change in the wage rate. In this situation, the supply curve does not shift to a new position. The change in the quantity supplied is determined by moving along the existing supply curve to the new wage rate. A change in the supply of labour indicates that there has been a shift in the entire supply curve. A shift of the supply curve to the right would indicate that more people are willing to work at this occupation regardless of the wage rate. Conversely, a shift of the supply curve to the left indicates that fewer people are available to work at this job.

What changes would bring about a shift in the supply curve for labour for a certain occupation? The supply curve would shift to the right if the population increased or more people trained for this occupation. The curve would shift to the left if unions restricted entry into an occupation or if many Canadians returned to college or university on a full-time basis. The movement of workers through emigration and immigration can also cause a shift in the labour supply curve. The topic of migration is discussed in this section.

To this point in the chapter, we have assumed that the individuals deciding to enter the labour force came from a fixed population. That is, the quantity of labour supplied to the market depended primarily on the wage rate and the response of individuals in the population to any changes in those wage rates. However, the distribution of the population is constantly changing. In Canada, there is internal migration as individuals and families move between provinces. Over the years, there has been internal migration away from the Atlantic provinces, Manitoba, and Saskatchewan to Ontario, Alberta, and British Columbia. Canada is also the destination of many international migrants. Canada's population and labour force have grown through international immigration but we have also lost labour force participants through emigration. In recent years, there has been substantial media coverage of the "brain drain" from Canada to the United States.

What impact does migration have on the supply curve for labour? The labour supply in the destination increases. The supply curve shifts to the right (S^2 in Figure 8.3, page 228). Regardless of the wage rate, more people are willing to work. Emigration shifts the labour supply curve to the left (S^3 in Figure 8.3) in

FIGURE 8.3

The Impacts of Migration on the Labour Supply Curve

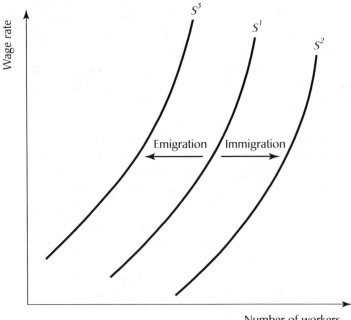

the country and province of origin. The supply curves in the figure can refer either to a regional labour supply within Canada or to the total domestic (Canadian) labour supply.

Why do individuals migrate internally within Canada or internationally? The literature treats the decision to migrate like it treats the decision to invest in education and training: the individual expects certain benefits from the move, which must be matched against the expected costs. If the benefits outweigh the costs, relocation to another province or country is the outcome.

One benefit from migration is monetary in nature. Individuals expect to be paid a higher wage rate and receive more benefits in the labour market of their destination. They hope the increase in the wage rate is not temporary and will continue throughout their working life. The fact that benefits are measured over one's working life explains why young people are more likely to relocate: for young people, the benefit of higher wages will accrue over a longer period of time. However, not all benefits from migration are monetary; some individuals may relocate for reasons of weather, culture, language, or crime.

Do migrants within Canada experience a monetary gain? The evidence seems to indicate that they do. In one study, those who migrated had increased their earnings by an average of 23% compared to the 4% increase for those who did not move. The impact on earnings is greater for younger workers than older workers. It is also greater for men who migrate than for women who migrate. Finally, a larger increase in earnings came to those who left lower-income provinces than for those who left Ontario and Alberta.

Part III: Microeconomic Theory of the Labour Market   NEL

The Brain Drain

W W W In recent years, Canadian newspapers have printed numerous articles on the large number of highly qualified Canadians leaving Canada to take up residence in the United States. This emigration was referred to as the "brain drain." Statistics Canada reports that 21 475 Canadians took up residency in the United States in 2000. This number was significantly more than the 12 948 Canadians who moved to the United States in 1999. Some of these individuals may be in the United States on a temporary work visa and may return to Canada. Nonetheless, there is a trend toward greater emigration to the United States. Florida is the most popular destination for those moving south, followed by California, Texas, New York, and Washington.

Of those who moved to the United States, 46% were professionals or managers. Canada is losing the skills that these people would have brought to the labour force. It is also losing the investment made by the taxpayer in educating these individuals, a loss estimated to be in excess of $10 billion. Further, the government of Canada is losing a great deal of income tax revenue when high-income earners leave the country.

Why do many Canadians want to migrate? Higher salaries in the United States attract qualified workers. Workers are also attracted by lower tax rates, exposure to leading-edge technologies, more opportunities for personal growth, and a warmer climate. Some analysts argue that emigration to the United States is relatively less than it was in the 1950s and that the current concern over emigration is simply a smokescreen for pressure on government to lower taxes. Others believe that the brain drain is slowing down. Still other analysts point to the high number of qualified immigrants arriving in Canada. Canada has more immigrants than emigrants each year. In fact, Toronto is the main destination for immigrants to the North American continent, and many of these immigrants are skilled and well-educated.

The expected costs vary depending on the distance of the move and the length of time required to find new employment. The costs also depend on how many individuals in the family are relocating. It is less expensive for one individual to relocate than for a family. This also helps explain why many migrants within Canada are young people. In addition, there is an opportunity cost to moving. The individual may have to sacrifice a job or government social assistance payments in order to relocate. One also must consider the cost of living at one's destination. If the economy there is expanding, it is likely that housing or accommodation prices will be higher than they were back home. There are, of course, also nonmonetary costs such as the difficulty in leaving family and friends.

The practice of comparing future benefits and costs will be discussed more fully in Chapter 12. In this chapter, let us simply state that the theory about the decision to relocate depends on expected benefits and costs. Do empirical results support the theory? Younger and better-educated workers are more likely than others to migrate, a finding that supports the contention that the benefits from migration accrue over a number of years. Within Canada, there is less migration between provinces that are farther apart. This finding supports the discussion of the costs of migration. Other factors influencing migration include the level of employment insurance benefits and social assistance benefits, the unemployment rates in both areas, the climate, and the ethnic composition of the population.

In Chapter 2, the concept of price elasticity was introduced. You will recall that price elasticity measures the response in the quantity demanded, or the quantity supplied, to a change in the price. The concept of price elasticity is also relevant for the labour market and is discussed in the next section.

Economic Rent

The labour supply curve for an occupation slopes up to the right. This implies that the more workers will be willing to work at a certain occupation, the higher the wage rate. An individual will be willing to work at this occupation for a relatively low wage rate. In other words, the individual's reservation wage rate is low. When an individual receives a wage rate in excess of his or her reservation wage rate, it is said that the person is receiving **economic rent**.

economic rent

wage rate received in excess of the reservation wage rate

The concept of economic rent is illustrated in Figure 8.4. For some individuals the reservation wage rate is W_1: they are not willing to offer their services to an employer for less than this wage rate. If the market wage rate were W_2, the individual would receive an economic rent of $W_2 - W_1$ for each hour worked. All individuals willing to work for less than W_2 are receiving an economic rent. The total economic rent paid to all individuals is shown by the shaded area in Figure 8.4.

FIGURE 8.4

Economic Rent

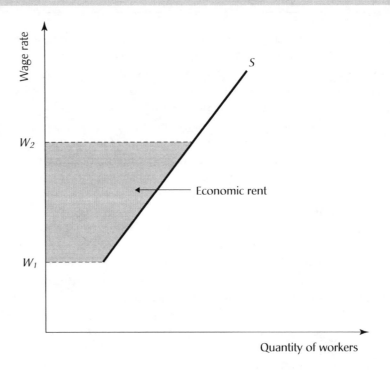

Why do employers not reduce an individual's wage rate down to the reservation wage rate for that person and eliminate economic rent? Reducing wage rates may not be possible. Minimum wage legislation may make it illegal to reduce the wage rate. Trade unions usually insist that all employees who perform a certain task get the same wage rate. Furthermore, an individual who is willing to work for a lower wage rate may not want to accept the lower rate if other employees receive a higher wage rate for the same work.

Rivalry among employers can lead to the payment of economic rent. This rivalry is evident in professional sports, where teams lure free-agent players away from the opposing teams. The desire to avoid paying economic rent has led, on occasion, to collusion among owners of sports franchises. The presence of salary caps (a maximum total payroll) in collective agreements between the players and the owners is a means of limiting the payment of economic rent.

Summary

The decision to work is analyzed by studying the demand for leisure. The price of leisure is the forgone earnings, or the opportunity cost, of not working. As one's wage rate increases, the price of leisure increases. As the price of leisure increases, less leisure is desired. The demand for leisure also depends on one's income. As the wage rate increases, and income increases, the demand for leisure increases. Thus, as the wage rate increases, there are competing influences on the decision to work more hours. The substitution effect focuses on the opportunity cost of not working and encourages an individual to work more hours. The income effect focuses on the ability of the individual to purchase leisure and encourages the purchase of more leisure.

The decision to participate in the labour force is influenced by a number of factors including age, family size, the presence of non-employment income, and the investment in education. The concepts of income and substitution effects can be used to analyze the impact of social assistance programs on the decision to look for work.

The individual labour supply curve may be backward bending. If, at high wage rates, the income effect dominates, the supply curve will bend backwards. The market supply curve is an accumulation of individual supply curves. The market supply curve is influenced by migration patterns. The wage rate elasticity of supply measures the responsiveness of the quantity of labour supplied in response to a change in the wage rate.

Key Terms

backward-bending supply curve for labour (page 223)

demogrant (page 219)

economic rent (page 230)

human capital (page 218)

income effect (supply) (page 214)

labour supply curve (page 223)

marginal tax rate (page 226)

normal good (page 214)

reservation wage rate (page 216)

substitution effect (supply) (page 214)

wage rate elasticity of labour supply (page 225)

Weblinks

Old Age Security and Canada Pension Plan
www.servicecanada.gc.ca/eng/isp/pub/factsheets/t4insert.shtml

Ontario Works
www.mcss.gov.on.ca/en/mcss/programs/social/ow/

Employment Insurance
www.servicecanada.gc.ca/eng/sc/ei/index.shtml

Marginal Tax Rates
www.econlib.org/library/Enc/MarginalTaxRates.html

Citizenship and Immigration Canada
www.cic.gc.ca

Discussion Questions

1. Would you work more hours in response to a wage rate increase? Would you work more hours in response to an increase in the wage rate paid to another family member? Explain.
2. What impact does a lower fertility rate have on the labour force participation rate? What impact would you expect an increase in the divorce rate to have on the labour force participation rate?
3. As the Canadian population ages, there are some concerns that the Canada Pension Plan is underfunded. That is, the plan may not have enough money to meet its expected obligations. If these concerns are valid, what implications does this have for the labour supply?
4. A negative income tax has been proposed as a form of guaranteed annual income. Under such a system, individuals whose income falls below a certain amount would receive a payment from the government. The size of the payment would vary according to the individual's income. For incomes above the cutoff, individuals would pay income tax based on the progressive income tax structure currently in place. With reference to the income and substitution effects, discuss the impact of a negative income tax system on the supply of labour.
5. A wage subsidy has been proposed as the best way to increase the incomes of the working poor. The subsidy would involve government

topping up the hourly wage rate of the individual who has been designated "working poor." Discuss the possible income and substitution effects associated with a wage subsidy.

6. What happens to economic rent when a rival professional sports league begins operation? Explain.

7. Is it possible that husbands' earnings influence the labour supply decision of wives, but wives' earnings do not influence the labour supply decisions of husbands? Discuss.

8. It is reported that in 2002, 62% of women with children under three years of age were in the labour force. This proportion compares with only 28% in 1976. Of women with children under 16, 72% are in the labour force. In your opinion, would a change in Canada's income tax legislation change these proportions?

9. New Zealand and Australia have abolished mandatory retirement. If Canada were to follow their lead, what would be the impact on the Canadian labour force?

Using the Internet

1. Go to the Citizenship and Immigration website at www.cic.gc.ca. Click on English and then click on Choose Canada > To Immigrate. Click on Skilled Worker Class Immigration and proceed through the steps to determine if you would have enough points to enter Canada as a skilled immigrant.

2. Go to the Ontario Works website, www.cfcs.gov.on.ca/CFCS/en/programs/IES/OntarioWorks/default.htm. Click on Income and Employment Supports. Click on Ontario Works. Write a one-paragraph summary of this program.

Exercises

1. Does personal wealth influence the dominance of the income or substitution effect with respect to the quantity of labour supplied to the market? Explain.

2. Discuss the arguments supporting a policy of mandatory retirement.

3. Critics of Canada's employment insurance program argue that the program discourages skill training and inflates the wage rate. Explain their reasoning.

4. Some trades and occupations require a certificate to practise that trade or profession. For example, a professional accountant may be required to have a CGA, a CMA, or a CA. Professionals such as lawyers and physicians must be licensed to practise. Draw a graph showing the impact that occupational licensing has on the supply of labour to a trade or occupation that requires occupational licensing.

5. What changes would cause the labour supply curve to shift to the left? to the right?

6. Explain the difference between the income effect and the substitution effect in response to a decrease in one's wage rate.

Economists use indifference curves to elaborate on the work–leisure model and the derivation of the individual labour supply curve discussed in this chapter. A map of indifference curves is presented in Figure 8A.1. Daily income earned through employment is presented on the vertical axis and hours of leisure are presented on the horizontal axis. Indifference curves are labelled I_1, I_2, and I_3. Each indifference curve represents a specific level of utility, or satisfaction, achieved by the individual when combining hours of leisure and hours of work. Depending on the wage rate, the number of hours of work will result in a specific daily income. All combinations of hours of leisure and daily income represented on I_1 provide the same amount of satisfaction to the individual. The individual is said to be "indifferent" between all the combinations of hours of leisure and daily income represented by I_1. Since the number of hours in a day is limited, an individual can only acquire more hours of leisure at the expense of sacrificing income. Conversely, more income can only be obtained by sacrificing leisure.

The indifference curve I_2 also represents combinations of hours of leisure and daily income that provide the same level of satisfaction to the individual. However, since the curve I_2 is farther away from the origin than I_1, I_2 represents a higher level of satisfaction to the individual than I_1. If we assume that individuals are interested in maximizing their satisfaction, they will seek to

FIGURE 8A.1

The Indifference Map

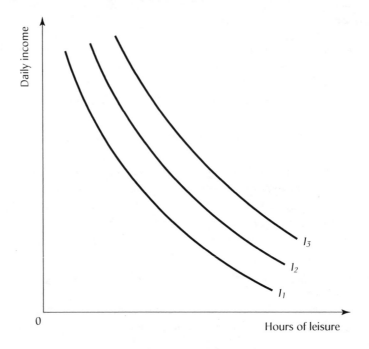

reach the indifference curve that is farthest away from the origin. That is, they will prefer more income and more leisure to less income and less leisure. Before discussing how an individual selects a given level of satisfaction, it is necessary to point out some characteristics of indifference curves.

- Indifference curves do not cross each other.

- Indifference curves do not cross the axes.

- The curves are convex to the origin. The shape of the curve is derived from the assumption that as the level of daily income increases, the extra (or marginal) satisfaction gained from acquiring more income decreases. Similarly, as the individual opts for more leisure, the marginal satisfaction obtained from more leisure decreases.

In addition to making assumptions about indifference curves, it is also important to assume that leisure is a normal good. That is, as one's income increases, more leisure would be purchased. It also must be assumed that individuals cannot live without income. Some income is needed to purchase food, clothing, shelter, and so on. An individual cannot opt for leisure 24 hours a day. In fact, individuals do need to sleep, so it is assumed in this appendix that only 16 hours per day are available to be allocated between leisure and income.

Figure 8A.2 introduces the concept of a time–budget line. For the purposes of this example, assume that an individual makes $10 per hour. If this individual works all 16 hours in a day, the total daily income earned is ($10 × 16) $160. If the individual works no hours in a day, the income earned is zero. All

FIGURE 8A.2

A Time–Budget Line

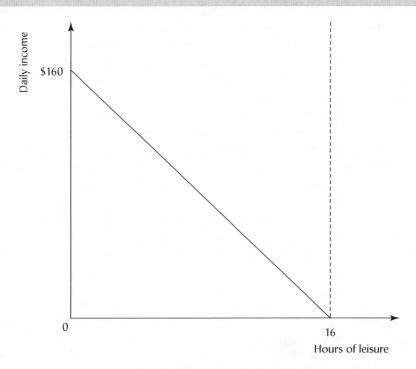

Selecting the Income–Leisure Combination

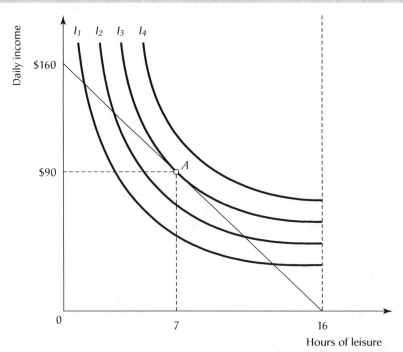

combinations of hours of leisure and daily income (at $10 per hour) are shown on the time–budget line. All combinations of hours of leisure and income shown on the time–budget line are possible to attain. Which combination of work and leisure should be chosen? The combination that touches the indifference curve that is farthest away from the origin. The point of tangency between the time–budget line and the indifference curve as shown by point *A* (Figure 8A.3) represents the combination of work and leisure that bring the highest level of satisfaction based on the individual's current wage rate. At this wage rate, seven hours of leisure and nine hours of work are chosen. The nine hours of work generate a daily income of $90.

How is the individual labour supply curve derived from this indifference curve map? As discussed in the chapter, the individual labour supply curve shows the response in terms of the number of hours offered for work when changes in the wage rate occur. Thus, it is necessary to introduce new wage rates into the diagram. New time–budget lines must be drawn to reflect the choices associated with higher wage rates (see Figure 8A.4). Depending on the wage rate, there will be a combination of hours of leisure and daily income that reaches an indifference curve as far away from the origin as possible. For example, at a wage rate of $10.50 per hour (daily income = $168), the best possible combination of income and leisure is point *B*. At a wage rate of $11 per hour (daily income = $176), the best possible combination is point *C*, and so on. If points *A*, *B*, and *C* are connected, the beginnings of a labour supply curve (see Figure 8A.5) have taken shape. The number of hours of work offered in relation to each wage rate can be determined by subtracting the number of hours of leisure from 16.

Wage Rates and Income–Leisure Combinations

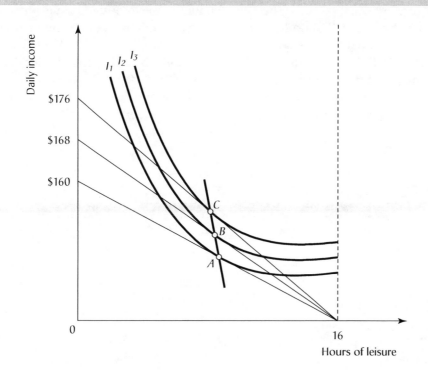

FIGURE 8A.5

The Beginnings of the Individual Labour Supply Curve

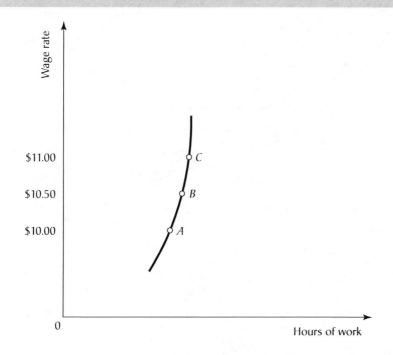

Appendix 8A: Indifference Curve Analysis of Labour Supply

If the backward-bending supply curve applies to this individual, the indifference map and time–budget line may appear as they do in Figure 8A.6. In the diagram, lines W_1, W_2, W_3, W_4, and W_5 represent time–budget lines for five different wage rates. The best combinations of income and leisure are represented by A, B, C, D, and E. A line running through these best combinations points to the beginning of a backward-bending supply curve for the individual. If an individual is provided with some non-labour income, the indifference map and time–budget line may appear as they do in Figure 8A.7. In the diagram, the time–budget line starts at a point above the horizontal axis. The daily income is a combination of earned and non-labour income.

FIGURE 8A.6

Derivation of the Backward-Bending Supply Curve for Labour

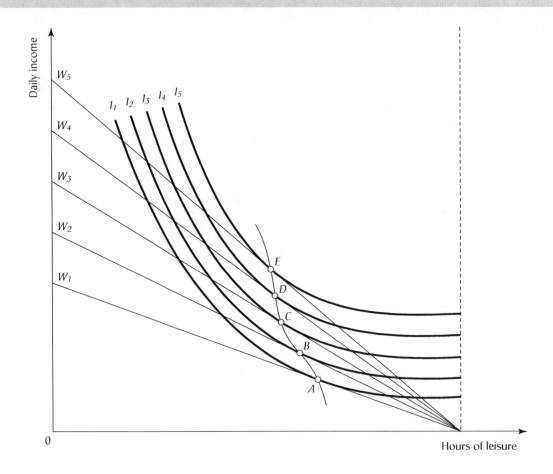

Income–Leisure Combination with Non-Labour Income

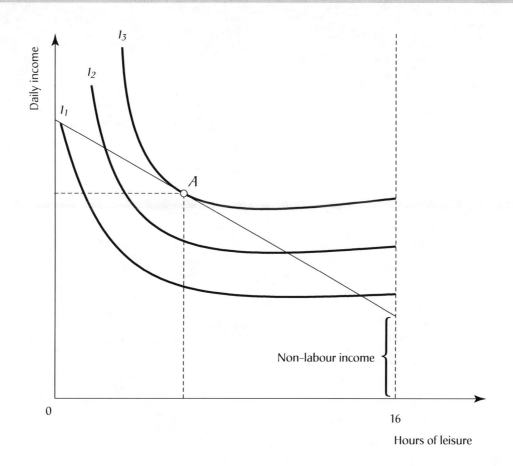

Appendix 8A: Indifference Curve Analysis of Labour Supply

Labour Market Decisions of Firms

Chapter Learning Objectives

After completing this chapter, you should be able to:

- define and describe each of the following terms: derived demand, law of diminishing returns, short run, long run, marginal productivity of labour, marginal revenue product, scale effect, substitution effect (demand), and quasi-fixed labour costs
- explain how the firm's demand curve for a specific occupation is derived
- explain how the demand curve for a specific occupation shifts to a new position
- discuss the factors that influence the wage elasticity of demand
- discuss the various factors that influence productivity in Canada
- discuss the types of quasi-fixed labour costs and how they affect the demand for labour

THE DEMAND FOR TRUCK DRIVERS

The demand for workers is derived from the demand for the goods and services that workers produce. The demand for truck drivers provides a good example of derived demand for students of labour economics. Revenue from trucking in Canada is in excess of $50 billion a year. Trucking companies handle 90% of the freight shipped within Canada and 70% of the freight going to the United States from Canada. Since Canada signed the Free Trade Agreement (FTA) and the North American Free Trade Agreement (NAFTA), the volume of trade between Canada and the United States has increased substantially. For example, exports to the United States doubled in the 10-year period after the signing of the FTA. Trucks cross the Canada–United States border more than 13 million times a year. The demand for shipping by truck has also increased because many Canadian manufacturers have switched to just-in-time inventories.

The trucking industry is populated by a few large firms and by thousands of medium-sized businesses and owner-operated trucks. The industry grows as the economy grows. As the trucking industry grows, the demand for truck drivers increases. In the 2001 Census of Canada, more men listed truck driver as an occupation than any other occupation. There are more than 263 000 truck drivers in the country and more than 400 000 people working in the industry. In spite of these numbers, there are not enough truck drivers to meet the current demand. The future ability of the industry to attract an adequate supply of truck drivers is not promising. The average age of a trucker in Canada is over 50 years; many will be retiring soon. Historically, many truck drivers were recruited from the farming industry and from the military. Since fewer people are going into farming and the military, the pool of possible truck drivers is drying up. The industry has asked the federal government to ease immigration restrictions for foreign truckers.

Introduction

The demand side of the labour market is represented by employers who require employees to produce goods and services. Consequently, the demand for workers is derived from the demand for the final product or service. If there is no demand for the final product or service, there is no demand for the workers who make that product or provide that service. If customers want the final product or service, there is a demand for workers to provide that product or service. Thus, the demand for workers is said to be a derived demand. Not only the demand for the product but the price of the product or service will affect firms' ability to pay wages. If the demand for a product increases, the price of the product will increase. The increase in price will likely be reflected in increased wage rates for employees. This chapter focuses on the relationship between the demand for the product and the demand for the workers to make the product. Chapter 10 will review the connection between the demand for the product and wage rates paid to employees.

The demand for workers also depends on the productivity of the worker. The demand for workers who are more productive is greater than that for those who are less productive. More productive workers can produce more goods and services, and are in greater demand from employers. Thus, workers who undertake training and further their education in order to improve their productivity can expect the demand for their services to increase.

This chapter introduces the theory behind the demand side of the labour market. The objective is to derive the demand curve for labour. The next chapter will combine the supply curve from Chapter 8 and the demand curve from this chapter to draw a picture of the labour market and the outcomes of the labour market: wage rates, and levels of employment.

The Demand Curve for Labour

The demand for labour will be discussed within the framework of two time periods: the short run, and the long run.

The Short Run

As mentioned in Chapter 2, economists refer to the short run as a period of time in which at least one factor of production cannot be changed. Factors of production are inputs into the production process, such as the building, workers, equipment, and so on. Normally, there is a period during which some of these factors cannot be changed. For example, a company may have leased a building for a year, so it is locked into the use of the building until the lease expires. For the next year, the building, which is one of the factors of production, cannot be changed. In economic terms, the short run for this company is a year. The building, which is capital, is fixed, but the number of workers can be varied. Labour is a variable factor of production. The short run may extend beyond a year; it may take longer than one year to expand a factory. The short run may also be shorter than a year; it may not take as long as a year for an office maintenance firm to buy a new truck, new cleaning equipment, new supplies, and so on.

Assume that a garment manufacturing company has leased this building for a year. If its sales expand, it will need to hire more employees. As new employees are hired, some efficiencies in production will be possible. Workers can divide up the jobs and begin to specialize. For example, some employees will cut the cloth. Others will specialize in sewing on sleeves or sewing on collars. The productivity of the workers will increase. Unfortunately, the increases in productivity achieved by hiring more workers will not continue indefinitely. The building is limited in size. There is only so much space in which the employees can work. At some point, the contribution of the next worker to the total output of the company will be less than that of the previous worker. The new employee has less of the fixed factor of production (the building) to work with than the previously hired employee. With less of the building to work with, the new employee's contribution to total output is less than that of the other employee. Economists refer to this reduction in the marginal output from the hiring of a new employee as diminishing returns. The **law of diminishing returns** states that as employment expands in the short run, a level of employment will be reached at which the next employee's contribution to total output will be less than the marginal contribution of the previously hired employee. Formally, the law of diminishing returns states that as more and more of a variable factor of production (workers) is added to a fixed amount of another factor of production (building), a point will be reached where the next worker's marginal contribution to output declines.

The law of diminishing returns only applies to the production time period known as the short run. In the long run, all factors of production can be changed or altered. A new building can be rented, more equipment can be purchased, more employees can be hired, and so on. The contribution of the next worker to total output is referred to as the marginal productivity of labour (MPL), which is illustrated in Figure 9.1A.

The numerical example in Table 9.1 can help explain the law of diminishing returns. In this example, as more employees are hired the number of shirts produced each day increases. The increase in the number of shirts obtained by

law of diminishing returns

in the short run, a point will be reached at which the extra contribution of the next worker to total output will be less than that of the previously hired worker

FIGURE 9.1A

Marginal Productivity of Labour

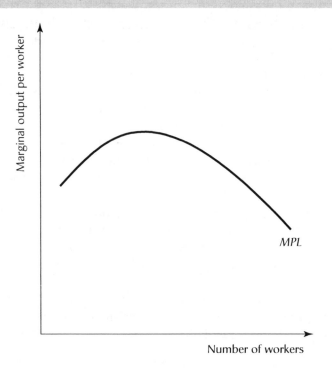

TABLE 9.1

Calculation of the Marginal Productivity of Labour

NUMBER OF EMPLOYEES	NUMBER OF SHIRTS PER DAY	MARGINAL PRODUCTIVITY OF LABOUR
0	0	
		> 5
1	5	
		> 8
2	13	
		> 9
3	22	
		> 8
4	30	
		> 7
5	37	
		> 6
6	43	
		> 5
7	48	
		> 4
8	52	

hiring one more employee is shown in the third column of the table. The MPL increases with the hiring of the second and third employees. The second employee adds eight shirts to the total output and the third employee adds nine shirts. The MPL increases as the work becomes more specialized. With the hiring of the fourth employee, the MPL begins to decline. At this point, diminishing returns from the hiring of more employees have begun to set in. Although total output continues to increase with each employee hired, the increases are smaller and smaller.

Not all companies experience diminishing returns with the hiring of the fourth employee. In some situations, hundreds of employees can be hired before diminishing returns are experienced. Since all firms must always be operating in a short-run situation when at least one input cannot be changed, all firms will eventually experience diminishing returns. Figure 9.1A is a graph of the MPL from Table 9.1.

The Decision to Hire

If the MPL of the next employee is less than that of the previous employee, should the new employee be hired? In order to make this decision, one must first convert the contribution of each successive worker to dollars. Since companies know how much they need to pay an employee in dollars, they need to determine the contribution of a new employee in dollars. The cost of the new employee and the contribution of the new employee can then be compared. In order to convert the contribution of a new employee to dollars, the MPL is multiplied by the **marginal revenue (MR)** obtained from the sale of the extra output. The marginal revenue is the addition to total revenue from selling one more unit of output. The dollar value of the product is called the **marginal revenue product (MRP)**.

$$MRP = MR \times MPL$$

marginal revenue (MR)

the extra revenue from selling one more unit of output

marginal revenue product (MRP)

the extra revenue obtained from selling the output of an additional worker

The marginal revenue product (MRP) is the dollar value of the contribution of each successive worker. A graph of the relationship between the MRP and the number of workers is shown in Figure 9.1B. Since the marginal product of labour (MPL) is a component of MRP, the shapes of the MPL and MRP curves are similar. Essentially there are two reasons why the MRP declines as the number of workers increases. First, the law of diminishing returns dictates that after a certain level of employment, the contribution of each new worker will be less than the contribution of the previous worker. Second, in a competitive market, the firm's demand curve slopes down to the right: the firm must lower the price of the product in order to sell more units. Thus, as more units are produced, the marginal revenue from selling one more unit decreases.

The firm's decision to hire a new employee will depend, in part, on the value of the new employee. It will also depend on the cost of hiring the new employee, which is the wage rate. If the value of the new employee to the company is greater than the cost of hiring the new employee, the decision would be to hire the person. If the reverse is true, the person would not be hired.

Once the wage rate is known, the MRP curve can be used to determine how many employees are hired. By comparing the wage rate with the MRP, the following decision rule can be applied.

- If wage rate > MRP, do not hire the person.
- If wage rate < MRP, hire the person.
- If wage rate = MRP, the employer is indifferent about hiring the person.

FIGURE 9.1B

Marginal Revenue Product

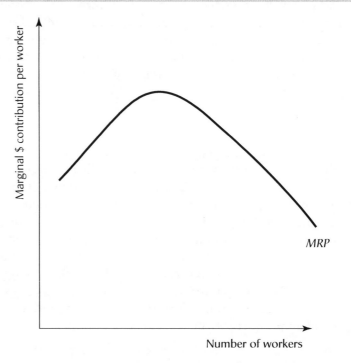

The decision to hire can be shown graphically in Figure 9.2. If the wage rate is W_1, the number of workers hired is L_1. If the wage rate is W_2, the number of workers hired is L_2. Thus, the MRP curve represents the firm's demand curve for a specific occupation. The curve displays the quantity of workers demanded in that occupation in relation to the cost, or the price, of adding one employee. More workers are demanded by employers at lower wage rates due to the decreasing marginal productivity of labour. Since the contribution of a new worker is less than the contribution of the previous worker, employers will only hire more employees if the wage rate is lower. Conversely, fewer workers are demanded at higher wage rates.

The demand for an occupation is influenced by the demand for the product, through the MR, and the MPL of the worker. If the demand for the product or service increases, its price will also likely increase. The MR from the sale of more of the product will increase, which results in increased MRP. If the MRP increases, the demand for labour increases, since the MRP curve represents the demand curve for labour. The demand for labour shifts to the right (MRP^2 in Figure 9.3A, page 248). A decrease in the MR shifts the demand curve for labour to the left.

If the productivity of employees (MPL) can be improved, and the MR does not change, the MRP and the demand for labour will increase (MRP^2 in Figure 9.3B, page 249). Conversely, a decrease in MPL will shift the demand curve for labour to the left.

FIGURE 9.2

Wage Rate and Number of Workers

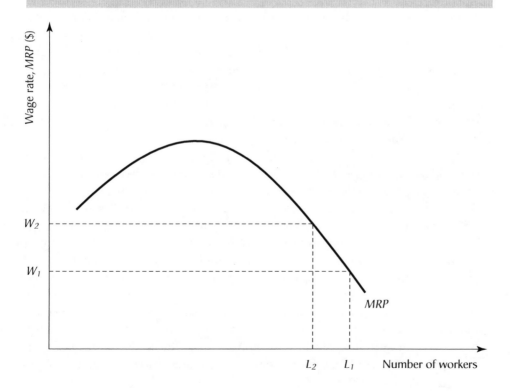

FIGURE 9.3A

Increase in Marginal Revenue

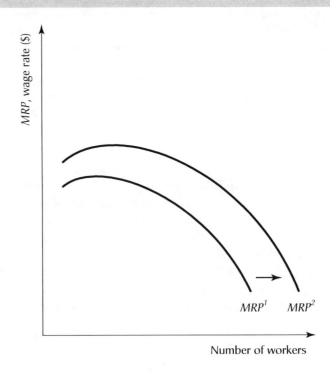

Employers do not usually talk of marginal productivity of labour and marginal revenue products. Since these terms are not used on a daily basis in business, one might assume firms do not use them in determining how many employees to hire. However, the lack of use in daily business practice does not make the concept useless or irrelevant. Firms that are successful in the marketplace must be following the principles discussed here. Employers must assess whether or not a new employee should be hired. That decision is based on a comparison of some measure of the contribution of the new employee to the firm and the cost of that employee to the firm.

Another criticism of the marginal productivity approach to labour demand stems from the fact that hiring is often accompanied by the purchase of new equipment. That is, the number of employees is not the only variable that changes in a firm as it expands. For example, a new employee may get a new personal computer to work with. If other factors of production are changing, the law of diminishing returns may not be relevant. You will recall that the law of diminishing returns applies only in the short run when at least one factor of production is fixed. If new equipment is purchased along with the hiring of a new employee, the productivity of the new worker may increase. Although it is true that the hiring of employees and the purchase of equipment often occur simultaneously, in many situations employees have been hired without any purchase of new equipment. In these situations, the marginal productivity of labour of the next employee can be determined.

FIGURE 9.3B

Increase in Productivity

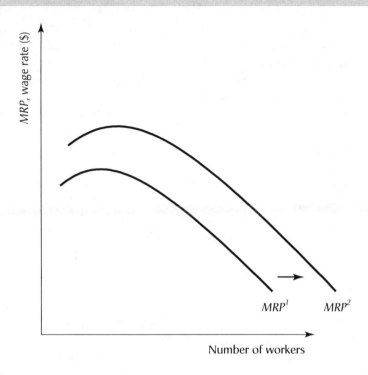

The Long Run

What is the shape of the demand curve for labour in the long run? In the long run, all factors of production are variable. As a firm expands, it moves from one short-run situation to another; it moves from a small operation to a larger operation. If the firm continues to expand, it will move into even larger premises. Regardless of what stage the firm is in, it is always in the short run; there is always one factor of production that cannot be changed easily. The long run is the *series* of short-run situations. The demand curve for labour slopes down to the right in the long run as well as in the short run; however, different influences come into play in the long run that affect the demand curve for labour.

In the long run, the demand curve for labour has a negative slope for two reasons: the scale effect, and the substitution effect. When wage rates paid to employees increase, the prices of products produced by those employees are likely to increase. Faced with higher prices, consumers buy less of the product. With less of the product being sold, the company needs fewer employees and cuts back the scale of its production. Conversely, if wage rates fell, the price of the product could be reduced. More of the product would be sold and more workers would be hired as the scale of production increased. The **scale effect** of a wage rate change refers to the change in the number of employees hired that results from changes in the amount of the product sold.

scale effect

the change in the number of employees hired as a result of changes in the amount of product sold

substitution effect (demand)

changes in the wage rate encourage employers to substitute capital for labour and labour for capital

In the long run, employers may be able to substitute capital equipment for workers. For example, robots may weld together pieces on an automobile. If wage rates increase, the substitution of capital for labour becomes more attractive. Fewer workers will be hired. Conversely, if wage rates decrease, there is an incentive to substitute workers for capital. More workers are demanded. The **substitution effect (demand)** refers to the substitution of capital for labour depending on the direction of the wage rate change. The substitution effect also applies when there is a change in the price of capital. For example, an increase in the price of capital could result in an increase in the number of workers employed as firms hire more workers instead of buying capital equipment. It is possible that workers in one occupation could be substituted for workers in another occupation. For example, labourers may be able to do the work of carpenters on a construction site. Nurses may be able to perform some of the duties assigned to physicians. Technologists may be substitutes for engineers and paralegals may be substitutes for lawyers.

Note that the scale effect and the substitution effect for demand operate in the same direction with respect to the employment of workers. If wage rates increase, both the scale and substitution effects reduce the quantity of labour demanded. If wage rates decrease, both effects increase the quantity of labour demanded.

So far in our discussion, the demand curve for an occupation represents only one firm's demand for a specific occupation. In order to get the overall, or market, demand for a specific occupation, such as a plumber, one must add together the demand curves for the individual firms. The market demand curve is drawn with the wage rate on the vertical axis and the number of employees (quantity of labour) on the horizontal axis (see Figure 9.4). Note that the axes for the market supply curve (Chapter 8) and market demand curves for an occupation are identical. In Chapter 10, the two curves will be combined on one graph to determine wage rate and employment levels.

In Chapter 2, the difference between a change in demand and a change in the quantity demanded was explained. That distinction applies to the labour market as well. A change in the wage rate does not result in a shift of the demand curve for labour. If the wage rate changes, the new quantity of workers demanded is determined by referring to the wage rate and the existing demand curve. A change in demand results in a shift of the demand curve. The demand curve for labour will shift if there is a change in the demand for the product or service provided by labour. For example, if there is an increase in the demand for restaurant meals, there will be an increase in the demand for workers to prepare and serve restaurant meals. The curve will shift if there is a change in productivity or a change in the price of a substitute, or complementary, resource to labour. For example, if robots and workers are substitutes in the production process, a decrease in the price of robots will decrease the demand for labour. A decrease in the demand for labour shifts the demand curve for labour to the left. If robots and workers are complementary in the production process, a decrease in the price of robots could lead to an increase in the demand for workers.

FIGURE 9.4

The Market Demand Curve for Labour

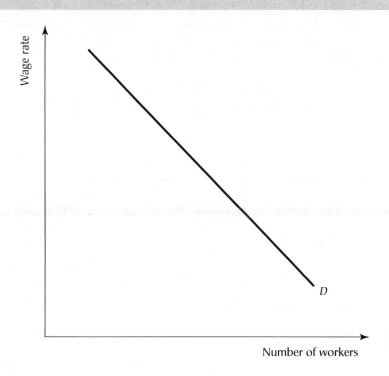

Wage Elasticity of Labour Demand

As we have seen, the number of employees a firm hires depends in part on the wage rate paid. Changes in the wage rate will bring about a change in the number of employees hired. The **wage elasticity of labour demand** measures the degree to which changes in the wage rate affect the quantity of employees demanded. The wage elasticity of labour demand is determined in a manner similar to the determination of price elasticity of demand (see Chapter 2):

$$\text{Coefficient of wage elasticity of demand} = \frac{\text{Percentage change in quantity of workers demanded}}{\text{Percentage change in the wage rate}}$$

wage elasticity of labour demand

the change in quantity demanded in response to a change in the wage rate

If the absolute value of the coefficient of wage elasticity of demand is greater than 1, the demand is said to be elastic. In an elastic situation, relatively small changes in the wage rate result in relatively large changes in the quantity of labour demanded. If the absolute value of the coefficient is less than 1, the demand is said to be inelastic. In an inelastic situation, similar changes in the wage rate result in relatively small changes in the quantity of workers demanded. What factors influence the wage elasticity of demand?

If a 5% increase in the wage rate led to a 3% reduction in the quantity of workers demanded, the coefficient of wage elasticity of demand would be as follows:

Coefficient of wage elasticity of demand = –3%/5% = –0.6

Discussions surrounding the wage elasticity of demand often omit the negative sign in the elasticity coefficient. The focus is only on the absolute value. Since 0.6 is less than 1, the demand in this situation is said to be inelastic. If a 1% increase in the wage rate resulted in a 2% drop in employment, the coefficient of wage elasticity of demand would be:

Coefficient of wage elasticity of demand = –2%/1% = –2

This example represents an elastic demand since the absolute value of the coefficient, 2, is greater than 1.

When calculating the coefficient of elasticity, the percentage changes are based on an average wage rate and an average quantity of workers demanded. For example, assume that the wage rate increased from $10 per hour to $11 per hour. In response to this increase in the wage rate, the quantity of workers demanded fell from 100 to 90. The change in the wage rate is $1 and the average wage rate is $10.50. Thus, the percentage change in the wage rate is 1/10.50 × 100%, or 9.5%. The change in the quantity of workers is –10 and the average quantity is 95. The percentage change in the quantity of workers demanded is –10/95 × 100%, or –10.5%. The coefficient of wage elasticity of demand is

Coefficient of wage elasticity of demand = –10.5%/9.5% = –1.105

What factors have an impact in the determination of the wage elasticity of demand?

Percentage of Labour Costs in Total Costs

If labour costs are a relatively small percentage of the total cost of making a product or providing a service, the demand for labour is likely to be inelastic. Relatively large changes in the wage rate will not affect total costs significantly. As a result, changes in the wage rate will not significantly affect the number of employees. For example, in office tower construction, the cost represented by plumbers' wages is small compared to the overall cost of the project. An increase in the wage rate paid to plumbers will not significantly increase the overall cost of the project. Therefore, there will be little reduction in the number of plumbers in response to an increase in the wage rate.

Conversely, if labour costs constitute a significant proportion of total costs, any change in the wage rate will have a major impact on total costs. This impact will result in a relatively large change in the number of employees. For companies that clean offices after hours, the majority of the costs are labour costs. If the wage rate paid to these employees increases, the overall cost of providing the service will increase significantly. The number of employees would be significantly reduced by the wage rate increase.

Number of Substitutes for Labour

If there are no substitutes for a type of labour, the demand for labour tends to be inelastic. There may be no substitutes because of government regulation. For example, only physicians can prescribe prescription drugs. Only qualified pilots fly airplanes. If the wage rate were to increase for either of these occupations, the quantity of workers demanded would change very little. In other situations, unions may have negotiated restrictions on the introduction of new technology or restrictions on contracting out work to non-union workers.

However, if there are several substitutes for a type of labour, the demand is likely to be elastic. Capital is not the only substitute for labour. Substitutes can be employees in other occupations. If the duties of a lawyer can be performed by a law clerk, wage rate increases for lawyers may result in a reduction in the number of lawyers. The wage elasticity of demand will likely increase as time goes on. New technologies can be developed and introduced into the production process. For example, new technologies are continually being introduced in construction and medicine.

Even where substitutes exist, it may not be easy for employers to use a substitute in place of their employees when wage rates increase. Assume there is an increase in the wage rate for a certain occupation. If there is a substitute for that occupation, there will be an increased demand for the substitute, which will drive up the price of the substitute. Companies that planned to use a substitute for labour may have to adjust those plans in light of the higher price for the substitute. If the supply of the substitute is elastic, the price increase in response to an increase in demand will be small and it may be relatively easy to switch to a substitute.

Price Elasticity of the Product or Service

If the product or service produced by labour has an inelastic demand, price increases will not significantly change the quantity demanded for that product. If workers producing the product or service get a wage rate increase, the price of the product will likely increase. However, if consumers do not respond to price increases by reducing the quantity demanded, employees are in a better position to achieve wage rate increases. For instance, necessities such as healthcare tend to have inelastic demands, and the wage elasticity of labour demand for workers in healthcare occupations is also inelastic. Conversely, if the demand for the product is elastic, consumers will respond to increases in the price by significantly decreasing the quantity of the product demanded. Employees in these industries will find it harder to achieve increases in their wage rates. An example of an industry with an elastic demand curve is restaurants; with many restaurants for consumers to choose from, the demand for each restaurant's product is elastic, and increases in employee wage rates are difficult to pass on to consumers.

The price elasticity of demand for products is influenced by government trade policy. Successive federal governments have pursued a policy of freer international trade. The removal of trade barriers opens up more competition in the product market, and with more competition, the demand for Canadian products becomes more elastic. As a consequence, the wage elasticity of demand for Canadian workers becomes more elastic. Because workers have a better opportunity to get a wage rate increase in conditions of an inelastic demand, unions generally oppose any reduction in trade barriers.

Why is the concept of wage elasticity important? Knowledge of the wage elasticity of demand for labour provides an indication of the employment effects associated with wage rate changes. For example, governments legislate minimum wage rates that are in excess of the current wage rate for a group of employees. How many workers are likely to become unemployed as a result of the minimum wage rate? The answer depends in part on the wage elasticity of demand. When the demand for labour is elastic, more workers are apt to lose their jobs than when the demand is inelastic. Unions also negotiate base wage rates for their members. The negative effects of these increases on employment also need to be determined. Unions are in a more advantageous bargaining position if the demand for their members is inelastic. Government-legislated pay equity usually results in higher wage rates for female workers. The size of the potential reduction in the employment of female workers hinges on the wage elasticity of demand.

The wage elasticity of demand can also have an impact on the total labour costs for employers when there is a change in the wage rate. If the demand for labour is inelastic and the wage rate increases, the total amount of money spent on wages will increase. The increase in the wage rate will not have a significant impact on the quantity of workers demanded. Conversely, if the wage elasticity of demand is elastic, an increase in the wage rate will lower the total labour costs. There will be a proportionately larger decrease in the number of people hired compared to the increase in the wage rate.

Closely related to the wage elasticity of demand is the concept of cross-wage elasticity of demand. An increase in the wage rate paid to one occupation, or group of workers, can lead to changes in the quantity demanded for workers in another occupation, or group. For example, an increase in the wage rate paid to construction carpenters might have an impact on the employment levels of other trades. If the wage rate increase given to carpenters increased building costs and ultimately, the price of buildings, consumers might react by reducing the quantity of new buildings demanded. A decrease in the quantity of new buildings demanded would lead to a reduction in the demand for other trades. Economists refer to the reduced demand for other trades as the scale effect. Since there has been a decline in the demand for the final product, the scale, or size, of the operation is cut back. The degree to which production will be reduced depends on the price elasticity of demand for the product. If consumers react strongly to price increases, production could be scaled back substantially. If, on the other hand, consumers do not react greatly to price increases, the scale effect will be small.

It is possible that an increase in the wage rate paid to one group may increase the quantity of workers demanded elsewhere. An increase in the wage rate paid to construction carpenters may encourage employers to look for substitutes for carpenters. They may hire more general labourers instead of carpenters. Economists refer to the increased demand for labourers as the substitution effect.

The coefficient for cross-wage elasticity of demand is determined as follows:

$$\text{Coefficient for cross-wage elasticity} = \frac{\text{Percentage change in quantity demanded for occupation A}}{\text{Percentage change in wage rate for occupation B}}$$

If the coefficient is negative, an increase in the wage rate paid to one group has reduced the quantity of workers demanded in another group. This situation often occurs with occupations that are complements in the production process. If the coefficient is negative, the scale effect is dominant. If the coefficient is positive, the substitution effect dominates. An increase in the wage rate paid to one group has increased the quantity of workers demanded in another group.

Labour Productivity

As mentioned in the beginning of this chapter, the demand for labour is influenced, in part, by the productivity of labour (MPL). If the productivity of labour increases, the demand for workers who achieve productivity increases. Chapter 10 will discuss the relationship between increases in the demand for labour and increases in the wage rate.

Much has been written in the past few years about the need for Canadian workers to improve productivity. Not only do productivity increases lead to wage rate increases, but they also help to control price increases and improve the overall standard of living for Canadians. If workers are more productive, firms can limit their price increases. If all workers are more productive, society can get more goods and services from the same amount of resources. In this section, we discuss the concept of labour productivity and the factors that influence labour productivity.

The total production of goods and services in Canada varies from year to year. The value of the final goods and services produced in a given year is referred to as **gross domestic product (GDP)**. The level of GDP in Canada depends, in part, on the resources that are available to Canadians. Canada's resources include land, labour, and capital. The land resource includes more than just the 10 million square kilometres that comprise Canada's land mass: it includes minerals, wild animals, vegetation, and water. Canada's population is the basis for the labour resource. The skills, levels of education, and training of the population are also part of the labour resource. The capital resource refers to human-made items that help us produce goods and services. Examples of capital are computers, factories, machinery, and airports.

gross domestic product (GDP)

value of the goods and services produced in a given year

Because this is a text on labour economics, the emphasis in this section is on Canada's labour resource. An increase in the number of workers will increase the amount of goods and services produced. Production increases can also be achieved if Canadian workers become more productive. In economic terms, total production can increase if productivity increases. **Labour productivity** is a measure of the relationship between the quantity of inputs

labour productivity

the output per worker

(workers) and the quantity of output. It is defined as the output per worker. For Canada, productivity is defined as the real GDP per employed person, or, to reflect changes in the hours of work, output per person-hour. The term "real" indicates that the GDP is adjusted for price increases. Because GDP measures the value of all goods and services produced in a given year, its value can increase simply by having prices increase. In order to reflect the goods and services actually being produced more accurately, real GDP is used to calculate productivity as opposed to nominal GDP (GDP at current prices).

If a small number of workers produce a relatively large quantity of goods and services, productivity will be high. If a large number of workers produce a relatively small quantity of goods and services, productivity will be low. The term "relatively" is used because we only know that Canadian productivity is high or low when it is compared to the productivity in other countries or when it is compared to Canadian productivity in previous years. Since not all countries measure productivity in the same manner, international comparisons of productivity are not straightforward. Some comparisons do, however, exist. The Bureau of Labor Statistics in the United States published the information shown in Table 9.2 on manufacturing output per hour for various countries. The numbers are in the form of an index, with the manufacturing output per hour in 1992 equal to 100.0. The growth in manufacturing output per hour for each country since 1992 is given by the value of that country's index in 2002. A higher index value for one country does not mean that it is more productive than another country. It simply means that the growth in productivity since 1992 has been greater. As shown in the table, Canada's growth in this measure of productivity has lagged behind that of many other nations.

The level of productivity is important for the Canadian economy, and so, too, is the rate of productivity growth. As indicated in Chapter 5, productivity growth is achieved when more output is produced with the same amount of inputs or, alternatively, the same level of output is produced with fewer inputs.

The factors that influence productivity are the focus of this section. Why is productivity growth important? Total output of goods and services increases with increases in productivity. As the level of production increases,

TABLE 9.2

Index of Manufacturing Output per Hour for Selected Countries, 2002 (1992 = 100.0)

Canada	117.9	Italy	113.0
France	153.3	Japan	140.7
United Kingdom	123.7	United States	151.9
Sweden	196.5	Norway	110.9
Netherlands	133.1	Germany	131.4
Belgium	143.4		

Source: http://data.bls.gov/cgi-bin/surveymost. Data retrieved on February 15, 2004.

incomes generated in production increase. As a result, the standard of living of Canadians increases. It is difficult for incomes to increase when productivity is not increasing. Productivity increases also allow prices to remain stable or to rise less rapidly. If labour productivity increases, payments to workers can increase without being accompanied by price increases. Furthermore, if Canadian prices are not rising as fast as those in other countries, Canadian products are more attractive to foreigners. In order to sell more goods and services to foreigners, we need more workers. Thus, productivity is not only related to incomes but also to employment.

Labour productivity growth may not be entirely due to improvements in the skill level of workers. Technological change, in terms of better machinery and equipment, can improve labour productivity. Studies of productivity in the United States have estimated that more than 40% of the increase in labour productivity can be attributed to technological change.

A more efficient use of resources can also improve productivity. That is, if resources (for example, workers) move from industries with low productivity to industries with high productivity, the overall level of productivity in the Canadian economy will increase. Decreases in the rate of productivity growth cannot be attributed solely to the fact that the workers are lazier than they previously were. As will be discussed shortly, many factors influence the level of Canadian labour productivity.

A summary of how productivity changes translate into changes in labour demand is shown below.

An increase in labour productivity → a decrease in the price of goods and services and/or an increase in wages → an increase in both domestic and foreign consumption → an increase in the production of goods and services → an increase in the use of machinery and equipment → an increase in demand for workers → an increase in overall employment, real wages, and the standard of living.

The main influences on the level of productivity growth in Canada can be divided into three groups. The first group of influences affect productivity in the economy as a whole. These are referred to as macro influences. They are the following:

- the structure of the economy
- economic conditions
- government policies

The second group of influences primarily affect the productivity level of the individual business firm. These are referred to as micro influences and are:

- the scale of business operations
- management techniques

The third group of influences straddles both of the first two groups. These factors influence both Canada's overall level of productivity and the productivity of the individual business firm. They are:

- quantity and quality of capital
- the labour force

Chapter 9: Labour Market Decisions of Firms

As the factors influencing productivity are discussed, you will notice that they are clearly interrelated. For example, the quality of management can influence the speed with which new technology is introduced. Economic conditions also affect the ability of the firm to produce on a larger scale.

The Structure of the Economy

The industrial composition of the labour force also influences productivity. The proportion of the labour force employed in both agriculture and manufacturing is continuing to decline. As mentioned in Chapter 5, most of the employment growth has been in the service sector of our economy, where it is more difficult to measure output than in either agriculture or manufacturing. It is also more difficult to measure productivity in the service sector. Consider the difficulties associated with measuring the productivity of lawyers, nurses, and firefighters.

Much of the increase in agricultural and manufacturing productivity over the last century can be attributed to improvements in machinery and equipment. The productivity of workers in these sectors is increasing through the introduction of new machinery; however, these sectors account for a declining proportion of total employment. In many situations, new machinery has allowed for the increase in output with fewer workers. On the other hand, can you replace nurses, police officers, and firefighters with machinery? Productivity increases are harder to come by in the service, retail, and government sectors, which are labour-intensive industries. Nonetheless, it is not impossible to get technical advances in the service sector. Examples of such advances are automated teller machines in banking and universal bar coding in the retail sector. The Centre for the Study of Living Standards reported in 2004 that productivity in Canada's service sector has made some impressive gains. The largest gains in productivity came from the finance, insurance, and real estate sectors. In spite of the improvement in productivity, the service sector in Canada is not as productive as the service sector in the United States. The reasons for the gap are that Canadian companies hire workers with lower levels of education, and Canadian companies invest less in research and development and in information and telecommunications technology.

Economic Conditions

Canadians are well aware of changing economic conditions. The economy expands when people, businesses, and government spend money. The level of economic activity eventually peaks and then heads toward a recession as the level of overall spending declines. Eventually, a trough is reached as the economy starts to pick up. How does the level of economic activity influence the measurement of productivity? When the economy slows down, employers cut back on hours of work. Employees no longer work overtime and some full-time employees are shifted to part-time employment. If productivity is measured as the output per employee, productivity will decrease. As employee hours of work and output decrease, the number of employees is unaffected and, as a result, the output per employee declines. Although some employee layoffs may take place, companies produce fewer products with almost the same number of employees. As the economy expands and spending increases, employees work more hours. Production per employee increases.

Slowdowns in economic activity affect goods-producing industries more than service industries and government. The demand for government-provided services and other services is more stable than that for manufactured products. Because recessions hit goods-producing or manufacturing industries harder than industries in the service sector, an economic slowdown will show drops in the overall level of productivity.

Government Policies

Governments can influence worker productivity in a number of ways. They can provide support through tax dollars or tax breaks for education and training. A better-educated labour force should be a more productive labour force. They can provide tax breaks for companies that provide skill training, or for companies that develop and introduce new technology. In addition, governments can ensure that school curricula are up to date and relevant to the workplace. The Organisation for Economic Co-operation and Development (OECD) has stated that although Canada spends more on education than other countries, the competence of our workforce in terms of literacy and numeracy is declining in comparison.

Government regulation of business has a large impact on productivity. For example, governments can restrict competition in some sectors of the economy by allowing monopolies to evolve in the public interest. The term

Labour Market Issue 9.1

Literacy and Wages

Literacy involves three measured skills:
1. the ability to understand and use prose (e.g., reading newspapers and books)
2. the ability to use and understand documents (e.g., job applications and travel schedules)
3. the ability to use and understand numbers (e.g., balance a chequebook)

A study of 12 countries divided individuals into five skill levels. A level of 3 was considered the minimum level required to handle the everyday demands of work and life. In Canada, only 57% of the population rated a level 3 or above. This can be compared with 75% of the population in Sweden.

The number of years of formal education is not always indicative of literacy. For example, 60% of adults in Sweden who did not complete the equivalent of a Canadian secondary school education scored well in the second category (documents). Only 27% of Canadians scored well in this category without completing secondary school.

Your number of years of schooling may help you get a job but in order to keep the job and receive promotions, you will need strong literacy skills. Employers associate literacy with productivity. More literate employees are better able to adapt to changing job requirements. Thus, more literate employees are higher-paid employees and are less likely to be unemployed.

"monopoly" refers to a "single seller." The lack of competition in highly regulated industries may reduce the need to become competitive. The federal government has taken some steps toward deregulating industries such as energy, telephones, and trucking.

International trade policies also influence competition. Tariffs may be imposed on imports to protect certain Canadian industries. Tariffs increase the cost of imported goods and thus help shift the demand from imported to domestic goods. Tariffs may temporarily help Canadian industries, but they make them less efficient in the long run. Continued tariff protection can prolong inefficiency. A major objective of the Canadian government in signing the North American Free Trade Agreement (NAFTA) was to increase the overall productivity of the Canadian labour force. It was hoped that the increased competition faced by Canadian companies would force them to be more productive. Also, Canadian companies would have a larger market where they could sell their goods and services. If companies could expand their sales and output, the productivity per worker should increase. Canada has had some previous experience with trade agreements and productivity. In 1965, Canada and the United States signed the Canada–United States Automobile Agreement, which permitted new cars to travel tariff-free between the two countries. This agreement resulted in greater output, employment, and productivity for the Canadian automobile industry.

A government's approach to managing the economy can also have an impact on productivity. Businesses that are comfortable with the government's economic policies may invest in Canada. If they do not agree with the government's policies, they may invest elsewhere. One aspect of economic management is taxes. The level of taxation is a major determinant of business confidence. Excessively high tax rates on both businesses and consumers may discourage investment in new plants and equipment. The monetary policies of the Bank of Canada with respect to stabilizing prices also increase the confidence level of business with respect to new investment.

The Scale of Business Operations

Rarely do companies begin their operations by producing a large output. As sales increase, the scale of the operation increases as well. Expanding output allows firms to take advantage of **increasing returns to scale**. That is, by doubling all their inputs (workers, size of building, etc.), they may cause output to more than double. Increasing returns to scale result in lower average costs and higher levels of productivity.

What factors permit increasing returns to take place? As the scale of the company expands, more efficient machinery and equipment can be used. Workers can perform more specialized functions, becoming more productive. Consider the situation in the automobile industry: Workers have very specialized individual tasks that result in a completed car. Can increasing returns to scale be expected to influence productivity indefinitely? Unfortunately, increases in size are accompanied by communication difficulties among individuals within the company, which increase average costs and reduce productivity. Large size can lead to inefficiencies and cost

increasing returns to scale

the percentage increase in output that is relatively greater than the percentage change in all the factors of production

International Trade and the Labour Market

The Canadian economy relies a great deal on international trade. Approximately one in four Canadian workers produces a product for export. Thus it is important that Canadian companies have access to foreign markets in order to sell their goods. Conversely, foreign firms want access to Canadian markets. During the Great Depression in the 1930s, many countries effectively closed their borders to foreign products. Many economists believe that the reduction in international trade extended the Depression.

After World War II, 23 countries including Canada signed an agreement to promote international trade. That agreement was called the General Agreement on Tariffs and Trade (GATT). Over the years, this agreement has led to reduced tariffs and quotas as well as non-tariff barriers to international trade. In 1995, the GATT was replaced by the World Trade Organization (WTO), which has more than 130 members.

Canada's commitment to freer trade goes beyond its membership in the WTO. In 1965, the Canada–United States Automobile Agreement was signed. This agreement permitted the duty-free movement of new cars and car parts between the two countries. With access to the U.S. market guaranteed, the Canadian automobile industry has significantly increased employment. The demand for cars made in Canada increased and the number of automobile workers increased as well. When automobile production moved to a larger scale, the productivity of automobile workers increased, as did their wage rates.

In 1989, Canada signed the Free Trade Agreement with the United States. This agreement reduced trade barriers between the two countries over 10 years. Mexico has since signed the agreement, now known as the North American Free Trade Agreement (NAFTA). What impact have these agreements had on the labour market? For Canadian companies that now have better access to foreign markets, those agreements have resulted in greater demand for their products. The derived demand for labour has also increased. Other Canadian companies are now experiencing more competition than before. The demand for their products has declined. Their demand for workers has also decreased. Changes in international trade patterns have forced some adjustment on the Canadian labour force.

The foreign demand for Canadian products and Canadians' demand for foreign products also depends on the foreign-exchange value of the Canadian dollar. Since the signing of the Free Trade Agreement, the value of the Canadian dollar has fluctuated between U.S. $0.66 and U.S. $0.89. When the foreign-exchange value of the Canadian dollar is low, Canadian products are more attractive to foreigners and foreign products are more expensive to Canadians. When the foreign-exchange value of the dollar increases, the reverse is true. Thus changes in the exchange rate also affect the Canadian labour market.

increases. To ward off the inefficiencies of size, many companies are experimenting with decentralization and concentrating production in smaller units.

Since the population of Canada is less than that of its main industrial competitors, our companies have a relatively small domestic market in which to sell their products. The scale of operations for many Canadian companies is often less than that for similar firms in other countries. Many Canadian firms are branch plants of multinational companies and may only be producing for the Canadian market. Can Canadian companies hope to expand their sales? Governments have attempted to open up foreign markets for Canadian products. Initiatives in this area include Canada's participation in the World Trade Organization (WTO), NAFTA, and other free-trade deals with countries such as Israel and Chile.

Management Techniques

In the last 20 years, Canadian companies have emphasized management style as a means of increasing productivity. Many books on management have been bestsellers. How can management influence the level of productivity? It is the responsibility of management to organize production and to establish administrative and decision-making structures within the organization. Management's attitude toward innovation is significant—does it have a positive attitude or is it reluctant to innovate? Productivity can be improved by introducing better machinery and equipment and by creating a positive atmosphere in the workplace. Good labour relations policies are a reflection of a positive atmosphere. Canada can have the best-trained workers and the most advanced equipment but will not be competitive in the marketplace unless management does its job.

A criticism of management techniques is that Canadian companies have been slow to introduce new technology. Several reasons have been put forth to explain this tardiness in adapting to new technology. First, the cost of the new technology has discouraged Canadian companies from adopting it. Second, many Canadian companies are not big enough to use the latest technology. Third, Canadian industry is characterized by a large number of branch plants of multinational firms, which may not have the authority or the resources to invest in the new technology. Fourth, it has been suggested that Canadian firms are slow to find out about new technologies.

Quality and Quantity of Capital

The amount of goods and services produced by an employee can increase if the employee has better machinery and equipment to work with. Farmers can be more productive tilling the land with a tractor as opposed to a manually operated hoe. Secretaries can produce more letters with a personal computer than with a typewriter. Automobile workers can produce more cars with the aid of robots. The more capital a worker has to work with, the more productive the worker is. The recognition of the contribution of capital equipment to productivity led Statistics Canada to calculate the Multifactor Productivity Index. This index indicates the level of productivity in an industry in consideration of all the relevant resources in the production process, not just labour. Employees are also more productive as the quality of the capital equipment improves. The speed of computers is constantly increasing and the software is constantly improving.

The Labour Force

The characteristics of the Canadian labour force also affect productivity. These characteristics include the age, health, education, and skill training of the members of the labour force. The average age of the labour force is increasing. Older workers have more experience, especially managerial experience, but they often have less formal education than younger workers. The aging of the labour force may also have an impact on the health of the labour force. The health of the labour force is also influenced by health and safety legislation. Attempts to reduce workplace injuries will result in a healthier labour force.

Two other influences affect the labour force in Canada. First, immigration has played a large role in the growth of Canada's labour force. Many immigrants enter Canada with needed skills; others need language training before they can become productive members of the labour force. Second, many skilled Canadians leave Canada for higher incomes in other countries, especially the United States, a phenomenon referred to as the "brain drain." The loss of skilled workers has a negative impact on productivity.

Several studies have been undertaken with respect to productivity levels in the Canadian economy. The C.D. Howe Institute projected that productivity will continue to increase until 2007 while the workers from the baby-boom generation are still in the labour force. After 2007, productivity levels will decline because of the labour shortages that will result from the large number of workers retiring from the labour force. Even after 2007, the labour force will have a large number of older workers who may be less productive. The Centre for the Study of Living Standards believes that competition is the most important element in determining where productivity increases will take place. Industries that are forced to compete will be forced to be more productive. Industries that are protected by government from competition will not be forced to be more productive. This protection from government can be in the form of a government-created monopoly or government-imposed restrictions on foreign ownership of certain Canadian businesses. The C.D. Howe Institute concurs that competition results in improved productivity. The Institute reports that in the first five years after the signing of the Free Trade Agreement, productivity increased by an average of 26% in industries that become subject to more competition. The Bank of Canada reports that there are four main factors in productivity growth: increased capital investment; the adoption of new technology; better management; and improved labour skills. Studies undertaken in the United States confirm that productivity increases occur in industries that are highly competitive. Much of the productivity improvement comes from technological and managerial innovations.

Quasi-Fixed Labour Costs and the Demand for Labour

The costs faced by firms can be divided into fixed costs and variable costs. Fixed costs remain unchanged regardless of the amount of output, such as property taxes. The amount of money paid in property tax does not depend on the amount of output. Variable costs change with the amount of output. Examples of variable costs are wages and salaries, energy costs, shipping expenses, and so on. These costs increase with the amount produced by the company.

There are certain non-wage costs to hiring employees that are not related to the hours that an employee works; they are known as **quasi-fixed labour costs**. These are not fixed costs because these costs are not totally independent of the amount produced. That is, the greater the amount produced, the more employees are needed. On the other hand, these costs are fixed per employee. Quasi-fixed costs include hiring and training expenses. Also included are government-legislated deductions from the payroll, such as

quasi-fixed labour costs
non-wage costs to hiring employees that are not related to the hours of work

employment insurance premiums and Canada Pension Plan premiums. There are also some deductions specific to the company such as health plan deductions and company pension plan deductions.

Hiring costs include advertising for and screening of applicants, record-keeping, issuing paycheques, and so on. There are also costs to training new employees, which can be direct or indirect costs. The direct costs include materials and the salaries of the trainers. The indirect costs, or opportunity costs, include the lost production from employees who are in training and from the capital equipment used for training and not for the production of goods and services. Since these costs can be substantial, the firm would like to minimize these expenses by keeping their employees for a long time. If employees leave the company, the expenses occur again when new employees are hired. It should be noted that there may also be expenses associated with terminating employees, which may encourage firms to maintain their workforce in the face of changing economic conditions.

Once training and hiring expenses have already been incurred, the company may prefer its existing employees to work longer hours rather than hire new employees and incur new expenses. Existing employees may work longer hours in spite of the premium pay earned by employees working overtime. Firms may also contract out certain tasks, such as cleaning services, rather than hire and train a cleaning crew, or opt for temporary employees from temporary help agencies. When a person is employed through a temporary help agency, the payroll deductions for the employee are made by the temporary help agency. The company using the temporary help is responsible for only the fee paid to the temporary help agency.

Summary

The demand for labour is a derived demand. That is, the demand for a specific occupation derives from the demand for the final product or service. The demand for labour also depends on the productivity of labour. The more productive the worker, the greater the employer's demand for the worker.

The firm's demand for labour is expressed in the marginal revenue product (MRP) curve. Changes in the demand for the final product change the price of the product and the marginal revenue (MR). Changes in MR change the MRP. Changes in worker productivity change the marginal productivity of labour (MPL). Changes in the MPL also change the MRP and thus change the demand for labour.

The demand curve for labour slopes down to the right. The negative slope is a result of two forces: the scale effect, and the substitution effect (demand). Higher wage rates may result in higher prices for goods and services. Quantity demanded falls with higher prices, so fewer workers are needed. Higher wages may also encourage employers to substitute capital for workers.

The wage elasticity of demand measures the percentage change in the quantity of workers demanded divided by the percentage change in the wage rate. The wage elasticity is influenced by the percentage of total costs represented by labour costs, the number of substitutes for labour, the availability of substitutes, and the price elasticity of the final product or service.

Increases in labour productivity allow for increases in incomes and for stable prices. The main influences on productivity can be divided into three groups: macro influences, micro influences, and factors that influence both the macro and the micro picture.

Not all labour costs vary with the number of hours worked. Certain labour costs are non-wage costs that vary with the number of employees hired. These costs include training and hiring costs, termination costs, and payroll deductions such as Canada Pension Plan.

Key Terms

gross domestic product (GDP) (page 255)
increasing returns to scale (page 260)
labour productivity (page 255)
law of diminishing returns (page 244)
marginal revenue (MR) (page 245)

marginal revenue product (MRP) (page 245)
quasi-fixed labour costs (page 263)
scale effect (page 249)
substitution effect (demand) (page 250)
wage elasticity of labour demand (page 251)

Weblinks

Canadian Trucking Alliance
www.cantruck.ca

Transport Canada
www.tc.gc.ca

Canadian Manufacturers and Exporters
www.cme-mec.ca

Discussion Questions

1. Identify two occupations that would have a positive cross-wage elasticity of demand. Identify two occupations that would have a negative cross-wage elasticity of demand.
2. Is the demand for airline pilots elastic or inelastic? Explain.
3. Who are the Luddites? What would be the impact of the Luddite philosophy on worker productivity? Explain.
4. It was suggested in the chapter that the presence of quasi-fixed labour costs encourages firms to pay premium rates of pay for overtime work as opposed to hiring new employees. Would changes to your province's employment standards legislation that increased the premium rate for overtime lead to more people being hired? Explain.
5. Economists have noted that the production of goods and services in our economy varies more than the level of employment. With reference to the material covered in this chapter, explain why this occurs.

Using the Internet

1. Access the Apparel Human Resources Council website at www.apparel-hrc.org/en/index_en.html. Discuss the human resources issues that the apparel industry in Canada is facing. To obtain some information on the apparel industry in Canada, access http://strategis.ic.gc.ca/epic/internet/inapparel-vetements.nsf/en/home.

Exercises

1. Describe the impact of freer trade between Canada and Latin America on the demand for labour in Canada and on the type of labour demanded.
2. Discuss how the productivity of employees can increase.
3. Why does the law of diminishing returns apply only in the short run?
4. State whether the wage elasticity of demand for each of the following occupations is elastic or inelastic. Explain your answer for each one.
   a. Dentist
   b. Data-entry clerk
   c. Chef
   d. Police officer
   e. Retail salesperson
5. Define two examples of quasi-fixed labour costs.
6. A payroll tax reduces the monetary contribution of each worker to the firm. Ontario has introduced a payroll tax to pay for healthcare in the province. Draw a diagram to show the impact of a payroll tax on the demand for labour. (Hint: The monetary contribution of a new worker is the MRP.)
7. a. Give an example of workers in one occupation being used as a substitute for workers in another occupation.
   b. Give an example of capital (machinery, equipment, etc.) being substituted for labour.
8. Determine the coefficient for wage elasticity of demand under the following conditions. An increase in the wage rate from $12 to $12.50 leads to a reduction of the number of workers demanded from 150 to 125.

Chapter 10

Wage Rate and Employment Determination

Chapter Learning Objectives

After completing this chapter, you should be able to:

- explain employment and wage rate determination in a competitive labour market and under conditions of monopsony
- use a graph to explain the impact of the minimum wage on the labour market
- use a graph to explain the impact of a payroll tax on the labour market
- explain the relationship between wage elasticity and the burden of paying a payroll tax
- explain how unions can influence the demand curve for labour
- distinguish between a craft union and an industrial union in terms of the ability to alter the supply of labour
- discuss the causes of unemployment

ESPANOLA: PAPER, LOGGING, AND MONOPSONY

Espanola, a town of approximately 5500 people, is situated on the Spanish River in Northern Ontario. Espanola is located 75 kilometres west of Sudbury, just south of Highway 17. Highway 6, which starts in Southern Ontario and continues north through Manitoulin Island, runs through the middle of the town. Espanola is located on the Canadian Shield and is the largest town in a region that includes the towns of Massey, Webbwood, McKerrow, and Nairn Centre. The forestry industry is the main employer in the area and the paper mill located in town is currently owned by Domtar. The mill produces hardwood and softwood pulp and is capable of producing 800 different types of paper.

Logging operations have been going on in the Espanola area for over 100 years. In 1911, construction began on the paper mill and the town has relied on the fortunes of the paper mill ever since. Employment at the mill has fluctuated over the years, and today the mill employs almost 800 people. At one time, the paper mill operated bush camps where the loggers cut down the trees for delivery to the mill; the loggers were employed by the mill, and many boarded at the camps. Today, the logging operation is outsourced; all the wood required to make paper is provided by private contractors.

The paper mill does not provide all the jobs in the town and the surrounding area; there are retail stores, restaurants, a hospital, government offices, and so on. The mill is, however, the major employer. In economic terminology, the mill is considered to be a monopsony. The term "monopsony" comes from a Greek word meaning "single buyer." The paper mill is the primary buyer of labour in the community and in the surrounding area. In past years, the mill represented a monopsony in the employment of loggers. Today there is not one employer of loggers, but many. The mill still represents a monopsony in the purchase of lumber. Because of the demand for lumber on the part of the mill, most of the wood in the area is sold to one buyer: the paper mill.

This short discussion of Espanola has introduced you to the concept of a monopsony. As you read the material on monopsony presented in this chapter, think of other labour markets in which a monopsony exists.

Introduction

In the previous two chapters, we discussed labour demand and labour supply curves as they relate to the individuals and firms in a competitive market. In this chapter, the individual labour demand and supply curves are aggregated and we analyze the overall labour market for a specific occupation. In a labour

Part III: Microeconomic Theory of the Labour Market

market, all the buyers and sellers of an occupation interact to exchange a service and establish a wage rate. Just as the firm's demand curve for a certain occupation slopes down to the right, so too does the market demand curve for that occupation. The market demand curve is simply the aggregation of the firms' demand curves. The factors that influence the demand curve for an occupation—the marginal revenue, or the price, of the final product or service and labour productivity—also influence the overall demand for that occupation.

The supply curve for an occupation slopes up to the right. As mentioned in Chapter 8, the opportunity cost of not working increases as the wage rate increases. Thus, as the wage rate increases, more people will be willing to work at that occupation. For some occupations, however, there is a cost to becoming qualified to work in that occupation: a lengthy education or a lengthy apprenticeship may be required. A relatively high wage rate is also necessary to attract individuals to these occupations.

This chapter begins with a discussion of wage rate and employment determination in a competitive market. It continues with a discussion of wage rate and employment determination under less-than-competitive conditions, followed by an analysis of the impact of government and trade union activity on the labour market. In an ideal labour market, wage rates would adjust to balance the quantity of labour supplied and the quantity of labour demanded. Changes in wage rates would ensure that all workers found employment. In the real world, there are always workers who are unemployed. The chapter concludes with a discussion of why the labour market often fails to balance labour supply and labour demand.

Wage Rate and Employment Determination in a Competitive Labour Market

The interaction between labour demand and labour supply in the market determines the equilibrium wage rate and the number of workers employed in that occupation. The determination of an equilibrium wage rate is identical to the determination of an equilibrium price (see Chapter 2). At the point of intersection of the demand and supply curves, the number of workers wanted by employers at that wage rate equals the number of individuals willing to offer their services at that wage rate. This state of affairs is referred to as equilibrium because it represents a balance in the labour market. If the wage rate is at the equilibrium level (W_1 in Figure 10.1, page 270), there is no tendency for either the wage rate or the level of employment (L_1) to change. If the current wage rate is below the intersection point (W_2 in Figure 10.1), the quantity of workers demanded by firms exceeds the quantity of workers who are willing to work. In other words, there is a shortage of qualified workers. The wage rate will increase as employers need to attract workers into this occupation.

If the wage rate is above the equilibrium level (W_3 in Figure 10.1), there is a surplus of individuals willing to work in this occupation. That is, more people are willing to do this job at the going wage rate than employers are willing to hire. There will be pressure on the wage rate to decrease. In Chapter 2,

FIGURE 10.1

The Labour Market

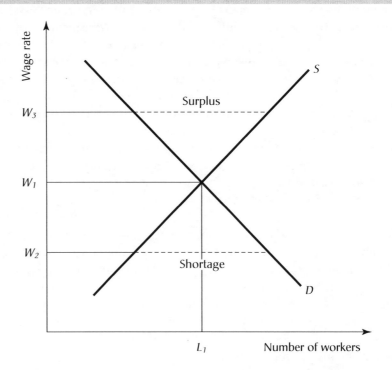

it was pointed out that there are some differences between labour markets and other markets. Wage rates do not decrease as easily as they increase. Economists state that wage rates are "sticky" in a downward direction. Prices for goods and services tend to decrease more quickly than wages, under similar demand and supply conditions. The sluggish nature of wages in response to downward pressure ensures that the surplus of workers will continue for a while. Why are wages slow to decrease? The market wage rate may not fall toward equilibrium if the wage rate was set in a collective agreement between union and management. Changes in the wage rate may be negotiated only when the current collective agreement expires. Another possibility is the presence of a government-legislated minimum wage rate, which makes it illegal to pay or accept a wage rate less than the legal minimum.

Can employers respond to the surplus of workers in ways other than by reducing the wage rate? Employers may respond by raising qualifications, which reduces the supply of potential employees. They may also reduce some of the benefits associated with the job that are not covered by the collective agreement or by legislation. For example, the number of coffee breaks could be reduced.

What causes market wage rates to change over time? Any factor that causes a shift in either the demand or the supply curve for an occupation will result in a change in the equilibrium wage rate. For example, an increase in the productivity of employees performing this occupation will shift the demand curve to the right (see Figure 10.2). The increase in demand will increase the equilibrium wage rate from W_1 to W_2. As the wage rate increases, more people are willing to work in this occupation and, as a result, the equilibrium level of employment rises from L_1 to L_2. An increase in the number of qualified college and university graduates may shift the supply curve to the right for some occupations (see Figure 10.3, page 272). This will decrease the equilibrium wage rate from W_1 to W_2 and increase the equilibrium level of employment from L_1 to L_2. As the wage rate falls, firms are willing to hire more workers (a movement along the demand curve).

Wage Rate and Employment Determination Under Conditions of Monopsony

When one firm is the only buyer of a certain type of labour, the firm is referred to as a **monopsony** (single buyer). Examples of monopsony are present in the Canadian labour market, such as a paper mill or a mine in a small town, or electrical utilities that hire nuclear engineers. The main feature of a monopsony with respect to the labour market is that the wage rate must be increased in order to attract more employees to the firm. A monopsony faces a supply curve for labour that slopes up to the right: more workers can be hired only if the wage rate increases. Since the monopsonist is the only demander for a particular type of labour in that market, any desire by the monopsony to increase

monopsony

a market in which there is only one buyer

FIGURE 10.2

An Increase in the Demand for Labour

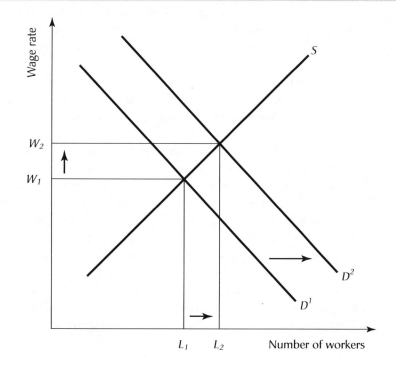

FIGURE 10.3

An Increase in the Supply of Labour

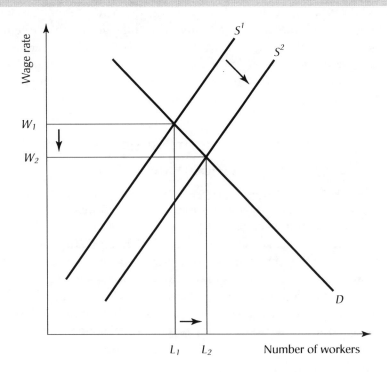

employment will increase the wage rate. If the wage rate paid to new employees is higher than the existing wage rate, all current employees in the same job category must receive the same compensation as the new employees. Therefore, the cost of hiring a new employee is not only the wage rate paid to that employee, but the increase in the wage rate paid to all existing employees as well.

The monopsony's demand curve for an occupation is identical to the market demand curve because the monopsony is the sole buyer of this type of labour. The supply curve of workers to the monopsony slopes up to the right. Under conditions of monopsony, wage rate and employment levels are not determined by the intersection of the demand and the supply curves. A marginal labour cost curve, derived from the supply curve, must be introduced to determine the wage rate and level of employment. The **marginal labour cost (MLC)** is the cost associated with hiring one more worker and is higher than the wage rate paid to that worker.

The marginal cost of labour is calculated as follows. Assume that a small electrical company in a remote geographical area has four electricians, with each earning $20 per hour. Business is improving and the company wants to hire an additional electrician. There are no unemployed electricians available, so the company must attract electricians who are already employed elsewhere. It is possible to get another electrician if the wage rate is increased to $21 per hour. The extra cost of hiring one additional worker is $21 + 4($1) = $25 per

marginal labour cost (MLC)

the additional cost of hiring one more worker

hour since the four current employees need to have their wage rate increased by $1 per hour. Note that the MLC per hour ($25) is greater than the wage rate per hour ($21). Table 10.1 shows the calculation of the MLC. The MLC schedule in the last column shows the change in the employer's cost of labour per hour for each additional worker hired.

Figure 10.4 (page 274) shows a graph of the labour market in the presence of a monopsony. It also shows the relationship between the MLC and the supply curve for labour.

The employment level under conditions of monopsony is determined by the intersection of the demand (marginal revenue product, or MRP) curve and the MLC curve (L_1 in Figure 10.4). In order to maximize profits, the monopsonist hires workers up to the point where

Marginal revenue product = Marginal labour cost

If MRP > MLC, the contribution of the next worker to the firm is greater than the cost, and the worker should be hired. If MLC > MRP, the cost of hiring one more worker exceeds the worker's contribution to the firm, so the worker would not be hired.

What wage rate is paid under conditions of monopsony? Once the level of employment is determined, the supply curve is used to determine the wage rate (see W_1 in Figure 10.4). Fewer employees (L_1) are hired under conditions of monopsony than under competitive conditions, because the level of employment in competitive conditions is determined where the demand curve intersects the supply curve (L_2 in Figure 10.4). Workers are paid less in a monopsony situation (W_1) than under competitive conditions (W_2) and are often said to be "exploited." However, since they are paid more than their reservation wage rate, they are willing to accept W_1.

Examples of pure monopsony in the real world are not numerous. Some have already been mentioned. Another example of a Canadian monopsony is the Canadian Football League, the only employer of professional football players. The model explained in this chapter is useful in situations where the wage rate must be increased in order to attract more workers to this occupation.

TABLE 10.1

Calculation of the Marginal Labour Cost

WAGE RATE	QUANTITY OF LABOUR SUPPLIED	TOTAL LABOUR COST	MARGINAL LABOUR COST (MLC)
$20	4	$80	
			> $25
$21	5	$105	
			> $27
$22	6	$132	
			> $29
$23	7	$161	

FIGURE 10.4

Wage Rate and Employment Determination Under Monopsony

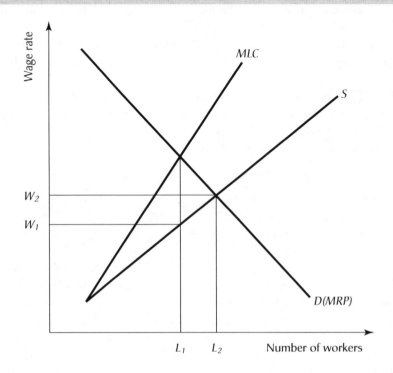

The Impact of Government Policies on the Labour Market

The labour market is one of the economy's most regulated markets. A review of the legislation that affects the labour market was presented in Chapter 3. This section looks at the implications of three government policies with respect to the labour market: the minimum wage rate, payroll taxes, and wage subsidies.

Minimum Wage Rate

All provinces and the federal government have enacted minimum wage legislation. Not all employees are covered by minimum wage legislation, but for those who are, the legal minimum wage rate is a wage floor. The wage rate cannot fall below the wage floor. Figure 10.5 illustrates a competitive labour market in which the equilibrium wage rate is $6.50 per hour. Groups of employees may argue that $6.50 is too low and employees should not be required to work at that rate. In response to these concerns, the government imposes a $7 per hour minimum wage rate. At $7 per hour, the quantity of workers demanded falls to L_D while the quantity of workers supplied increases to L_S. There is a surplus of workers at the minimum wage rate. A surplus of workers in the labour market is referred to as unemployment. Thus, the imposition of a minimum wage rate has created some unemployment in the labour market.

FIGURE 10.5

The Minimum Wage Rate

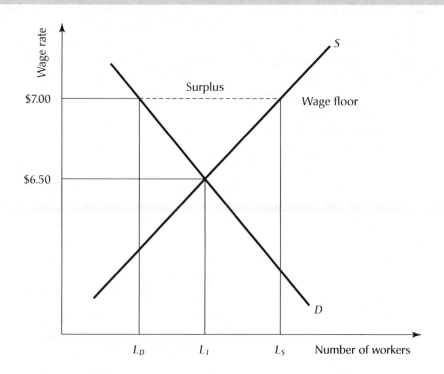

The extent of job losses that result from the imposition of the minimum wage rate depends on the wage elasticity of demand for labour. If the wage elasticity of demand for labour is inelastic, wage rate increases will not have a significant impact on the number of workers employed. However, when demand for labour is elastic, the reduction in employment would be much greater because employers respond relatively more to wage rate changes. The wage rate elasticity of demand is likely to be elastic for unskilled and semi-skilled workers. Thus, any increase in the minimum wage rate that applies to them will result in larger job losses than for other occupations.

When we predict the number of job losses that result from imposing or increasing a minimum wage rate, we assume that all other factors influencing the demand for labour remain constant. In the real world, however, a variety of changes can shift the entire demand curve to the right or to the left. For example, an increase in the overall demand for workers could come about as a result of an improvement in economic conditions, which would shift the demand curve for labour to the right. Such a shift would put upward pressure on the equilibrium wage rate. A shift of the labour demand curve to the right reduces the negative impact of the minimum wage rate on employment levels. Governments tend to increase the minimum wage rate when economic conditions are good, and freeze the minimum wage rate when the economy is in a slump.

Empirical studies measuring the extent of the negative impact of minimum wage rate increases on employment levels are inconclusive because so many factors on both sides of the labour market are changing over time. There is some evidence that increases in the legal minimum wage rate decrease employment opportunities for youth and for low-productivity groups in the labour force. As Figure 10.5 (page 275) shows, the impact of the minimum wage is not felt only on the demand side of the labour market. Higher minimum wage rates encourage more individuals to enter the labour market, but if the employment opportunities are not available, the new entrants to this occupation may find themselves unemployed.

Who earns the minimum wage in the Canadian economy? In 1998, Statistics Canada compiled a profile of minimum wage workers. Some of the characteristics of minimum wage workers are listed below.

- Young people, aged 15 to 24 years, comprised approximately 58% of all minimum wage workers.

- Close to 20% of all young people who have jobs are earning the minimum wage.

- Approximately 60% of all young minimum wage earners are students living at home with their parents.

- There are more female minimum wage earners than male. For those over 25, two-thirds of the minimum wage earners are women.

- Most minimum wage earners are part of a family. About 14% of all minimum wage earners are their family's sole income earner either because they have no spouse, or because the spouse is unemployed.

- Part-time jobs make up 62% of the minimum wage jobs.

- About 28% of all minimum wage earners work in the beverage and food industry.

Labour Market Issue 10.1

The Minimum Wage Rate and Poverty

The objective of minimum wage rate legislation is not always evident. When questioned about the objectives behind a legislated minimum wage rate, politicians and bureaucrats are often at a loss to explain the rationale behind increasing the legal minimum wage rate. Proponents of the minimum wage have listed the following as objectives of the legislation:

- to prevent employers who, in the absence of minimum wage rate legislation, may resort to the payment of substandard wage rates and exploit workers with little bargaining power

- to force employers to make their operations more efficient
- to help reduce poverty among the working poor

For the purposes of our discussion here, we will focus on the minimum wage rate as a tool in the fight against poverty. In line with this goal, proponents of higher minimum wage rates argue that earnings from employment should be higher than the income received from social assistance. Earnings from employment at the legal minimum wage rate should exceed what a family of four receives on social assistance. If the minimum wage rate guarantees an

Part III: Microeconomic Theory of the Labour Market

income in excess of social assistance benefits, the extent of poverty among the working poor will be reduced.

However, there are a number of reasons why the legal minimum wage rate may not be an effective tool in the fight against poverty.

First, low hourly wage rates are only one cause of poverty. Poverty can also stem from low hours of work, unemployment, the size of the family, and the health condition of family members. Changes in the hourly wage rate are not sufficient to deal with all of these factors. For example, if someone is already unemployed, increases in the hourly minimum wage rate provide no assistance in the fight against poverty. In other instances, a large family may be the primary cause of a poverty-like existence. It is not likely that employers would pay those with large families a higher hourly wage rate.

Second, if increases in the minimum wage rate help alleviate poverty, why not increase the rate substantially, for example to $50 per hour? Increases in the legal minimum wage rate result in unemployment for some workers: the higher the minimum wage rate, the more unemployment. It is very difficult to determine exactly how many workers lose their jobs as a result of increases in the minimum wage rate; still, economists know that some individuals become unemployed as a result of minimum wage rate increases. Higher minimum wage rates also pose a barrier to employment for other prospective employees. Those who become unemployed as a result of an increase in the minimum wage rate are often those with fewer employment skills. How can they acquire those skills if they are not working? Furthermore, how does one gain employment experience when one is unemployed?

Third, in many jurisdictions, several classes of workers are exempt from minimum wage coverage. For example, in some provinces, domestic servants and agricultural workers are exempt from coverage. Increases in the minimum wage rate do not help these individuals.

Fourth, the impact of increases in the minimum wage rate on poverty depends on the characteristics of low-wage earners. A majority of low-wage earners are young people. The majority of these workers are single and have no dependants. They may also belong to an affluent family. These individuals receive more money working than they would receive on social assistance since it is unlikely that they would be eligible for social assistance. Low-wage earners who lose their job do not necessarily qualify for social assistance. Many individuals who are working at low wages have a spouse who is employed. The loss of the low-wage worker's job may not put the family in a poverty situation.

Although not directly related to the alleviation of poverty, the minimum wage rate should help reduce the disparity in wage rates between occupations. That is, increases in the minimum wage rate should narrow the wage differential between occupations. Minimum wage rate increases tend to narrow the wage gap between occupations initially but, over time, the wage differentials reassert themselves. For example, assume that your job normally pays $0.25 per hour more than the lowest-paid job in the factory, which is the legal minimum wage rate. An increase of $0.25 in the legal minimum wage rate would result in your wage rate being equal to that of the lowest-paid job in the factory. You would be anxious to re-establish the differential between the wage rate that you receive and the wage rate paid for the lowest-paid job. Empirical studies have shown that the wage differentials reassert themselves within a year of a legal minimum wage rate increase.

Payroll Taxes

In order to raise revenue, governments legislate payroll taxes to be paid by employers. That is, employers must pay a tax based on the size of their payroll. Well-known payroll taxes in Canada include the Canada Pension Plan and employment insurance. The conventional wisdom is that the burden of paying the payroll tax is a tax on employers. In fact, the burden of a payroll tax is also borne, in part, by employees in the form of lower wage rates and lower levels of employment.

The imposition of a payroll tax results in a shift to the left of the demand curve for labour. Firms will only hire the same number of employees if the payroll tax can be offset with a lower wage rate. Alternatively, firms will hire fewer employees if the wage rate cannot be lowered. Figure 10.6 is a graphical representation of the impact of a payroll tax on wage rate and employment levels. The equilibrium wage rate is W_1 before the imposition of the payroll tax. The demand curve shifts down by the amount of the tax. Why does the demand curve for labour shift down by the amount of the tax? You will recall from Chapter 9 that the firm's demand curve for an occupation is the marginal revenue product curve. This curve represents the monetary contribution of each new worker to the company. If the employer is required to pay a payroll tax for each employee, the monetary contribution of each new employee is reduced by the amount of the tax.

The new equilibrium wage rate (W_2) is determined by the intersection of the new labour demand curve (D^2) and the labour supply curve. The equilibrium wage rate has not decreased by the full amount of the tax. Because the equilibrium wage rate did not decrease by the full amount of the tax, both the employer and the employee share the burden of paying the tax. The employees' contribution to paying the tax is represented by the reduction in the wage rate and by the loss in employment. The employer's portion of the payroll tax is the difference between the amount of the tax and the reduction in the wage rate.

FIGURE 10.6

Impact of a Payroll Tax on the Labour Market

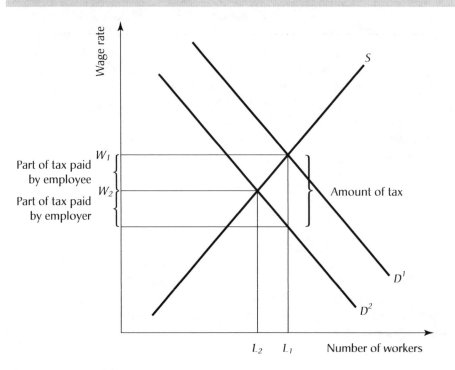

The proportions of the tax paid by employers and employees partly depend on the wage elasticity of demand and supply.

- If the demand for labour is inelastic, employment levels do not fluctuate greatly with a change in the wage rate. Both the wage reduction that results from a payroll tax and the corresponding decrease in employment are relatively small.

- If the demand for labour is *elastic*, the opposite occurs: the equilibrium wage rate decreases to a greater extent and the job losses are also greater.

In Figures 10.7A and B, an identical payroll tax is applied to situations of an inelastic demand (steep curve) and an elastic demand (flat curve) for labour. In both, the wage rate falls from W_1 to W_2. In the inelastic situation, the wage rate reduction is relatively small compared to the elastic situation. In the case of an inelastic demand for labour, the burden of paying the payroll tax falls mainly on the employer. In the case of an elastic demand for labour, the burden falls mainly on the employee.

The impact of a payroll tax also depends on the wage elasticity of supply for labour. If the labour supply is inelastic, the equilibrium wage rate decreases relatively more than under conditions of elastic supply. In Figures 10.8A and B (pages 280–281), an identical payroll tax is applied in conditions of an inelastic labour supply and an elastic labour supply. The

Figure 10.7A

Impact of a Payroll Tax (Inelastic Demand)

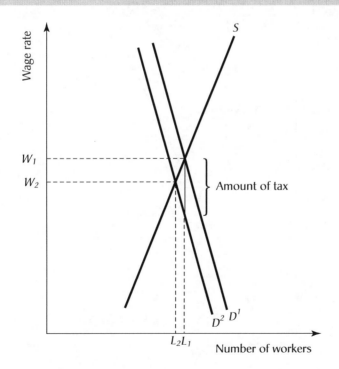

FIGURE 10.7B

Impact of a Payroll Tax (Elastic Demand)

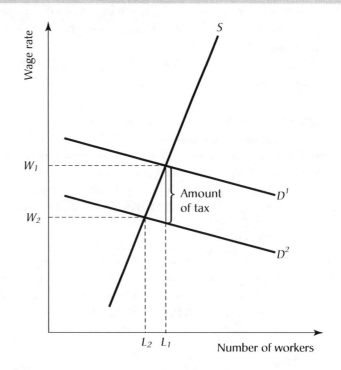

FIGURE 10.8A

Impact of a Payroll Tax (Inelastic Supply)

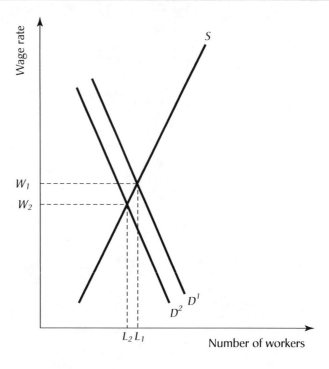

FIGURE 10.8B

Impact of a Payroll Tax (Elastic Supply)

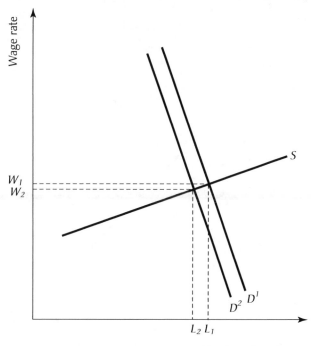

Number of workers

wage rate falls from W_1 to W_2 in both. The wage rate reduction is much smaller in the situation of an elastic labour supply. In terms of the reduction in wage rates, the employees bear the greater burden of a payroll tax under conditions of inelastic labour supply.

Wage Subsidy

Consider the impact of a wage rate subsidy paid to the employer on the labour market. A **wage rate subsidy** is the opposite of a payroll tax. That is, the government pays part of the hourly wage rate for each employee, or each new employee. If a payroll tax shifts the demand curve for labour to the left, a wage rate subsidy will shift the demand curve for labour to the right. The wage rate subsidy will increase the monetary contribution of the employee to the firm. In addition to the contribution to production, the new employee also brings a payment made by the government. A shift of the demand curve for labour to the right will increase the wage rate and increase the level of employment (see Figure 10.9, page 282). The wage rate subsidy has increased the wage rate from W_1 to W_2. Government may use a wage rate subsidy to increase the employment levels of certain groups in the labour force, such as youth.

wage rate subsidy

a payment by government to an employer to assist in paying wages

Figure 10.9

Impact of a Wage Rate Subsidy on the Wage Rate

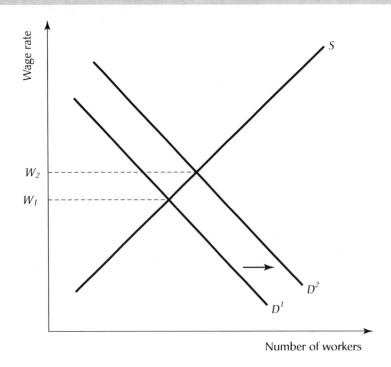

The Impact of Unions
on Wage Rates and Employment

One goal that workers have when voting to be represented by a union is to increase the wage rate. Obtaining wage rate increases from the employer is not unions' only objective in negotiating with management, but for many unions it is the primary objective. This section describes how unions attempt to obtain wage rate increases for their members.

Wage rates are determined by the interaction of demand and supply in the marketplace. If unions are to be successful in obtaining wage rate increases, they must be able to cause a shift in either the demand or the supply curve, or both. We will first look at ways by which unions can increase the demand for the workers they represent.

The Impact of Unions on the Demand for Labour

The demand for any worker is derived from the demand for the product or service that the worker provides. Unions could increase the demand for the product by advertising it, but union advertising is not common since many people in the union movement believe that product promotion is the sole jurisdiction of the company. However, when an industry is facing increased competition, especially from imports, unions find it necessary to become involved in product promotion. For example, the International Ladies'

Garment Workers Union ran advertisements on television promoting North American–made clothing. The union also set up booths in exhibitions that provided information on clothing and fabrics. The Canadian Automobile Workers union promoted the buying of cars "your neighbours help to build" in order to meet the challenge from imported automobiles. Labour organizations have also run "Buy Union Made" or "Look for the Union Label" campaigns. In Ontario, the union representing the electricians and the association representing the electrical contractors have jointly sponsored radio advertisements promoting companies who employ union members. These campaigns aim not only to shift the demand curve for labour to the right but also to change the elasticity of demand for labour by making the demand for the product less elastic. In order to deal with the pressure from offshore competition, unions have lobbied the federal government to create trade barriers. If the prices of imported products increase due to tariffs and other trade barriers, consumers may increase their demand for domestic goods—thereby increasing the demand for labour.

Unions can also help shift the demand curve for their members to the right by improving the productivity of their members. This can be done through upgrading courses and other training. Labour productivity may also increase if unions permit management to introduce the latest technology into the operation.

Unions have also used featherbedding to maintain the demand for their workers. That is, featherbedding techniques attempt to stop the MRP curve from shifting to the left. **Featherbedding** involves retaining jobs and workers who would otherwise be made redundant by technological change. For example, in the railroad industry, trains continued to employ firemen long after steam engines had been replaced, and it is only in recent years that the caboose was removed from trains. It is easier to maintain jobs through featherbedding when the industry does not face much competition. In construction, unions have resisted technological advances such as plastic pipe, which has reduced installation time. As competition in the marketplace intensifies, featherbedding disappears. Firms that face tough competition for their products are forced to introduce the latest technology.

featherbedding

retaining workers who would otherwise be made redundant by technological change

The Impact of Unions on the Supply of Labour

In order to examine the impact of unions on the supply side of the market, it is necessary to distinguish between craft and industrial unions. All the members of **craft unions** possess a certain skill, such as electricians or plumbers. The first unions in North America were craft unions. **Industrial unions** organize all workers in an industry, such as steel or automobiles. Members of industrial unions can be skilled tradespeople or unskilled workers. Industrial unions represent a variety of skills.

Craft unions attempt to shift the supply curve to the left, thereby increasing the wage rate. For example, the supply curve will shift to the left if a lengthy apprenticeship period is required to acquire the skill. High initiation fees and union dues may discourage workers from entering this trade. Craft unions may pressure the federal government to limit the number of immigrants, especially

craft union

a union whose members all possess a certain craft or skill

industrial union

a union whose members all work in the same industry

those who possess the same skills as the union members. Some collective agreements call for a closed shop, meaning that the employer can only hire union members. Other collective agreements specify a journeyman–apprentice ratio (the number of apprentices who can work on a job is limited by the number of journeymen on that job). Governments can also help shift the supply curve to the left by legislating that only certain trades can perform certain functions. Professional associations in such occupations as law, accounting, and medicine operate in a manner similar to craft unions in order to restrict the supply of labour.

The impact of craft unions on the supply of labour is shown in Figure 10.10. A shift of the supply curve from S^1 to S^2 increases the equilibrium wage rate from W_1 to W_2, which decreases the number of workers from L_1 to L_2. The drop in employment affects union membership.

Industrial unions cannot control the supply of labour by insisting on long apprenticeships or bargaining for closed shops in collective agreements. These unions insist on a wage floor or else the members will go on strike to back their demands (see W_2 in Figure 10.11). The supply curve is altered as shown in the diagram. The new supply curve is W_2aS. Since no one is permitted to work for less than the wage floor, the section of the supply curve below that level does not exist.

FIGURE 10.10

Impact of a Craft Union on the Supply of Labour

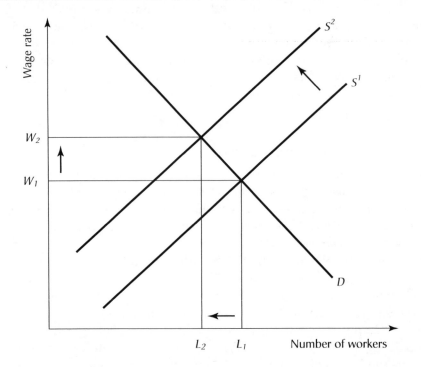

Part III: Microeconomic Theory of the Labour Market

FIGURE 10.11

Impact of an Industrial Union on the Supply of Labour

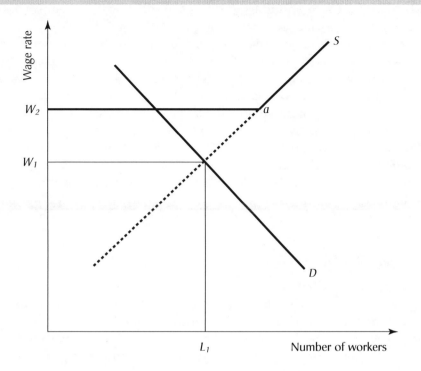

The ability to get a wage rate increase depends on the wage elasticity of demand for labour. If the demand is elastic, an increased wage rate may result in a relatively large drop in employment and a decline in the total wage bill paid to members. The interests of union members anxious to get a wage rate increase must be balanced against the wishes of other members who are anxious to keep their jobs.

Empirical Evidence

Do unions succeed in raising wage rates? Most studies indicate that unions do influence wage rates although the extent of that influence is difficult to determine. Many argue that the unions' ability to get wage rate increases for their memberships is contingent on the industry in which they work. Unions have accepted wage freezes when companies have been in financial difficulty. Some unions have negotiated lower wage rates in a new collective agreement in order to get their members back to work. Some collective agreements contain the requirement that some jobs be paid at the minimum wage rate. Workers do not need a union to get the minimum wage.

Canadian studies conducted on the effects of unions on wage rates have estimated the union impact on wages to be an increase anywhere from 10% to 30%. One must be careful in interpreting these studies, however, as many were conducted during the 1970s, when the labour market was different from today's. Some studies focused solely on manufacturing, while others looked at all industries. The impact of unions on wage rates is likely to vary by industry and by individual firm within an industry. It is also possible that the presence of unions in an industry affects the wages paid to employees of non-union firms in the industry. Employers may increase the wage rate of non-union workers in order to ward off union organizing attempts. Increases in wage rates achieved through collective bargaining may reduce the number of workers employed. The terminated workers will then compete for jobs with non-union workers, increasing the supply of non-union workers. The increased supply of non-union workers may put downward pressure on non-union wage rates, which will widen the gap between union and non-union wages. Unions' success at improving the working conditions of their members cannot be measured solely by looking at the impact on wage rates, however. Unions also have an impact on the employment relationship by negotiating for fringe benefits (such as health plans) and some non-monetary benefits (such as seniority and work assignments).

Causes of Unemployment

This chapter has explained how equilibrium wage rates and levels of employment are determined. The discussion now shifts to the question of why the labour market may not easily establish an equilibrium between demand and supply. The focus in this chapter has been on the equilibrium wage rate. We now shift focus to the other outcome of the labour market process—jobs. Using our knowledge of how markets operate, we will now examine why there are always some workers without jobs. We have already seen in this chapter how minimum wage rate legislation can create an excess supply of labour (unemployment). In the following sections, we will focus on two additional reasons for unemployment: job search, and rigid wage rates.

Job Search

Job search is the result of imperfect information in the labour market. Unemployed workers often do not know where jobs are available and employers with vacancies are not always aware of all the individuals with adequate skills seeking work. **Job search** is the process of matching workers with appropriate jobs. Workers differ in their tastes and skills, jobs differ in their attributes, and information about job vacancies filters slowly through the various labour markets. It takes time to check want ads, inquire of friends and relatives, apply to companies, and weed out acceptable jobs from unacceptable ones. Because it takes time to find an appropriate job, the process of job search usually involves periods of unemployment. What determines the length of search and thus the duration of unemployment?

One key factor often singled out in the analysis of job search is the reservation wage rate. As mentioned in Chapter 8, the reservation wage is the lowest wage the unemployed worker will consider acceptable. Suppose an unemployed worker has searched vacancies and has received a job offer.

job search

the process of matching workers and available jobs

The worker will compare the wage offered by the company with his or her reservation wage, and accept the job only if the wage offered exceeds or equals the reservation wage.[i] If a person has a relatively low reservation wage rate, suitable job offers will be received more readily and the period of unemployment will be short. A high reservation wage rate will result in a lengthy period of search and thus unemployment.

What determines a worker's reservation wage? In deciding upon a reservation wage, a person must balance the benefits versus the cost of each choice. The marginal or additional benefit that is associated with a higher reservation wage rate once a job is found is a higher rate of pay received in this job than in other jobs. In order to obtain a higher reservation wage rate, certain additional or marginal costs must be incurred. For example, a longer period of unemployment will usually be necessary before a job can be found at that rate. As long as the marginal benefit associated with a certain reservation wage rate exceeds the marginal cost, it is worth the wait to acquire employment at that wage rate, or at any wage rate where the marginal benefit exceeds the marginal costs. Realistically, factors such as the person's pay on the previous job, the customary standard of living, and wages earned by friends or relatives also affect the reservation wage rate.

A model of job search based on a comparison of the benefits and costs of search leads to the conclusion that any factor that reduces the costs of unemployment will increase the length of job search and the duration of unemployment. A major factor in the cost of unemployment anywhere is the unemployment compensation program instituted in a country. The cost of job search generally includes direct costs such as transportation costs, fax and phone bills, or fees of employment agencies as well as the opportunity cost of income forgone while being unemployed. An unemployed person with no income during the period of unemployment faces a high opportunity cost of job search. In this situation, the reservation wage rate is likely to be low and search to be short. The more generous are unemployment benefits, or the longer the period over which benefits can be received, the lower the opportunity cost of job search will be. Low opportunity costs of job search result in a higher reservation wage rate for the individual and a greater likelihood of remaining unemployed.

Wage Rate Rigidity

Another explanation of unemployment is wage rate rigidity, that is, the downward inflexibility of money wage rates. It is much easier for wage rates to increase than to decrease. Since wage rates are not quick to decrease, they are referred to as rigid. Rigid wage rates cause an imbalance between the number of people seeking employment and the number of vacancies available. They do not allow the labour market to reach a point of equilibrium. The problem caused by rigid wage rates is illustrated in Figure 10.12 (page 288).

---

[i] Of course, the acceptance of a job offer depends on other factors as well, such as working conditions, reputation of the company, and commuting time.

FIGURE 10.12

Rigid Wage Rates

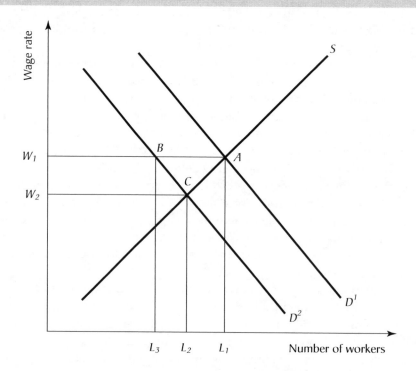

To see how rigid wage rates cause unemployment, let us assume that Canadian households reduce their spending. As sales of consumer goods decline, firms reduce their desired level of employment, which is represented by the leftward shift of the labour demand curve to D^2. At the prevailing real wage of W_1, employment falls to L_3 (point A to point B), leading to demand-deficient unemployment ($L_1 - L_3$). If wage rates were flexible downward, the excess supply of labour in the market would result in a bidding down of wage rates until a new equilibrium were established at the wage rate of W_2, where the demand and supply of jobs are equal again (point C). The fall in the wage eliminates the amount of demand-deficient unemployment both by inducing firms to increase their hiring and by causing some of the unemployed to drop out of the labour force. Should wage rates be rigid in the downward direction, this equilibrating process would not take place, and unemployment would persist. Because wage rates are indeed sticky even in the face of substantial unemployment, this downward inflexibility offers an explanation for both cyclical and structural unemployment. The question, then, is why do wage rates not fall during periods of high unemployment?

One source of wage rigidity is labour unions. The majority of collective agreements have two- or three-year terms, so wage rates in unionized industries cannot readily respond to short-run increases in unemployment. Why would firms restrict their flexibility with long-term collective agreements? One answer is the costs involved in collective bargaining can be time consuming and expensive. There is thus a tradeoff between the costs of locking workers and firms into contracts for longer periods of time and the costs of wage negotiations. The optimal tradeoff for the length of a collective agreement seems to be between one and three years.

Even if longer contracts are preferred, they could be formulated in a way that allows wage rates to adjust downward in case the economy moves into a recession. Workers and firms could agree to a fixed employment level rather than a fixed wage level in their contract. However, contracts that guarantee jobs rather than wages are very rare. One reason is the application of the seniority principle in unionized firms. When layoffs occur, workers with seniority are usually the last ones out and the junior workers bear the brunt of layoffs. If senior workers hold most of the power in the union, they will prefer contracts that call for layoffs rather than wage rate cuts during hard times since they are less likely to be laid off.

Even labour markets unaffected by union wage rates exhibit downward inflexibility. Although non-union firms are not bound by any explicit, written agreement to follow a layoff policy over a policy of wage rate cuts, in most cases there appears to exist an unwritten agreement or implicit contract that such a policy will be followed. Implicit contracts are sometimes called the "invisible handshake." Because they are unwritten, it is difficult to confirm their existence; however, the fact that layoffs are the primary method by which firms adjust in economic downturns, even in non-unionized markets, speaks for their existence.

A related argument holds that workers are less concerned about their wages in absolute terms than they are about how they fare compared to other workers in other firms and industries. It is the relative wage rate that determines an individual's position in the income distribution. Because income comparisons largely determine workers' social status in society, workers will resist a reduction in their wage rates out of fear that it will lower their standing. The only way they would agree to wage rate cuts is if they knew that all other workers were receiving similar cuts. It is difficult to reassure any one group of workers that all other workers are in the same situation, and they, therefore, will resist any cut in their wages. There may thus be an implicit understanding between firms and workers that wages will not be lowered in order to avoid making workers worse off than their counterparts in other firms.

When wage rates are set above the equilibrium level, there is a surplus of workers wanting to work at that job. A form of job rationing needs to take place. **Job rationing** refers to the practice of employers paying wages that create an excess of workers seeking employment and a shortage of jobs. This practice may be legally required as, for example, by minimum wage legislation, or it may reflect the employers' decisions to pay wage rates that exceed the equilibrium level.

Job rationing occurs when firms themselves pay a wage higher than that mandated by supply and demand. Why would firms want to keep wages high even in the presence of an excess supply of labour? After all, higher wages add to their costs. The answer is that wages are not the only factor affecting labour

job rationing
practice of employers paying wages that create an excess of workers seeking employment and a shortage of jobs

Chapter 10: Wage Rate and Employment Determination

cost. The other major factor is labour productivity. Firms want their workers to be productive because higher productivity lowers cost. Paying higher wages might prove profitable if the higher wages raise the productivity of workers. How can higher wage rates lead to higher labour productivity?

Higher wage rates can lead to a reduction in worker turnover. High turnover increases production costs; it is also costly for firms to hire and train new workers. Even after they are trained, newly hired workers are often not as productive as experienced workers. The higher the wage rate, the more financially attractive it is for workers to stay with that firm and the less likely they are to quit.

A second reason for paying a higher wage rate than the equilibrium wage rate is that higher wages may reduce "shirking." In many jobs, workers have some discretion over how hard they work. As a result, firms often try to monitor the efforts of their workers. Monitoring, however, is costly and sometimes even impossible. A firm can respond to this problem by paying wage rates above the equilibrium level. Paying a wage rate higher than the competitive wage rate makes it costly for workers to lose their jobs if they are found shirking. Also, when a firm hires new workers it cannot accurately assess the quality of those workers before they start working. By paying higher wages, firms can attract a pool of higher-qualified applicants.

efficiency wages

wage rates paid in excess of the equilibrium level in order to increase productivity

Economists refer to wage rates paid in excess of the equilibrium level as **efficiency wages** because wages have an effect on workers' productivity. Unemployment arising from efficiency wages is similar to unemployment caused by minimum wage rates. In both cases, wage rates are higher than the level required to balance the quantity of labour supplied and the labour demanded. However, while minimum wage laws prevent firms from lowering wages, efficiency wage theory argues that firms deliberately keep wages above the equilibrium level.

Summary

The equilibrium wage rate in a labour market is determined by the intersection of the labour demand and the labour supply curves. If the wage rate is lower than the equilibrium level, the quantity of workers demanded will exceed the quantity supplied. Pressure will be put on the wage rate to increase. If the wage rate is greater than the equilibrium wage rate, downward pressure will be exerted on the wage rate. If the wage rate is at the equilibrium level, there is no tendency for the wage rate to change.

The imposition of a minimum wage rate on the labour market results in a surplus of workers. In the labour market, this surplus is called unemployment. The imposition of a payroll tax results in a lower wage rate and lower levels of employment. The impact of the payroll tax on wage rate and employment levels depends on the wage elasticities of demand and supply for labour.

Unions attempt to increase the wage rate paid to their members by shifting the demand curve for labour to the right or by altering the supply curve. Craft unions may be successful in shifting the labour supply curve to the left but industrial unions can only alter the shape of the supply curve.

Three main causes of unemployment are job search and rigid wage rates. The length of the job search is influenced by the person's reservation wage rate. The choice of the reservation wage rate is influenced by the marginal benefits of a high wage rate and the marginal costs associated with a larger job search. Rigid wage rates refer to the fact that wage rates do not fall that easily in response to an excess supply of labour. Job rationing occurs when wage rates are paid in excess of the equilibrium level.

Key Terms

craft union (page 283)
efficiency wages (page 290)
featherbedding (page 283)
industrial union (page 283)
job rationing (page 289)

job search (page 286)
marginal labour cost (MLC) (page 272)
monopsony (page 271)
wage rate subsidy (page 281)

Weblinks

For wage subsidies
www.hrsdc.gc.ca/en/home.shtml

Discussion Questions

1. Identify examples of monopsony (or near monopsony) in the economy.
2. What payroll taxes do employers pay in your province or territory?
3. Some newspaper editorials have recommended abolishing the minimum wage rate because of its negative impact on employment. What would be the consequences in the labour market if governments were to repeal minimum wage legislation?
4. Does an increase in the minimum wage rate result in a transfer of wealth from one group in the labour force to another? Explain.
5. Are employers likely to introduce labour-saving technology when faced with increases in the minimum wage rate?
6. One reason for employees wanting to be members of a trade union is higher wages. List other possible reasons.

Using the Internet

1. Access the HRSDC website, www.hrsdc.gc.ca/en/home.shtml. Under Business, click on Partnership and Funding. Under Partnership Initiatives and Funding Programs, click on Wage Subsidies. Write a one-page summary of this program citing objectives and eligibility.

Exercises

1. Why are payroll taxes referred to as "job killers"?
2. "There is a positive impact of increases in income associated with an increase in the minimum wage rate; this impact outweighs the negative impact of lost jobs." True or false? Explain.
3. Using a graph in your answer, discuss the impact of government paying $2 per hour toward the wages of each student hired for the summer by a private firm.

Appendix 10A: Wage Rate Changes and Unemployment

One factor that appears to have an impact on the wage rate is the unemployment rate. The British economist A.W. Phillips related the percentage change in wage rates to the unemployment rate for the years 1861 to 1957. He used percentage wage rate changes as the dependent variable and the unemployment rate as the independent variable. There was an inverse relationship between the two variables that seemed to last over the period covered by the study. That is, as the unemployment rate increased, the percentage increase in wage rates decreased.

Why does this inverse relationship hold? In times of low unemployment, there is a strong demand for labour. For many occupations, that demand exceeds the available supply. The shortage of workers at the going wage rate puts pressure on the wage rate to increase. The market adjusts to a higher equilibrium wage rate. The greater the excess demand for labour, the greater the increase in wage rates. When the demand for labour decreases, the unemployment rate increases and the pressure to increase wage rates is reduced. There may even be pressure for the wage rate to decrease, although, as we have discussed, wage rates tend to be more "sticky" downward than upward.

In Figure 10A.1, the relationship between percentage increases in the wage rate increases and the rate of unemployment appears as P^1. Is this relationship a constant one? That is, does the line P^1 remain the same year after year? Research indicates that the relationship is not stable. Over the years, the graph of the relationship has moved to the right, as indicated by P^2. Unemployment rates are thus now associated with higher wage rate increases than in the past. Alternatively, the wage rate increases are associated with higher levels of unemployment. Why has the relationship changed?

Various reasons have been put forth to explain the fact that the trade-off between the unemployment rate and increases in wage rates has deteriorated. These reasons include:

- A more generous employment insurance scheme, introduced in the 1970s, which has allowed some individuals to remain unemployed rather than to seek work.
- Changes in the size and composition of the labour force have occurred, in part because of the entrance of "baby boomers" into the labour market and the increased participation rate of women.
- Canadians began to expect high levels of price increases through the 1970s and 1980s and these expectations found their way into negotiated wage rate increases.
- The decline in the foreign exchange value of the Canadian dollar caused prices for imports to increase, which also increased prices. Price increases have led to wage rate increases.

Relationship Between Percentage Wage Rate Changes and the Unemployment Rate

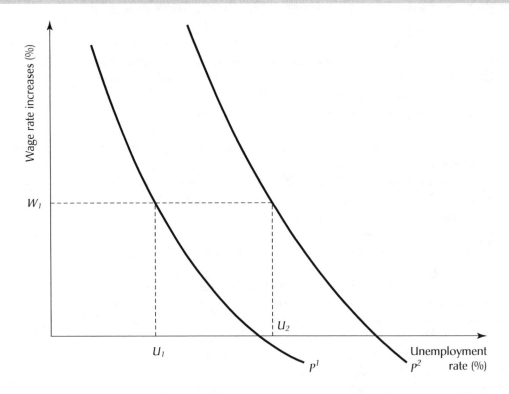

Since Phillips published his findings in the 1950s, the relationship between wage rate increases and the unemployment rate has been extended to price increases (inflation). Analysts have focused on measuring the relationship between price increases and the unemployment rate.

Chapter 11

Wage Rate Differentials

Chapter Learning Objectives

After completing this chapter, you should be able to:

- explain how adjustment lags result in wage rate differences between occupations
- define the following terms: wage structure, compensating wage differentials, and equalizing differences
- list job characteristics that can contribute to equalizing differences
- describe how the presence of labour market barriers results in wage rate differentials
- discuss the personal characteristics associated with the wage structure
- describe various factors affecting the wage gap between men and women
- explain why discrimination occurs in the labour market
- discuss the government policies designed to combat employment and pay discrimination

PARALEGALS: A CASE OF OCCUPATIONAL LICENSING

One goal of this chapter is to explain the wage rate differences between occupations. There are several reasons why not everyone earns the same wage rate. One reason is the existence of barriers that prevent workers from moving into higher-paying jobs. One such barrier is occupational licensing. To work at a trade or a profession, it may be mandatory that one obtain the necessary qualifications or licence. This introductory reading discusses the situation of paralegals.

Does all legal work in a province need to be handled by lawyers? If the answer is no, then there may be a need for someone with legal training who is not a lawyer. In other words, there may be a need for a paralegal. Specifically, a paralegal is a non-lawyer who works independently performing legal services before boards, tribunals, or some courts for a fee. How can the public be guaranteed that a paralegal is qualified to handle the situation? Lawyers are concerned that paralegals are not qualified to handle certain cases. Lawyers are also protective of the legal monopoly that has been created over the years.

In 1999, the Ontario government appointed Peter Cory, a retired Supreme Court of Canada justice, to examine the role of paralegals in the provision of legal services. His recommendations were as follows:

- paralegals could perform some of the family law and real estate work now performed by lawyers, such as drawing up simple wills, undertaking uncontested divorce proceedings, and representing vendors in real estate transactions
- paralegals should be allowed to swear affidavits and undertake simple incorporations. In the area of criminal law, however, they should not be allowed to handle summary convictions. In the area of criminal law, they should be able to perform work in the following areas of the criminal code: vagrancy; using slugs and tokens; defacing coins; falsifying employment records; and public nudity.
- paralegals should be licensed after successful completion of a two-year college course
- the paralegal industry should be regulated to prevent untrained and irresponsible persons from performing paralegal work
- an independent body should be established to regulate paralegals
  The following websites will provide more information on the market for paralegals.
- Paralegal Society of Ontario: www.paralegalsociety.on.ca
- Paralegal Discussion Paper:
  www.lsuc.on.ca/news/pdf/may1304_paralegal.pdf

Introduction

Why does your neighbour earn more money than you do? Why do professional athletes earn so much money? Much has been written in recent years about the earnings difference between men and women—why are men paid, on average, more than women? Why is there a difference in wage rates between different occupations? This chapter will explain why the differences in wage rates exist.

The focus in this chapter will be on the **occupational wage structure**, the differences in wage rates among the occupations that exist in the labour market. Wage rate differences encourage workers to seek out occupations that are most productive. If we assume that most people want to earn a high wage rate, workers will move to those occupations that pay more. In this manner, workers gravitate toward jobs in which they are most productive. Having individuals work at occupations in which they are most productive benefits society: not only are individual earnings higher, but society gets products and services provided more efficiently. Differences in wage rates also encourage individuals to develop their skills and invest in their training. If all occupations paid an identical wage, why would someone incur the expense of additional education or training?

The discussion of wage rate differences is divided into four categories:

- adjustment lags
- labour market barriers
- compensating wage differentials
- personal characteristics

occupational wage structure

differences in wage rates between occupations in the labour market

Adjustment Lags

You will recall from the earlier discussion that wage rates tend to move toward a condition of equilibrium in the labour market. That is, if the wage rate is currently above the equilibrium level (W_1 in Figure 11.1, page 298), there will be pressure to lower the wage rate toward equilibrium. As the wage rate is reduced, the quantity of workers demanded increases and the quantity of workers willing to work at that occupation decreases. At the equilibrium wage rate (W_e), the quantity of workers demanded equals the quantity of workers supplied to that occupation. The market is in equilibrium. Conversely, if the current wage rate is below the equilibrium wage rate (W_2), there is pressure to increase the wage rate to the equilibrium level. As the

FIGURE 11.1

Labour Market Equilibrium

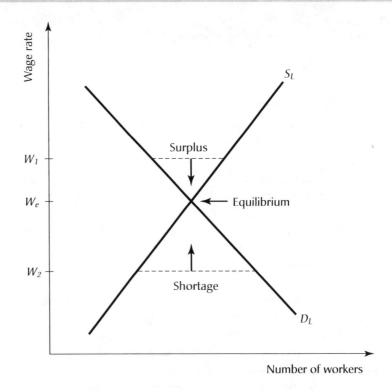

wage rate increases, the quantity of workers demanded by employers decreases and the quantity of workers willing to work at that occupation increases.

The difference in wage rates between two occupations may result from an **adjustment lag** as workers and employers react to changes in the wage rate. It takes time for the quantity of workers supplied to an occupation to increase. If wage rates are higher in one occupation than in others, it may take time for the information about the wage rate differences to be disseminated throughout the labour market. Workers do not instantly quit their jobs and move on upon hearing about the wage rates paid on other jobs.

It may also take time for employers to respond to changing wage rates. Assume that the equilibrium wage rate for an occupation falls. Employers may not be able to quickly change the wage rate for their employees. In situations where a collective agreement is in effect, wage rates remain at the current levels until the collective agreement expires. Legislation such as pay equity and the minimum wage rate may also prevent employers from lowering wage rates.

To further illustrate the concept of adjustment lags, imagine two occupations, *A* and *B*, with different wage rates (see Figure 11.2). The wage rate in occupation *A* is currently higher than the wage rate in occupation *B*. If we assume that workers want to earn more money and also that the jobs are similar in attractiveness, workers would move away from the occupation with the lower wage rate (*B*) to the occupation with the higher wage rate (*A*). In the

adjustment lag

period during which workers and employers react to changes in the wage rate

FIGURE 11.2

Wage Differentials Between Two Occupations

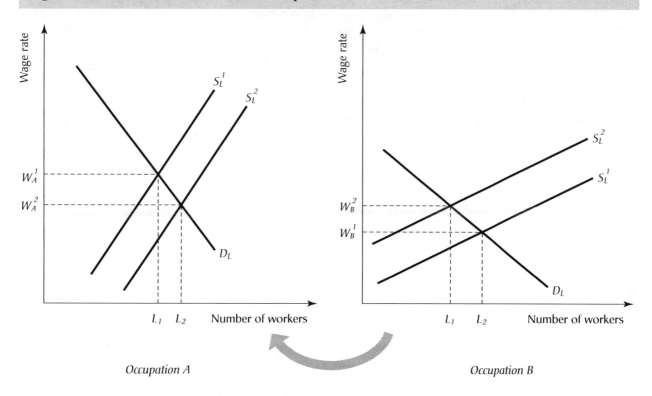

Occupation A   *Occupation B*

market with the lower wage rate, the supply of workers would decrease. The reduction in supply (a shift of the supply curve to the left) would increase the wage rate for this occupation (see the graph for occupation *B*). In the market with the higher wage rate, the supply curve would shift to the right with the increase in supply of workers willing to do this job. The wage rate in this market would be reduced.

In the market for occupation *B*, the wage rate increases as a result of the flow of workers out of occupation *B* to occupation *A*. In the market for occupation *A*, the wage rate decreases as a result of the flow of workers from occupation *B* into occupation *A*. The wage rate differential between the two occupations narrows.

As long as there is movement of workers from one occupation to another, the wage rates in the two occupations will get closer together. The wage rate differential will eventually disappear.

Labour Market Barriers

Wage rate differentials may appear because of adjustment lags in the labour market. These wage rate differentials are temporary. However, most wage rate differences between occupations are not temporary. The presence of barriers in the labour market is another factor that creates differences in the wage rate. The concept of labour market barriers is discussed in this section.

We have seen that workers move from lower-wage jobs to higher-wage jobs. This movement tends to equalize wage rates between occupations. If something interfered with the flow of workers from one occupation to another, the supply of workers in one occupation would remain high while the supply of workers in the other occupation would remain low. The wage differential between the occupations would continue to exist. If workers are restricted in their mobility from occupation *B* to occupation *A*, then the wage rate will remain lower in occupation *B* than in occupation *A*. The restrictions on mobility of workers from one job to another are called **labour market barriers**.

The distinction between a labour market barrier and an equalizing difference is that an equalizing difference acts as a magnet that keeps workers in lower-paying jobs, while labour market barriers prevent workers who want to switch jobs from moving to higher-paying jobs.

The following are labour market barriers:

- lack of information
- discrimination
- geography and language
- union-imposed regulations
- government regulations
- lack of education or training

The presence of labour market barriers means that the labour market is not as competitive as we assumed it to be in our discussion of demand and supply. Although some barriers (e.g., geography) may be difficult to eliminate, the removal of labour market barriers will make the labour market more competitive. Workers will move more freely between occupations and wage rate differentials will be reduced.

A discussion of each of these barriers follows. Note that some are easier to remove than others; for example, it is easier to overcome a lack of education and training than it is to remove the barriers imposed by government regulation.

Lack of Information

Thousands of different occupations exist in the Canadian labour market. It is virtually impossible for anyone to be aware of all the various occupations he or she is qualified for. As long as people are unaware of other occupations that can utilize their skills, they will remain in the lower-paying occupation. The federal government has attempted to rectify this barrier with the establishment of Human Resources Development Centres. Private placement agencies fill a similar role in the marketplace.

Discrimination

People are often denied an equal opportunity to develop their potential capability, or they are denied a wage equal to what others of the same capability are paid. **Pre-market discrimination** occurs when people have been deprived of the equal opportunity to develop their natural abilities and talents during the early pre-employment years. Pre-market discrimination, for example,

labour market barriers

restrictions on the mobility of workers from one job to another

pre-market discrimination

denial of equal opportunities to develop natural abilities and talents during pre-employment years would occur if children from a specific region or minority group received inferior schooling or inadequate health services. For example, children of Aboriginal families living on reserves often encounter pre-market discrimination. **Market discrimination** occurs when job assignments, promotions, or wage rates are based on characteristics unrelated to job performance. These characteristics may be the person's age, gender, or colour of skin. The distinction between pre-market and market discrimination is important because differences in hiring, promotion, or pay often reflect pre-market discrimination rather than market discrimination. If an Aboriginal worker receives less pay for the same job than a non-Aboriginal worker, it may be that the non-Aboriginal worker has had more education or training, which makes that person more productive. In this case, wage rate differentials would not be the result of market discrimination. Differences in educational attainment levels may reflect discrimination at the school level. But discrimination within the educational system is not the fault of the individual employer.

market discrimination
different responsibilities and benefits based on characteristics unrelated to job performance

Labour market barriers that arise from discrimination are often not easy to detect. Ideally, in order to detect discrimination, we would compare two groups whose productivity is assumed to be equal—such as men and women, or members of visible minorities and the majority. If women received lower wage rates than men with similar productivity levels, or if members of visible minorities received lower wages than other workers with similar productivity levels, we would argue that the wage rate differential is the result of discrimination. However, discrimination normally takes more subtle forms than unequal wages for equal work. For example, employers can restrict women or members of visible minorities to inferior jobs, thus justifying the lower wages paid to them.

As long as individuals are prevented from access to certain jobs because of gender or skin colour, existing wage rate differentials are likely to remain. Governments address occupational barriers through human rights legislation that makes it illegal to discriminate on the basis of age, gender, creed, race, and other characteristics in hiring or promoting.

Geography and Language

It may not always be easy to relocate to where the higher-wage jobs are. There are costs associated with moving to another city or province. Furthermore, the higher-wage job may be in a location with a higher cost of living. More expensive housing can be a barrier to the mobility of workers. There may also be social costs associated with relocation: it is often difficult to move away from friends and family. When children are involved in the move, their needs must also be considered. If one's spouse is also employed, relocation may be more complicated.

Language can also be a barrier to mobility. In Canada, the inability to speak one of the official languages may prevent a move to a higher wage rate job. Quebec's current language laws may not only discourage workers from moving to Quebec but may also inhibit francophone residents of Quebec from migrating interprovincially. The federal government has reaffirmed that many of those in senior civil service positions must be bilingual.

Union-Imposed Regulations

Collective agreements between union and management can restrict the mobility of labour between occupations. In industries such as construction, the union practices of a closed shop and a hiring hall affect the labour market. In a closed shop, the company can only employ members of the union, so prospective employees must be a member of the union before being hired. In a hiring hall situation, the union supplies workers to the employer and attempts to place local workers first.

Government Regulations

Provincial governments have legislation that restricts the movement of workers from province to province. Restrictions have been imposed on the transferability of trade certification; that is, although a worker may be certified to practise in one province, the certification may not be valid in another province. The Canadian Constitution gives the provinces the right to pass legislation limiting the number of non-residents able to work in certain occupations.

Municipal governments can set regulations for such businesses as hot dog vending or taxicab driving. These restrictions often dictate who can work in that field and where they can work.

Provinces and municipalities can also issue licences for certain businesses and occupations. Licences provide revenue for governments and, if the fee is very high, restrict entry into the trade. The main argument in favour of licensing is that it promotes public health and safety. To ensure that standards are maintained, licence applicants may have to pass an examination or serve an apprenticeship. The difficulty of the examination and the length of the apprenticeship can act as labour market barriers: tougher examinations and lengthier apprenticeships restrict entry into the trade or profession. Because occupational licensing restricts competition, the cost of the services provided by licensed occupations is higher than it otherwise would be. The quality of the service may also be lower than it would be with more competition. Licensing arrangements exist for the following occupations, among others: dentists, veterinarians, physicians, architects, actuaries, lawyers, and optometrists.

Tax laws restrict the interprovincial movement of workers. Travel and living expenses are not deductible for temporary employment away from home.

Lack of Education or Training

Many occupations have educational qualifications: someone who does not have the required educational credentials cannot work at these occupations. Furthermore, if a specific amount of education is required to enter an occupation, employees want to be compensated for the time and expense involved in getting the education or training. Many studies have established the existence of a positive correlation between the level of education and wage rates. Expenditures on education and training are an important aspect of the labour market. Chapter 12 is, therefore, devoted to discussing the returns received from investments in education and training.

Compensating Wage Differentials

The theory of compensating wage differentials recognizes that jobs differ in terms of their attractiveness. Jobs or occupations with unattractive attributes will require a higher wage rate in order to attract individuals to those occupations. Attractive occupations may be desirable in spite of lower wage rates as the positive aspects of the job compensate individuals for the reduction in wages.

What are unattractive working conditions? The most undesirable attribute of an occupation is the risk of injury or illness. Studies that compared occupations on the basis of risk of death or injury found that, all else being equal, such risks are associated with higher wage rates. When studying the impact of risk on wage rates, we must assume that all other working conditions are the same, although this is not likely to be the case. It is difficult to find two jobs that are identical except for any one aspect. There are many variations in employment conditions. Also, it can be difficult to measure risk.

Other working conditions listed as undesirable are extensive physical effort, especially lifting; a stressful work environment, especially where the work must be performed at a fast pace; unattractive hours of work such as shift work and weekend work; the risk of unemployment; noise; smoke; and extreme temperatures in the workplace. Apart from the risk of death or injury, other working conditions considered to be unattractive appear to have a negligible impact on wage rates.

In theory, when the working conditions of an occupation are undesirable, the wage rate paid to workers in that occupation is adjusted upward. A higher wage rate becomes necessary to attract workers into that occupation. The increase in the wage rate that compensates workers for undesirable conditions is referred to as a **compensating wage differential**. The size of the differential in relation to each unattractive attribute of a job is difficult to measure, because it is difficult to single out the impact of certain characteristics on the wage rate. Furthermore, individual preferences play a role here. Some people prefer shift work to a regular 9-to-5 routine. Some prefer outdoor work to office work. Although unattractive to many, some working conditions may appeal to others. Nonetheless, in order to attract workers into some occupations, the wage rate must be increased.

Wage differentials can also be viewed from the positive aspects of certain occupations. Some jobs are conducted in clean and safe conditions. Some jobs may be close to home, or they may have employment security. Some occupations have a degree of status associated with them, or flexible hours or long holidays. Where positive aspects of a job are present, individuals may accept a lower wage rate with the recognition that the positive aspects of the job compensate for the reduction in pay. These positive features of a job are referred to as **equalizing differences**. They act as a magnet, attracting individuals to lower-paying jobs. The size of the equalizing difference can be measured by determining the amount of money necessary to convince someone to leave a lower-paying attractive job for a higher-paying unattractive job.

compensating wage differential
increase in the wage rate that compensates workers for undesirable working conditions

equalizing differences
the features of a job that compensate for wage rates that are lower than in other jobs

Legislation Related to Risk in the Workplace

Empirical evidence suggests that higher earnings are associated with the risk of a fatal injury. However, the nature of employment is constantly changing and the amount of money necessary to compensate individuals for risk is changing as well. Occupational health and safety legislation has made many workplaces safer. In addition to having better safety equipment and procedures available, workers now have more information on hazardous substances. What impact does the presence of health and safety legislation have on the determination of wage rates?

If the risk of injury on the job is reduced through the use of better equipment or better procedures, the amount of the risk premium paid to workers who work in risky jobs is also reduced. On the other hand, the new legislation may make workers aware of dangers in the workplace, and once they are aware that certain substances are hazardous, workers may demand a wage premium to work at that occupation.

The presence of workers' compensation benefits may also reduce the compensating wage differential associated with unsafe conditions. If workers believe that the probability of loss of income due to injury is reduced because of workers' compensation payments, the premium required to work at a risky job may also be reduced. If a publicly operated workers' compensation program were not in effect, some employees would take out private insurance against wage loss. Those employees would demand a wage rate increase to cover the cost of the insurance.

The availability of employment insurance benefits may reduce the compensating wage differential between jobs with varying risks of unemployment. That is, prior to the introduction of a federal employment insurance program, employees who worked in jobs where the risk of unemployment was high sought higher wages to compensate for this risk. Government policy reflected this concern about job loss. The minimum wage rate for construction workers, who often have periods of unemployment, was higher than the minimum wage rate for other workers. Conversely, others would accept jobs with lower wage rates where the risk of unemployment was low. Prior to the 1970s, a job in the public sector was considered to be a "job for life." In return for this level of job security, many public-sector jobs had wage rates lower than comparable private-sector jobs. If employment insurance is available to all employees, workers need not seek out more secure jobs at lower pay, nor demand higher wage rates for less secure jobs, because they will receive some income in the event of a layoff or termination.

A survey of employees revealed the following attributes of a job to be the most attractive: job security, short hours and long vacations, promotion and training opportunities, low pressure/stress, lack of responsibility, prestige, superior geographic location, low danger, and non-monetary fringe benefits. There is some evidence that individuals will accept a lower wage rate to work in a location with a low crime rate, less pollution, or a lower population density. It also appears that individuals will accept a lower wage rate to avoid snow or to acquire extra sunshine.

In addition to non-monetary benefits of a job, there are also monetary fringe benefits. Employers may spend more than one-third of their payroll on monetary fringe benefits such as company pensions, bonuses and profit sharing, and group health plans. Differences in monetary fringe benefits can also lead to differences in money wage rates. Rather than offer a higher wage rate, some employers may offer more monetary fringe benefits.

Personal Characteristics

Another approach to explaining wage rate differentials between individuals is to focus on the personal characteristics associated with earners of higher wage rates. What characteristics distinguish high-wage earners from low-wage earners? These characteristics are discussed below.

Higher education is assumed to provide more cognitive knowledge either in terms of general communication skills and problem-solving abilities or in terms of occupation-specific competencies. It also may reflect a higher achievement motivation, discipline, and other personality traits often associated with productivity. Workers who are more productive are likely to be paid more. As mentioned earlier, empirical studies have confirmed the positive relationship between the amount of schooling and earnings.

Workers differ not only in terms of the number of years of schooling received and the level of degrees or certificates obtained, but also in terms of the quality of schooling. Does it matter where someone got a degree or diploma? Given that employers grade academic institutions, there is clearly a perception among employers that the college or university providing the education matters.

The longer an individual has been in the labour force, the more productive that person is likely to be.[i] There has been more opportunity for on-the-job training. When the relationship between training and wage rates is studied, the number of years of work experience is often used as a proxy for training, because it is difficult to measure how specific the training was. More years of service with an employer are likely associated with more opportunities for advancement within the company.

Not all individuals have equal ability. Some physicians are better than others. Some hockey players are better than others. In fact, in professional sports, a small difference in ability may translate into a large difference in earnings. One player is not a perfect substitute for another.

There is a positive relationship between the socioeconomic status of the family and earnings. If the parents are professionals, they may encourage their children to further their education. The parents may also have the finances to make that possible, and they may be able to introduce their children to people who can help them land a good job. Also, parents who are professionals expose their children to these types of jobs, so the children are aware that they exist.

Note that there is a great deal of interaction among these variables. For example, it is likely that individuals who come from a wealthy family will be able to afford more years of schooling. They may also be able to afford a higher-quality education. Nonetheless, individual characteristics do matter when it comes to earnings.

---

[i] Increases in productivity are not directly related to years of work experience throughout all of one's working life. As an individual approaches the age of retirement, his or her productivity may start to decrease.

Discrimination and Male–Female Wage Differentials

In discussing labour market barriers as a source of wage differentials, we briefly discussed the subject of discrimination. We will now take a closer look at discrimination and the role that it plays in the wage difference between male and female workers.

Empirical Evidence on Male–Female Wage Differentials

Statistics indicate that the earnings of women are less than the earnings of men. Does this mean that women are paid less than men just because they are women? Obviously not. As we have pointed out in this chapter, there are many other factors besides gender that can affect earnings. One such factor is the number of hours of work. On average, men work for pay more hours than women: 39.8 hours versus 35.2 hours per week. If one controls for differences in hours worked by men and women, for instance if one compares hourly wages, the gender gap is reduced to about 75% to 80%. Another factor is age: as the wage differential has narrowed over the years, one would expect that gender wage differences would be smallest among young workers. Indeed, that is what one finds. In the mid-1990s, women aged 55 and over who worked full-time earned on average 64% of the wages earned by male workers in the same age bracket. Their daughters and granddaughters, aged 15–24, earned on average 86% of the earnings of men in the same age group.

Marital status is another significant factor. The ratio of average earnings of females compared to males is very much reduced if one compares single men and women. The ratio is close to 0.9 or 90%. For single women in specific age groups or with certain educational levels, the difference is even less. The earnings of single women aged 35–44 were almost 95% of those earned by single men of the same age. The wage gap disappears entirely when one looks at the most educated members of that age group—single men and women with a university degree. In contrast, earnings between married men and women differ significantly. This indicates that married men and women choose different life and career paths from those chosen by single men and women.

There are many other potential factors that can affect the wage gap: absenteeism, labour market experience, seniority, health, and training. It is estimated that almost 20% of the wage gap can be explained by workplace characteristics—especially the incidence of part-time employment. Women are more likely to work in establishments that have a higher proportion of part-time employment than others, and part-time wage rates tend to be lower than full-time wage rates. Why are women overrepresented in part-time jobs? The answer to this question is not fully understood. It may be that part-time employment offers more flexibility, which is an attractive employment attribute. Women are also less likely to work in teams than are men. Women are less likely to have their earnings tied to productivity and performance. Another 20% of the wage gap can be explained by the differences in the industries within which men and women work. Women tend to be concentrated in low-wage industries. Finally, men have been in the workforce for a longer period of time than women. Wages tend to increase with experience.

Economists have devoted considerable effort to disentangling the various effects and separating them from the effect of gender. The idea is to estimate the male–female wage differential that remains after controlling those factors that account for productivity differences between male and female workers. Wage rate differences that reflect productivity differences are considered non-discriminatory. The wage rate gap that remains after productivity-related differences are taken into account is the unexplained or "residual" amount. It cannot be attributed to productivity differences and, therefore, is chosen as a measure of discrimination.

Theories of Discrimination

What does economic theory tell us about discrimination? In the following we will focus on market (or employment) discrimination, not because pre-market (or pre-employment) discrimination is unimportant, but because its causes are largely beyond the field of economics. We look at two theories of discrimination. One is based on prejudice, the other on lack of information.

Prejudice by Employers

Prejudice describes a subjective feeling of dislike for an individual or group. A common feature of prejudice is that the person tries to create a distance from the disliked individual or group, which can take several forms. One form is physical distance. What happens if employers distance themselves from individuals or groups by not hiring them, for instance by not hiring women?

Suppose we look at a group of firms that discriminates against women and a group that does not. Assume that the labour demand curves for both groups are identical. However, the supply curve of labour for the non-discriminating firms must lie farther to the right than for the discriminating firms. Men and women can work for the non-discriminating firms, whereas only men can work for the discriminating firms. Because of the larger supply of labour to the non-discriminating firms, wage rates will be lower. Women are restricted to work for the non-discriminating firms, so their wage rates are on average lower than those of men. Men's average wage rates are composed of the lower wage rates paid by non-discriminating firms and the higher wage rates paid by discriminating firms. The observed wage rate differential between men and women can be explained by the discrimination against hiring women.

Can these wage differentials persist over time? It depends. The discriminating firms pay a price for their prejudice: by excluding women, they must pay a higher wage rate. The non-discriminatory firms have a cost advantage because they pay a lower wage rate. In competitive labour markets, the discriminating firms will be driven out of business over time, and the gender wage gap will disappear. If, however, the discriminating firms are protected from competition, they will be able to remain in business. In protected industries, such as government-regulated industries, there is less competitive pressure to maximize profits. Thus, firms that choose to discriminate can maintain their discriminatory practices. However, they will pay a price for discriminating by earning lower profits than they otherwise could have.

Prejudice by Workers

Another source of discrimination may come from prejudice of fellow workers, which is often a more powerful source of discrimination because the motives are generally stronger. Employers are not always in contact with their workers; prejudice among fellow workers, on the other hand, is fuelled both by competition for jobs and close personal contact at work.

In short, when employers are the source of discrimination, competitive forces tend to reduce discrimination over time. When workers are the source of discrimination, prejudice will remain for a longer period of time. Assume that men do not like to have women as their supervisors. If men fail to cooperate in the workplace, female supervisors will be less efficient in their work compared to their male counterparts. Hence the female supervisors will earn lower wage rates. The wage rate gap between male and female supervisors caused by the prejudice of workers can persist even in the long run. There is no mechanism in place that would force the gap to disappear over time.

Discrimination as a Result of Imperfect Information

A second explanation for market discrimination is the imperfect information that is available to employers when they hire workers. An employer can never be sure of a worker's actual productivity at the time of hiring. Employers, therefore, often use personal characteristics of workers in the screening process as indicators of their productivity. Some of these personal characteristics are individual in nature, such as years of education, previous work experience, or test scores. Others are group characteristics, such as gender or race. The use of group characteristics in screening job applicants gives rise to **statistical discrimination**.

statistical discrimination

discrimination that results from imperfect information in the screening process of job applicants

For discrimination to take place, two workers of equal productivity must be paid different wages based on a criterion such as gender or race. How might this occur? Imagine a firm wants to hire a new worker. The firm's newspaper ad has attracted several male and female job applicants who have different levels of education and work experience and different labour force attachments. To choose the most productive worker, the firm will screen the applicants based on characteristics that it considers directly linked to a worker's productivity. Assume that the firm will use only two characteristics: level of education and gender. If the level of educational attainment were a perfect predictor of productivity, the firm might only hire college or university graduates. Male and female workers with equal educational attainment would receive equal wage rates. If education were an imperfect predictor of productivity, the employer would use additional characteristics that are correlated with job performance to improve the screening process. In this example, the only other observable characteristic is gender.

It is a fact that only women can give birth. It is also a fact that many, not all, women who have babies quit their jobs (at least for a while) to look after their babies. The employer knows this. However, what the employer does not know is which of the female applicants of child-bearing age are likely to withdraw from the labour force for this reason. If the employer knew, he or she would treat equally all applicants with the same educational level and the same long-term job commitment. Instead, because of imperfect information, the employer presumes that all female applicants of child-bearing age are likely to quit in order to raise a family. Therefore, the employer would likely prefer to hire a male applicant.

Women whose careers have been interrupted to raise children may have a lower level of productivity than other women of comparable age and educational attainment. Thus employers may systematically prefer male to female workers of equal educational level, giving rise to lower wage rates for women. Are these wage differentials discriminatory? On a group basis, they are not, to the extent that the differences in wage rates reflect actual differences in productivity. On an individual level, they are discriminatory. Those female applicants who are identical to male applicants in terms of personal qualifications, including job commitment, are rejected based on the fact that they are female.

Policies to Combat Discrimination

Governments in Canada have enacted a wide range of legislation aimed at combating discrimination in the labour market.

Equal Employment Opportunity Legislation

Discrimination, as we have seen, can affect different aspects of employment: hiring, promotion, dismissal, or pay. Equal employment opportunity legislation attempts to prevent discrimination in hiring, promotion, and dismissals. Provinces include this legislation in their Human Rights Code, so complaints regarding employment discrimination are considered by the province's Human Rights Commission. If the parties involved in a complaint cannot resolve the issue, a board of inquiry takes on the case and makes a final decision.

Affirmative Action Legislation

Affirmative action goes a step further than equal employment opportunity legislation. In addition to requiring that firms and other organizations end discriminatory practices, it requires them to demonstrate that they are actively making efforts to locate and to hire members of the following four designated groups: women, members of visible minorities, people with disabilities, and Aboriginal people. These four groups have most frequently been subjected to discrimination. Affirmative action or equal opportunity legislation so far applies only to industries that fall under federal jurisdiction.

affirmative action

policy that promotes employment equity for women, members of visible minorities, people with disabilities, and Aboriginal people

Affirmative action legislation has not been without controversy. One criticism is that affirmative action really amounts to a system of employment quotas. Another criticism is that it forces companies and other organizations to hire unqualified workers simply because they belong to one of the designated groups. Proponents counter that, without affirmative action, employers who discriminate would simply claim they could not find qualified female or minority workers. The problem is that one cannot decide on purely objective grounds who is qualified and who is not. Supporters of affirmative action also argue that, even if some reverse discrimination is involved, it is justified as a compensation for past discrimination.

Equal Pay Legislation

All Canadian jurisdictions have legislated equal pay for equal work. Under the provisions of this legislation, men and women who perform the same work within the same establishment must be paid the same wage rate. Equal or same work is generally interpreted in a rather broad sense, that is, as similar or substantially similar work. Differences can appear in the wage rate between men and women on the same job if a piecework arrangement is in effect or if seniority is factored into everyone's wage rate in the firm.

Pay Equity or Equal Value Legislation

The impact of equal pay legislation is limited because men and women are often not performing the same or similar work in a firm. To remedy the resulting wage disparities, further legislative initiatives have been proposed and partly implemented. Legislation that ensures that men and women are paid equally for work of equal value is known as pay equity legislation. Under this legislation, companies must pay the same wage rate to male and female employees performing different tasks if these tasks are deemed to be of equal value. The value of a job is determined by a job evaluation scheme, instead of being established in the market. Such a scheme compares male-dominated jobs with female-dominated jobs. The legislation establishes factors by which to determine the value of a job, including physical effort, skill, educational requirements, responsibility, and working conditions. Points are assigned to each factor and added up for each job. Male-dominated jobs are then compared with female-dominated jobs with the same total point score. If, for example, wages in female-dominated jobs are 20% lower than wages in male-dominated jobs with the same point score, the wage rates assigned to female-dominated jobs are adjusted upward.

In Chapter 3, we listed some of the jurisdictions that have implemented pay equity legislation. Here, we will focus on some of the arguments that have been brought forward in the debate over pay equity legislation. Critics of the legislation charge that comparing the values of different jobs on the basis of a common set of characteristics is like trying to compare the values of oranges and apples on the basis of their nutritional value. In the case of oranges and apples, the subjective preferences of consumers play a large part in determining the demand for and, therefore, the prices of the two fruits. Even if oranges and apples had an identical nutritional value, the price of oranges might be much higher than that of apples if consumers preferred the taste of oranges. The same applies to different jobs. Critics point out that just because a job held by men has the same value—in terms of point score for skills, responsibility, and so on—as a job held by women, this does not imply that the two jobs should have the same wage. If a majority of women prefer certain jobs, and therefore expand the supply of labour to these jobs, it can be expected that wage rates in these jobs will be lower.

Another argument against pay equity legislation is that it will lead to serious inefficiencies in the labour market by creating chronic surpluses in some occupations and shortages in others. Job evaluations might give carpenters (a male-dominated occupation) and social workers (a female-dominated occupation) who are both employed in the public sector an equal point score; salaries in these two occupations would, therefore, be adjusted so that they are equal. If carpenters earned higher salaries than social workers before the implementation of pay equity legislation, the result would be an increase in the supply of people wanting social worker positions.

Opponents of pay equity legislation further argue that such legislation will cause many women to lose their jobs by raising the relative wage of women. The imposition of an increase in the wage rate brought about by pay equity legislation is similar to the imposition of a higher minimum wage rate. There will be fewer workers demanded, especially if the wage elasticity of demand is elastic. Also, there may be fewer job opportunities because employers who are faced with a major pay equity settlement may relocate to jurisdictions that do not have pay equity legislation.

Critics also argue that the process of determining the true value of jobs is inherently subjective. A job's evaluation score depends on which factors are included in establishing the value of a job and on the weight given to each factor. Both decisions are affected by the values and beliefs of the evaluator. Not surprisingly, the same jobs have received different ratings when evaluated by different people.

Proponents of pay equity legislation discount most of the criticism. First, they admit that, in a competitive market, differences in supply and demand may lead to differences in wages for jobs that have the same measured characteristics. They maintain that real-world wage differentials between men and women do not arise from competitive market forces but are mostly the result of women being crowded into certain occupations due to discrimination and sex stereotyping. The fact that pay equity legislation negates market-determined wage differentials is thus desirable because these differentials represent past and present discrimination.

Second, they argue that job evaluation can be done far more objectively than the critics of the legislation seem to admit. The objectivity comes from standardized evaluation procedures.

Third, proponents dispute the negative effects of the legislation on economic efficiency and on the employment of women. They point to the experience of other countries such as Australia and Great Britain. Australia has had pay equity legislation since 1969. Since that time women's pay has risen from 66% to more than 85% of men's. Major labour market imbalances do not seem to have emerged. In Great Britain, pay equity laws were toughened in 1983. The legislative changes and their enforcement do not seem to have caused major market distortions in that country.

Empirical research on various aspects of pay equity legislation is still insufficient to draw firm conclusions on its pros and cons. Nevertheless, some tentative conclusions have emerged. In jurisdictions where pay equity legislation has been in force for some time, the gender wage gap has been reduced, in some cases considerably so. Negative employment effects for women seem to have been minimal.

Summary

Occupational wage structure refers to differences in wage rates between different occupations. Wage differences between occupations may be the result of adjustment lags, as it takes time for workers and employers to adjust to wage differences. Wage differences arising from adjustment lags are generally of a temporary nature.

Occupations differ from each other in terms of both undesirable and desirable attributes. Jobs with undesirable attributes generally have to pay higher wages to compensate for the undesirable conditions. Jobs with desirable attributes often lead workers to accept lower wages. For the total of advantages and disadvantages to be equalized among occupations, wages must rise or fall by enough to equalize or compensate for the differentials, which are usually of a long-term nature.

Wage differentials between occupations generally cause workers to move from the lower-paid to the higher-paid occupations. Movements between occupations may be hindered by labour market barriers, which may be the result of discrimination, lack of information, different geographical location of employers and employees, language, or union- or government-imposed regulations.

Discrimination is often cited as the main reason for the wage gap between men and women. Although the gender wage gap has been decreasing over the last decades, men still earn more than women on average. There are many factors that affect the earnings differential between men and women such as differences in hours of work, work experience, training, absences from work, and seniority. It has been found that even if the major factors leading to productivity differences are taken into account, there remains a wage gap between men and women. This residual or "unexplained" part of the overall wage difference is often chosen as a measure of discrimination.

Labour market discrimination occurs when people of equal productivity are paid different wages, are hired into different jobs, or receive unequal training or promotion opportunities on the basis of characteristics such as gender, race, age, or religion. The source of discrimination can be found in prejudices of employers or fellow workers or in imperfect information regarding a worker's true productivity.

Several policies have been designed and partly implemented to reduce discrimination in the labour market. Equal employment opportunity legislation and affirmative action legislation address discrimination in hiring and promotion. Equal pay legislation and pay equity legislation address discrimination in pay. Equal pay legislation requires that men and women who perform the same or substantially similar work in the same establishment must be paid the same wage rate. Pay equity legislation prescribes that men and women receive the same pay in different jobs as long as these jobs are considered to be of equal value.

Key Terms

adjustment lag (page 298)
affirmative action (page 309)
compensating wage differential (page 303)
equalizing differences (page 303)
labour market barriers (page 300)

market discrimination (page 301)
occupational wage structure (page 297)
pre-market discrimination (page 300)
statistical discrimination (page 308)

Weblinks

Status of Women Canada
www.swc-cfc.gc.ca/pubs/0662327535/index_e.html

Canadian Human Rights Commission
www.chrc-ccdp.ca/pay_equity/default-en.asp

Pay Equity in Canada—Steven Brooks
www.policy.ca/PDF/20010126.pdf

Discussion Questions

1. Political pressure to pass occupational licensing legislation usually comes from the people employed in the occupation rather than from consumers. Why?
2. Only a few women are employed as airline pilots, and only a few men are employed as dental hygienists. What could account for this pattern?
3. How can a seniority system perpetuate discrimination?
4. Some argue that the wages of equally productive men and women will converge over time in a competitive labour market and that wage differentials that result from discrimination will not persist in the long run. Discuss.
5. Discuss the pros and cons of pay equity legislation. Which side of the debate do you think has the stronger argument?

Using the Internet

1. Access the Steven Brooks website (www.policy.ca/PDF/20010126.pdf). Write a summary of the arguments for and against pay equity legislation.

Exercises

1. Do jobs with undesirable attributes pay more than jobs with desirable attributes, or is it the other way around? Explain.
2. Occupation A and occupation B are identical except that occupation B requires people to work at night. Assume that some people prefer night jobs, but others do not. Will the wage in occupation B be higher, lower, or equal to that in A? Why?
3. Draw labour market diagrams for two regional labour markets, A and B. In region A, a particular occupation is paid a higher wage than in region B. As a result, workers in that occupation move from region B to region A. Show the effect of the movement on the occupation's wage structure in both regions. What geographical barriers could prevent workers' moving from region B to A?
4. What is meant by statistical discrimination?
5. Why is equal employment opportunity legislation generally considered to be insufficient to abolish the segregation of women into female-dominated jobs?

Chapter 12

Education, Training, and Earnings Differentials

Chapter Learning Objectives

After completing this chapter, you should be able to:

- describe the typical pattern of age–earnings profiles for different levels of education
- explain the cost–benefit analysis of investment in postsecondary education
- outline the changes in returns to postsecondary education over time
- discuss the impact of education and other factors on the distribution of individual earnings
- contrast the signalling approach with the human capital approach to investment in education
- distinguish between general and specific training

THE RISE IN STUDENT DEBT

In 2000, about 270 000 students graduated from public college and university programs in Canada. Drawing on data from the 2002 National Graduates Survey (NGS) of the Class of 2000, a recent Statistics Canada study reports that about half of those who graduated in 2000 owed student debt upon graduation.[1] While government student loan programs were the major source of student borrowing, almost one in five college and bachelor's graduates borrowed from other sources to finance their education.

At the college level, graduates with only government student loans owed, on average, $12 500 at graduation, while those with only non-government debt owed $7100. The 8% of students who had borrowed from both sources owed, on average, $19 200. The corresponding figures for bachelor's graduates were $19 500 for those with only government student loans and $9500 for those with only non-government debt. The 11% of graduates who owed to both sources owed, on average, $32 200.

Student debt has increased considerably in recent years. The average debt from government student loan programs carried by college graduates in 2000 increased by 21% compared to the debt of students who graduated in 1995 and by 76% compared to the class of 1990 (in 2000 constant dollars). Students in bachelor's programs owed about 30% more than the class of 1995, and 76% more than the Class of 1990. These increases mirror the rise in tuition fees over the 1990s. Average undergraduate tuition fees (in current dollars), for example, more than doubled in 10 years, an increase from $1872 in 1993–1994 to $4024 in 2003–2004.

Pursuing a college or university education is an investment in human capital that involves costs and benefits. Given the rising tuition fees and debt loads facing young people, are the benefits of a postsecondary education outweighing the cost? Considering the increasing enrollment rates in postsecondary education programs in recent years, the answer of many Canadians appears to be yes.

Introduction

In Chapter 11, we looked at various factors explaining differences in wage rates. This chapter examines the role of education and on-the-job training as a source of earnings differentials. The study of the effects of education and training on the labour market is the core of what economists call human capital theory. The central idea of this theory is that expenditures on education and training are investments that individuals make in themselves in order to increase their market skills, productivity, and earnings. To explain earnings differentials, human capital theory focuses on individual differences in years of schooling and length of on-the-job training.

The chapter is divided into three sections. The first section examines formal education as a type of human capital investment. The concept of a rate of return to human capital investment is introduced and we explore why differences in years of education among individuals are expected to lead to differences in earnings. In the second section, we focus more closely on the causes of individual differences in investment in schooling, particularly on factors such as individual ability, financial opportunity, and so on. The third section of the chapter is devoted to on-the-job training and the implications of different types of such training for earnings differentials.

The Pattern of Education and Earnings

Is there any truth to the old maxim, "If you want to get ahead, get an education"? Consider the evidence shown in Figures 12.1A and B (pages 318–319), which make use of **age–earnings profiles**. Such profiles show annual earnings for people of different ages who have had the same amount of schooling. Profiles of average annual earnings for Canadian men and women are drawn for five educational levels: (i) fewer than nine years of elementary schooling; (ii) nine to thirteen years of elementary and secondary schooling but no high school certificate; (iii) high school certificate; (iv) some postsecondary education such as trade certificates but not a college certificate or university degree; and (v) a certificate/diploma or degree from a college or university. The profiles are for year-round full-time workers only. We can see in these two figures that education and earnings are strongly related. Men and women with more education make more money, as shown by the successively higher level of each age–earning profile.

At first glance, these figures strongly support the belief that additional education results in higher earnings. Whether further education is a good investment, however, requires more analysis. It is necessary to compare the increased earnings from additional years of education and the additional costs. While a postsecondary degree or certificate does lead to higher earnings for most people, the investment nevertheless may not be worthwhile when one considers the rising costs of obtaining a postsecondary education.

age–earnings profile
average hourly or annual earnings for people of different ages with the same level of education

Investment in Education

When individuals incur expenses to further their education, to acquire a new skill, to relocate to a new job, or to improve their health, they are investing in themselves. Economists refer to this spending as investment in human capital. Our discussion of human capital will focus on investment in education and training. While most individuals treat schooling as an investment in their future, schooling is also seen by many people as a consumption good. That is, individuals spend money on education for the pleasure and the satisfaction of the experience. There are certain psychic benefits associated with the learning experience and the social life while being at college or university.

FIGURE 12.1A

Annual Earnings by Age and Education, Canadian Males, 1995

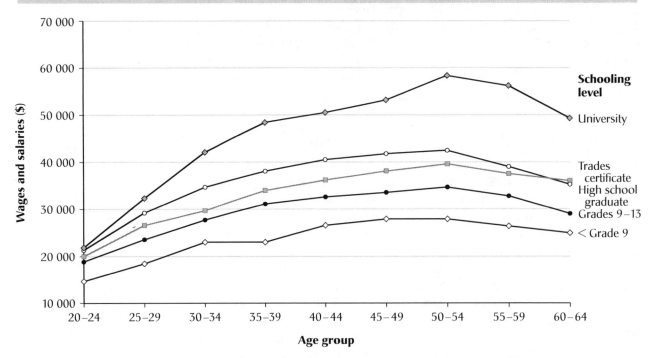

Note: Earnings are average wage and salary income of full-year (49+ weeks), full-time (30+ hours per week) workers.

Source: Authors' tabulations from the 1996 Census Public Use Microdata Files, Statistics Canada.

The Investment Decision

cost–benefit analysis

a comparison of the costs and benefits of an investment

When is additional education a good investment? One way to find out is to compare the cost of the investment with the benefits derived from it. This is called a **cost–benefit analysis**. There are two types of costs accruing to the individual: direct costs and opportunity costs. Direct costs include tuition fees, books, and other educational expenses. They may also include the increase in living and travel expenses associated with living away from home. An opportunity cost is the lost income that a person could have earned had he or she been working rather than attending college or university. Opportunity costs depend on the labour force experience and skills of the individual who is sacrificing an income to attend school. A chartered accountant with 10 years' work experience who returns to school to earn a computer science degree will have much higher opportunity costs compared to a freelance writer with two years' part-time work experience who is enrolling in a certificate program in journalism. Balanced against these costs are the benefits obtained from spending on education. These benefits may be monetary or non-monetary. Pursuing more education may allow an individual to select a job that is associated with relatively higher wages, attractive working hours, or social status and prestige.

FIGURE 12.1B

Annual Earnings by Age and Education, Canadian Females, 1995

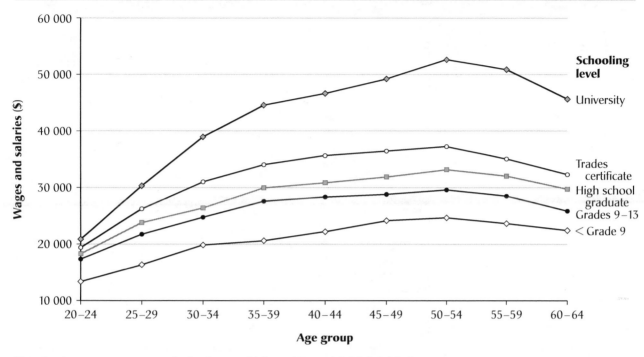

Note: Earnings are average wage and salary income of full-year (49+ weeks), full-time (30+ hours per week) workers.

Source: Authors' tabulations from the 1996 Census Public Use Microdata Files, Statistics Canada.

To apply the cost–benefit approach, consider the following. After finishing high school at age 18, should an individual seek full-time employment with the goal of working continuously until age 65? Or should the individual attend university for four years from ages 18 to 21 inclusive and then work continuously from age 22 to retirement at age 65? From the perspective of human capital, the answer depends on the costs in comparison to the monetary benefits. Figure 12.2 (page 320) illustrates the age–earnings profiles resulting from the two different investment strategies. Entering the workforce at age 18 produces the profile indicated by the label "High school." Pursuing a university degree is described by the profile labelled "University." The costs and benefits of attending university can readily be seen. The direct costs are shown by the area where the university profile lies below zero on the vertical axis. The size of the direct costs depends on such factors as whether the individual enrolls in a professional or liberal arts program, obtains a scholarship, lives in residence, and so on. The indirect costs or forgone earnings are indicated by the earnings that a high school graduate would receive in the first four years of employment. Had the individual not gone to the university, he or she would be earning this money. The size of these opportunity costs depends on the earnings that a high school graduate is able to make and

FIGURE 12.2

Benefits and Costs of Four Years of University Education

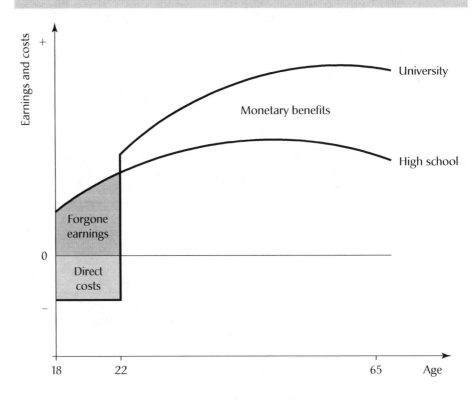

whether or not the university student works part-time while in school. Although not shown in Figure 12.2, the opportunity cost of attending university may extend several years beyond age 22 if the university graduate begins work at a lower salary than what the high school graduate is earning at age 22. Finally, note that the opportunity cost of attending university outweighs the direct cost in Figure 12.2. The lost earnings from even a relatively low-skilled full-time job generally exceed the direct expenses of attending a postsecondary institution. With rapidly rising tuition fees and falling relative wages for less-skilled workers, the composition of total costs as described in Figure 12.2, however, may be reversed in the near future.

The monetary benefits of a university education are the higher after-tax earnings that the university graduate is able to command in the job market. In Figure 12.2, these monetary benefits are given by the difference between the age–earnings profiles for high school and university.

Following the cost–benefit approach, the question about the investment in four additional years of postsecondary education is resolved by the following criterion: If the benefits exceed the costs, the investment is worthwhile. If the area labelled "Monetary benefits" in Figure 12.2 is larger than the area indicated by direct costs and forgone earnings, the investment should be undertaken. Alternatively, if the costs exceed the benefits, the investment will not be advisable. This rule, however, is not as simple as it sounds. The dollar values of the costs and benefits are not directly comparable. Costs and benefits accrue at different points in time. The costs of acquiring the university degree in the example are incurred over four years, while the benefits are obtained over many years in the future. To compare the benefits with the costs, both must be calculated in terms of their present value.

Let us have a look at the procedure usually used to compare present and future receipts and outlays.

Present Value

Would you rather receive $1000 now or $1000 a year from now? The answer is straightforward. If you had $1000 now, you could invest it in a savings account, term deposit, Treasury bill, or bond, and receive interest. Suppose you invested $1000 for one year at a rate of interest of 10%. Then at the end of the year you would receive $1000 \times .10 = \$100$, which, with the return of the principal $1000, would give you

$$\$1000 + \$1000 \times 0.10 = \$1000(1 + 0.10) = \$1100$$

The future value (FV) of $1000 received now would be $1100 a year from now.

If you invested the $1000 for two years at 10%, compounded annually, the future value of the $1000 at the end of that time would be

$$FV = \$1000\,[(1 + 0.10)(1 + 0.10)] = \$1000(1 + 0.10)^2 = \$1000 \times 1.21 = \$1210$$

The future value of a sum of money (Y) in year (n) if invested at a given rate of interest (i) is given by the formula:

$$FV = Y(1 + i)^n$$

The formula tells us how much a sum of money invested today at a given interest rate will be worth in the future.

Let's turn the argument around and ask: What is today's value of a sum of money received in the future? Or applied to the previous example: What is the **present value** (PV) of $1100 received at the end of a year worth now, given an interest rate of 10%?

Since the future value of $1000 at the end of the year is

$$FV = \$1000(1 + 0.10) = \$1100$$

the present value of $1100 is

$$PV = \frac{\$1100}{(1 + 0.10)} = \$1000$$

Similarly, the present value of $1210 received at the end of two years is

$$PV = \frac{\$1210}{(1 + 0.10)^2} = \frac{\$1210}{1.21} = \$1000$$

The general formula for the present value of a future sum of money (Y) received in year (n) is:

$$PV = \frac{Y}{(1 + i)^n}$$

present value

the current value of a future sum of money

The formula permits us to translate amounts received at different dates in the future into their equivalent current value. Once we have translated those amounts into their current value we can add or subtract them directly. The present value of Y dollars is also called the discounted present value. The term "discounted" comes from the fact that the income received in a future year is discounted, with $1/(1 + i)$ being the discount factor. The interest rate (i) is sometimes called the discount rate. The discount rate is a measure of what we lose by receiving our money later rather than now. It is the *opportunity cost* of not having the money sooner. Since the interest rate is always positive, the discount factor is always less than 1. Having a dollar next year is worth less than having a dollar today.

The PV formula shows that the present value is determined by two factors: the length of time, indicated by n, and the interest rate. The more distantly in time the payment is received, that is, the larger n is, the lower the present value of the same Y dollars. The higher the discount rate i, the lower the present value. For example, if $i = 5\%$, the value today of a dollar next year is $1/1.05 = 95$ cents; if $i = 10\%$, the value today of a dollar next year is $1/1.10 = 91$ cents. The interest rate, or discount rate, is influenced by current financial markets. If the interest rate on savings deposits at banks, for example, is high, the opportunity cost of spending this money on education is high.

Let us return now to our example of the decision whether to invest in a university or college education. Assume a person receives income after graduation each year until reaching age 65. To determine the monetary benefits from the investment in four years of postsecondary education requires calculating the present value of the income stream earned by the high school graduate and college graduate up to retirement.

For the high school graduate, the present value of the stream of income (PV^{HS}) is:

$$PV^{HS} = Y_{18} + \frac{Y_{19}}{(1 + i)} + \frac{Y_{20}}{(1 + i)^2} + ... + \frac{Y_{64}}{(1 + i)^{46}}$$

where Y_{18} is the income received in the year of graduation, Y_{19} is the income received next year (when the graduate is 19), and so on. The last income received before retirement is Y_{64}.

The university graduate starts receiving income only at age 22. Since the decision of whether to invest in more education is made at age 18, the first income received at age 22 has to be discounted over four years. The income received at age 23 has to be discounted over five years, and so on. The present value of the stream of income for the university graduate (PV^U) is:

$$PV^U = \frac{Y_{22}}{(1 + i)^4} + \frac{Y_{23}}{(1 + i)^5} + ... + \frac{Y_{64}}{(1 + i)^{46}}$$

Converting the income streams of the high school and university graduates into their present value has a dramatic impact on the relative benefits of a postsecondary education. As we saw earlier, the more distant the receipt of income, the more heavily it is discounted and the less its present value. This fact clearly bears on the decision of whether to invest in postsecondary education. The high school graduate earns an income from age 18 to 22. Because

Part III: Microeconomic Theory of the Labour Market

of its immediacy, this income is discounted relatively little. The university graduate, on the other hand, forgoes current income for the promise of higher income in the future. Because these higher earnings are not realized for several years, they are worth considerably less in terms of their present value. Assume that the university graduate obtains a job at 22 years of age, that the student expects to retire the day before turning 65, and that the earnings estimated over that work life amount to $2 433 000 (in 1992 dollars). Using a discount rate of 5%, the present value of this income stream would be reduced to $629 000. Suppose the person had instead entered the labour market after graduation from high school and that the estimated earning stream from age 18 to the end of 64 would be $1 753 000. Discounted with 5%, the present value of the total income would be $503 000. While both income streams are greatly reduced in value, the income stream of the university graduate is reduced the most when converted to present value. The difference in total lifetime earnings of $680 000 ($2 433 000 – $1 753 000) is reduced to $126 000 ($629 000 – $503 000), once the earnings are discounted over the respective work lives.

So far we have looked only at the monetary benefits of pursuing a postsecondary education compared to entering the labour force directly after high school graduation. Since the investment decision is based on a comparison of benefits and costs, we now have to include the cost of university studies. The university graduate incurs costs over four years. The costs at ages 19, 20, and 21 must be discounted back to age 18. The present value of the costs (PV_C) is

$$PV_C = C_{18} + \frac{C_{19}}{(1 + i)} + \frac{C_{20}}{(1 + i)^2} + \frac{C_{21}}{(1 + i)^3}$$

Assume that the costs of pursuing a four-year degree are $15 000 for the first year, $16 000 for the second year, $18 000 for the third year, and $20 000 for the fourth year. The discounted value of the total cost of $69 000 using a discount rate of 5% would be:

$$PV = \$15\ 000 + \frac{\$16.\ 000}{(1.05)} + \frac{\$18.\ 000}{(1.05)^2} + \frac{\$20.\ 000}{(1.05)^3}$$

$$= \$15\ 000 + \$15\ 238.10 + \$16\ 326.53 + \$17\ 277.12$$

$$= \$63\ 841.75$$

Subtracting the present value of the costs from the present value of the income stream in the previous formula yields the *net present value* of the income stream. In our example, the net present value of the income stream for the university graduate is $629 000 – $63 841.75 = $565 158.25. Once the net present value of alternative income streams is determined, the following decision rule can be applied: select the human capital investment that yields the highest net present value. If the net present value of the investment in a university education is higher than the net present value of the income stream received after graduating from high school, then the investment in university education is worthwhile. In our example, the investment should be undertaken because the net present value of the postsecondary education, $565 158.25, is larger than the net present value of the income stream received by the high school graduate, $503 000.

Internal Rate of Return

internal rate of return

the discount rate that equalizes the present values from both the benefits and the costs of an investment

An alternative way to decide whether postsecondary education is a good investment is to calculate the **internal rate of return** and to compare it with the market rate of interest. The internal rate of return is the discount rate (i), which equalizes the present values of the costs and benefits from a decision to invest in postsecondary education. If the internal rate of return of an investment is greater than or equal to the market rate of interest, the investment in education is profitable.

Another way to look at the internal rate of return is to describe it as the discount rate that equalizes the net present values of two income streams. In our example, the internal rate of return would be the interest rate that makes the net present value of a high school graduate's lifetime earnings equal to the net present value of the lifetime earnings of a university graduate. The meaning of the rate of return can be illustrated with the help of Figure 12.2 (page 320). If the discount rate were zero, the value of the income stream of the university graduate would far exceed the lifetime income of the high school graduate. As the discount rate increases, the earnings of both graduates are discounted more than at a lower interest rate. As the discount rate increases, the earnings of a university graduate need to be much higher than those of a high school graduate in order for the net present value of the university graduate's earnings to be greater than those of the high school graduate. At some value of i, the present values of the age–earnings profiles of the high school and university graduates will be equal. This value of i is the internal rate of return: it is the minimum rate of return the university graduate needs to make on the investment in postsecondary education.

Private and Social Rates of Return

In addition to individual, or private, costs and benefits of postsecondary education, there are social costs and benefits. To assess the costs and benefits of spending on education, it is necessary to estimate both the private rate of return and the social rate of return. The **private rate of return** is the yield on the investment in education that is received by the person making the investment. The **social rate of return** measures the yield to society from the resources spent on education.

private rate of return

yield on the investment in education received by the person making the investment

social rate of return

yield to society from the resources allocated to education

The cost used in calculating the private rate of return significantly understates the true cost of obtaining a postsecondary education. Education is heavily subsidized by taxpayers' dollars. Also, many students receive financial assistance from family members and scholarships from various organizations. To calculate the social rate of return, costs must include expenditures by government and non-profit institutions as well as expenditures by students and families.

On the benefit side, the returns from education are calculated on income before taxes. If we assume that firms pay workers an income equal to their productivity, the income received by graduates indicates their contribution to society. A more productive labour force is better able to provide higher quality

Labour Market Issue 12.1

Who Should Pay for Higher Education?

WWW Who should go to college or university? One answer could be, "those best qualified to benefit from higher education, regardless of family background, gender, or race." But there is the question of cost. Postsecondary education is expensive. Who should pay for it? There are two sides in the debate.

One side argues that higher education is essentially a private investment. People who undertake the investment benefit from it through higher lifetime income. Some also enjoy the learning experience. So why should postsecondary education be provided at public expense? Why shouldn't it be sold to cover cost?

Although undergraduate arts tuition fees, for example, have increased in Canada on average by 115% from $1872 in 1993–94 to $4024 in 2003–04 (the increases range from 57% in British Columbia to 167% in Alberta), students still pay less than 30% of the cost of their education. The largest portion is paid by government. Students thus receive a big scholarship and they receive this without regard to financial need: students from rich families benefit the same way as students from poor families do. Studies show that individuals from higher-income families are more likely to attend postsecondary institutions than individuals from lower-income families. Government subsidies to reduce tuition thus provide assistance to predominantly higher-income families rather than to lower-income families. Government spending on higher education involves an income transfer in the wrong direction, from the lower- to the higher-income families.

For these reasons, it is argued, the student, and not society, should bear the cost of higher education.

The other side argues that postsecondary education should be provided at less than full cost to all students because the benefits from education accrue not only to the individual student but also to society at large. A better educated labour force is likely to be a more productive one, which will result in more and better quality products. Scientific and medical advances are associated with a better educated population. Those who receive a postsecondary education are also likely to earn higher incomes and pay more taxes. Higher tax revenues allow governments to redistribute income to lower-income families. There should be a higher standard of living for all Canadians. The argument that education benefits all of society is made to support free elementary and secondary education, so why stop at the end of high school? Why not extend the same reasoning through to college and university level?

If the price of higher education is closer to its full cost, students from low-income families will be less able to afford higher education. Someone who wishes to buy a major item, such as a car or a house, can save a certain amount of money over time and then can borrow the rest, putting up the car or the house as collateral on the loan. It takes time for a student to save the necessary funds, during which the student grows older and passes beyond the usual age of attending college or university. The option to borrow does not exist because, unlike in the case of a car or house, there is no collateral to put up.

But do the student loan programs offered by the government not provide sufficient funds for students? Studies indicate that students from low-income families are more risk averse. They are reluctant to take large loans because their families cannot be counted on to repay the loans if they run into problems later. Even if loans are available, high tuition set at or close to full cost will deter these students from attending a postsecondary institution.

goods and services at a lower cost. Society also receives other benefits from spending on education. Further education makes for better informed and more responsible citizens. This suggests that the social return calculated from pre-tax earnings is a minimum return—the floor of a true overall return. Some benefits may be difficult to measure in terms of dollars and cents.

Implications of Human Capital Theory

An objection sometimes made against human capital theory is that people do not really make decisions in the manner just described. Few college or university students would calculate the rate of return to a postsecondary education. Nonetheless, evidence suggests that the decision to attend college or university is significantly influenced by the benefits and costs of postsecondary education. The usefulness of this approach to educational expenditures can be determined by comparing its predictions with actual behaviour.

Effect of Costs on Enrollment

One prediction is that any factor that reduces the cost of a college or university education should lead to an increase in postsecondary school enrollments. Scholarships, fellowships, and tuition waivers reduce the direct costs of higher education and should make educational investment more attractive. Increases in tuition fees or reductions in low-cost student loans would have the opposite effect. A reduction in the opportunity costs would also raise the rate of return to education, making college or university attendance more attractive. Many colleges and universities have recognized this fact by offering evening classes so that students may continue to work, either full-time or part-time, thus reducing the forgone costs of higher education. Research supports the prediction that postsecondary enrollments are sensitive to the costs of education.

Timing of Education Over One's Work Life

Another prediction is that investment in education will vary with age. Younger people will benefit more in monetary terms from a postsecondary education than older people. The reasons are twofold. First, older persons have fewer years of work life remaining during which to recoup the costs of the additional education. Second, as workers age, their earnings increase as a result of more work experience, training, and seniority. This increases the opportunity cost of leaving work to further one's education. The opportunity cost of leaving a job at age 40 to attend college or university is much higher than the opportunity cost at age 20. While educational patterns have been changing more recently, the vast majority of postsecondary students are still in younger age groups (18–24), as the theory suggests.

Labour Force Attachment

A third prediction is that people with a weak labour force attachment will invest less in education. The fewer years spent in the labour force, the less time there is to recoup the cost of education. This prediction seems to be supported by the trend in labour force participation rates and university enrollment of women. In the late 1940s, about 25% of women were in the labour force, compared to 85% of men. At that time, most undergraduate degrees were awarded to men. More than 50 years later, in 2003, close to 62% of women were in the labour force, many pursuing full-time careers. For these women, a postsecondary education became a much more attractive investment. The stronger labour force attachment of women has increased the attractiveness of educational expenditure. As we noted in Chapter 4, today women obtain more than half of all undergraduate degrees in Canada.

Earnings Differentials

Fourth, human capital theory predicts that people with more education should also have higher earnings in their peak work years. This prediction is supported by the age–earnings profiles in Figures 12.1A and B (pages 318–319). There are three reasons for this prediction:

- Higher earnings are necessary to compensate for the costs associated with additional schooling. If the earnings of a postsecondary graduate were no greater than those of a high school graduate, there would be little financial incentive to attend college or university. For the same reason, the annual earnings of a medical doctor must exceed those of a person with a four-year degree to keep the rate of return to a medical degree competitive.

- People with more education have fewer years in the labour force in which to recoup their investment in schooling. The high school graduate, for example, has 47 years of earnings between ages 18 and 65; the person with a Ph.D. may have only 35 years or so (from age 30 to 65) in the labour force. Fewer working years plus additional costs require that actual dollar earnings be greater for people with more years of schooling in order to induce them to invest in human capital.

- Higher earnings from education are not received until relatively later in life and are heavily discounted in terms of their present value. The earnings of doctors or lawyers are received relatively far in the future compared to those of high school graduates. To make investment in education attractive, dollar earnings must be greater for persons with more years of education as a reward for postponing earnings and consumption.

Changes in Private Returns Over Time

The rate of return on postsecondary education can vary over time. It is not a constant value. Using the supply and demand framework, in Figure 12.3 (page 328) we show how changes in the supply of and demand for workers with postsecondary degrees have affected the rate of return to postsecondary education from the early 1960s to the late 1980s. Notice the difference in notation on the axes of Figure 12.3 as compared to earlier labour market diagrams. On the vertical axis is the rate of return instead of the wage rate. The two variables are closely linked. As wage rates for college- and university-educated workers increase, so do rates of return, all other things remaining the same. On the horizontal axis is the number of workers who graduated from college or university expressed as a proportion of the total labour force.

In times of a high rate of return to college or university education, many new students will be attracted to pursuing postsecondary education. Conversely, a low rate of return will deter many potential entrants. This response to changes in the rate of return is described by the supply curve S in Figure 12.3. The supply curve relates the fraction of college or university students in the labour force to the rate of return to college or university education. The supply curve slopes upward. With a higher rate of return, more students will continue on to college or university. Corresponding to this supply curve is the demand curve D, describing employers' hiring plans for educated workers, which slopes downward. When the rate of return to postsecondary degrees/certificates is high, implying higher additional pay for college or university graduates, firms prefer to use fewer workers with a postsecondary education.

Point A describes the equilibrium rate of return for an undergraduate university degree in the late 1960s. After-tax returns for a university undergraduate education were generally estimated at between 10% and 15%. The rapid growth in the population with postsecondary degrees or certificates during the 1970s shifted the supply curve to the right. The expansion of the educated labour force resulted from the entry of the baby-boom generation into the

FIGURE 12.3

Supply of and Demand for College/University Graduates

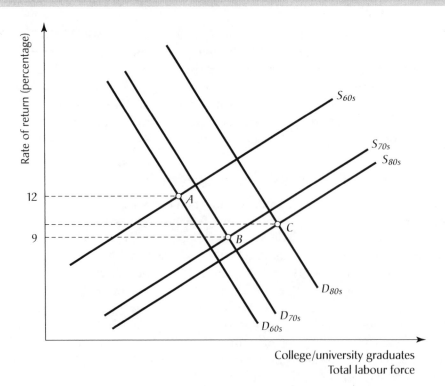

Part III: Microeconomic Theory of the Labour Market   NEL

labour market. Since demand did not increase as much, earnings of college/university graduates dropped and as a result the rate of return to a college or university education declined significantly during the 1970s, as shown by the intersection at point *B*. Estimates of the private after-tax rate of return for the decade range from 7% to 13%.[2] The decline in the rate of return was reversed in the 1980s, when the demand for workers with postsecondary degrees or certificates shifted out significantly. At the same time, fewer educated baby-boomers entered the labour force. Postsecondary education became a better investment in the 1980s than it was in the 1970s, as is reflected in point *C*.[3]

Unfortunately, estimates on returns to schooling in Canada for recent years are lacking.

In Chapter 7, we noted the growing polarization of earnings between low-skilled workers and high-skilled workers. The polarization is an indication that returns to education may have increased in recent years. As employment has shifted from the primary resource and manufacturing sectors to the dynamic services industries, the demand for skilled, educated workers has increased. Other factors noted in Chapter 7 that are having a positive effect on the demand for skilled/educated workers are increasing international competition and continual technological change.

Education and the Distribution of Individual Earnings

One of the social issues that raises major concern is the inequality of income. Since the largest component of income for most people is the amount earned from work, income inequality reflects inequality of earnings. According to 2001 Census data, 41% of Canadian workers earned less than $20 000, while nearly 13% earned $60 000 or more.[4] What can account for this wide dispersion in earnings between individuals? Human capital theory suggests a number of important factors such as years of schooling, quality of schooling, age, mental ability, and family background. To isolate the impact of each factor on earnings, economists have used the statistical method of linear regression to estimate human capital earnings functions. The dependent variable in an earnings function is an individual's annual earnings; the independent or explanatory variables are all the factors thought to influence earnings.

The simplest earnings function would include only years of schooling, or highest educational level attained. Studies of that kind have found that differences in years of schooling among individuals can account for only a small portion of the overall difference in earnings—between 10% and 15%. As shown in the age–earnings profiles in Figures 12.1A and B (pages 318–319), individuals with the same level of education have very different levels of earnings depending on their age at the time the data are collected. By including an age variable in the earnings function, approximately 30% of the dispersion in earnings can be accounted for by differences in schooling and age. If differences in age and schooling account for only 30% of the differences in individual earnings, other factors must be important in explaining earnings differentials.

Ability

Particular attention has been given to the role of ability as a cause of individual earnings differentials. People with greater ability often will invest more in education and training. If a measure of ability is not included in the earnings function, the higher earnings of the individual will be mistakenly attributed to the effect of extra schooling, when, in fact, both the amount of schooling and earnings may be due to the individual's greater ability.

Disentangling the effects of ability and schooling on earnings is fraught with problems. One problem concerns the measurement of ability. Earning an income involves many different dimensions of ability, ranging from a soprano singer's ability to hold a high C to the quick reflexes of a professional boxer to the ability of an electronics engineer to solve complex mathematical problems. Most often, however, ability is treated as synonymous with intelligence or mental capacity. To obtain an empirical measure of intelligence, most studies have used intelligence quotient (IQ) test scores, or scores on various types of aptitude tests. Whether or not IQ scores are a valid measure of intelligence is open to debate. Studies have found a strong positive relationship between IQ and educational attainment. People who are "smarter" generally also have more education.

The results of these studies have been criticized on several counts. One criticism is that measured IQ scores fail to capture many aspects of ability. This failure reduces the estimated impact of ability on earnings. A salesperson with a relatively low IQ may be highly successful and earn large commissions because of the ability to be a smooth talker. Second, ability itself may be to a large extent the result of another variable—family background.

Family Background

Family background includes such factors as parents' income, education, occupational status, and connections. Children raised in families of higher socioeconomic position may score better on IQ tests as a result of better care and parental instruction. This possibility is at the heart of the old nature versus nurture debate. How much is difference in IQ scores due to heredity or to the environment in which one is raised? The more important nurture is, the more important family background becomes as a determinant of both educational attainment and earnings and the less important inherited intelligence becomes.

How to disentangle the independent effects of family background, ability, and education on earnings is an unresolved problem. A novel approach to resolve the problem is to use large samples of identical and fraternal twins. The advantage of these samples is that identical twins do not differ genetically while fraternal twins do. This allows researchers to identify the effect of differences in ability on the earnings of persons who have identical family backgrounds. In one study that did not control either for ability or for family background among the twins in the sample, the rate of return to additional schooling was found to be 8%. When the influence of family background was controlled for, the rate of return fell to 6%. When both family background and genetic ability were introduced into the earnings function, the rate of return fell to 3%. The implication of these findings is that about two-thirds of the estimated effect of additional education on income was really due to the fact that those individuals who obtained more education were also of higher ability, or had a more favourable family background.

School Quality

Another factor that might lead to differences in earnings is variation in school quality. If two people of equal ability made the same dollar expenditure on schooling, but one received schooling of higher quality, presumably that person would receive higher earnings and a greater rate of return. As with ability, there are obvious difficulties in obtaining a measure of school quality. One approach has been to include in the earnings function a variable for average expenditures per student in the individual's school district. Studies using this approach found that attendance in higher-quality schools had a significant positive effect on earnings.

The Link Between Education and Earnings

The age–earnings profiles and empirical studies convincingly show a strong link between years or levels of formal education and the earnings of an individual. Why does more education lead to higher earnings? The answer, according to human capital theory, is that more education leads to higher productivity, which in turn is reflected in higher earnings. Additional schooling is viewed as enhancing those abilities that make people more productive at work. These abilities include logical reasoning, communication and writing skills, as well as more specific job skills learned in accounting, engineering, and other professional courses. The reason a community college graduate earns more than a high school graduate, or business majors earn more than history majors, is that they have skills that employers consider to enhance productivity and are willing to pay extra for.

Education as a Signal

Some economists disagree with the argument that more education makes a person more productive. They maintain that the primary reason that education and earnings go hand in hand is because employers use educational credentials such as degrees and certificates as a screening device. According to this view, the educational system is a means of finding out who is productive rather than a system that increases the productivity of workers. Remember that at the time of hiring, employers are not sure of the actual productivity of an applicant. To improve the probability that the best worker is chosen, prospective employees can be given aptitude tests or other tests. References can be checked. In addition, firms use educational credentials as an indicator to sort

signalling

the use of educational credentials as an indicator of a worker's potential productivity

or screen prospective workers into those most likely to be high- and low-productivity employees. When employers use the level of education as a signal of an applicant's potential productivity, it is known as **signalling**. According to the human capital approach, education and earnings are positively related because education itself increases a person's productivity on the job. Following the signalling approach, more education leads to higher earnings because employers have found that educational credentials are a reliable signal concerning trainability and subsequent productivity on the job.

The Job Competition Model

An example of the screening view of education is provided by the job competition model. Most job skills are not acquired before one enters the labour market. Rather, they are obtained through on-the-job training and learning by doing. One can view the labour market as primarily a training market where firms have training slots to be filled at the bottom of the job ladder and workers compete to be hired. From the firm's perspective, the decision regarding which worker to hire is not based on who will work for the lowest wage, but rather on who is most trainable. Because the firm is uncertain about which applicant can be trained at the least cost, it must screen or sort the applicants into a queue, from highest expected productivity to lowest based on each worker's signals. From the viewpoint of the applicants, the competition in the labour market is over obtaining access to the firm's job ladder (hence the name job competition model). To obtain access sets off a race among workers to acquire the background characteristics and credentials that employers value most.

The role of education in the job competition model is quite different than in the human capital model. According to the job competition model, education does not itself lead to greater productivity for workers. Rather, it identifies the workers who possess the character traits such as intelligence, discipline, perseverance, and communication skills that are necessary for success on the job. As in the human capital model, additional years of education result in additional earnings. These extra earnings from education, however, are *not* a payment resulting from the productivity of the person's human capital. Instead, they are a payment for the individual's pre-existing ability and intelligence that education signals.

These two views of schooling have created considerable debate over the social benefits of additional expenditures on education. According to the human capital approach, additional resources devoted to education are an important source of economic growth because they represent an investment in upgrading the work skills and productive capacity of the nation's workforce. From a screening perspective, the social benefits from additional expenditures on education are more dubious. At its best in this context, education adds to productivity by enabling firms to identify superior-quality employees. At its worst, the main effect is to set off a "paper chase" as workers invest in ever higher educational degrees in order to compete for jobs. An example is the trend toward increasing professionalization of occupations that ties professional status to educational certificates. Access to a growing number of occupational positions is monitored through educational credentials. The increasing dependence of occupational status on educational certificates causes individuals to make higher educational investments in order to achieve these certificates. As more and more people satisfy the educational entrance requirements for certain occupations, firms respond with educational upgrading of these occupations. This process has been called the "inflation of educational certificates."

Empirical Evidence

A number of studies have attempted to sort out to what degree the positive relationship between education and earnings is caused by screening and productivity. The results are not clear cut. Some empirical tests conclude that years of schooling and various types of academic credentials raise a person's income regardless of any productivity that may have been acquired in the educational process. For example, one study looked at the starting salaries of university graduates who majored in economics. The authors' idea was that if earnings are strictly related to productivity, then economics majors who took jobs that used their academic training should be paid more than those who took jobs unrelated to their field of study. They could find no difference in the starting salaries of the two groups, leading them to conclude that employers were using a university degree in economics as a means of screening applicants. An additional piece of evidence that education is used as a screening device is the so-called sheepskin effect. Studies have typically found that the rate of return on the last year of high school (for example, Grade 12) is much higher than the rate for the penultimate year (Grade 11). Such findings suggest that acquiring a high school certificate or diploma has a large effect on earnings that exceeds whatever additional knowledge was gained in that one extra year of education.

Other studies conclude that education has direct effects on productivity. One study compared the years of schooling obtained by self-employed workers with those of contractually employed workers. If education were only used as a screening device, one would expect self-employed people to have lower educational levels. People who planned on being self-employed would invest in only the amount that could be justified from a productivity point of view, while salaried workers would invest in additional schooling for its value as a credential. The study, however, found only negligible differences in educational levels between these two groups.

Independent of empirical evidence, there is a sound economic reason to doubt that education serves only as a signal for screening purposes. If education had only a signalling function, firms and workers alike would probably have found a less costly method of identifying worker productivity. The fact that education continues to be used as a central screening device indicates that it improves the skills of workers in a way that firms value.

On-the-Job Training

Formal education is one type of human capital investment. On-the-job training (OJT) is another one. OJT offered by employers varies from formal programs that are very much like classroom instruction to the simple forms of learning by doing (e.g., observing others). Relatively little is known about the extent of employer-based training in Canadian industry. This is partly due to the problem of defining what constitutes training. One "survey of surveys" suggests that roughly one-third of firms in Canada provide formal training. Estimates of the incidence of training (percentage of employees who received training) are considerably higher—between 60% and 70%—when informal training is included.[i] According to the 2003 Adult Education and Training Survey, an estimated 4.8 million workers participated in formal job-related training in 2002.[5] This represents about one-third of Canadian workers aged 25–64. Participants received on average 150 hours of training, which translates to about 25 days of training a year based on a training day of six hours. Seven out of every ten participants received some form of training support from their employers. The support ranged from providing the training, and paying for the training (either directly or by reimbursing an employee), to allowing a trainee to work a flexible schedule to accommodate training. Since 1997, the proportion of workers receiving some support from their employers in formal job-related training has declined. An increasing number of adult workers appear to take formal, job-related training on their own and at their own expense.

A few studies have compared the training efforts in Canada with those in other countries and concluded that Canadian firms train employees less than their counterparts in other major industrialized countries.[6] These conclusions are based on a range of indicators including the percentage of employees receiving training, the percentage of firms providing training, private-sector expenditures on training, and the incidence of apprenticeship training. In contrast, a Statistics Canada study using average training hours per employee as a measure of the level of training concludes that Canada's training effort is average when compared to the training level of the five European countries included in the study and the United States.[7]

On-the-job training is as much a form of human capital investment as a college or university education is since it involves costs and benefits. Where the training is clearly a separable activity, these costs can be identified fairly straightforwardly. The direct costs include the salaries of training staff and the operating and capital costs of equipment used in training. Where training takes place concurrently with production, the costs, although of the same general kind, may be more difficult to measure. Some of the trainees' time and that of their supervisors or co-workers is used in training; output is therefore less than it would be if all workers were fully trained. For the same reason,

[i] What is the distinction between formal and informal training? Two examples of definitions: The Human Resource Training and Development Survey defines formal training as programs that have "an identifiable structured plan and objectives designed to develop a worker's skill and competence." Informal training, as defined by the Small Business Panel Survey, includes training "acquired by working under normal work or production conditions, either with an experienced worker or under the direction of a supervisor."

capital cost may be higher than normal. Material may be wasted or products may be defective due to the trainee's inexperience. Workers may also bear some of the costs of acquiring OJT by agreeing to work at reduced wages during the training period. The benefit to the firm is that its workforce becomes more productive, which will result in greater profits. Workers benefit because they gain additional skills and experience that increase their earning power and bargaining strength in the labour market.

General and Specific Training

It is conventional to make a distinction between general and specific training. **General training** is training that increases a worker's productivity not only in the firm providing it, but also at other firms. An example is apprenticeship training for crafts such as electrician or carpenter where the skills learned are of general value throughout the industry. Computer skills or supervisory skills are also often transferable. Less formalized types of training such as how to operate a word processor or a bulldozer also work to enhance an employee's productivity both in the firm providing the training and in other firms. **Specific training** increases the worker's productivity only in the firm providing it, such as training in the operation of a firm's wage payment

general training

training that increases the worker's productivity not only in the firm providing the training but also in other firms

specific training

training that increases the worker's productivity only in the firm providing the training system or an assembly line job. Skill specificity may arise out of unique features of the firm's product. A computer engineer employed by IBM, for example, would develop many skills of value to IBM, but this knowledge may be of far less value to another company with computers of different design. Although few types of OJT are truly specific in nature, many job skills do have a firm-specific component. Furthermore, regardless of whether a person is a clerk, salesperson, or manager, with experience on the job each worker in the firm acquires a detailed knowledge of the organizational structure and operation of the firm that is itself a valuable but very firm-specific type of training.

Benefits and Costs of On-the-Job Training

For OJT to be undertaken, it must promise a rate of return competitive with other investments. The rate of return is a function of the benefits and costs of training, which are illustrated in Figure 12.4.

The horizontal line EG at W_A gives the wage and marginal revenue product (MRP) of the untrained worker over a work life. The stepped line $ABCD$ gives the wage and marginal revenue product of the worker who undergoes training. During the training period, the worker's wage and marginal productivity (W_0) is lower than it would have been had the worker chosen alternative employment. After training the wage rate and marginal

FIGURE 12.4

Benefits and Costs of On-the-Job Training

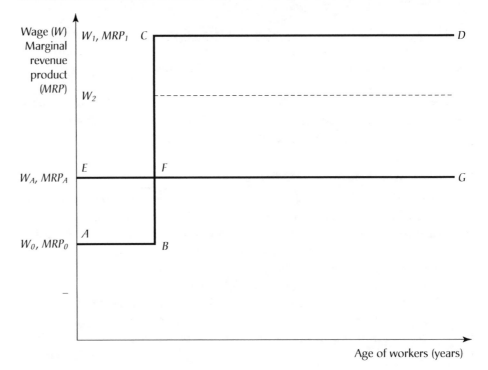

Part III: Microeconomic Theory of the Labour Market

productivity increase to W_1.[ii] The cost of training is the value of production forgone during the training process, shown by the area $AEFB$. The economic benefit is the increase in production that training makes possible, shown by the area $FCDG$. For training to be a good investment, the present value of the stream of output (in dollars) generated by the worker receiving training (the profile $ABCD$) must be at least as large as that of the output stream if no training were provided (the profile EG).

If we assume that training is a good investment, who bears the cost and reaps the benefit: the firm or the worker? The answer depends on whether the training is general or specific in nature. With general OJT, it is the worker who bears the cost of training. Without training the worker's marginal productivity is MRP_A. Competition among firms ensures that the worker is paid a wage rate W_A corresponding with this level of productivity. If the firm were to bear the cost of training, it would have to continue to pay the worker W_A even though productivity during training is only MRP_0. What inducement does the firm have to do this? In the case of general training, the answer is none. The productivity of a worker who completes the training rises to MRP_1. If the firm were able to still pay a wage of only W_A, the difference between the value of output produced and wage paid (the distance FC) would provide it with a return on its investment. Because general training is transferable, however, were the firm to pay less than W_1 the worker would quit and find employment at a firm willing to pay a wage equal to his or her productivity. Competition for labour and the transferable nature of general training make it impossible for the firm to pay a wage less than W_1. At this wage, the firm is unable to recoup its investment, so it is unwilling to bear the costs of general training. Because firms have no incentive to pay for general OJT, the workers must pay for it. The cost of general training is the drop in productivity from MRP_A to MRP_0. A worker can pay for general training by agreeing to work during the training period for a wage of only W_0. Workers have an incentive to bear this cost since once training is completed, the wage they can demand in the market will rise to W_1, providing the return on their investment.

If on-the-job training is firm-specific, it is the firm that bears the cost. Because specific OJT is non-transferable, once training is completed the productivity of the worker at any other firm in the labour market is still only MRP_A. Even though the firm that provided the training receives a level of production worth MRP_1, it need not pay the worker more than W_A since that person can do no better elsewhere. In this case the worker has no incentive to work for a lower wage of W_0 during training since it is the firm that reaps the benefit. To induce workers to acquire specific training, the firm must bear the cost of training by paying the original unskilled wage of W_A even though the worker's productivity is only MRP_0. The return on its investment is the difference between the worker's higher productivity MRP_1 and the wage W_A that it pays after training.

[ii] For simplicity, it is assumed the worker receives one "dose" of training and that the economic value of the training does not depreciate over time.

In practice, the post-training wage rate paid by the firm in the case of specific training is generally higher than the minimum W_0. One possible wage might be W_2, shown by the broken line. The reason for the wage increase is that specific training creates a situation in which the firm and the worker have some power over the other. Should the worker quit, the firm will lose its investment in training, so the firm is induced to share a portion of its return $(W_1 - W_A)$ with the worker. The firm, however, also has power over the worker. Should the worker demand a wage rate so high that it would eliminate the firm's return on its investment, the worker would be laid off. This would cause a financial loss to the worker, who could only earn the lower wage rate of W_A at any other firm.

Implications of On-the-Job Training

Whether training is general or specific has a number of implications for understanding the pattern of several labour market outcomes.

Employee Turnover

Specific on-the-job training provides a strong incentive to both firms and workers to reduce turnover from quits and layoffs. Employee turnover is costly to a firm because the firm loses its investment in specific training. Workers with specific training also stand to lose by leaving (or being forced to leave) because there is no other employer at which their productivity and their wage will be as high. One would expect, therefore, fewer quits and layoffs among workers who have relatively more specific training.

Minimum Wage

A frequent criticism of minimum wage laws is that they may lead firms to reduce the amount of general OJT provided to workers, particularly younger workers. An employer has little incentive to bear the costs of training youths because of their relatively high turnover rates. To make training attractive to the firm, the young worker must invest in himself or herself by working at a relatively low wage rate such as W_0 in Figure 12.4 (page 336). The incentive to do so is that with some experience the young worker can move to a better job with higher earnings. A minimum wage law may prevent the provision of training if it places a wage floor at a level of W_A. At this wage rate, the employer no longer finds it profitable to provide general training because the cost exceeds the worker's productivity.

Job Ladders and Internal Recruiting

Firm-specific training is also an important factor in explaining the development of job ladders and internal recruitment within firms. For many types of production processes, a vertical or hierarchical set of job tasks build on one another. They are often sufficiently unique to a firm that they can only be learned by workers starting at the bottom and working up. If all job skills were acquired through general OJT, there would be no internal labour markets since firms could readily hire a worker in the external labour market. The more important specific training is as a source of job skills, the less reliant the firm is on outside recruitment. Internal promotion and advancement will be the preferred means of filling job vacancies.

Age–Earnings Profiles

If employers expect workers to stay with them for a longer period, they will be more willing to offer specific training because there is a longer pay-out period on the investment. Workers will also be more willing to undergo training if they expect to stay with the firm longer or if they are younger. In both cases, they too have a longer time over which to reap the returns on the investment. These considerations suggest that the fraction of time spent on training will be highest early in a work life. Sometime late in the work life, it will neither pay for them to accept nor for the firm to offer any more training. There is not sufficient time left in the work life to make the investment pay off.

The pattern of declining investment in OJT during the work life carries specific implications for the age–earnings profiles observed in Figures 12.1A and B (pages 318–319). A worker's earnings capacity rises rapidly early in the work life because of the large investment in OJT. Actual earnings reflect this rapid rise in the earlier stage of the work life. A worker's stock of human capital is depreciating all the time. As time devoted to training is decreasing, the negative effect of the depreciation of skills begins to outweigh the positive impact of the diminished additional investment in additional skills. Earnings drop more rapidly near the end of the work life when the stock of skills is still depreciating and is no longer augmented by additional investment in on-the-job training.

Summary

Education is an important investment in human capital. It entails costs and benefits to the individual and to society. The costs to the individual are the direct cost of tuition, books, and other expenses and the indirect cost of the forgone earnings. The monetary benefit is the higher income the person expects to earn. For society, the costs are the opportunity costs of the tax dollars spent on education. The economic benefits are the increased production made possible by a more skilled (educated) workforce.

There are several methods one can use to find out whether or not an investment in education is worthwhile. Two methods discussed in the text are the present value method, and the internal rate of return method. The private and social rates of return are likely higher than those estimated with these two methods since education also yields non-monetary benefits.

Private rates of return to postsecondary education in Canada were relatively high in the 1960s. They declined in the 1970s and rose again during the 1980s. The increase in the 1980s was mainly due to an increase in the demand for higher-educated workers.

To quantify the effects of education on earnings, economists estimate earnings functions. Individual factors other than education affect earnings, including age, ability, and family background. In estimating earnings functions it is difficult to separate out the contribution of these interrelated factors to earnings.

There is some debate about why earnings and education are closely related. According to human capital theory the reason is that education increases productivity and higher productivity is reflected in higher earnings. The signalling approach argues that education is used by firms as a screening device to separate the more able from the less able applicants. Empirical evidence supports both views.

Investment in human capital can also take the form of on-the-job training. General training increases an individual's productivity to many potential employers. Because skills from general training are transferable between companies, the trainee bears the cost of general training. Specific training increases an individual's productivity only in the firm that provides the training. Since the skills are not transferable, the firm bears the cost of specific training. The distinction between general and specific training is useful in understanding employee turnover, the effect of minimum wage legislation on firms' training efforts, recruitment policies of firms, and the shape of the age–earnings profiles.

Key Terms

age–earnings profile (page 317)
cost–benefit analysis (page 318)
general training (page 335)
internal rate of return (page 324)
present value (page 321)

private rate of return (page 324)
signalling (page 332)
social rate of return (page 324)
specific training (page 335)

Weblinks

For information on the National Graduates Survey
www.statcan.gc.ca/imdb-bmdi/5012-eng.htm

For the Statistics Canada publication "Education Matters"
www5.statcan.gc.ca/bsolc/olc-cel/olc-cel?catno=81-004-X&CHROPG=1&
lang=eng

For statistics on postsecondary education
www.caut.ca

For information on the 2003 Adult Education and Training Survey
www.statcan.gc.ca/daily-quotidien/040430/dq040430b-eng.htm

For an international perspective on employee training
www5.statcan.gc.ca/bsolc/olc-cel/olc-cel?lang=eng&catno=89F0096X

Discussion Questions

1. The age–earnings profiles in Figures 12.1A and B (pages 318–319) rise steeply early on, then flatten and eventually fall. Explain the falling part of the earnings profile.

2. Empirical studies have found that the rate of return declines with additional years of education. How could you explain this? Does the "sheepskin effect" contradict the findings of a diminishing rate of return?

3. In Canada, postsecondary education is heavily subsidized by the government. Students do not bear the full cost of their education. What are the reasons for public subsidies? While there may be good reasons for subsidizing postsecondary education, there are also drawbacks. Explain what these drawbacks are.

4. Human capital theory predicts that people with weak labour force attachment will invest less in education. Why?

5. Why are the costs of general training most likely to be borne by the trainee, whereas in the case of firm-specific training the costs are shared by the employer and the trainee?

6. There are strong reasons for expecting underinvestment in training programs with a large element of general skills, on the part of employers as well as employees. Present a brief explanation for this underinvestment.

7. Which type of vocational training will most likely require more government subsidies: general training, or firm-specific training? Explain.

Using the Internet

Go to the Statistics Canada website at www.statcan.ca. Follow the links: Our Products and Services, Internet Publications (Free), Education, 81-595-M Culture, Tourism and the Centre for Education Statistics—Research Papers. In the chronological index, look up the report "Education and labour market pathways of young Canadians between age 20 and 22: An overview." The report, using data from the Youth in Transition Survey, provides an overview of the major pathways between high school, postsecondary education, and the labour market undertaken by Canadian youth. Some youth, for example, start out in the workforce directly after secondary school, others pursue postsecondary studies full-time, and still others combine school with work. Some take advantage of the "second chance system" to return to school after having started out in the workforce.

1. Compare your own transitions from high school to postsecondary education and the labour market to the major pathways described in the report. Do your own educational and labour market pathways closely resemble those taken by the majority of young people surveyed in the report, or do they differ from their pathways?

2. Reflecting about your choice of pathways, list the factors that influenced your education or work choices. Did any of the human capital investment considerations discussed in Chapter 12 enter your education and career choices?

3. After having made the transition from school to full-time work, do you expect to return to school or to take training courses at one point in your future work life?

Exercises

1. Based on the human capital approach, explain graphically why medical doctors work on average more hours per week than most other professions.

2. If firms fill most jobs by promotion from within, what does this reveal about the type of training they provide their employees?

3. Assume that after graduating from high school you had to decide whether to enroll in an apprenticeship training program or to enroll in a certificate program at a community college. What economic criteria would you apply in making this decision?

4. Assume that you are deciding whether or not to acquire a four-year university degree in economics. Your only consideration at this moment is the degree as an investment for yourself. The direct costs per year are the tuition fees of $1500 and purchases of books and other course material of $400. The government pays the university an amount equal to four times the amount of the tuition fees to cover the cost per student. If you do not go to university, you will earn $20 000 per year as an acrobat during the first four years with a salary increase of 5% from the fifth year on. With a university degree, however, you know that you can earn $30 000 per year as a circus manager for the first four years after graduation with an annual increase of 6% thereafter. Because of the nature of the chosen occupation, your time horizon for the investment decision is exactly 10 years after graduating from university; that is, if the investment decision is to be worthwhile it must be so within a 10-year period. The market rate of interest is 5%. Would you make the investment in the degree? Use either the present value or internal rate of return approach for your calculation.

5. Suppose educational certificates and degrees are used as a screening device by firms and are responsible for the higher earnings of college and university graduates. Why might the private rate of return to college or university be relatively high, yet the social rate of return be relatively low?

References

[1]Allen, M., and Vaillancourt, C. (2004). *Class of 2000: Profile of Postsecondary Graduates and Student Debt*. Culture, Tourism and the Centre for Education Statistics— Research Papers. Ottawa: Statistics Canada (Catalogue no. 81-595-MIE20040016).

[2]Vaillancourt, F., and Henriques, I. (1986). "The Returns to University Schooling in Canada." *Canadian Public Policy*, 12: 449–458.

[3]Freeman, R., and Needels, K. (1995). "Skill Differentials in Canada in an Era of Rising Labour Market Inequality." In D. Card and R. Freeman (Eds.), *Small Differences That Matter*. Chicago: University of Chicago Press.

[4]Statistics Canada. (2003). 2001 *Census: Analysis series. Earnings of Canadians: Making a Living in the New Economy*. Ottawa: Minister of Industry (Catalogue no. 96F0030XIE2001013), p. 24.

[5]Peters, V. (2004). *Working and Training: First Results of the 2003 Adult Education and Training Survey*. Ottawa: Statistics Canada (Catalogue no. 81-595-MIE – No. 015).

[6]Betcherman, G. (1992). "Are Canadian Firms Underinvesting in Training?" *Canadian Business Economics*, 1: 25–33.

[7]Kapsalis, C. (1998). "An International Comparison of Employee Training." *Perspectives on Labour and Income*, 10. Ottawa: Statistics Canada (Catalogue no. 75-001-XPE): 23–28.

APPENDIX

Chart 1

Working Age Population in Canada and the United States, 1976–2011

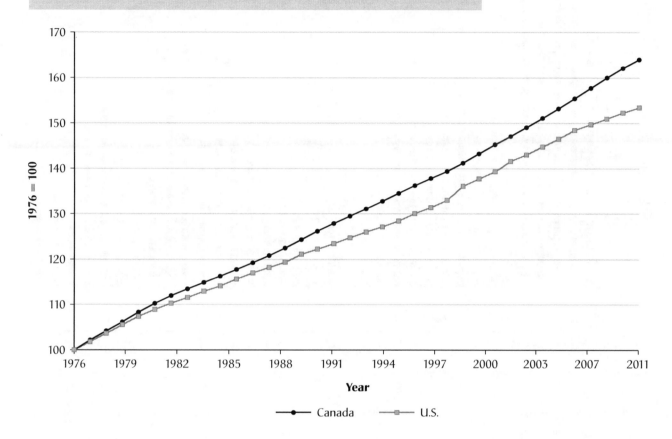

All labour market data (except for population) refer to population aged 15 and over in Canada and 16 and over in the United States.

Source: Statistics Canada CANSIM, Table 282-0002 and Table 051-0001

CHART 2

Labour Force in Canada and the United States, 1977–2011

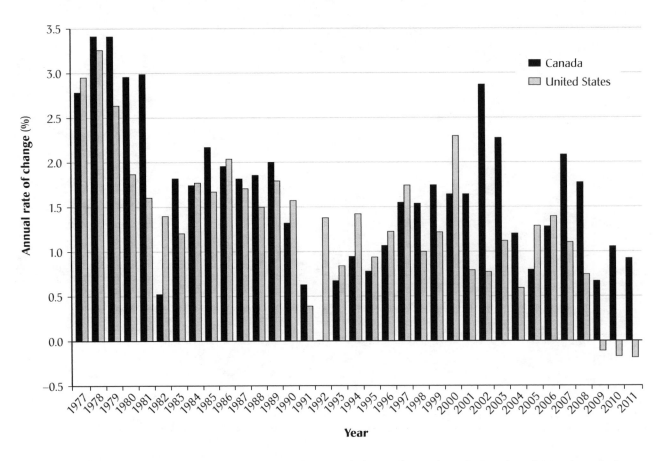

All labour market data (except for population) refer to population aged 15 and over in Canada and 16 and over in the United States.

CHART 3

Employment in Canada and the United States, 1977–2011

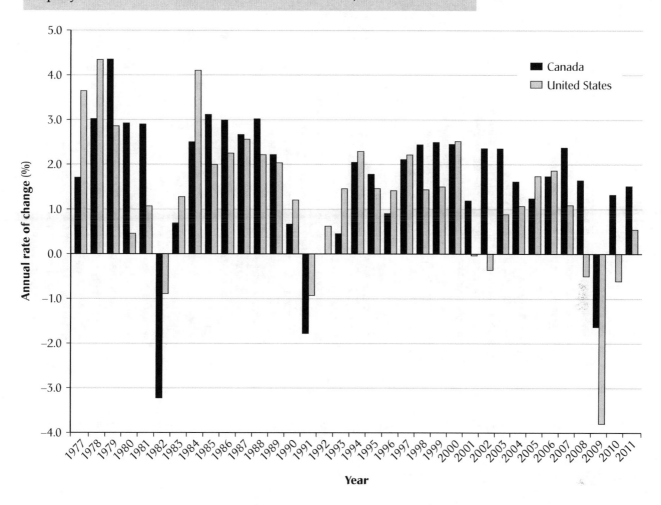

All labour market data (except for population) refer to population aged 15 and over in Canada and 16 and over in the United States.

CHART 4

Unemployment in Canada and the United States, 1976–2011

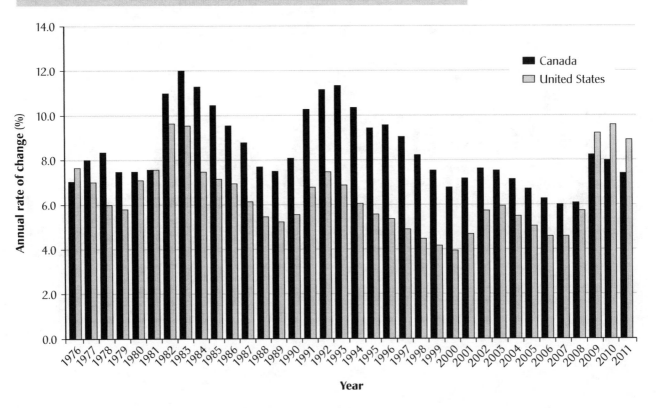

All labour market data (except for population) refer to population aged 15 and over in Canada and 16 and over in the United States.

Source: Statistics Canada CANSIM, Table 282-0002 and Table 051-0001

Glossary

actual working hours total hours actually worked (5)

adjustment lag period during which workers and employers react to changes in the wage rate (11)

affirmative action policy that promotes employment equity for women, members of visible minorities, people with disabilities, and Aboriginal people (11)

age–earnings profile average hourly or annual earnings for people of different ages with the same level of education (12)

aggregate labour demand the total number of jobs made available by firms, government agencies, and non-governmental organizations (5)

average labour productivity the output produced per worker in a given period (7)

backward-bending supply curve for labour a supply curve for labour that switches from a positive slope at lower wage rates to a negative slope at higher wage rates, with the substitution effect dominating at low wage rates and the income effect dominating at high wage rates (8)

base wage rate the wage rate that applies to the lowest-paid classification for workers in a bargaining unit (7)

birth rate the number of births per 1000 of population (4)

business cycle the more or less regular pattern of expansion and contraction in economic activity around full employment output (4)

Canada Labour Code labour standards and practices for industries that fall under federal jurisdiction, and for their employers and employees (3)

change in demand a shift in the demand curve resulting from a change in a factor, other than the price, that influences the demand for a product or service (2)

change in supply a shift in the supply curve resulting from a change in a factor, other than the price, that influences the supply of a product or service (2)

change in the quantity demanded a movement along the demand curve in response to a change in the price of the product or service (2)

change in the quantity supplied a movement along the supply curve in response to a change in the price of the product or service (2)

circular flow model a visual model of the economy that shows how goods and services and money flow between households and firms via markets (2)

civilian working-age population (labour force source population) the Canadian population aged 15 years and over excluding full-time members of the Armed Forces, institutional residents, persons living on Native reserves, and residents of the Yukon, Nunavut, and the Northwest Territories (4)

command economy an economy in which the decisions about resource allocation are made by the state (1)

compensating wage differential increase in the wage rate that compensates workers for undesirable working conditions (11)

Consumer Price Index (CPI) a measure of the price of a basket of goods and services bought by a typical family (7)

cost–benefit analysis a comparison of the costs and benefits of an investment (12)

craft union a union whose members all possess a certain craft or skill (10)

cyclical unemployment (demand-deficient unemployment) unemployment that arises because the economy does not generate enough jobs for those seeking one (6)

demand curve a graph of the relationship between the price of a good and the quantity demanded (2)

demand-deficient unemployment see *cyclical unemployment* (6)

demand for labour the stocks of job vacancies and employed workers (2)

demogrant a lump sum payment to an individual based on membership in a particular demographic group (8)

dependency rate the ratio of retirees to taxpaying workers (4)

derived demand the demand for workers that is derived from the demand for goods and services (2)

diminishing returns additional output decreases as a result of hiring one more worker, when other factors are fixed (2)

discouraged workers persons who want a job but have given up looking for work (6)

duration of unemployment the average time each person spends unemployed (6)

economic rent wage rate received in excess of the reservation wage rate (8)

efficiency wages wage rates paid in excess of the equilibrium level in order to increase productivity (10)

employed describes a person who works for pay or profit during the reference week of the Labour Force Survey (4)

employment equity all barriers to employment have been removed and equitable treatment of employees exists (3)

employment rate the ratio of employment to working-age population (5)

Engel's law expenditures on necessities such as food are a decreasing proportion of one's income as real income increases, while expenditures on rent and clothing remain constant and expenditures on luxuries increase in proportion (5)

equalizing differences the features of a job that compensate for wage rates that are lower than in other jobs (11)

equilibrium price the price at which the quantity demanded equals the quantity supplied (2)

factor market the market in which factors of production are exchanged (2)

factors of production the inputs used to produce goods and services (labour, land, and capital) (2)

featherbedding retaining workers who would otherwise be made redundant by technological change (10)

fertility rate the number of births per 1000 women aged 15 to 49 years (4)

fiscal policy changes in government spending and taxation (6)

flow variable a variable whose quantity is measured per unit of time (2)

Fordism a mass production system that combines a small group of highly skilled managers and technically trained personnel with a workforce having relatively low educational attainment and vocational skills organized in a vertical hierarchy (2)

free-market economy an economy in which the decisions about resource use are made by private households and firms (1)

frictional unemployment unemployment associated with the normal turnover of labour that is inevitable in a well-functioning labour market (6)

fringe benefits job-related benefits paid by the employer (5)

full employment when the actual rate of unemployment equals the natural rate of unemployment (6)

functional flexibility internal labour market rules that give employers greater freedom to move employees from one job to another within the firm (5)

functional income distribution the share of national income going to the owners of the factors of production, labour, and capital (7)

general training training that increases the worker's productivity not only in the firm providing the training but also in other firms (12)

globalization the integration of countries through growth in foreign trade and foreign investment (2)

gross domestic product (GDP) value of the goods and services produced in a given year (9)

gross national product (GNP) the total income earned by Canadians in a given year (7)

hidden unemployed discouraged workers who do not show up as unemployed on the Labour Force Survey (6)

hours paid hours for which workers are paid regardless of whether they were working or not (5)

human capital human resources considered in terms of their contributions to the economy, as in skills, education, etc. (8)

incidence of unemployment the proportion of people in the labour force entering the state of unemployment in a given period (6)

income effect (demand) the effect of changes in price on how much a consumer can buy with a given income (2)

income effect (supply) the change in hours of work caused by a change in income (8)

income elasticity of demand the relationship between changes in real income and changes in the quantity demanded (5)

increasing returns to scale the percentage increase in output that is relatively greater than the percentage change in all the factors of production (9)

industrial union a union whose members all work in the same industry (10)

inflation an increase in the overall level of prices in the economy (7)

internal labour market personnel policy of firms by which job openings are filled from within the ranks of firms' own employees (1)

internal rate of return the discount rate that equalizes the present values from both the benefits and the costs of an investment (12)

invisible hand the price mechanism that coordinates individual actions in a market (1)

job rationing practice of employers paying wages that create an excess of workers seeking employment and a shortage of jobs (10)

job search the process of matching workers and available jobs (10)

labour force the number of people who are either employed or unemployed (4)

labour force participation rate the percentage of the working-age population that is in the labour force (4)

labour force source population see *civilian working-age population* (4)

labour hoarding practice of firms to retain workers during a downturn in the economy in order to avoid the possibility of temporarily laid off workers' no longer being available when the economy returns to normal levels (7)

labour income earnings and supplementary labour income combined (7)

labour market the interaction of buyers and sellers of labour services (2)

labour market barriers restrictions on the mobility of workers from one job to another (11)

labour productivity the output per worker (9)

labour's share labour income as a ratio of total income (GNP) (7)

labour supply curve a graph showing the number of hours of work offered in relation to the wage rate (8)

law of diminishing returns in the short run, a point will be reached at which the extra contribution of the next worker to total output will be less than that of the previously hired worker (9)

law of downward-sloping demand there is an inverse relationship between the price and the quantity demanded (2)

long run a period of time during which all factors of production can be changed (2)

marginal benefit the additional benefit (1)

marginal cost the additional cost resulting from doing something (1)

marginal labour cost (MLC) the additional cost of hiring one more worker (10)

marginal productivity of labour (MPL) extra output obtained by adding one more worker or having a worker work one more hour (5)

marginal revenue (MR) the extra revenue from selling one more unit of output (9)

marginal revenue product (MRP) the extra revenue obtained from selling the output of an additional worker (9)

marginal tax rate the proportion of any additional income earned that is paid in taxes (8)

marginal workers workers with a weak attachment to the labour force (6)

market the interaction of buyers and sellers, in which a price is established and a product or service exchanged (2)

market discrimination different responsibilities and benefits based on characteristics unrelated to job performance (11)

mixed economy a combination of the command system and the free-market system (1)

monopsony a market in which there is only one buyer (10)

moonlighting multiple jobholding (5)

monetary policy changes in money supply by the Bank of Canada (6)

mortality rate the number of deaths per 1000 of population (4)

natural population growth the difference between the numbers of births and deaths (4)

natural rate of unemployment the unemployment rate that exists when the economy is functioning at full capacity (6)

net wages gross wages minus taxes and other payroll deductions (7)

nominal wage the rate of payment to workers in current dollars (7)

non-standard employment employment that is not full-time for a full year (5)

normal good a good for which demand increases as one's income increases (8)

normative statement a statement about how the world ought to be (1)

not in the labour force describes a person who is neither employed nor unemployed (4)

numerical flexibility a company's practice of contracting out and making greater use of temporary or part-time workers to improve flexibility in its workforce (5)

occupational wage structure differences in wage rates between occupations in the labour market (11)

open economy an economy in which imports and exports represent a large percentage of overall economic activity (5)

opportunity cost value of the best forgone alternative when a decision is made (1)

own-account self-employment entrepreneurs without paid employees (5)

part-time employment the number of people working less than 30 hours per week on their main job (5)

pay equity equal pay for work of equal value (3)

payroll tax a tax levied on employers, based on the level of employment, usually proportional to the firm's payroll (5)

personal income distribution the share of national income going to groups of families or individuals (7)

positive statement a statement about how the world is (1)

pre-market discrimination denial of equal opportunities to develop natural abilities and talents during pre-employment years (11)

present value the current value of a future sum of money (12)

price elasticity of demand the responsiveness of quantity demanded to a change in price (2)

price elasticity of supply the responsiveness of quantity supplied to a change in price (2)

private rate of return yield on the investment in education received by the person making the investment (12)

product market the market in which goods and services are exchanged (2)

profit the difference between revenues and costs (1)

quasi-fixed labour costs non-wage costs to hiring employees that are not related to the hours of work (9)

real average labour income total annual labour income, adjusted for inflation, divided by average annual number of paid workers (7)

real wage the quantity of goods and services that can be bought with the nominal wage (7)

recession a period during which the total production of goods and services falls for at least two consecutive quarters (4)

reservation wage rate the lowest wage rate an individual is willing to work for (8)

salaried worker worker paid by the week or longer time period (7)

scale effect the change in the number of employees hired as a result of changes in the amount of product sold (9)

scarcity limitation of a society's resources (1)

seasonal unemployment unemployment resulting from the decline in the number of jobs at certain times of the year (6)

severance pay a lump-sum payment to an employee upon termination of employment (3)

shortage a situation in which quantity demanded is greater than quantity supplied (2)

short run a period of time during which at least one factor of production remains fixed (2)

signalling the use of educational credentials as an indicator of a worker's potential productivity (12)

social rate of return yield to society from the resources allocated to education (12)

specific training training that increases the worker's productivity only in the firm providing the training (12)

standard working hours the number of hours in a standard workweek as established by law, collective agreement, or company policy (5)

statistical discrimination discrimination that results from imperfect information in the screening process of job applicants (11)

stock variable a variable whose quantity is measured at a given point in time (2)

structural unemployment unemployment resulting from a mismatching of workers and job opportunities based either on skills or on geography (6)

substitution effect (demand) (labour market) changes in the wage rate encourage employers to substitute capital for labour and labour for capital (9)

substitution effect (demand) (product market) changes in price encourage consumers to substitute one product for another (2)

substitution effect (supply) leisure and work hours are substituted for each other as the wage rate changes (8)

supplementary labour income non-wage benefits received by an employee (7)

supply curve a graph of the relationship between the price of a good and the quantity supplied (2)

supply of labour the stocks of employed and unemployed workers (2)

surplus a situation in which the quantity demanded by consumers is less than the quantity supplied (2)

technological unemployment unemployment due to advances in technical and organizational know-how occurring at a faster pace than the ability to find new uses for labour (6)

total factor productivity the increase in output obtained from the same amount of inputs into the production process (5)

total income the total of labour compensation and unearned income (7)

Toyotism an organizational model involving flexible management forms of semi-independent groups linked laterally rather than vertically (2)

underemployed describes workers who are obliged to take part-time jobs although they prefer to work full-time (5)

unemployed describes a person without work, available for work, and looking for work (4)

unemployment hysteresis the dependency of the natural rate of unemployment on the actual unemployment rate (6)

unemployment rate percentage of the labour force that is unemployed (6)

union density ratio of the number of employees belonging to a union to the total number of paid employees (3)

utility the satisfaction or well-being a household receives from consuming a good or service (1)

wage earner worker paid by the hour or the day (7)

wage elasticity of labour demand the change in quantity demanded in response to a change in the wage rate (9)

wage rate the price of an hour of work established in the labour market (2)

wage rate elasticity of labour supply the responsiveness of quantity supplied to changes in the wage rate (8)

wage rate subsidy a payment by government to an employer to assist in paying wages (10)

Index

Page numbers in **bold** indicate key terms. Page numbers followed by an *f* indicate material within figures.

Ability
  and earnings differentials, 330
  and wage rate differentials, 305
Aboriginal peoples
  excluded from civilian working-age population, 72
  unemployment, 157
Absenteeism
  and aging labour force, 80
Actual working hours, **132**
Adjustment lags, 297–99, **298**
Affirmative action, **309**
Age
  and decision to work, 215–16
  and earnings, 198–99
Age composition of the labour force, 76–81
Age discrimination, 56
Age–earnings profile, **317**
Aggregate labour demand, **107**
Aging of the labour force
  and absenteeism, 80
  and corporate organizational structures, 78
  and job advancement, 78
  job turnover rates, 80
  long-duration unemployment, 80
  and occupational shortages, 81
  and part-time work, 80
  and the Social Security system, 78–80
Aging of the population, 72, 75–76
  labour force turnover rates, 80
Alberta
  minimum age, 50
  statutory holidays, 52
  vacations with pay, 52
Anti-Inflation Program (AIP), 196
Apprenticeship system, 156
Asia, immigrants from, 84
Auto industry, Canadian, and globalization, 42–43
Average labour productivity, **190**. *See also*
    Productivity; Labour productivity
Average weekly earnings, changes in, 193–94

Baby-boom, 72
  and age structure of the population, 77–78
  aging of, 75

and fertility rates, 76
Backward-bending supply curve for labour, **223**–24
Bank of Canada, monetary policy, 196–97
Base wage rates, **194**
Beach, C., 199–200
Bell Canada, 311
Benefits, non-wage, 184
Betcherman report, 117
Birth control, 94–95
Birth rate, **75**
Blacks, foreign-born, and unemployment, 157
Brain drain, 70, 227, 229, 263
Brain gain, 70
British Columbia
  freedom of belief, 56
  immigrants to, 87
  minimum age, 50
  statutory holidays, 52
  vacations with pay, 52
Business cycle, **81**
Business licensing, 302

Canada Labour Code, **49**
Canada Pension Plan (CPP), 78–79
  as payroll tax, 50
Canada–United States Automobile Agreement,
    260, 261
Canadian Automobile Workers (CAW), 283
Casual jobs, 127
Centrally planned economy. *See* Command economy
Chain rule, and labour force participation rate, 88
Change in demand, **25**
Change in quantity demanded, **26**
Change in supply, **27**
Childcare, subsidized, 222
  and tax laws, 223
Children
  and decision to work, 216–18
  decline in numbers per family, 94–95
  opportunity cost of, 95, 216–18
China, immigrants from, 84
Circular flow model, **37**
Civilian working-age population, **72**
Clark, Colin, 113

COLA (cost of living allowance) clauses, 131, 195
Collective bargaining, and wage decline, 201
Command economy, **9**
Compensating wage differential, **303**
Competition, 260
Constitution Act, 1867, 49
Consumer Price Index (CPI), **186**
Consumption time, 213
Contract jobs, 127
Contracting out, 116
Cory, Peter. 296
Cost–benefit analysis, **318**–21
Craft unions, **283**
Cyclical unemployment, **168**

Daycare, 222
Decision making, optimal, 10–11
Deferred payments, 184
Deindustrialization, 118
Demand, derived, 39
Demand, market, 24–26
    change in, 26
    change in quantity demanded, 26
    downward-sloping, law of, 24
    factors influencing, 24
    income effect, 24
Demand curve, **24**
Demand curve for labour, 243–51
    decision to hire, 245–48
    factors of production, 243–48
    long run, 249–50
    short run, 243–48
Demand-deficient unemployment, **168**
Demand for labour, **40**
    input of unions on, 282–83
    and quasi-fixed labour costs, 263–64
Demand for leisure, 214
Demogrant, **219**
Demographic changes, and non-standard
        employment, 129
Dependency rate, **79**
Derived demand, **39**
Deskilling of labour force, debate over, 118–20
Diminishing returns, **26**
Disappearance of the middle class, 131, 199–202
Discouraged workers, **145**–46
    in Newfoundland, 142
Discrimination, 300–1
    affirmative action, 309–10

employer prejudice, 307–8
equal employment opportunity legislation, 309
equal pay legislation, 310
equal value legislation, 310–12
and imperfect information, 308–9
male-female wage differences, 306–7
pay equity, 310
policies to combat, 309–12
theories of, 307–9
worker prejudice, 308
Domestic population. *See* Population
Douglas, Paul, 188
Downsizing, 89
Duration of employment, **153**–54

Early retirement, factors affecting, 90
Earnings, **183**–84
    age gap, 198–99
    and education, 317, 333
    gaps, 197–202
    gender gap, 197–98
    occupational polarization, 199–202
Earnings differentials
    ability, 330
    education as signal, 331–32
    and family background, 330–31
    and human capital theory, 327
    and school quality, 331
Echo generation, 75
Economic hardship, and unemployment rate, 147–48
Economic rent, **230**–31
Economically active, 147
Economically inactive, 147
Economists as policy makers, 14
Economy, circular flow model of, 37
Education
    and decision to work, 218
    and distribution of individual earnings, 329–31
    and earnings, 317
    job competition model, 332–33
    labour force participation, 89, 94
    and skill differential, 200
    unemployment, 156, 158
    and wage rate differentials, 305
    who pays for, 325
Education investment, 317–25
    changes in private returns, 327–29
    cost–benefit analysis of, **318**–21

earnings differentials, 327
effects of costs on enrollment, 326
and human capital theory, 326–27
internal rate of return, 324
labour force attachment, 326–27
net present value of, 323
present value of, 321–23
social rate of return, 324
vs. work life, 326
Educational sector, labour shortages in, 81
Efficiency, 6
Efficiency wages, **290**
Employed, **71**
Employment
changes in level of, 107–11
contracting out, 116
deskilling debate, 118–20
factors causing shift to service sector, 113–17
full, 167
hours of work, 132–36
international competition, 116
non-standard, 120–32
occupational shifts, 117–20
and productivity rates, 113–15
service-sector, shift to, 111–13
shifts in the composition of, 111–20
unions' impact on, 282–86
white-collar jobs, 117
Employment agencies, 165
Employment determination
and wage rate in a competitive labour market, 269–71
and wage rate under monopsony, 271–73
Employment discrimination, **56**
Employment equity, **56**
Employment growth, 1947–2003, 107
Employment insurance (EI), 304
and Canadian unemployment, 161–63
and decision to work, 220–22
and labour force participation rate, 89
legislation, 57–58
and natural rate of unemployment, 170–72
as payroll tax, 50
premiums, 129–30
unemployment and, 148
Employment Insurance Act, 1997, 58
Employment rate, **108**, 109
vs. unemployment rate, 149–50
Employment relationship, long-term, 34–35

Employment standards
federal and provincial jurisdiction for, 49–50
hours of work, 51
minimum age, 50
minimum wage, 53
overtime pay, 51–52
pay equity, 53–54
severance pay, 54–55
statutory holidays, 52
vacations with pay, 52
Engel, Ernst, 115
Engel's law, **115**–16
Equal employment opportunities, 309
Equal pay legislation, 310
Equalizing difference, 300, **303**
Equilibrium price, **29**
change in, 30
Equity vs. efficiency, 6–7, 8
Espanola, 268
Europe, immigrants from, 83–84

Factor market, **37**–38
Factors of production, **37**, 243–44
Family allowance program, 219
Family background, and earnings differentials, 330–31
Family income, 199–200
Family size, and work, 216–18
Featherbedding, 283
Federal government
statutory holidays, 50
vacations with pay, 52
See also Government
Fertility, and work, 216–18
Fertility gap, Canada vs. United States, 76
Fertility rate, 72, **75**
declining, 76
Fiscal policy, **168**
Flow variable, **39**
Fordism, **22**
Foreign exchange rate, 23
Free market economy, 9–**10**
Free rider problem, 335
Free trade, 261
Freedom of belief, 56
Frictional unemployment, **164**
Fringe benefit, **129**–30
Full employment, **167**

Functional flexibility, 131
Functional income distribution, **191**

General Agreement on Tariffs and Trade (GATT), 261
General Social Survey (GSS), 127
General training, **335**
Germany, 115
Globalization
    and Canadian auto industry, 42–43
    and labour markets, 41–43
Government
    downsizing, 89
    federal jurisdiction in labour market, 49
    provincial jurisdiction in labour market, 49–50
    role in market economy, 6–7
    trade policy, 253
    See also Federal government
Government policies
    impact on labour market, 274–82
    and labour productivity, 259–60
    minimum wage rate, 274–76
    payroll taxes, 277–81
    wage subsidy, 281–82
Government regulation
    employment insurance, 57–58
    employment standards, 50–54
    health and safety, 57
    human rights, 56
    union–management relationships, 58–59
    workers' compensation, 57
Gross domestic product (GDP), **255**–56
Gross national product (GNP), **188**

Health and safety legislation, 57
Healthcare, labour shortage in, 81
Hidden unemployed, **145**
Holmes, Sherlock, 67
Home workers, employment standards for, 51–52
Hourly wages, changes in, 193–94
Hours paid, 132
Hours of work, 51, 132–36
    changes in distribution of, 135–36
    factors affecting, 134–35
Human capital, **218**
Human capital theory, and education investment,
        326–29
Human resources management (HRM), nature of, 8
Human rights, 56

Idleness, 213
Immigrants
    assessed classes, 84
    classes of, 84–85
    destinations of, 87
    deteriorating labour market position of, 86
    non-assessed classes, 84
    origins of, 83–84
    rising skill levels of, 85–86
    underutilization of, 70–71
Immigration
    and the business cycle, 81
    and demographic factors, 82–83
    effects of, 87
    and labour, 263
    and the labour force, 72
    net, 81
    points-based system, 85–86
    and population base, 81–88
    and recessions, 81
    target plans for, 84–85
Immigration and Refugee Protection Act (Bill C–11), 85
Immigration policies, 15–16
Incidence of unemployment, **152**
Income, non-employment, 218–22
Income effect (demand), **24**
Income effect (supply), **214**
Income elasticity of demand, **116**
Incomplete information, in labour markets, 35
Increasing return to scale, **260**
Index of real hourly wages, 185–86
Indifference curve of labour analysis, 234–39
Indifference map, 236
Individual supply curve, 222–26
Industrial relations. *See* Labour relations
Industrial restructuring, 173
Industrial union, 283
Inefficiency, 6
Inflation, 131, **186**
Information, sources of, 67–68
Information-based work, 119–20
Information economy, 119
Information technology, and the economy, 119–20
Innovation, 22
Institutional forces
    corporate personnel policies, 12
    internal labour market, 12
    and labour markets, 12–13
    unions, 12–13

wage rates, 12–13
Intelligence quotient (IQ) tests, 330
Interest rate, 23
Internal labour market, **12**
Internal migration and labour supply curve, 227–29
Internal rate of return, **324**
International Ladies' Garment Workers Union, 283
International trade, 41
  and the labour market, 261
  policies and competition, 260
Invisible hand, **12**
Involuntary part-time workers, 124–25

Japan, 92, 115
Job competition model, 332–33
Job losers, 153
Job rationing, **289**–90
Job search, **286**–87
Jurisdiction in labour market
  federal government, 49
  provincial governments, 49–50

Knowledge-based economy, 119–20

Labour
demand for, 40
  market supply curve for, 227–31
  supply of, **40**
Labour compensation. *See* Labour income; Wages
Labour demand
  skilled vs. unskilled workers, 200
Labour economics, **7**
  relevance of, 7–8
Labour economists, role of, 6–7
Labour force, **71**
  age composition of, 76–81
  aging of, 72
  Canadian, growth of, 72
  changes in skills composition of, 118–20
  components of, 71–74
  dependency rate, 79
  employed, 71
  gender composition of, changes in, 95–97
  growth rate of, 72
  immigration as source for, 72
  not in the, 71
  and population base, 75–88
  underutilization of immigrants, 70–71
  unemployed, 71

withdrawals from, 74
Labour force participation
  changes in, 88–95
  and children, 216–18
Labour force participation rate(s), **73**–74, 88–89
  calculating, 88
  male vs. female trends in, 88–89
  and marriage break-ups, 95
  men, 90
  and labour-saving technology, 95
  provincial 98–99
  and standard of living, 95
  social attitudes and, 92
  women, 90–95, 96
  youth, 97–98
Labour force source population, **72**
Labour Force Survey (LFS), 71, 107, 127
  measuring unemployment, 144
Labour hoarding, **191**
Labour income, **184**
  changes in average weekly earnings and hourly
    wages, 193–94
  changes by sector, 192
  changes in total, and labour's share, 188–91
  functional income distribution, 191
  personal income distribution, 191
  real average, 192
  sources of information about, 188–97
Labour market(s), **23**
  competitive, and wage rate and employment
    determination, 269–71
  diversity among jobs and workers, 35
  factors of production, 37
  features of, 33–37
  federal jurisdiction within, 49
  flow approach, 39–41
  fragmented nature of, 35–37
  government intervention in, 59
  and globalization, 41–43
  impact of government policies on, 274–82
  lengthy employment relations, 34–35
  and national economy, 37–39
  nature of, 7–8
  people supply labour services, 33–34
  stock approach to, 41
  and use of supply and demand curves, 36–37
Labour market barriers, 299–302, **300**
  discrimination, 300–1
  geography, 301

government regulations, 302
  lack of education or training, 302
  lack of information, 300–1
  language, 301
  union-imposed regulations, 302
Labour market equilibrium, 298*f*
Labour market outcomes, 11
Labour market process, 11–14
  institutional forces, 12–13
  market forces, 11–12
  sociological forces, 13–14
Labour productivity, **255**–63
  economic conditions, 258–59
  factors affecting, 258–63
  government policies, 259–60
  labour force, 262–63
  management techniques, 262
  quality and quantity of capital, 262
  and scale of business operations, 260–61
  structure of the economy, 258
  studies about, 263
Labour relations
  federal and provincial jurisdiction for, 49–50
  nature of, 8
Labour services, supplied by people, 33–34
Labour supply, 71
  factors affecting, 72
  and the fertility rate, 72
  indifference curve analysis of, 234–39
  wage rate elasticity of, 225
  women, 72
Labour supply curve, **223**
  backward-bending, 223–24
Labour's share, **188**
Law of diminishing returns, **244**
Law of downward-sloping demand, **24**
Leisure,
  demand for, 214
  price of, 214, 220
Literacy, and wages, 259
Long run, **26**, 249–50
Low wage earners, 182
Luxuries, 31–32

Macroeconomic performance, Canada and U.S.
  compared, 160
Major wage settlements, 195
Malthus, Thomas R., 155
Mandatory retirement, 217

Manitoba
  freedom of belief, 56
  pay equity, 54
Marginal benefit, **10**
Marginal cost, **10**
Marginal labour cost (MLC), **272**
Marginal productivity of labour (MPL), **113**, 245
  calculation of, 245
Marginal revenue (MR), **245**
  increase in, 248*f*
Marginal revenue product (MRP), **245**–46
Marginal tax rate, **226**
Marginal workers, **146**–47
Market, **23**. *See also* Labour market
  equilibrium price, 29
  shortage, 29
  surplus, 28
Market discrimination, **301**
Market forces
  and labour markets, 11–12
  price mechanisms, 11
  rationing, 11
Market mechanism
  demand side, 24–26
  price determination, 28–30
  price elasticity, 30–33
  supply side, 26–28
  workings of, 23–37
Market supply curve for labour, 227–31
Mass production system. *See* Fordism
Maternity leave, 48
Men
  employment rate, 110
  labour force participation rates, 90
  life expectancy, 90
  moonlighting, 125–26
  part-time work, 121–22, 123
  self-employment, 126
Middle class, disappearance of, 131, 199–202
Migration, internal
  and labour supply curves, 227–29
Minimum age for employment, 50
Minimum wage rate, 53, 274–76
  and poverty, 276–77
  who earns, 276
Mixed economy, **10**
Monetary policy, **168**, 196–97
Monopoly, 259–60
Monopsony, 268, **271**–73

Moonlighting, **125**–26
Mortality rate, **75**
  and labour force, 74
Multinational corporations, 41
Multiple jobholding, 125–26

National Income and Expenditure Accounts, 188
Natural population growth, **75**
Natural rate of unemployment, **167**
  demographic shifts, 169–70
  and employment insurances, 170–72
  industrial restructuring, 173
  shifts in, 169–74
  and technological change, 173
Necessities, 31–32
Net immigration, 81
Net present value, 323
Net wages, **183**
New Brunswick
  hours of work, 51
  pay equity, 54
  statutory holidays, 52
  vacations with pay, 52
Newfoundland and Labrador
  freedom of belief, 56
  hours of work, 51
  pay equity, 54
  statutory holidays, 52
  vacations with pay, 52
  workers' compensation, 57
Nominal wage, **184**
Nominal wage rates, changes in, 194–97
Non-employment income, 218–22
  demogrant, 219
  employment insurance, 220–22
  subsidized childcare, 222
  welfare, 219–20
Non-market work, 213
Non-standard employment, **120**–32
  and business uncertainty, 130–32
  and demographic changes, 129
  factors affecting, 128–32
  and functional flexibility, 131
  multiple jobs, 125–26
  and numerical flexibility, 131
  own-account self-employment, 126–27
  part-time work, 121–25
  reasons for, 128–32
  reducing costs, 129–30

  temporary work, 127–28
Normal good, **214**
Normative statements, **14**–16
North American Free Trade Agreement (NAFTA), 41,
  42, 260, 261
North West Territories (NWT)
  vacations with pay, 52
  statutory holidays, 52
Not in the labour force, **71**
Nova Scotia
  hours of work, 51
  minimum age, 50
  pay equity, 54
  statutory holidays, 52
Nunavut
  statutory holidays, 52
  vacations with pay, 52

Occupational earnings polarization, 199–202
Occupational wage structure, **297**
Offshoring, 106
Old Age Security benefit, 219
Older workers
  earnings, 198–99
  labour trends for, 80
  productivity, 215
  self-employment, 127
On-call jobs, 127
Ontario
  emergency days for workers, 96
  Equal Opportunity Plan, 56
  immigration to, 87
  minimum age, 50
  statutory holidays, 52
On-the-job training, 334–39
  age–earnings profiles, 339
  costs and benefits of, 336–38
  employee turnover, 338
  general, 335
  implications of, 338–39
  internal recruiting, 338–39
  job ladders, 338
  minimum wage, 338
  specific, 335
OPEC oil price increase, 196
Open economy, **116**
Opportunity cost, **9**
  and decision to work, 215–16
  of having children, 216–18

Optimal decision rule, 10–11
Organisation for Economic Co-operation and
    Development (OECD), 259
Outsourcing, in computer services industry, 106–7
Overtime, 223–24
Overtime pay, 51–52
Own-account self-employment, **126**–27

Paralegals, 296
Parental leave, 48
Part-time work, **121**–25
    involuntary, 124–25
    and job market restructuring, 123–24
    older workers, 80
    in service sector, 122–23
    women vs. men, 121–22
Pay equity, **53**–54
    arguments against, 311
    arguments for, 312
Payroll taxes, 50, **129**–30, 277–81
Perfectly inelastic supply curve, 32
Personal income distribution, **191**
Plateauing, 78
Population
    aging of, 7, 75–76
    dependency rate, **79**
    domestic, growth of, 75–76
Population base
    age structure of labour force, 76–81
    changes in, 75–88
    and immigration, 81–87
Positive statements, **14**–16
Postindustrial state, 113
Poverty, and minimum wage, 276–77
Pre-market discrimination, **300**
Present value, **321**–23
    formula for, 321
Price determination, 28–30
    equilibrium price, 29
    surplus, 28
Price elasticity of demand, **30**–32
    factors affecting, 31–32
    formula for, 31
    luxury vs. necessity, 31–32
    percentage of income spent on product, 32
    and substitutes, 31
Price elasticity of supply, **32**–33
    formula for, 32
    and time factor, 32
Price mechanism
    and efficiency, 6

and rationing, 11
Primary-resource industries
    productivity rates, 113–15
Prince Edward Island
    freedom of belief, 56
    hours of work, 51
    pay equity, 54
    statutory holidays, 52
    workers compensation, 57
Private rate of return, **324**
Product market, **37**–38
Productivity
    and age, 215
    changes, and labour demand, 257
    increase in, 249
    and shift to service economies, 115
    See also Labour productivity
Productivity growth rates, in service sector vs. goods-
    producing sector, 113–15
Profit, **10**
Profit-maximizing rule, 273

Quasi-fixed labour costs, **263**–64
Quebec
    employment equity regulations, 56
    freedom of belief, 56
    hours of work, 51
    immigrants to, 87
    minimum age, 50
    statutory holidays, 52
    vacations with pay, 52
Quebec Pension Plan (QPP), 79

Rationing, and scarcity, 11
Real average labour income, **192**
    negative growth rates, 192
Real income increases, and service sector
    employment, 115–16
Real wage, **185**
    changes in, 194–97
Recession, **81**
Rent, 23
Reservation wage rate, **216**, 223, 286–87
Retirement
    deciding on, 216,
    mandatory, 217

Salaried worker, **183**
Saskatchewan
    statutory holidays, 52
    vacations with pay, 52

Scale effect, **249**
Scarcity, **9**
  and market forces, 11
Seasonal jobs, 127
Seasonal unemployment, **166**
Self-employment, 106
  own-account, 126–27
Service sector
  contracting out, 116
  increased demand for services as inputs, 117
  and international competition, 116
  part-time work, 122–23
  productivity growth rates and employment in,
    113–15
  real income increases, and employment in, 115–16
  shift to employment in, 111–13
  structure of, 112
Severance pay, **54**–55
Sexual orientation, 56
Shortage, **29**
Short run, **26**, 243–48
Signalling, 331–**32**
Skilled trades, declines in, 119
Skills composition of labour force, changes in, 118–20
Slotsve, G., 199–200
Social rate of return, **324**
Social security system
  and aging labour force, 78–80
  beneficiary/worker ratio, 79
  dependency rate, 78–80
  ratio of working-age to retirement age
    population, 79
Sociological forces
  and labour market, 13–14
  cultural values, 13
  custom, 13
  social norms, 13
Specific training, **335**
Standard working hours, **132**
Statistical discrimination, **308**
Statistics, 67
Statutory holidays, 52
Stock options, 184
Stock variable, **39**
Structural unemployment, 166–**67**
Student debt, 316
Subsidized childcare, 222
Substitutes, 31
Substitution effect (demand), **24, 250**
Substitution effect (supply), **214**
Supplementary labour income, **184**

Supply, 27
  change in, 26–28
  change in quantity supplied, 27–28
  factors affecting, 26
  price elasticity of, 32–33
Supply curve, **27**
Supply of labour, **40**
  and unions, 283–85
Surplus, **28**
Survey on Employment, Payrolls, and Hours
  (SEPH), 195
Survey of Job Opportunities, 145
Sweden, 92

Tariffs, 260
Technological change, 22, 173
  and labour compensation, 201
Technological unemployment, 173
Temporary work, 127–28
Term jobs, 127
Time–budget line, 235–36
Toronto, immigrants to, 87
Total factor productivity, **113**
Total income, **184**
Total labour supply, 71
Total revenue, **31**
Toyotism, **22**
Tracking, 156
Trade unions. *See* Unions
Training tax, 335
Truck drivers, 242
Turnover rates, older workers, 80

Uncertainty, in labour markets, 35
Underemployed, **124,** 146
Unemployed, **71**
Unemployment
  Canadian, characteristics of, 150–51
  Canadian and U.S. compared, 160–64
  causes of, 286–90
  cyclical, 168
  demographic differences in, 155–58
  different measures in Canada and U.S., 163–64
  discouraged workers, 145–46
  duration of, 153–54
  and education, 156, 158
  and employment insurance availability, 161–63
  female, 157
  flow analysis of, 153
  frictional, 164–65
  hidden causes of, 144–48

hidden unemployed, 145
hysteresis, 172
inactive job seekers, 144–45
incidence of, 151–53
job search, 286–87
long-duration, 80
and macroeconomic performance, 160–61
marginal workers, 146–47
measuring, 143–44
and minimum wage rate, 274–76
natural rate of, 167
occupational, 157
regional differences in, 158–60
seasonal, 166
structural, 166–67
types of, 164–68
underemployed workers, 146
wage rate rigidity, 287–90
youth, 155–57
Unemployment rate, **144**
Canadian trends in, 150
vs. employment rate, 149–50
as measure of economic hardship, 147–48
Union density, **60**–61
by occupation, 61
Union–management relationships, legislation
regarding, 58–59
Unions
and the demand for labour, 282–83
impact on the supply of labour, 283–85
impact on wages and employment, 282–86
membership in, 59–61
and rigid wages, 288–89
and wage decline, 201
Unit labour cost, 186
United Kingdom, 92
United States, 92
unemployment in, compared to Canada, 160–64
Universal Declaration of Human Rights (U.N.), 56
Unskilled workers, relative wage decline among,
200–2
Utility, **10**

Vacations with pay, 52
Visible minorities, unemployment, 157

Wage earner, **183**
Wage elasticity of labour demand, **251**–55
factors affecting, 251–55
number of substitutes for labour, 252–53
percentage of labour costs in total costs, 252

price elasticity of the product or service, 253–55
relevance of, 254
Wage rates, **23**
causes of changes in, 270–71
economic rent, 230–31
elasticity of labour supply, **225**–26
empirical evidence re union impact, 285–86
and employment determination in a competitive
labour market, 269–71
and employment determination under monopsony,
271–73
sticky, 270
Wage rate differentials
adjustment lags, 297–99
compensating, 303–304
labour market barriers, 299–302
male–female, and discrimination, 306–7
personal characteristics, 305
Wage rate rigidity, 287–90
Wage rate subsidy, **281**
Wages
deferred payments, 184
earnings, 183–84
earning gaps, 197–202
as labour income, 184
and literacy, 259
and long-term employment relationship, 34
measuring, 183–84
nominal vs. real, 184–87
in non-permanent jobs, 128
non-wage benefits, 184
overtime rate, 223–24
premium rate, 223–24
real wage, 185
sources of inequality in, 200–1
stock options, 184
unions' impact on, 282–86
unit labour cost, 186
Welfare, 219–20
and employment earnings, 221
West Germany, 92
White-collar jobs, 117
Women
earnings gap, 197–98
and flexible work time, 94
increased employment opportunities, 94
labour force participation rate, 72, 89, 90–95, 96,
109–10
moonlighting, 125–26
non-standard employment, 129
part-time work, 121–22, 123

rise in real hourly earnings, 94
rising educational levels of, 92–93
self-employment, 126
temporary work, 128
unemployment, 157
university education, 198
Work
  and age, 215–16
  education investment, 218
  factors affecting decisions, 215–22
  and family size, 216–18
  and fertility, 216–18
  individual supply curve, 222–26
  marginal tax rates and, 226
  and non-employment income, 218–22
  See also Labour force participation
Workdays lost, and older workers, 80
Workers' compensation benefits, 304
Workers' compensation legislation, 57
Workforce. *See* Labour force

Working conditions
  attractive, 304
  unattractive, 303
Work/leisure tradeoff, 213
Workplace Hazardous Materials Information System
  (WHMIS), 57
Workplace risk, legislation for, 304
World Trade Organization (WTO), 41, 261

Youth
  earnings gap, 198–99
  employment rates, 110
  freedom of belief, 56
  labour force participation, 97–98
  and minimum wage, 276
  moonlighting, 125
  and non-standard employment, 129
  and part-time work, 124
  statutory holidays, 52
  unemployment, 155–57